'A Good Disruption *convincingly argues that to reconcile growth, planetary boundaries and human well-being we have to step into the engine room of our industrial system and make it net-positive by design. The good news is that this is no longer a dream – but a choice. A choice we must make.'*

Paul Polman, CEO, Unilever

'An essential, eye-opening book for the urgently needed paradigm shift away from the depleting economic models of today towards a more positive dynamic for the economy, natural resources and people.'

Antoine Frérot, Chairman and CEO, Veolia

'Inspired and inspirational ... in its portrayal of what we can do and create if we anticipate, think, design and organize. It is beautifully written by those who know how to deliver as well as how to analyse. It is a tremendous achievement.'

Professor Lord Nicholas Stern, IG Patel Professor of Economics and Government, London School of Economics and President of the British Academy.

'A Good Disruption *makes a compelling case for redefining economic prosperity, unlocking creativity and kickstarting regenerative cycles in the digital age.'*

Ellen MacArthur, Founder, the Ellen MacArthur Foundation

'Dramatic technological progress promises exciting new products and a rising level of conventionally measured prosperity. But it cannot on its own solve the huge environmental problems created by today's stunningly wasteful economy. A new model of economic growth is essential – and A Good Disruption *describes it. Combining thought-provoking theoretical frameworks, eye-catching facts, and strong focus on how the necessary change can in practice be achieved, this well-written book should be read by anyone who wants a prosperous and environmentally sustainable world.'*

Adair Turner

A Good Disruption

Redefining Growth in the Twenty-First Century

Martin R. Stuchtey, Per-Anders Enkvist and Klaus Zumwinkel

Bloomsbury Business
An imprint of Bloomsbury Publishing Plc

B L O O M S B U R Y
LONDON · OXFORD · NEW YORK · NEW DELHI · SYDNEY

Bloomsbury Business

An imprint of Bloomsbury Publishing Plc

50 Bedford Square   1385 Broadway
London   New York
WC1B 3DP   NY 10018
UK   USA

www.bloomsbury.com

BLOOMSBURY and the Diana logo are trademarks of Bloomsbury Publishing Plc

First published 2016

© Martin R. Stuchtey, Per-Anders Enkvist and Klaus Zumwinkel, 2016

British Library Cataloguing-in-Publication Data
A catalogue record for this book is available from the British Library.

ISBN: HB: 978-1-4729-3978-4
ePDF: 978-1-4729-3980-7
ePub: 978-1-4729-3979-1

Library of Congress Cataloging-in-Publication Data
A catalog record for this book is available from the Library of Congress.

Cover design by Liron Gilenberg Gilboa
Cover image © v_alex/iStockphoto

Typeset by Fakenham Prepress Solutions, Fakenham, Norfolk, NR21 8NN
Printed and bound in Great Britain

To our families – for giving us the support, the space and the reason to write this book.

Table of Contents

Foreword

We are in a time of unprecedented disruption – with a pace and scale of change unlike anything we have seen before. Businesses, governments and entire economies are undergoing massive shifts in the ways they organize and create value – with significant implications for leaders, workers and whole societies.

We at McKinsey are privileged to meet with and advise many of the world's top leaders, across the public and private sectors. We are consistently hearing that leaders feel the 'clock speed' of change has accelerated. New technologies, changing demographics, the 're-rise' of Asia, and the dramatic increase in the 'interconnectedness' of our economies are all changing our world – and will continue to do so. The way we produce, consume, work, learn, travel and interact will all change radically over the coming years. This disruption is at the heart of the book that Per-Anders, Martin and Klaus have written – a terrific take on the impact that disruption will have.

To many, disruption appears to be a threat. The leaders of large corporations know that the changes we are seeing are testing their companies' ability to adapt and thrive. *A Good Disruption* helps leaders see the opportunities that come with these changes. The book argues that these changes may allow us to reconcile economic growth, social inclusion and environmental sustainability – goals some have long considered competing. The book also goes a long way to explain how the future global economy could look, if we take advantage of the opportunities that disruption presents us – an economy based more on new renewable energy systems; increasingly decoupled from material inputs; and with new ways of organizing cities and food supply chains. The authors argue that the future could provide enormous value for society, with little or no negative impact on the natural world. They have a positive, exciting vision – and describe an opportunity that we should not let pass.

A Good Disruption also reminds us of the increasingly short-term nature of decision-making – and the risks that this poses. We at McKinsey, together with many other committed organizations and individuals, have worked extensively on this topic in recent years, through the 'Focusing Capital on the Long Term' effort. We are seeing more and more evidence of growing short-termism – such as an increasing focus on quarterly results, high CEO turnover, underinvestment in long-term projects, short-term profit taking, and overleveraging. Short-termism is costing stakeholders such as pension schemes, insurance funds and university funds – all of which have important commitments to future generations. And a culture of short-termism – as makes clear – creates social and environment costs in the trillions of dollars.

A Good Disruption makes the case that our over-reliance on short-term performance measures contributes significantly to short-term decision-making. Furthermore, a focus on GDP growth alone is unlikely to deliver the society we aspire to live in. The focus on short-term earnings is failing to help companies navigate towards long-term value creation for all of their stakeholders – shareholders, customers, employees and suppliers. New metrics are needed to keep today's large, complex institutions on course. As *A Good Disruption* argues, we also need to rethink the way we evaluate corporations. We have to account for the systemic risks they carry, the quality of capital and people they have built, the role they play in society, and their ability to renew themselves.

All these points are important topics for any CEO or politician and for those who advise them – and require our attention. The authors call for business and government leaders to 'up their game' and drive systemic change. They call for leaders, not managers; long-term stewards, not short-term maximizers; and cross-sector conveners, not vested interest lobbyists.

I am delighted that three former McKinsey Partner colleagues, all of them good friends, are raising these important points – blending sound analysis, mature foresight and good story-telling.

A Good Disruption captures the shifts we all need to make in this time of change – and provides a positive, actionable agenda on how to shape what the authors call the 'great reconciliation'.

Dominic Barton
Global Managing Director
McKinsey & Company

Acknowledgements

This book would not exist were it not for the coincidence of three benign circumstances: families that allowed us to lose track of time and take on this project on top of everything else. In fact it was the dinner table debates at home with our wives and children that convinced us that writing this book would be time well spent. We also owe it, and the experience that feeds it, to the clients we worked with during our forty-six collective years at McKinsey & Company. Their trust and collaboration created eye-opening insights and provided reality and relevance checks for the thinking that we develop throughout the book. And finally, it is the result of meeting exceptional people who encouraged us and offered invaluable support.

There are many we should thank: Jeremy Oppenheim from SystemiQ Ltd and Michael Jung provided precious insights along the way. Others joined in, many of them icons in this domain: Janez Potočnik, Robert Ayres, Ellen MacArthur, Andreas Merkl, Andrew Morlet, Ernst-Ulrich von Weizsäcker, Joss Bleriot, Ken Webster, Ashima Sukhdev, Wilhelm Merck, Anders Wijkman, Stefan Heck, John Bernstein, Thomas von Mitschke, Johannes Meier and Thomas Kausch. The partners of System iQ Ltd. helped us as did many former McKinsey colleagues including Morten Rossé, Steven Swartz, Hauke Engel, Ivan Mihow, Saif Hameed, Sander Defruyt, Adrien Vincent, Helga Vanthournout, Rob Opsomer, Yoni Shiran, Marco Albani, Shannon Bouton, Kerstin Humberg, Dorothee d'Herde, Steve John, Markus Hammer, Ken Somers, Ruben Korenke, Jürg Käppli, Stephanie Hubold, and Brodie Boland. We are also very grateful to a team of unrelenting supporters who walked with us through the daily work of writing the book, page by page: Britta Riedel, Janike Reichman, Pia Heden, Heide Stuchtey and Janna Jung-Irrgang. We are indebted to our friend and partner Dominic Barton for providing the foreword. He helped us to navigate the terrain between the short and the long term during our McKinsey years. Last, but clearly not least in appreciation, we are very grateful to our five interviewees who not only took the time to share their perspectives but also gifted us with unforgettable moments and conversations: Bishop Heinrich Bedford-Strohm, Professor Lord Nicholas Stern, Professor Dr Michael Braungart and Jean-Marc Duvoisin.

Introduction

The debate that ultimately led to this book took place in the summer of 2015 in Brussels, Belgium. A few months earlier, the European Commission had made public that it would release its 'Circular Economy Package' before the end of 2015, laying out its vision for how the European economy should move towards a better and more circular use of resources. Everyone involved recognized the importance – the package would in effect set the direction for Europe's resource-related policies for the next five to ten years – and this had turned Brussels into a melting pot of reports, position papers, roundtables and speeches, all laying out their different views about what the package should and should not contain.

The debate was fascinating to follow. First because it opened our eyes to the sincerity and importance of the EU to address long-term challenges in a political context of growing short-termism and populism. And second, because it revealed just how little agreement there is on the relationship between resources, the economy and the environment, and what direction an advanced economy like Europe should set for its future resource use. There was total disagreement on even 'basic' questions: Is Europe using resources reasonably efficiently today, or is there a big opportunity for improvement? Will Europe's competitiveness suffer if it tries to change the way it uses resources, or will a system whereby materials recirculate rather offer a competitive advantage, reducing cost and volatility? Would investing in a transition towards a circular economy stimulate growth, or would it simply divert public funds and attention from other more important and urgent matters: refugees, bank reform, trade agreements? How will the technology disruption change the resource equation? Should policy-makers even get involved, or will the market itself find the optimal solution? The debate provided a microcosm that showed how bereft the world is of guiding principles, economic criteria and inner compasses when it comes to questions of natural resources, and how decision-makers struggle to get it right every time they dedicate more land for construction, choose between power generation technologies, or design new products.

We also threw our log into the fire. Together with our good friend and ally Dame Ellen MacArthur, we published a report entitled *Growth Within: A Circular Economy Vision for a Competitive Europe* in June 2015, in which we investigated some of these questions. Some of the analyses from that report are discussed later on in this book, while the entire report is available online.

The Circular Economy package was eventually published in December 2015 one year after Commissioner Potočnik had first tabled it. History will tell whether it was just another piece of environmental legislation, as critics suggested, or one of the first major policy efforts towards a new definition of how advanced economies should produce and consume. But already by the early autumn of 2015 we had decided not to wait for the verdict but to push ahead, because the questions at hand felt too important and too exciting. This was the start of a journey that took us deeper and deeper into different academic disciplines, from incumbent industrial giants to technology firms in Silicon Valley, and from environmentalists to free-market economists.

Technology was a common denominator across all our discussions, and felt to many of our discussion partners like the defining trend. Big data, 3D printing, driverless cars, robotics, artificial intelligence, the internet of things, intelligent materials, cheap solar power, electric vehicles, sharing business models – in almost every sector of the economy, a disruption seemed imminent. Technology firms pointed out how they could solve resource issues while at the same time providing consumer benefits. Incumbents were worried they would get 'Ubered-away', with huge job losses and stranded assets as a consequence. Policy-makers felt powerless in the face of what one of them called a 'digital tsunami', but at the same time, many were excited about the new possibilities. The environmental community was upbeat after the Paris climate agreement and the recent advances in solar, wind and battery technology, but at the same time pointed out that the global community is far overstepping planetary boundaries, year on year.

The mosaic that started to appear was both intriguing and schizophrenic. We were intrigued on the one hand by the huge opportunity that technology holds in almost every economic sector, and we could see clearly how the disruption is now quickly reaching the resource-heavy parts of the economy. But on the other hand, we were also struck by the major concerns expressed by almost everyone we talked to: an economy plagued by low growth, unemployment and inequality, and a set of seemingly intractable environmental issues becoming ever more pressing. The disruption could clearly impact some of these issues, but on the current path, it was very unclear whether the change was for better or for worse. It seemed to us we don't just need a disruption, we need a good disruption. As we reviewed area after area, we became increasingly convinced that ensuring a good disruption might be the defining challenge for business and policy-makers over the next decade. This is crucial for all the above reasons, but perhaps most of all for environmental ones, since there are more and more signs from the global ecosystem that we are leaving what the Planetary Boundaries research team calls the 'safe operating space' in irreversible ways, which will have real consequences for the lives of ourselves, our children and grandchildren.

The key question of the book

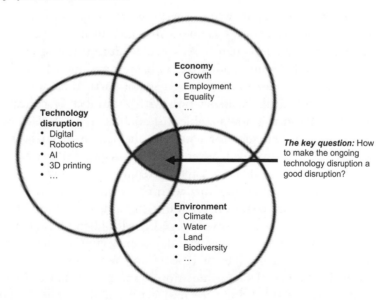

Fig. 0.1

A Good Disruption does not provide all the answers – how could it, given its huge scope, the fast development, and the complexity of issues? We have tried to paint a comprehensive picture, rather than go deeply into one individual area, so we have had to use a broad brush. We have put on paper what we believe is a better growth model for the physical part of the economy – which turns out to be about half of it – now that the disruption is coming, and given the massive environmental issues. We are aware that this opens us up to accusations of both naivety and arrogance. After all, isn't it both unrealistic and cynical to suggest deep changes to a growth model that has in many ways served us so well over the last decades, and in which we are so massively invested? We chose to provide this alternative vision anyway, because it is so clear from the data that tinkering around the edges of the current growth model will not get us anywhere close to our ultimate goal. When it comes to the resource-related parts of our economy, we need a deep redesign. The following section, 'A new narrative emerging', summarizes our entire argument, while subsequent chapters provide more nuance, evidence and colour.

So who are we to tell this story?

Martin R. Stuchtey grew up in wellington boots and ended up in a tent in Africa as a young geologist in search of mineral-bearing rock formations. He subsequently returned to Europe and exchanged his khakis for a dark suit, graduated in business and joined McKinsey for almost twenty years, ultimately as a senior partner. He worked across all industries until, in association with a number of colleagues, he initiated McKinsey's now sizeable sustainability practice. He developed green growth strategies for countries, helped to green large multi-nationals and developed government strategies for better resource use. Two topics particularly captivated him: the future of water and the circular economy. Together with the World Bank and Nestlé, he initiated a global coalition for water stewardship – the '2030 Water Resources Group' – and worked together with Ellen MacArthur for five years on the economics of a circular economy. With her foundation he co-authored a number of reports on the economic and business rationale of an accelerated transition towards a circular economy, and travelled the world giving speeches, lectures and interviews about the new resource economy. Together with his former McKinsey colleague

Jeremy Oppenheim, Martin founded SystemiQ, a principal and venture catalyst for system-level change in the environmental space. Martin is also a university professor for resource strategies and management at Innsbruck University. But then he tries to walk the talk, often uphill: his alpine farm absorbs much of his physical energy. He runs it with the help of his wife and their six children, sometimes his university students and, once again, in wellington boots.

Per-Anders Enkvist is a physicist by training, and worked at McKinsey from 1999 to 2015, the last seven years as a partner in the sustainability practice which he co-founded together with Martin and a group of partners. He started his consulting career working across the energy and manufacturing industries, but soon got passionate about resource strategy and sustainability topics, becoming increasingly disturbed by the deep disconnect between business practices and the natural resource world and concerned by how little of what we know about carbon, water, oceans and land is translated into information on which decision-makers can act. In 2006, he developed McKinsey's global greenhouse gas abatement cost curve: a comprehensive mapping of greenhouse gas reduction opportunities in all major sectors and world regions – essentially a global menu of emission reduction opportunities, prioritized according to cost. Ever since, this cost curve with its clear concepts of volumes, costs and benefits has become a lingua franca for all those who believe that economic thinking should govern the path towards a low-carbon economy. Since then, he has consulted on resource strategy and sustainability topics across the world, including low-carbon energy strategies, corporate sustainability transformations, the circular economy, climate change strategies and green growth. Per-Anders is the founder of Material Economics, a consulting firm specialized on resource strategy and sustainability tranformations, which currently absorbs all his professional energy. He lives outside Stockholm with his wife and three children.

After ten years as a McKinsey consultant, **Klaus Zumwinkel** left his position as senior partner to become CEO of the largest German mail order group, and subsequently of the German postal service. He also served on many boards, including Lufthansa, Allianz, Morgan Stanley and Deutsche Telekom, chairing the latter. In these assignments his aim was directed to one single overarching question: how to transform and renew large, often state-run, companies and turn them into successful global players. In his nineteen years as CEO, he turned Deutsche Post, now Deutsche Post DHL, into the logistics backbone of the global economy and a globally recognized brand. Under Klaus's leadership, DP DHL grew and developed like few other companies before: from approximately €10 billion in revenue to €54 billion, and almost 500,000 employees. In total, Deutsche Post DHL acquired and integrated more than 170 companies during Klaus's leadership and entered 150 new national markets. Today, the company stands for global reach, an operating philosophy envied by other companies, and a strong and diverse management team. Before Klaus stepped down as CEO, he started an ambitious GoGreen campaign and a programme to improve the environmental footprint year on year. A period of self-reflection followed. One key question that captured Klaus's particular attention was the conflict between 'green' and 'profitable'. He felt that the CEOs who collectively command the largest part of the planet's resources, and the financial capital that determines how we produce and live, are left to operate without an economic and legal framework fit for our increasingly populated world. He dedicated the foundation which he now leads, aptly called SUN[1], to the exploration of that very economic framework.

So we share a deep interest in resource economics and green innovation, but also years of immersion in the economic mainstream with some of the largest corporations and according to the rules of a very competitive game: building high-performing organizations, driving efficiencies, delivering superior returns and fulfilling customer demands. This is a world unable to accept a vision that does not offer new business and eventually growth opportunity. But it is also a world, we found, that is hungry for a new narrative of how, in the twenty-first century, we can continue to grow on a planet of 10 billion people or more.

A new narrative emerging

'Can you tell me a story?'
'What kind of story?'
'One with a good ending.'

Child and father

Wherever we went, and whoever we talked to over the last years, three questions kept coming up: Will growth get 'back on track'? Where is the massive technology disruption taking us, our jobs and our income? And, is there a way to combine our insatiable need for more growth and wealth with a finite planet, which is showing increasing signs of overuse and depletion?

CEOs, scientists, government officials, students, religious leaders ... they all expressed similar concerns: that our current growth model is spurring inequality, anxiety and populist backlash and is broadly at odds with our social vision, the planet and out concept of a good life. And they felt that the demand for renewal was more urgent than ever, now that the financial crisis has stolen a big part of our economic self-confidence, when accelerating technology seems to dictate the pace and direction of our lives, and where the global dimensions of our environmental challenges are getting ever more clear.

These concerns have become mainstream, entering our living rooms, boardrooms and classrooms. Scepticism about the long-term viability of our current economic engine is spurred by public leaders from Pope Francis to Ban Ki Moon, and from Unilever's Paul Polman to BlackRock chief banker Laurence Fink, who says that 'Short-term thinking pervades our most important institutions, from government to households. We've created a gambling culture in which we tune out everything except the most immediate outcomes.'[1]

But so far, we are desperately short on answers. Our current growth model has worked miracles, and has lifted billions out of poverty into a rewarding and prosperous life. And we have invested immensely in it. So meddling with it seems reckless at best, given there are another few billion who look forward to joining the global middle class. And yet there is no escaping the overwhelming evidence that says we are destroying our planet at breathtaking speed, and that our societies are fragmenting at a level not seen since the Second World War.

We believe the technology disruption can offer a core part of the solution. Not by itself: after reviewing a lot of research about its implications, we are as concerned as ever about the impact of the disruption, on its current path. But guided by a new narrative and set of principles, we believe it can provide an answer to many of the above questions – a massive opportunity at our fingertips, to go from merely a disruption, to a good disruption.

I. Our affair with growth

We are in the midst of an amazing global development. To recognize that, it is perhaps necessary to step back from the daily news about rollercoaster markets, unemployment, currency crises and austerity. But looking at the data for the last few decades, it is hard to come to any other conclusion. In 1990, the size of the global economy was €23 trillion, as measured in real Gross Domestic Product (GDP) terms. In 2015, only twenty-five years later, it had tripled to 78 trillion. In 1990, 1.9 billion people were living in extreme poverty. By 2015 that number had been cut by more than half, to 830 million, while in parallel the global middle class had almost tripled. And most citizens of advanced economies today command goods and services that were beyond the reach of even kings and emperors only 200 years ago.[2,3]

The social development that went hand in hand with the economic journey is even more startling. The number of children of primary school age who did not attend school dropped from 100 million in 2000 to 57 million by 2015. The illiteracy rate of adolescents decreased from 17 per cent in 1990 to 9 per cent today. Child mortality dropped by more than half during the same period, and maternal mortality rates dropped by 45 per cent. The population with access to piped drinking water doubled. The share of internet access in the global population grew from 6 per cent in 2000 to 43 per cent in 2015. The list goes on and on.[4]

Compared to previous economic growth, the pace and scale of this prosperity increase is mind-blowing. When the first industrial revolution started in the UK in the eighteenth century, it took over 150 years for the country to double its GDP per capita, with a population of less than 10 million at the beginning of the journey. The US achieved the same doubling of GDP per capita in fifty years, also starting with about 10 million people. China and India did it in only twelve and sixteen years, respectively, and with a combined population of about 1.8 billion people at the start of their journeys – close to 200 times as many people and 10 times the speed of the UK industrialization. The sheer force of new demand hitting global markets is 2,000 times higher.[5]

Fuelled by natural resources

If one steps into the engine room and tries to understand the historic growth engine, one of the most striking findings is that the success is largely built on *transforming natural capital*, the economist's word for natural resources, into other forms of capital. This was obvious in the early industrialization. Ores and coal were being transformed into metals, and thence into products. Limestone was transformed into cement, and thence into houses and bridges. And forests were transformed into timber, heat and steam, and used to power machines and railways. Over time, we learned to tame ever more types of natural capital, and use it to create ever more advanced products. This is well known and described in any textbook on the industrial revolution. What is less understood is that the old growth recipe of transforming natural capital into other forms of capital still plays a huge role in economic growth, even in the most advanced economies. Until today, after three industrial revolutions, a significantly expanded service sector, and with more than 50 per cent of the population living in cities, our model of economic value creation remains remarkably similar to the early days of industrialization. The evidence abounds: low oil prices remain the single most important economic stimulus, they are celebrated by oil importers and often spark stockmarket fireworks. And they wreak havoc in economies like Russia, Saudi Arabia, or Brazil that are riding on programmes of massive resource extraction. Even many advanced economies such as Australia, Canada and Norway remain massively dependent on resources. If we move downstream, we see a similar pattern. At the heart of our economy are still large resource-intense value chains. In Europe the three resource-intense value chains of housing, food and mobility represented a full 51 per cent of GDP in 2013, 46 per cent of employment, and 63 per cent of household spending.[6]

In academic economics the role of energy and resources in driving economic growth is finally starting to attract more recognition. Historically, labour and capital were always regarded as the two most important input factors, at least since Nobel laureate Robert Solow formalized the neo-classical growth theory in the mid-1950s (notably in a world of 2.8 billion people when resource use was order-of-magnitude lower than today). In this theory, natural resource and energy use are seen as a result of growth, not a driver of it. But the neo-classical theory could only explain about half of the empirically observed growth, with the remaining 'Solow residual' long being qualitatively attributed to synergy effects between labour and capital productivity improvements, but without a quantitative theory to explain it. Over the last decade, however, a new school of economic thinkers has instead started to model energy and natural resources as a third major input factor on a par with labour and capital, a very intuitive assumption for natural scientists. Doing so led to massively different conclusions: more natural resource input, and more productive use of it, turned out to explain about half of the entire economic growth of the twentieth century in the countries studied. In other words, it explained almost all of the Solow residual, and suggested a much bigger role for natural resources in explaining growth than conventional economics has it, also for advanced economies.

So we should not let talk about a 'service economy' or 'knowledge economy' fool us into believing natural resources are not important for growth: much of the services are highly resource-related (transport, real estate, food, household goods, etc.) and much of the knowledge is about physical products and value chains.

This matters. If we don't appreciate how crucial natural capital still is to our economic success, we will undermanage natural capital and the planet's ability to provide it, and we will under-react to the threat that the ever more evident depletion of this natural capital poses to our future economic success. We are confronted with a huge story – a story not only of environmental degradation but of diminishing returns of our current resource-intensive industrial model. If growth is to an important extent built on natural capital, and that capital is being depleted, then what will that do to our economy?

A bank run on natural resources

As we elaborate throughout the book, our resource-intensive model comes with profound economic, social and environmental implications. None of these are entirely new. The environmental issues have been intensely debated at least since the 1960s. So far they have been perceived primarily as undesirable side-effects of industrialization, but largely disconnected from the economy, and unable to really hurt economic growth. What is perhaps less clear to non-specialist readers is how dramatically this situation has changed over the last decades. Since the mid-1980s and with ever-increasing speed, environmental depletion has reached a global scale and scope where it actually starts to threaten the viability of our model of wealth creation itself. Our economy has grown so big, so fast, that it is quickly depleting the very same natural capital on which it thrives. In a way, it is falling victim to its own success.

Climate change is clearly the most-discussed environmental threat, with its dire foreseen consequences for sea levels, storms, droughts, biodiversity, and loss of bioproductivity at large. But there are a number of other global environmental issues that many earth scientists would argue are equally serious:

- *Freshwater shortage.* Most of the global population is expected to live in regions with moderate to severe freshwater deficits by 2030, a third even in regions where less than 50 per cent of the water demand can be met.[7] The reason is the unquenched and unmanaged thirst of the agricultural, industrial and – increasingly – energy sectors.
- *Nitrogen and phosphorous.* The global flows of these two crucial food nutrients are deeply disturbed due to agriculture fertilization practices. Fossil phosphate is a key ingredient in synthetic fertilizers, but can primarily be mined at high concentration levels in Morocco and the Western Sahara, and there are many question marks about its long-term supply, at least at cost levels close to the current. Probably worse, up to 70 per cent of the phosphorus currently ends up in lakes and oceans, where it causes eutrophication and dead

zones, rather than being brought back to the fields.[8] We are literally throwing an essential food nutrient, which is hard to substitute and which has limited supply, into the sea at a fast pace.

- *Ocean depletion and pollution.* The decline of fisheries has been a serious local issue for many years, but has now reached global proportions. As a global average, the fish catch per dollar of expenditure (labour, equipment) has gone down a staggering 83 per cent since 1975.[9] Ocean pollution has also become a global problem during the last decades. As an example, there will be more plastics than edible fish in the oceans by 2050 if the current plastics pollution of 8–12 million tons per year continues.[10]

- *Biodiversity loss.* Finally, and possibly most concerning of all, we are losing biodiversity at a rate of 8–100 times higher than the natural background rate, leading scientists to talk about the sixth mass extinction, much larger and more comprehensive than previous ones.[11] This is no longer just about organisms that non-specialists have never heard of. A recent scientific inventory concluded that up to 75 per cent of large animals are at risk of extinction, including household names such as tigers, leopards and gorillas.[12] We have truly stepped into the Anthropocene.

We could have made the list longer, and included phenomena like topsoil depletion, desertification, saltwater intrusion, ocean acidification and deforestation. Our point is not to scaremonger but to show that there are now global threats to almost all of our most crucial natural resources: land, water, air, nutrients and fauna. The well-regarded Planetary Boundaries research team has identified nine dimensions for planetary health, and now believe four of those boundaries have already been trespassed.[13]

The Global Footprint Network uses another striking way to synthesize our natural resource use: every year they calculate the biological surface area needed to sustainably produce all the natural resources used that year. 1970 was the first year the total biological area was larger than the available area on the planet and the global economy went into the 'red'. Since then, we have continued to use ever more resources, and in 2015, we used a full 1.6 planets, with most rich countries using between two and five times more than their share.[14]

The environmental movement is sometimes accused of unnecessary alarmism, but reviewing the key environmental facts to write this book led us to conclude that sounding the alarm might be quite appropriate in the present situation.

This is deeply problematic for many reasons. From a strictly economic point of view, the key point is that the productivity of our natural resource systems is dropping (there are ample examples throughout this book) as a consequence of overuse, depletion and contamination, raising questions about how effective our historic growth recipe of transforming natural capital into other forms of capital will be in the future.

Another underdiscussed insight is that a large share of our environmental issues can be traced back to our use of materials and products. As one proxy, we looked at the total global environmental damage costs as calculated by UN-supported TEEB (The Economics of Ecosystems and Biodiversity)[15] and split it by root cause. It turns out 60-65 per cent of the costs were material-related and 35-40 per cent were energy-related. So while our energy demand and the combustion of fossil fuels is a major resource challenge, our material use is arguably an even bigger one. This material use has received much less attention than the energy aspect in environmental discussions to date.

There are two important nuances to this environmental argument that we want to stress. First, the world is not broadly 'running out' of metal and fossil resources. For many large mineral categories, the so-called reserve-to-production ratios, which measure how big the proven reserves of different resources are compared to their annual use, are steadily growing, meaning that new findings are made faster than old ones are depleted. So the world is not running out of iron or oil any time soon. There are important exceptions to this general rule though. The EU, for instance, has twenty materials on its 'critical raw material' list, and most of the fifty elements that make a smartphone are rare functional metals such as europium, dysprosium and thulium, in some cases even originating from one single mine.[16] Instead it is our biological systems that are starting to default, and our economy depends on the productivity of those systems in ways that we failed to recognize in the past.

Second, we want to acknowledge that some planetary borrowing from the future might well be defendable. For instance, nature is the major asset of many poor countries, so the fact that they 'use' some of it to achieve a basic standard of living and to build other forms of capital stock is hard to criticize. But now almost all countries are borrowing, simultaneously, at an ever higher pace, and the richest countries are borrowing the most. To us, that does not look like prudent borrowing with a plan to repay. It looks like a bank run on natural resources.

Growing poor?

Perhaps the year 1985 will be remembered as the start of the great divergence. It was in that year that GDP – our predominant economic success metric – started to fundamentally diverge from many of the other key metrics of human well-being: labour income, income distribution and natural capital. Since then, a number of ambitious efforts have been undertaken to develop a new compass to steer our economy in a way that reconciles the two megatrends hidden in those numbers: on one hand, an amazing economic and social progress, but on the other hand, major environmental depletion. Disturbingly, all of these efforts come to a similar conclusion: that 'real' growth, if one adjusts for the natural capital destruction, is anaemic, substantially lower than GDP growth. This is important: if 'real' growth is much lower than we think, it also means our current economic growth engine is less successful than we think. So let us review three of the key efforts:[17]

- The Inclusive Wealth Index (IWI), a UNEP-supported effort led by a group of prominent economists, aims to measure long-term sustainable wealth. It defines wealth as a country's total capital stock, including manufactured capital, natural capital and human capital, and it defines growth as the development of that total capital stock. The underlying idea is that the key determinant of the future well-being of a country's population is how well the country's total capital stock (its 'productive base') is maintained and developed, not its income here-and-now (as GDP measures). Across 140 countries, the disturbing conclusion in the latest IWI report is that global growth of Inclusive Wealth for the twenty years between 1990 and 2010 was a mere 32 per cent, compared to a GDP growth of 187 per cent for the same period. Eighty-two of the 140 countries in IWI's dataset are actually growing poorer in per capita terms when environmental damage costs are included, as natural capital is depleted faster than other types of capital are built. And still only a few of the environmental issues above were included in the IWI's calculations, so they potentially underestimate the natural capital destruction.[18]

- The Genuine Progress Indicator (GPI) instead starts from GDP growth, and then adjusts for a number of environmental and social factors to arrive at what it considers to be genuine growth. Globally, GPI growth has been close to zero between 1990 and 2005. While trajectories vary from region to region, the pattern remains largely consistent: a widening gap between GDP and GPI.
- The Economics of Ecosystems and Biodiversity (TEEB) and economic consultancy Trucost in 2013 took on the Herculean task of estimating the total cost of damages to natural capital across all major types of earth systems and across the world. They estimated the total cost at a staggering 13 per cent of global GDP – an enormous number, yet one that will continue to grow on our current development trajectory. They then went on to compare this cost to the size and profits of the extractive and primary processing industries that cause most of the depletion, and identified that none – none! – of those industries would be profitable today if they had to carry their environmental damage costs. This poses an enormous problem and risk at the heart of our global economy. In the energy industry, the risk of stranded fossil assets has been much discussed in recent years (the 'carbon bubble' debate), but according to Trucost's analysis, the total environmental bubble is 2–3 times larger.[19]

There is some controversy around the methodology for each one of these metrics – as there is for GDP – but together they point to an inescapable conclusion: that GDP is no longer a lead indicator for progress and wealth, and that underneath the still-positive GDP growth numbers a much less favourable story is unravelling. A lot of the GDP growth we are measuring might in fact be borrowing from the future rather than real progress. Our real economic progress seems to be much slower than we think and may even be negative in some countries. Are we growing poor?

Waste, waste everywhere

Ironically our attempt to borrow growth at the expense of our natural capital stock is happening in the face of massive waste in our economic system. We deplete natural capital to produce manufactured capital, and then we massively underutilize that same manufactured capital for which we have paid so dearly. The heart of the issue is that our centuries-long freeriding of natural resources has made the economy highly wasteful in how it uses energy, materials and products.

As part of the *Growth Within* report described in the Introduction, we investigated waste in the European economy, revealing a surprising wastefulness. This is important to our argument, so let's look at some of the key numbers here, and then go into more detail later on in the book.

In 2012, the average European directly needed 13.5 metric tons of materials to support his lifestyle, or a full 260 kilograms per week.[20] In value terms, Europe loses a full 95 per cent of the material and energy value after one use cycle, whereas material recycling and waste-based energy recovery represents only 5 per cent of the original raw material value.[21] Even recycling success stories like steel, PET and paper lose 30–75 per cent of the material value in the first use cycle. Partly, this is because only a share of the volumes is actually recycled. But more importantly, the value of the material is severely reduced because it is mixed with so many other materials that it can only be reused in low-value applications. So on average, Europe uses lots of materials, uses them only once, and leaves them downgraded for future generations. The same is true globally, even though patterns of material reuse vary slightly across the world.

If we broaden our perspective, the current level of structural waste becomes even more breathtaking: Take mobility. Here, capable car manufacturers have optimized productivity for a century – at the product level. At the systems level, the picture looks radically different: a European car is parked 92 per cent of the time. Another 3 per cent of the time is lost to congestion and looking for parking, so the car is only driven productively about 5 per cent of the time. And then only 1.5 of its five seats are occupied. Combining these figures, we arrive at a surprisingly low car utilization of less than 2 per cent. In the US, this number is even lower. And remember that many families have one or more years of disposable income tied up in their car. The numbers are similar from an energy point of view: the average deadweight ratio is about 12:1,[22] and only about 20 per cent of the chemical petroleum energy in the oil well is translated into kinetic energy for the car. Multiplying the two numbers, we find that less than 2 per cent of the chemical energy of the petroleum in the well actually ends up transporting people. The same story from a land perspective: up to 50 per cent of inner-city land is devoted to road mobility, if one includes both roads and parking spaces. But even at rush hour – which is typically 5–10 per cent of the time – cars cover only 10 per cent of the average city street. So the result is a surprisingly low 1–2 per cent utilization from whatever perspective we use, for one of the economy's largest capital categories.

Similar numbers are presented later on in the book for the housing and food value chains. All in all, these numbers show an unexpected amount of waste for some of our largest value chains, that together comprise about half of our economy and 70–80 per cent of our resource use.

This is important: if one takes a system view on our largest value chains, there is so much waste that reducing it even slightly represents a massive economic and environmental opportunity. Put differently, there is a tremendous opportunity to get much more economic value out of our existing infrastructure, products and materials. As we show in the book, new technology and business models are now available to achieve this, if the development is steered the right way. That is the core of the 'good disruption' opportunity.

But before we go to the solution, how did we get ourselves into this situation of wastefulness and overuse, which we think few people are happy with? At a practical level, the answer many economics textbooks give is that there haven't been high enough prices on environmental damage and the 'polluter pays' principle has not been observed. At a deeper level, we believe the answer is that natural resources were long seen as abundantly available and free for all. Therefore, natural capital was not included when people started to define wealth, capital, economic progress, and the market-based capitalist system, nor when the basis of our current economic theory and metrics was defined – in a world of 1 to 4 billion people. This in turn created a belief system that still runs deep: that capital and economic progress should be thought of as separate from natural capital, or at most weakly linked through 'externalities' that change markets marginally. And it worked so well. But now, with many natural resources being stretched by a global population potentially heading towards 11 billion, with consumption per head quickly increasing, and with mankind already acting outside the safe operating space of the planet, we need to recognize that major externalities are the norm rather than the exception. In some cases they dwarf the economic benefits. We need to rethink deeply.

Sustainability – the broken dream

Our mismanagement of natural resources is not news, and there has been an active battle to preserve the environment for more than a century. The history of environmentalism fascinates with pioneers (from Rachel Carson to Chico Mendes), crises (from Seveso to Exxon Valdez), battles (from poaching to ocean plastic debris) and wins (from Montreal to Paris). In a way, it is a reflection of modern history itself.

The first set of real environmental laws was enacted in the UK already in the late nineteenth century, and the first environmental organizations were also formed at that time (e.g. the Sierra Club in 1892). Crucially, the focus of the early legislation and influencing groups was on environmental *conservation*, either through protecting land areas or species, or banning dangerous substances. Over the last century, the conservation approach has scored many victories: controlled use of lead and mercury, banning DDT, PCB and other chemical compounds, modern waste management, among many others. Most of the issues were local or national, and environmental protection was a game of black-listing substances and undesired business practices, and enforcing compliance. For businesses, it was another boundary condition, no more.

During the 1980s and 1990s, this changed. It became clear that the conservation approach, for all its great achievements, was insufficient to tackle the environmental issues of the day: the first signs of climate change, ocean acidification, land degradation, the ozone hole, city smog, deforestation. Many of these issues were international, and to complicate matters, many of them were linked to increased resource use, which was at the same time crucial for the industrial take-off of poor countries.

As a consequence of this shift in issues and perspective, the global environmental strategy broadly changed focus from conservation to *eco-efficiency*. It was no longer enough to protect particularly important forests, lakes or species, or to ban particularly dangerous substances; the entire economy had to use natural resources as efficiently as possible. Environmental stewardship started to be everyone's business, and all companies, countries and consumers were expected to be eco-efficient. Eco-efficiency was also one of the key outcomes of the UN's Rio de Janeiro Earth Summit in 1992, and later the World Business Council for Sustainable Development (WBCSD) was formed with the idea of eco-efficiency at its heart.[23] Eco-efficiency is still the dominant global environmental strategy. Most advanced economies have a long string of environmental regulations that set eco-efficiency standards for different sectors: fuel standards for vehicles, energy efficiency standards for buildings, and water efficiency standards for appliances, to mention just a few. And most companies have eco-efficiency at the heart of their sustainability efforts.

Unfortunately, eco-efficiency, for all its good intentions and achievements (we do not want to imagine a world without it), is now also proving inadequate as a response to global environmental and social challenges. That might sound harsh, but eco-efficiency has now been the strategy of choice for over twenty-five years, and still we are observing an *accelerating* global environmental deterioration, at a scale and speed that threatens both global earth systems and economic progress itself. That does not mean eco-efficiency was wrong; it would probably have been impossible to gather political support for anything else – it was a source of economic – not merely environmental – benefit and innovation – and bought us precious time.

There are two core problems: First, the incremental eco-efficiency product improvements that most industries and countries achieve are dwarfed by their sheer volume growth, from economic growth and from the so-called rebound effect. Second, sustainability efforts are primarily focused on the products themselves, and on cleaning up the energy system, whereas there is much less effort on addressing the system-level waste we pointed at above. The result? All the curves on absolute resource use – which is what matters to our global environmental issues – keep rising, not declining. Between 1995 (when eco-efficiency had been broadly established) and 2010, iron demand grew by 81 per cent, plastics demand by 83 per cent, and fossil fuel-related greenhouse gas emissions by 48 per cent, to take just a few examples. So the inescapable truth is that the super-demand cycle for planetary resources is on and exerting higher pressure today than 20–25 years ago when the eco-efficiency strategy was established.

The world is caught in a trap: efficiency improvements are far too slow. But accelerating the improvements comes at a cost that many consider too high, and believe would stand in the way of growth. Car emissions provide an interesting case in point. The Obama administration's fleet standards for car makers are targeting 54.5 miles per gallon (mpg) in 2025 (compared to 30 mpg today), the European Union is aiming at 60.6 and China at 50.1. But in parallel, the numbers of cars globally is expected to double, from about one billion today to two billion by 2030.[24] The net effect is an *increase* in global greenhouse gas emissions from cars, even if auto manufacturers manage to reach the aggressive mpg targets.

This predicament is getting more acute all the time. A look forward confirms: even though the financial crisis has let some of the steam out of the resource boom, almost all forecasts suggest natural resource overuse will not only remain, but grow. The national climate plans submitted to the Paris climate negotiations in December 2015, for instance, sum up to a 25 per cent *increase* in global primary energy demand until 2030.[25] So while there is plenty of reason to be upbeat about the Paris agreement, the first wave of commitments was far from sufficient. It is becoming blatantly clear that greening based on eco-efficiency is not fast enough: 'Being less bad is no good,' as Michael Braungart and William McDonough provocatively formulated it in their seminal book *Cradle to Cradle*.[26] So in spite of all the achievements of eco-efficiency, it seems we are coming to the end of the second era of environmentalism, and we are in great need of a redesign and a new set of rules.

To sum up this diagnostic part of our argument: the last 30 years have been a great economic success if one uses today's measure (GDP), and this success has to a large extent been achieved through transforming natural capital into other forms of capital. But this historic growth model is now becoming a victim of its own success, since the economy's size is causing a massive global depletion of natural capital, which reduces the future effectiveness of the historic growth formula. Already today, 'real' growth is much lower than reported GDP growth, much of which is borrowed from the future. It seems our current growth model needs a deep re-think. Today's sustainability approach – eco-efficiency – is inadequate, but the solution could be a new set of principles that we have not started to define, embrace and enact.

II. Accretive economics – recapitalizing the economy

If eco-efficiency is not the answer to make the ongoing disruption a good disruption, then what is? If we could wish to achieve one thing with this book, it would be to accelerate that discussion by providing some of the required facts and perspectives. We are aware that it will take years, and countless debates, articles, pioneers and pledges to fill the imagination gap we currently face. How could it be different for a change of that magnitude? But allow us to throw our log onto the fire.

At the highest level, we believe two major changes are needed. First, addressing the system waste we identified above needs to become a major priority, including both the waste in the largest systems, and the waste inherent in our one-way material flows. This holds a major economic as well as environmental opportunity. Second, we believe the 'less bad' eco-efficiency norm needs to be replaced by a 'good' norm, which we will call 'net-positive' or 'accretive'. Let's explore each of these changes, how they are made possible by the technology disruption, and then show how they can take the world a big step towards a good disruption.

From eco-efficiency to planet compatibility – three pillars

What does a planet-compatible economic model look like? We believe a useful way to describe it is in term of three major pillars, all enabled by the technology disruption, and together making it possible to combine increased wealth with a prospering planet:

- *Abundant clean energy.* Renewable energy technologies have been through an amazing improvement journey over the last decade, beating all expectations on both cost and volume development. Solar photovoltaics, to take one example, have decreased more than 70 per cent in cost over the last decade. Renewable energy costs are now broadly on a par with incumbent fossil alternatives. Even in China – the largest coal-based economy – 2015 coal demand was actually lower than in 2014,[27] and the local coal industry is in crisis. So the shift to a low-carbon energy system is real in a way it was not ten years ago; it is happening fast; and it is now happening for economic as much as environmental reasons. This 'clean energy' pillar is the only pillar the world is ambitiously addressing today. We describe this in more detail later on, and also bring another important message: once the energy system is clean and low cost, it will act as a major boost to innovation and economic progress, the way cheap fossil fuels did in the past. So once the clean transition is made, the strategy should be to flood the economy with cheap clean energy, and to use it efficiently.
- *A 'cradle-to-cradle' material bank.* A circular material system, where materials, components and products are reused many times or safely returned to the environment, is the second pillar. It has huge economic benefits, as today's one-way material use is very wasteful, and would also address all the negative environmental and health impacts from our current material use. As we will discuss, most materials can be reused almost endlessly as long as they are kept pure, products are designed for disassembly and better recovery and tracing systems are put in place. At first sight, it might look like a hassle for companies to have to comply with such design rules, but consider this: with a set of relatively basic product design rules, today's giant waste industry could be turned into a giant mine,

serving many of our material needs. Material recovery is in many cases not profitable today, because today's product design makes the end-of-life value of most products close to zero by glueing, welding and mixing different materials and additives together. But with good design principles, the asset inventory of a country could turn into a 'bank' of materials and a true competitive advantage, and it would unleash a wave of innovation and renewal, as companies redesign their products to take advantage of the new material source. We will show what such a system could look like, and that technology development has made it possible in a way it was not a decade ago.

- *High-productivity regenerative systems.* We are starting to recognize how much system architectures matter. Even the best products fuelled with abundant renewable energy and designed for reuse will not allow us to build an accretive economy if not embedded into high-productivity systems. Systems are the new unit of change. Higher utilization through sharing, virtualization of activities to avoid physical products in the first place, better integration of products into systems (such as mobility systems, cities, food systems) and less wastefulness through better system design – all of these are huge but under-leveraged opportunities. And again, due to technology, they are feasible today in a way they were not a decade ago. Sharing of cars and houses, for instance, was not attractive to large consumer groups before the smartphone, but is now growing explosively. Sharing and virtualization might in fact be among the most powerful environmental levers we have – a radically new perspective compared to e.g. the turn of the century. We show later on how three of our largest value chains – mobility, food and housing – are today severely under-developed compared to their economic and environmental potential, and we show that if we can only improve these three systems, we will already have come a long way towards a good disruption.

Of course, outlining these pillars at a high level is the easy part, but we drill a few levels deeper in the book and talk about what mix of technology, innovation, policy and behaviours we think is needed to establish each of them. Once these three pillars start to fall into place, we will enter a virtuous cycle. Abundant clean energy and good design principles will allow us to circulate products and materials many more times through the economy, and to cheaply disintegrate them into their material components. High-productivity systems will in turn make both energy and materials cheaper and increase the value of products. So all three pillars are needed and mutually reinforcing. Too many discussions have been focused on one pillar only. Over the last decade, particularly during the climate change debate, all attention has been on renewable energy. We are only starting to understand the importance of a cradle-to-cradle material system and the importance of both to be embedded in high-productivity systems. So the three-pillar model represents a major change compared to today's environmental efforts, and a very attractive economic growth opportunity. As we will discuss, the two last pillars are also essential to achieve the 1.5°–2°C climate commitment which 195 countries made at the Paris conference.

New norms, new behaviours

We also believe it is now time to change the eco-efficiency norm itself. Being 'less bad' is clearly not good enough, as described above. It should be a basic societal norm of all economic activities that their total net impact, including their impact on manufactured capital, natural capital and human capital, is actually positive – in other words, that the economic activity in total does more good than harm – over the lifetime of the asset (and including after-life uses). We call such an activity 'net-positive', when we refer to individual decisions, or 'accretive' when we want to emphasize that such activities increase the capital base of a country.

This is a simple, almost obvious, idea, and a counter-question we often get asked is: but are most companies, consumers and governments not already acting this way, to the best of their abilities? A few are, but having spent the last thirty collective years advising companies and governments on strategy as well as on environmental topics, we can safely say that this idea represents a massive shift in mindset and expectations among the vast majority of business and political leaders. Today, almost all are in the eco-efficiency and reductionist mindset; in other words, the bar they set for themselves is to cause less damage than comparable countries or competing firms. Pick up the sustainability report of any major corporation today, and you will find it full of statistics on how the company is more eco-efficient than last year (i.e. that it is 'less bad'). But, crucially, you will – on average – also find that the company's total environmental footprint has actually increased (i.e. that the total environmental damage is larger this year than last). And look through any government report on its environmental initiatives, and you will find it dominated by eco-efficiency policies like fuel standards and energy efficiency. So a net-positive principle represents a massive shift in the aspiration companies and governments set for themselves, in their mindset, and how they evaluate success.

The idea of a net-positive, or accretive, norm has many roots. It builds on Paul Collier's suggestion that we should see ourselves as custodians of natural resources, and that we are allowed to use and consume them as long as what remains leaves the next generation better off than otherwise. It benefits from Hawken's and Lovins' *Natural Capitalism* thinking, and it incorporates Walter Stahel's push to maximize the utilization of any capital that we take into operation in the framework of *performance economy*. It feeds from Michael Braungart and William McDonough's *Cradle to Cradle* thinking, which lays out how all products should be designed to keep the value in materials and components high for the next use cycle. And it builds on the UN-sponsored natural capital accounting work.

But so far, these notions have not become mainstream, and among the companies and governments we work with, only a small minority seriously consider them. We believe this is largely because they are seen as too aspirational, almost unrealistic, and therefore have often been shelved as long-term opportunities.

We will argue in this book that this must no longer be the case. In fact, new technology has made a net-positive principle not only realistic, but attractive for a broad range of products and services – a claim that was hard to make in the past. The combination of dramatic performance improvements of renewable energy technologies and new digital technologies that allow order-of-magnitude better use of materials and products, together makes the net-positive equation balance in a way it did not ten years ago. Natural capital damages are much cheaper to minimize or remove than a decade ago, and the material and product value can now often be maximized through sharing, digitization and re-manufacturing in ways it previously couldn't.

Crucially, a net-positive principle does not imply a 'back to nature' economy where all use of natural resources is frowned upon. Plenty of natural resource uses, even of finite materials such as metal ores, can be defended within this framework. The only thing the principle requires is to use a definition of the capital base that is broad enough to cover the elements most people care about, estimate the main impacts of the economic activity across its lifetime on this capital base and be able to show that in total, it causes more good than harm to our aggregate state of capital.

Let us give one example now – metals – and then many more throughout the book. Mining of metal ores inevitably causes nature some scars, and turning ores into metals is a highly energy-intense process, today largely fossil fuel-based. Does this mean we should abstain from using metals in an economy that refrains from eroding natural capital? No. Many impact analyses of metals come out positive already with today's practices, since metals enable a long range of hugely value-adding products. But now imagine if clean energy had been used to produce the metal, and if the metal is built into products and handled in a way so that it can be reused over and over again (new technology has made both things realistic and profitable). Then it would not be hard to motivate economically or morally why extracting the metal in order to create a working material stock was beneficial. Quite the opposite: a good supply of clean high-performing materials circulating in the economy would be an invaluable asset to hand over to our children. We would have accreted our capital stock. When thinking through different product categories, it turns out many of our products are not accretive today: they are dissipated and lost at best, and massively contaminating at worst. But with the technology now available, this can in many cases change. And for those products that cannot realistically be made net-positive – is that not a very good thing for policy-makers, investors and consumers to know?

At the beginning, these calculations will feel awkward, and few decision-makers will have a sense for what health costs or freshwater depletion damage costs 'should' be. But quickly decision-makers will develop an intuition for what the numbers should look like, and these more comprehensive calculations will become part of the everyday decision-making of companies. Eventually, passing the 'net-positive test' might one day be as obvious for companies as passing the profitability test is today. And it might be more intuitive than we think: after all, capital accretion is the hidden norm by which many family businesses and private households are run – not for short-term income but for long-term wealth accumulation.

The power of net-positive thinking

But will it make a difference? This is another common counter-question we get asked. Surely most companies and governments are already doing their best, given their competitive situation and public budgets, so why would it help to raise the bar even further?

We believe that if a net-positive, or accretive, principle was broadly established, it would make a huge difference, in at least three ways. First, it would change everyday company decisions. Norms matter for such decisions. Most companies would never use child labour even if they could get away with it, and most companies today have radically different norms about gender equality, corruption, health and safety, than they had just a few decades ago. So norms matter, and they can change over time. And norms are at their most effective in precisely the sort of situation we are in, where decision-making is spread over many individuals, where it is hard to create formal regulations and when circumstances change quickly over time. Thinking about it, we find it almost surprising that when it comes to resource stewardship, there isn't currently any such broadly established norm, beyond that of doing a little less harm than last year.

Second, it would create a new competitive dynamic. Consumers would start to regard it as a basic quality requirement that the products they buy do more good than harm (a conclusion that is impossible to draw from today's dizzying array of certificates, labels and product claims). Why should consumers accept anything less? Investors could set similar requirements. And with the transparency that new digital technology offers, it is much easier and cheaper than a decade ago to trace a product and verify how it has been put together. This will also mean a new standard for how companies compete. At first, being regenerative and circular will be a powerful marketing argument for companies that can show their products are actually doing good, all key things considered. Then net-positive products will become a hygiene factor, and a market standard. Companies won't be able to afford to not comply, and companies that produce too much waste such as end-of-use plastic, CO_2 or idle car capacity will be regarded as undermanaged. For companies, having an appealing vision and set of values is also a competitive advantage in the labour market: in the interview in Part V of this book, Jean-Marc Duvoisin, the CEO of Nespresso, explains that companies without such appeal have to pay significantly more to attract young talent.

Finally, if this new social norm was established, it would accelerate formal environmental regulation. Isn't the answer to all of these issues tougher environmental regulations? is another counterquestion we often get. Economists would often call this the 'polluter pays' principle, or say that externalities should be priced – this is the standard recommendation most economics textbooks give for ensuring public goods are not overused. We are all for better externalities pricing, and agree it is a crucial precondition for establishing a planet-compatible economic model. However, this has been the textbook recommendation for many decades, and still it has not happened. Why? Because changes of this magnitude have to start from ideas, values and convictions. First, companies and voters need to be convinced that the transformation is needed, attractive and realistic. Then, and only then, technical rules and formal prices can follow. Externalities pricing is today perceived as a burden to the economy, and many voters don't see the need for a transition in the first place, so in reality it is today risky for political leaders to move ahead and impose stricter environmental legislation.

So what we suggest is in fact very different from just proposing externalities pricing: we suggest that companies, consumers, governments, NGOs and investors start to discuss and experiment with the principle of capital accretion or net-positive, and start asking it of the products they buy. When a share of them find out that – with new technology – the benefits are tangible, it will spread and start becoming a new norm. When this norm is sufficiently well accepted, it will in turn create the political preconditions for formal externalities pricing of the scale required. So a quite different approach, one led by ideas and norms.

Impact on the economy

To make the vision more concrete, we applied it to the European economy, and specifically to its mobility, food and housing systems. Then we worked with an academic team to model the quantitative economic and environmental consequences. The results blew us away. If this vision was to materialize, European GDP could increase by as much as 7 percentage points until 2030, relative to a 'business as usual' development. Clearly, there are major uncertainties involved when modelling big economic shifts. But for all the flaws and difficulties of choosing the right input metrics, they provide a direction – a large positive impact. And that makes intuitive sense: if one can use new technology and smarter policy to reduce the massive amounts of structural waste inherent in our largest systems, and do so at a comparatively low additional cost, this should have a major positive impact. This cost decrease of basic human needs would effectively act as a wage increase for European households, and be proportionally largest for low- and middle-income households. In parallel, the modelling showed that greenhouse gas emissions could drop by as much as 83 per cent until 2050,[28] in line with what is needed to stabilize climate change at 1.5–2 degrees, and we found no evidence that such a model could not offer at least as much employment as today's model.

Imagine also the innovation and renewal that such a transformation would unleash in the economy: net-positive products, a high-value material bank, low-waste mobility and food systems. Major opportunities to cut waste in our largest value chains. When discussing with CEOs, we sometimes use the 'lean operations' analogy. When lean pioneer Toyota changed the ambition level for its operations and supply chain from 'incrementally reduce cost' to 'eliminate all waste', this new lens allowed them to discover a whole new range of improvement opportunities that no one had thought about before.[29] It also led to a huge boost in product improvements and productivity gains within Toyota, since it mobilized the organization to innovate around a common ambitious norm. This propelled Toyota to become the world's largest and most profitable car manufacturer, and made the 'lean' approach a standard for manufacturing firms. We believe a principle of net-positive could be an equally unambiguous, simple and powerful notion, and could unleash a similar innovation.

At a deeper level, an accretive principle would mean the global economy would actually be on a development pathway towards combining prosperity and planet. As should be clear by now, we are not on such a pathway today. But a new principle of capital accretion will also mean we resolve the deep paradox that today sits at the heart of our economy: the more successful we are at growing the economy, the longer we live and the more children we have, the more we destroy our surrounding environment and the more socially skewed the outcomes will be. As long as we are in the depletive model, we can never truly celebrate – either birth – or growth. An accretive economy would instead be one of abundance: the more we grow, the better for future generations, and for our planet.

These results gave us encouragement that a shift in the direction we propose could provide an answer to the question that today's model fails to answer: how we can continue to increase shared prosperity without destroying the productivity of our natural capital base.

III. The technology disruption – necessary but not sufficient

We are in the midst of a major technology disruption and an industrial shake-up. That matters hugely for our discussion, because our ability to feed ourselves, to lead good lives and to grow the economy is not a function of planetary constraints and population size. It is the technology we use and the systems we install that govern the difference between scarcity and abundance. The system of hunting and gathering fed 5 million people, that of agriculture 800 million. Industrialization provided a basis for 5 billion people to thrive.[30] But – as we have amply demonstrated – not for 7 or 11 billion. A new technology platform is needed to reconcile people and planet. And it is arriving in a massive storm that is already scaring many incumbent companies stiff. The technologies behind these shifts are improving at a fast pace: smartphones, artificial intelligence, 3D printing, biomaterials, quantum computing, robotics, big data, automation, and many others.

This technology disruption will, over the next two decades, deeply transform the economy's big physical value chains, in the same way it has already transformed information sectors like banking, communication and entertainment. We will look at mobility, food and housing, and we will show that for almost every large segment in these value chains, there is not only one but several blockbuster technologies and business models that are commercially attractive today, or close to it, and that look to have a profound impact over the coming five to ten years on intractable challenges such as externalities, free-riding and overuse: driverless cars, precision agriculture, 3D-printed houses, cheap clean energy, or the internet of things. In the words of Cisco CEO John Chambers, 'the impact is likely to be five times bigger than the internet revolution'. The stakes are enormous, given how important these value chains are for our way of life, employment, economy and natural capital.

Disrupted – for better or worse?

On one hand, this disruption creates a fantastic opportunity for implementing the vision laid out above: it makes it practically doable and economically attractive. We have the most powerful tool in history right at our fingertips.

But on the other hand, on the current trajectory, the disruption won't solve our natural capital issues, nor will it help solve our major social issues around income equality and cohesion. There is, in fact, a fairly strong body of evidence to suggest the disruption might instead aggravate both sets of issues. And it raises the bar, since such large and important value chains will be impacted. It seems we are heading for a bad disruption.

For *natural capital*, the issue, as already described above, is that per-unit improvements are vastly outweighed by volume increases. Economic growth increases demand, and when new technology on top of that decreases per-unit prices, experience shows that people will request more cars, food and houses (the so-called rebound effect). At first sight, this looks like good news: consumer benefits increase and the economy grows. However, it also increases absolute resource use in many cases when it should instead decrease. And in some of these value chains, the volume growth would in practice negate many of the benefits: if car access became much cheaper per kilometre, there is every reason to believe inner cities would get more congested, outweighing much of the original advantages.

The impact of technology on *economic growth* is hotly debated. We will review both sides of the argument in detail later in the book, but so far, the numbers seem to be on the side of technology sceptics: growth in output per worker in the US, for instance, has decreased during the last decades of technology disruption, not increased.

According to the majority of research, *inequality* will likely increase as a result of the disruption: less-qualified work is often easier to automate, and digitization means the 'superstars' can increase their reach and value-add.

For *employment*, the research is more split: for instance, an ambitious 2013 study from Oxford examined the top 700 types of employment and found that 47 per cent of jobs were at risk of being digitized.[31] Others point out, however, that large sectors such as healthcare will need more employees in future, that fears of major employment destruction have never materialized in previous technology disruptions, and that employment can often be managed by smart policy.

What's more, there is a broad sense among many consumers, companies and governments that they are at the mercy of a global technology tsunami, gushing over their communities, business models or constituencies in ways they cannot control. Technology is to many synonymous with loss of control. This is a huge challenge to our democratic societies at large.

For us, this situation is deeply disturbing. There are literally hundreds of millions of savvy innovators at work all over the world, in all sorts of sectors and positions, yet it is arguable whether the total result of that innovation is even positive and, as we showed above, in many cases it is unclear whether our wealth is even increasing. We will explore how this can be, and also what the latest research says about how governments can steer innovation and technology development without destroying it.

These are all crucial reasons for governments and the broader society to become more engaged in managing the effects of the technology disruption, and to define principles and boundary constraints to make it net-positive and ultimately a good disruption – a useful one.

IV. Crossing the chasm

It is evident: the new accretive model powered by renewable energy, operating a cradle-to-cradle material bank, and embedding products into high-productivity regenerative systems differs fundamentally from the current industrial model. The old and the new model are separated by a chasm with regard to the ways we produce, consume, share benefits between producers and consumers, measure success and – most importantly – use our natural resources. The chasm is deep and wide: it consists of inherited infrastructure (from power plants to incinerators), established business practices (from stock write-downs to faster fashion cycles), rules and regulations (from price-based public procurement to trade restrictions of post-use equipment), incentives (from sales to cost targets), mindsets and our limited ability to reimagine the world. Even if we fully embraced the power of the new economic model, we are locked into the old one in an all-encompassing way. Yes, we are advancing it based on new technology and it is changing its face every day. But deep inside it continues to be extractive, exploitative and exhaustive and not at all geared towards growing our common stock of human, social, natural and man-made capital.

We have failed on transformations of much lower and more incremental ambition, such as medical or education reform. How can we believe in resetting the entire operating system of our global economy at a moment when governance is failing on a global scale, the spectre of isolationism returns, short-term capitalism reigns and confidence falters? We think we can. The opportunity is at our fingertips and it is our choice to use it. There are five reasons for our optimism.

Reason 1: A burning platform

The world will not move without a very clear case for action. Over the next 10 years, we must act. For a long time it seemed a matter of opinion, but now facts are inescapable and numbers unequivocal: we have ten years to initiate the shift from depletion to accretion in order to avert a crisis. The productivity of our natural systems such as agriculture is unable to keep pace with demand. In 2010 for the first time population growth exceeded the yield growth of grain[32] – a Malthusian moment that must not (as history shows) but can go wrong. In 'business as usual' mode we will transgress the safe operating space of all earth systems in time; this has already happened in four out of nine earth systems, according to the Stockholm Resilience Centre. Over the next ten years we will likely transgress at least another two, massively affecting the productivity of our natural systems and the economy as a whole.[33] Often these warnings have been dismissed as alarmist. Many environmental missions have faced such a reproach: the effort to ban DDT, Germany's battle to stop acid rain, or the wake-up call of the Club of Rome. Yet sometimes you can ring an alarm bell too soon – ample evidence shows that early warning was the reason why some of those gloomy predictions did not materialize. However, firemen report that most casualties from fires in public places are not the result of panic and over-reaction but of delayed response. There is a point in ringing the alarm bell on time.

And we *can* act: inaction over the next ten years would mean missing a historic window of opportunity. The Paris climate agreement brought a momentum and a strengthened political mandate. By relentlessly exposing the gap between 'intended nationally determined contributions' (INDCs) of approximately 2.6 degrees and the collective global commitment (1.5 degrees), it rendered the current industrial and energy system unviable[34] – a historic step indeed, providing the tailwind to rethink and challenge some fundamental economic assumptions. Then there is the economic imperative to avoid stranded assets in the trillions. Over the next ten years we will be investing $60 trillion into infrastructure alone.[35] If it is based in the old model of energy generation and industrial production and consumption, this would be the single biggest stack of stranded assets in history. And lastly, we are reaching 'peak child'. Today we have 1.9 billion children, which is likely to be the highest number ever in human history – it has not been and will not be higher.[36] Socializing this peak generation into a new economic vision – renewable energy, healthy products, performance selling, asset sharing and reinvestment into natural systems – will ripple through the rest of the century. If we were to touch all 15-year-olds by 2025 with this new vision, and they were to pass on the new normal to their successors, 75 per cent of the human years lived in this century would see and live the new model – an opportunity we cannot possibly miss. The costs of depletion of this opportunity for a reset have never been more conspicuous, tangible or real. We have a case for change.

Reason 2: An intuition reset is within reach

The major barrier towards a rapid transition out of our depleting industrial model is our imagination gap. We grew up during a time when coal power was much cheaper than solar power, when gasoline cars performed much better than electric, when virgin materials were cheaper than recycled. But that gap is closing now and our ability to envisage a different future might create a unique tipping point. Thomas Kuhn's 1962 book *The Structure of Scientific Revolutions* established the concept of 'paradigm shifts'. What is a household name today was an eye-opener in the mid-sixties. Kuhn's core argument was this: most scientific research happens within established belief systems, paradigms, such as classical mechanics, or Bohr's atomic model. Researchers use these paradigms to explain more and more phenomena, through experiments and theory development. But then, over time, observations and new discoveries are made that are inconsistent with the prevailing paradigm. At first, scientists try to assimilate such anomalies into the existing paradigm. But as more and more incommensurable observations stack up, the old paradigm falls into crisis, as its inability to explain reality gets ever more obvious. The search for a new paradigm starts. For quite some time the old and the new paradigm coexist and compete, until the old one ultimately demises. We end up with a new intuition of reality, see the

Fig. 0.2

world in a new 'gestalt' and often wonder how we could ever have seen it differently. Kuhn visualized the concept of a gestalt shift through a now-famous drawing that can be seen both as a duck and a rabbit. If we have always seen the duck, we cannot see the rabbit. Once we learn to see the rabbit, it is impossible to go back and only see the duck.[37]

In a way this book describes a perfect duck and a perfect rabbit. Let's start with today's duck: in this view of the world, the global economy is generating unprecedented wealth. Through a capitalist system of markets, ownership, competition and innovation, it is lifting billions of people from poverty to middle class and towards prosperity. Yes, economic growth inevitably creates some costs to human health and the environment, but every time these costs are getting too high we put remedies in place. Natural resources are in general amply available and cheap, and whenever they get scarce, price signals encourage innovation that in turn finds workarounds. Improvements in exploration, mining, transport, production, distribution and supply chain management are keeping costs down in spite of growth, and make products affordable to the billions who sweep into the global economy. Making any substantial changes to this model could jeopardize its success and is a reckless thing to suggest. To many, this is the gestalt of our current economy – a perfect duck.

Fictitiously looking backward to the present day creates a very different gestalt – a perfect rabbit. We will be shaking our heads over the old normal: investing hugely into assets that we then massively under-utilize, burning in two hundred years the fossil fuels that took millions of years to be created even when knowing the dangers, hauling billions of tons of industrial production to landfills after single use, running a global agricultural system on mineral fertilizers which predictably will be available for only a few decades and allowing the entire available stock of mineral phosphate to be washed into the sea, or building cities that are inaccessible for everyone not owning a car. Against a new paradigm, future generations won't be able to understand that we did not see and react to the massive anomalies that were stacking up. They will ask: 'What were you thinking?', the same way we do when it comes to slavery, voting rights for women, or spraying DDT all over our food. When you had all the technology at your fingertips, they will ask, what then caused the imagination gap? We cannot overinvest in drawing the gestalt of an accretive system, in looking back at ourselves from the future and in questioning today's normal. System-level change always starts with visioning and stretching our beliefs. And it ends – as Thomas Kuhn describes – with a shift in our world view that is much faster and more fundamental than we could ever imagine.

Reason 3: The explosion of expressive power

When Malaysian Airlines flight MH370 disappeared on 8 March 2014, Digital Globe provided high-resolution satellite imaging to web users who browsed pixel-by-pixel in the search for airplane debris. The response was phenomenal; at one stage the website recorded more than 100,000 visits per hour. Users could tag images which were later reviewed with algorithms. The database turned out to be the most important resource for guiding the search for the missing plane.[38] A similar crowdsourcing platform, 'Tomnod', has been deployed since 2014 to pinpoint forest fires in Sumatra, again by creating complete near-time transparency on new fires, often triggering on-the-ground action by government or activists.[39] The technology disruption not only helps us to build the systems which will house, feed, move and warm us in the future, it also enables change itself. There are more examples. Greenpeace forced toymaker Mattel to disband palm oil derived packaging for its signature dolls Barbie and Ken dolls through channelling protesters onto Mattel's Facebook and Twitter pages. More than 200,000 emails were directed to Bob Eckert, Mattel's CEO.[40] The Extractive Industries Transparency Initiative, which aims to create transparency and accountability around use of natural resources, transformed the global mining industry. While it was launched as an initiative of the UK government under Tony Blair, it quickly grew through the support of the global grass-root community. Today more than 51 countries implement EITI standards and report revenues, tax income of $1.847 trillion of mining activities and their use of the proceeds.[41]

We cannot overestimate the social dynamics of the internet revolution. The availability of many-to-many media is so fundamentally different from the one-to-one communication enabled by the telephone or one-to-many communication enabled by radio and television that it will determine the path our society is taking. 'The moment we're living through [...] is the largest increase in expressive capability in human history,' Clay Shirky says. Fighting corruption in China, exposing neglect in old people's homes, controlling effluents on an industrial site or keeping MPs honest – web-empowered citizens and social media groups are massively shifting the balance of power, the speed and direction of societal change.[42] Clearly this sparks new challenges such as the loss of personal accountability and privacy. And yet, the disruption seems made for the system-level change needed in our economic model. Over and above the power to expose resource use, to monitor ecosystem health, to share assets and products, and to trace materials through their use cycles, it is the ability to express public dissent, to convene user communities and to socialize a new paradigm that will pave the way for a new economic model.

Reason 4: The rise of the meso-economy

Many still regard the economy as consisting of two types of stakeholders. On one hand, self-interested companies are competing in perfect or near-perfect markets based on the microeconomics of supply and demand. On the other hand, states are making rules for those markets, and steer aggregate supply and demand based on different macroeconomic beliefs. In this world, any transition towards a circular and regenerative economy is slow and difficult. The business sector is pointing at government, saying it needs better rules and a level playing field to be able to change. And governments say that before they can take the risk of introducing new regulation, they need some companies to show initiative and prove that new business models and technologies are indeed viable. Locked in a chicken-and-egg dynamic, businesses only react to market rules set by the state, and the state refuses to act because it fears for economic activity, employment and growth. In such a world, a system shift towards the three-pillar, net-positive economy is an impossibility.

This two-sector view of the world is simple and elegant – but increasingly wrong. Economists such as Nobel laureate Ronald Coase have long criticized microeconomic theory for failing to properly describe the real-life contractual relationships between companies, and increasingly so in new markets where property rights are far from clear and transaction costs are high.

Luckily, there is a new meso-economy emerging which has already proved to be a force for good. It occupies a fast-growing terrain right in between the two polar endpoints of micro and macro. More and more economic activity is relational and not transactional by nature, and it happens between relevant stakeholders: companies, banks, universities, governments and consumers. The meso-economy is emerging in three different forms.

First, it takes the form of non- or pre-competitive collaboration. More and more companies are joining forces with others in their relevant sector or system in order to redefine the rules of the game. For example, H2 Mobility is a consortium of Air Liquide, Daimler, Linde, OMV, Shell and Total aspiring to explore and promote the use of hydrogen in mobility. The Project Mainstream consortium initiated by the World Economic Forum, the Ellen MacArthur Foundation and McKinsey's Center for Business and Environment comprises ten companies that share an ambition to take circular products and services mainstream. Eighty of the world's largest pension and sovereign wealth funds have joined forces in the P80 Group to cooperate on sustainable investment. Increasingly companies view such collaborations as being highly strategic and the pre-eminent instrument to shape their market environment. Some of the most game-changing plots in the battle for better resource stewardship are the result of business consortia signing up to a joint mission: the Carbon Disclosure Project, which provides transparency on companies' carbon emissions; the Marine Stewardship Council; the New Plastic Economy project and the Tropical Forest Alliance.

Second, we see the renaissance of the cooperative. In Germany, cooperative banks have gained 1 million new customers since 2008 and have been praised by chancellor Angela Merkel as the 'model of the future'.[43] Throughout the world, cooperatives outgrow the overall economy. They operate in agriculture, energy, social infrastructure and increasingly in the digital space. They come with the benefit of including all users and importantly, they work in imperfect markets where the market price for a service is hard to determine.

And finally, nonprofits are becoming much more professional, and are fast increasing their impact. They bundle resources, develop dependable strategic and operational plans, measure impact and offer opportunities for the best talent.

This matters, because the meso-economy is increasingly morphing into the epicentre of systemic change. While market-based transactions and the macro-economic steer of vigilant governments remain important (particularly when it comes to controlling externalities), the sphere where lock-in is overcome has moved to the meso-economy.

Reason 5: New capitalists

There is a debate about whether capital is becoming more short-term or long-term. Both are true. There is hard evidence for increased short-termism and cash preference on the one hand, and particularly public capital markets are not delivering their promise as agents of breakthrough, systemic innovation. But there is also a swiftly growing segment of long-term and impact-oriented capitalists and active governments. It is growing in scale and conviction and has the power to drive system change. Catalytic capital can play a major role in escaping our linear lock-in and there will be more of it. Impact capital funds are growing by a staggering 37 per cent per annum.[44] In Europe socially responsible investment (ESG – Environmental, Social and Governance) already constitutes 10 per cent of direct investments and investments managed by the asset management industry. These investments have grown by over 30 per cent per annum since 2009.[45] Some environmental funds such as Generation Investment have consistently outperformed the market. Importantly, major institutional investors such as mega-asset manager BlackRock or Canada Pension Plan Investment are changing perspective: moving from a 'renter' to an 'owner' mindset, reducing the frequency of trade and taking more active board positions. And finally, public sector funding is increasingly striving to embrace the systemic nature of the change that lies ahead. The European Union has granted €650 million to circular economy projects and opened up its Horizon 2020 fund of €24 billion to circular economy projects.[46] The new capitalists don't enter the stage with a different set of morals but with a new set of insights. The systemic risk that has been accumulating in portfolios is mounting. And now they have to move beyond system boundaries in order to redeploy the significant stocks of cash that sit in pension funds, life insurances and cash-rich companies and which today are locked into low-yield and one-day stranded 'old economy' assets.

We have seen before how fast this goes as soon as investors realize that the growth prospect of an asset class are bleak: coal companies have lost almost all of their market capitalization over the last years, and fossil-based utilities have also taken a massive beating in only a few years. So long-term, activist capital together with the other four aspects we elaborated are reasons for optimism but not complacency. What is needed is a chain of knock-on effects that will take us into an upward spiral. There are indications that this chain is already in motion.

Entering the upward spiral

How can we take our industrial engine on a different path over the next ten years? We won't try to lay out a plan for the transition – it is far too unpredictable for that. Let us instead look at a similar transition that has been going on for a while – that of climate change mitigation and clean energy and see what we can learn from it. While very far from completion, it is an exciting learning case which demonstrates that systemic change is the result of neither macro- and microeconomic policy nor singular super-innovations. Instead it is the result of accelerating reinforcement and knock-on effects between different types of economic actors.

The story of climate mitigation and clean energy is one of tipping points, positive reinforcement between stakeholder groups, vested interests and the power of good examples. The academic community started to send serious warnings of global warming already in the 1970s and 1980s, and began calling for an end to fossil fuels. But the mere thought was so entirely irreconcilable with the technology and economy of the day that their calls were largely seen as unrealistic. Decision-makers saw the rabbit and could not see the duck. But over time that changed. The warnings led to a debate, to funded research, to multilateral action, to grass-root protests and ultimately produced a policy tipping point, the UN's Framework Convention on Climate Change (UNFCCC), which was negotiated at the Rio de Janeiro Earth Summit in 1992, and later followed up with the Kyoto protocol in 1997.

Research grants and subsidies to renewable energy increased, although these technologies were still far out of the money. Pioneering companies started to invest real research and development resources, and costs for the new technologies started to decrease fast, making a clean energy transition economically viable. In parallel, ever more academic research was done, creating a better fact base on the serious effects of global warming, and leading to an emerging conviction among most electorates that this was an issue to take seriously – another tipping point. This, in turn, created the political preconditions for Europe to introduce its cap-and-trade system in 2005, another tipping point.

Now suddenly climate regulation had a major financial impact and was on everyone's lips. We would characterize 2005–10 as the years of awakening and conviction by the business community, at least in Europe. As business consultants, we saw how industry's attitude evolved by the month. All the input from the resource boom, CO_2 prices, the Copenhagen negotiations, academia and technology companies created a broadly held conviction that clean energy systems and resource productivity were major business themes for the coming decades, and indeed survival criteria for companies. Another tipping point had been reached. Research and development investments shifted quickly, and fantastic technology stories started to emerge in solar photovoltaics (PV), battery technology, electric cars and many other areas. Moore's law, originally describing the evolution of chip performance, took hold of many segments: the improvement pace reached such heights that companies needed to make major research and development investments just to keep up with competitors, and these investments of course further accelerated the pace of development.

By 2009–10, the genie was out of the bottle: not even the combination of the financial crisis, the shale gas boom and the resulting dip in fossil fuel prices was enough to halt that development. Certainly, these years were tough for many clean energy companies, but the disruptively fast growth of the clean energy sector continued.

In parallel, the attractiveness of the 'old' system deteriorated fast, sending it into crisis. In the European electricity industry, growth of the incumbent power generation technologies turned negative, resulting in low utilization, a dramatic drop in electricity prices, massive write-downs and plummeting share prices. These new economics – with renewable energy technologies soon being the cheapest – were a crucial reason why the Paris agreement could be negotiated in late 2015.

Now, writing in early 2016, we would say it is a broadly held belief that our energy future is a clean and renewable one, both in the Western world and increasingly in developing economies, and most companies we know agree that the transition is entirely possible without prohibitive costs. The duck is quickly turning into a rabbit. Much remains to be done, of course, but it is an amazing development. Only fifteen years ago, all the odds were stacked up against this revolution: relative costs, economies of scale, vested interests, voter sentiment and company mindsets all suggested a fossil future was the safe bet.

What can we learn? That changing systems is an iterative process between all stakeholders mentioned above, where a step forward from one group makes it easier for the others to reach the next level, creating an upward spiral. That beliefs and paradigms are highly effective in steering action and investments, and that they can and must change in parallel with 'hard' policies. That system-level change is driven by tipping points, implying that change often happens much faster than preconceptions suggest. But perhaps most importantly, that such transitions are inevitably about innovation, in technology, business models, governance and thinking at large.

We believe a similar dynamic is possible for our broader capital-accretive agenda, and that it is indeed crucial to set in motion the same type of mutual reinforcement and upward spiral. We see some version of the net-positive principle and the three pillars as the new paradigm. For those who agree with us that this is an attractive, liberating vision to pursue, it translates to the following broad priorities for each stakeholder group: governments should work to put disincentives for environmental and health damages in place – this is the economics textbook answer to how to deal with externalities, and an important part of the solution. However, they should also acknowledge that today they do not have the political mandate to introduce strong enough legislation, and currently are only able to change resource pricing at the margin. Therefore, they should take a completely new approach: They should jockey for pole position in creating material banks and establishing criteria for high-productivity regenerative systems in the same way they started doing it for the low-carbon energy systems. This will take many years. A first step is to acknowledge the inherent opportunity in each of these pillars, their current wastefulness, and broaden the political discourse from 'climate and energy' to include 'materials' and 'systems'. And then get to work on the myriad of regulatory changes, tax adjustments, public-private partnerships, and public investments that are needed to create the same upward spiralling dynamic as for renewable energy. The ongoing technology disruption will provide a strong tail-wind if well captured, as we will demonstrate throughout the book.

Equally important, policy-makers need to help establish the vision that a net-positive and circular economy is not only possible, but also realistic and attractive and a way to own the 'moral high ground' during the tide of technological changes ahead of us.

Governments must further act as entrepreneurs and innovators. Radical innovation requires a 'knowledge-hungry' state that invests where the private sector will not. As Mariana Mazzucato points out in her paper, 'The Entrepreneurial State', many of the major breakthroughs in digital, biotech or energy have in fact been on the back of foresighted, long-term national 'systems of innovation'. The transition ahead provides ample opportunity for such breakthrough and market-creating innovation: implementing 'product IDs' – cheap chips or QR codes that make assets smart and trackable is one such opportunity. It would allow consumers and society to have the same control over the use cycle of a product as large companies have today. This is entirely possible with today's technology, and would enable an enormous amount of innovation and new markets within sharing, re-use, and re-manufacturing.

Non-government actors, too, have to recognize the opportunity. Investors have to see the long-term opportunity that comes with the largest infrastructure renewal programme in history and the need to derisk their portfolios. Companies have to see the market opportunity for higher quality products, higher margin service contracts and resource independence. The workforce and trade unions have to recognize the employment opportunity, labour intensity and wealth of new skills needed to build the three pillars, as well as acknowledging that more jobs and better, more equitable access to services will help close the dangerous inequality gap. Academia and research institutions have to see the massive redesign opportunity and huge demand for innovation in materials, product design, industrial processes and business models. And finally, consumers will realize the benefits of higher quality, lower costs of service and more choice.

Activating any of these will spark a positive dynamic and catalytic effect on others – an upward spiral 'beyond the political trenches', a joint vision and more generosity as we move from a doctrine of scarcity to one of abundance.

Use it or lose it

We have found significant endorsement and support for our observations and conclusions. We know from our discussions and public talks that the young generation in particular is easily mobilized around a vision that could be as transformational as the creation of the EU internal market, a WTO free trade agreement or the shift from a socialist to market-based system in eastern Europe have been at the time. In fact the young refuse to accept the old answers. That does not mean that their views will be translated into meaningful action of the scope and speed we need. We could easily lose the decisive twenty to thirty years as there are some very safe seats on the backbenches. Mobilizing around the theme of a net-positive, accretive economy calls us into a collective take-off mode. What does it take to mobilize decision-makers and society at large towards the magnitude of changes that we are proposing? We have talked to five exceptional leaders, asking them exactly this question and hearing their perspective on system-level change: a church leader, a leading climate economist, a Nobel Peace Prize laureate, a CEO and a breakthrough scientist. You can read the interviews in Part V of the book. They all gave us optimism and opened our eyes to different avenues through which change will walk. They also made us aware that the question at stake is not only one of a higher-performing, lower-risk economy. It is not only about rebuilding our capital. It is more than that – it is perhaps the central human project that reconnects us to our planet, bridges social divides and reconciles us with future generations. And they made us realize that the time is now. Throughout our history, phases of scepticism, disorder and anxiety have been alternating with episodes of momentum and collective confidence. These have proved to be turning points – sometimes for bad and sometimes for good. The key reason why we have written this book is to point to the massive opportunity ahead of us. It's ours to lose. We could not think of a more exciting, more rewarding, and more deserving time to live in.

The table below summarizes the change in narrative that we have tried to describe in this chapter, and that we will explore more deeply in the rest of this book.

	From ...	... to
Part I	We are continuing to grow our economies	Underlying growth is much lower than GDP growth, and close to zero
	GDP is the best available metric of economic progress	Capital accretion metrics are now available and provide a better view
	Environmental challenges are local and episodic	We are facing a global, pervasive and accelerating environmental crisis
	Environmental degradation is the price for social progress	Social distortions and environmental damage are hugely correlated
	Resources might become scarce	Some resources are scarce, but the productivity and absorption capacity of earth systems are exhausted
	Competition has made our big physical value chains efficient	There is massive system waste even in mature value chains
	The environment is under threat	The economy and assets in the trillions are under threat
	The answer to our environmental issues is to become more eco-efficient	Eco-efficiency is good but insufficient – we need an entirely new norm for treating natural capital

	Eventually we will grow green	An entirely new pathway is required
Part II	An industrial economy without depleting the environment is impossible	New technology has over the last decades made an accretive economy feasible
	It is hard to say whether we are on track	The concept of a net-positive economy based on circular principles provides straight-forward, absolute criteria
	Hard fiscal incentives are what matter for environmental protection	Norms, values and beliefs about the future have huge influence on company decisions
	Transforming energy systems is the key to sustainability	Transforming material systems is at least as important
	Markets have optimized our big physical value chains	Our big physical value chains are severely under managed compared to their economic and environmental opportunity
	Greening is prohibitively expensive	Eradicating system waste is attractive economically and environmentally
	Sustainability can only be measured in comparison to others	There are objective and absolute standards for capital accretion
Part III	Technology will have much less impact on physical value chains than on informational ones	New technologies will deeply transform our big physical value chains starting in the next decade
	Technology is the ultimate solution for the environment	Technology is necessary but far from sufficient

Innovation and human ingenuity is lifting us to new levels	Research is very split over whether the effect of the current wave of innovation is positive or not
Technology development is essentially unmanageable	Technology development can be steered towards the solutions we want
Digitization will, on balance, increase the rate of material consumption	Digitization helps build feedback-rich systems which revolutionize the way we use the material world

Part IV

System change is hard, if not impossible	There are at least five reasons why system change could succeed this time round
The shift will take many decades	Within the next ten years we can reach a tipping point
Real change requires a massive shift in policy	Changes are the result of multiple actors taking synchronous action
Micro- and macroeconomic policies are key	An emerging meso-economy is also key
We should improve our current products and material systems	We must develop and grow new, better products and systems

PART I: OUR AFFAIR
WITH GROWTH

Chapter 1

Desired – celebrating growth

When the relative growth rate is constant, the quantity undergoes exponential growth and has a constant doubling time.

Wikipedia

We are addicted to growth, and we have reasons to be. In the twentieth century we invented a relentless growth engine that is unprecedented in history. During the twentieth century, the global economy grew from $2 trillion towards $37 trillion. That growth has changed our lives and the level of material well-being beyond imagination. In a local supermarket we just counted 56 different cereals and 122 different wines. The growth has occurred not just in the West but throughout the world: in the year 2000, 5.2 billion people were properly nourished, 1.6 billion drove cars and by 2014 close to 1.8 billion belonged to the global middle class.[1,2,3,4] Global poverty numbers – now less than 890 million – are decreasing and continue to do so with every percentage point of global GDP growth.[5] The same thing is happening to the gap between global incomes (now at $2,920) and OECD median incomes (now at $10,717).[6,7] The last century has been a true economic miracle a reason to explore outcomes, drivers and consequences.

1.1 A global *Wirtschaftswunder* – the extraordinary century

We all know the economic miracle that has transformed our lives. But reviewing the facts makes it look yet more astounding: Between the years 1000 and 2000 the economy grew from $0.1 trillion to $37 trillion (constant 2005 $): 98 per cent of that growth happened after 1820, 97 per cent in the twentieth century and 86 per cent of it in the second half of that century (see Figure 1.1). Twenty-one per cent of the material wealth that was ever created in history was manufactured between 2000 and 2014.[8] Before the nineteenth century, growth was essentially unknown and quality of life had to be based on non-material wealth and the promise of redemption.

These numbers tell the story of an industrial age which took most of the world by force. The first industrial revolution around 1820 was the starting point of a new economic era. It redefined societies, the balance between labour and capital, the relationship between countries, civilization and our environment and man and its creator. It marks a productivity explosion through new technologies, amplified through an ever-increasing amount of labour inputs and a social order amenable to an accountable and effective division of labour.

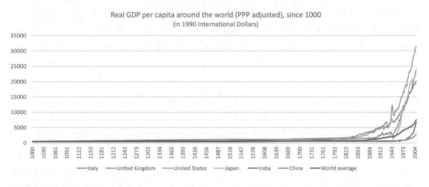

Real GDP per capita around the world (PPP adjusted), since 1000 (in 1990 International Dollars)

SOURCE: OurWorldInData.org (2016)

Fig. 1.1

By the end of the twentieth century the industrialized countries, EU, US and Japan, dominated the global economy by a leap. They accounted for around 65 per cent of the global GDP with 12 per cent of the population. And they globally defined the lifestyle, since in parallel, health, education and mobility had improved to unprecedented levels. Employment, social cohesion, political moderation, infrastructural renewal – all of these have been shown to correlate positively with economic growth. This, in turn, stabilized industrial societies. Growth continues to be the most effective inclusion programme. 'Slower growth makes distributional conflict inevitable,' says 2015 Nobel laureate economist Angus Deaton, 'because the only way forward for me is at your expense.'[9] To many, it is much simpler. Says Richard DeKaser, an economist with the US bank Wells Fargo: 'Most people agree, I think, that output, and hence, their ability to consume should improve. This is sort of the American Dream – things get better as you look toward the future.'[10]

1.2 Asia and Africa – impending super-growth

Future growth will have a massively different geographic pattern. In 2012, global GDP was about $72 trillion. Until 2025 a full $45 trillion – or three times the current US economy – will be added, an amazing leap in prosperity. Of this growth, 75 per cent will come from the developing world.[11]

The pace and scale is mind-blowing. Let's bring it into perspective. When the first industrial revolution started in the UK, it took 154 years for it to double GDP per capita in the UK, which had a mere 9 million people at the beginning of the journey. The US completed the same journey during the nineteenth century in fifty-three years, starting with about 10 million people. China did it in twelve (!) years, starting with more than a billion people, and finally in India it took sixteen years, with just over 800 million people. And of course, the Chinese and Indian developments are playing out in parallel, which means the total number of people affected is about 200 times larger, and the pace of change simultaneously about ten times faster than for the UK industrialization. So the sheer force of economic development is about 2,000 times higher.

This is a fantastic development – there is no other word for it. In 1990, 47 per cent of the population in the developing world was living in extreme poverty (defined as a disposable income of less than $1.25 per day), or a total of 1.9 billion people. By 2015 that share had decreased to just 14 per cent, or 836 million in total. In contrast, the middle-class population (defined as more than $10 per day in disposable income) almost tripled during the same time, and now makes up half the population in the developing world.

The social improvements that go hand in hand with the economic development are even more encouraging. The number of children of primary school age who did not attend school had dropped from

100 million in 2000 to 57 million by 2015, and the literacy rate of people aged between 15 and 24 years has increased from 83 to 91 per cent, with women making up for most of the improvement. Under-5 child mortality has dropped by more than half during the same period, from 90 deaths per 1,000 live births in 1990 to 43 in 2015, and maternal mortality rates reduced by 45 per cent during the same period. The population with access to piped drinking water rose from 2.3 billion in 1990 to 4.2 billion in 2015. The share of internet access in the global population has grown from 6 per cent in 2000 to 43 per cent in 2015; a total of 3.2 billion people now have access to the internet.[12]

There is a second continent on the rise. Africa has been a sleeping lion. In the 1980s and 1990s GDP amounted to less than 2 per cent per year.[13] After 2000 growth across the continent leaped to a formidable 5 per cent, sometimes propelled and sometimes hindered by commodity markets which still account for a quarter of GDP. Economies grow on the back of domestic demand driven by their growing populations. Africa will earn the population dividend. It is the continent with the fastest growing population. Since 2000 population numbers grew by more than 370 million, from 814 million to almost 1.2 billion in 2015. Population growth is slowing, but far more slowly than demographers expected. The latest UN estimates expect population to soar to 1.7 billion by 2030 and to 2.5 billion by 2050. By 2100 Africa is expected to be a 4.4 billion continent. This is an increase of over 2 billion compared with the UN 2004 estimate.[14]

For the global economy, the key implication is that the middle-class is quickly expanding through income and population growth. McKinsey Global Institute estimates that this group grew from 1.2 billion in 1990 to 2.4 billion in 2010, and that it will almost double again until 2030, to 4.2 billion people. In total, that means another 3 billion consumers from 1990 to 2025, and it also means that for the first time, a majority of the world's population will be consumers by 2025. If one looks specifically at those people having an annual income of $20,000 per annum or more – the level of income most Europeans and Americans enjoy today – there will be a total of about one billion by 2030, and 600 million will live in developing countries.[15] Prosperity finally stops being a western privilege.

1.3 Built on growth – the bedrock assumption

This century-long and hugely successful growth journey now followed by the East and the South has made the world used and addicted to growth. For more than seven generations and since the beginning of the industrial revolution, the Western world has been enjoying significant annual growth rates of around 2 per cent per annum. Non-growth is unthinkable. We started to discount future growth into all aspects of life – economically, socially, politically. Economically, positive interest rates essentially reflect growth expectations minus any risks incurred along the way. The same holds true for any stock price in excess of that motivated by historic dividends. When McKinsey's finance experts deconstruct the value expectations embedded in share prices, they find that on average, 70–90 per cent of a company's value comes from expected growth, more than three years out.[16] Socially, the world economy has built growth into pension schemes and public sector budgets. In Germany, 8 per cent of GDP was dedicated to pension commitments in 2014. That share will grow to 10–11 per cent over the next 15 years if the economy grows at historic rates. Without growth, the share will be 13–14 per cent.[17] This is unthinkable and unaffordable. The claims created in the past are repayable only in a growth environment. Politically, too, growth continues to be the most attractive political currency and the most robust re-election agenda. The fact that pre-election growth drives the incumbent's popular vote is well established. In post-war US elections, the economic growth of the second and third quarter of any election year explains a large share of re-election results.[18] For Paul Krugman, the evidence is clear enough to suggest that depressing growth for the first half of a term can help re-election.[19]

Perhaps unsurprisingly then, growth is often at the centre of political agendas. Already in 1946, US President Harry Truman established the Council of Economic Advisors, commissioned to ensure continued growth and take the US out of its post-war quagmire. Over the following decades, many governments followed suit: Germany passed its stability and growth laws in 1967, Canada in 2012. It is noteworthy that, over time, the focus has shifted, drifting from balanced growth within the 'magical rectangle' of stable prices, low employment, balanced trade and steady growth[20] towards plain growth, at almost any price.

In summary, growth has become the 'normal', the underlying economic assumption of our entire society, and the default mechanism of progress and development.

Chapter 2

Fuelled – resource-based growth

Fire is the basis of all craft. Without it, man could not persist.

Hesiod, 700BC.

A few months back, one of us drove past the nodding oil donkeys that characterize the Texan landscape so recognizably. Texas started its oil production in 1898, and peaked in 1972 at a daily production of 3,500 barrels. During the same period, the US economy grew from 417 billion to $5,134 billion.[1] The question of whether the availability of cheap energy was a key driver of the growth is an obvious one and dominated the discussion that evening. 'I only did a business degree and looked at growth economics in a rush,' a young colleague said, 'but it struck me that there was very little talk about the role of energy and resources.' A major misconception of traditional economics is that it vastly underplays the importance of energy and resources for economic growth. This, in turn, makes countries focus insufficiently on securing a long-term competitive supply of resources and energy, and on ways to turn these assets into economic value.

2.1 Resources – the missing piece in Solow's puzzle?

Growth theory is a well-worn discipline. Every generation of theorists has added its spin. Adam Smith and David Ricardo were first to explain what drives growth and stagnation; they are the fathers of classical growth theory. According to them, capital, labour and land define our economic output. Smith saw few limits to our ability for making these factors productive. The most fundamental weakness of the classical model was its inability to provide a quantitative explanation of growth, and how powerful different levers were in providing it. Clearly, this was getting in the way of deriving good practical advice from the theories.

In 1956 and 1957 Nobel laureate Robert Solow solved that issue in two seminal papers.[2,3] His 'neoclassical' theory quantitatively explains growth as the result of two primary input factors, labour and capital, and their respective productivity. In most developed economies, labour is found to explain ~70 per cent of growth, and capital the remaining ~30 per cent, with these shares being relatively constant over time. There was one major problem though: empirical data on input and productivity development only equate to at least half of the observed GDP growth rate over time. This result held true for long time series and for many countries. The unexplained growth, which is often called the 'Solow residual', Solow attributed to *technological progress* in the broad sense of the word; that is, he assumed it came from a synergy effect from combining better labour practices with more productive capital investments. This is still the prevailing view in economics, even though some now refer to the same phenomenon as a 'total factor productivity' effect. To this date, there is little quantitative microeconomic understanding of this other half of growth and how it can be managed. More than half of our growth engine remains a black box.

Notably, energy and resources are not seen as important input factors in this theory. Part of the capital formation is of course power plants and mining equipment, but the energy and resources themselves are seen as abundantly available intermediate products, not as inputs, and without a direct link to growth. In most developed economies, energy and resources account for 6.7 per cent of total value-add,[4] and according to the neoclassical theory, this is seen as a good proxy for their importance for growth. Ultimately, the effect has been that the supply and conversion of energy has not received much interest from economists and economic policy-makers as a determinant of future growth.

2.2 Economists' awakening – resource and growth

This view of the world may be about to change. Over the last fifteen years, research has started to suggest a much bigger role for energy and other natural resources in explaining economic growth. This makes intuitive sense from an economic history point of view. Taming wind and hydro energy, and inputting them into the economy, once allowed mechanization of grinding, pumping, sawing, irrigation and many other laborious tasks, freeing up men and horses for other more productive tasks. Taming coal and vastly increasing the amount of energy put into the economy was crucial for the first industrial revolution. While our modern economy has of course moved on from horses and steam engines, it is still striking how many industries continue to depend heavily on natural resources: food, transport, construction and all primary material production, for instance. So looking at how much energy and other natural resources are put into the economy, and how productively they are used, seems like a plausible place to go looking for the Solow residual.

That is just what Ayres et al. (2005)[5] did. From his overly humble INSEAD study Robert Angres drew open the curtain and identified *exergy*, or more precisely *useful work*, as a third major primary input to economic growth, next to labour and capital. Exergy and useful work are thermodynamic terms, and their definitions are important for understanding Ayres's results. Exergy is the *potential work* that can be achieved in a physical system. It is different from energy, which is always conserved. As an example, there is an enormous amount of energy stored as low temperature heat in our oceans, but most of it cannot be used productively, because what matters are temperature differences. This potential work is then turned into *useful work* through all sorts of conversion processes (of both energy and materials). For instance, the exergy of a litre of gasoline is turned into useful transport work through the efficiency of a car and specifically its internal combustion engine. Ayres et al. estimated the total amount of potential work supplied to the US economy year by year through the twentieth century by adding up the exergy content of the major resources inputted into the economy, and then multiplied with year by year estimates of how productively that potential work was used, to estimate the *total useful work supplied to the US economy year by year.* Simply put, they tested the hypothesis that energy and other natural resources should be regarded as a third major input to economic growth, next to labour and capital.

The results were startling. Through this approach, Ayres et al. were able to explain much of the Solow residual for the US economy during the twentieth century with high statistical accuracy – that is, they were able to show that the amount of exergy added to the economy, and the productivity with which this exergy was converted into useful work, explained a large part of the 'missing' growth.

These results have since been confirmed for other countries and time series. Voudouris and Ayres (2014) redid the analysis for each of the EU-15 countries, and were able to explain a significant share of their respective Solow residuals between 1970 and 2010.[6]

This is a hugely important conclusion: how much resources are put into an economy, and how productively they are used, seem to be very important factors in explaining economic growth, in some of the studies mentioned above even explaining up to half of the total economic growth.

These results do not mean that technological progress is unimportant for growth – it clearly is. They simply mean that most technological progress is captured within labour, capital and resource productivity, and that there is limited need to apply an additional synergy factor 'on top' to explain total economic growth. In short, resources matter.

2.3 Oil prices – the variable beyond control

Other researchers have used other approaches to reach a similar conclusion: that energy and other natural resources are much more important than mainstream economics assumes. James Hamilton (1983, 1996, 2009) observes that all but one of the eleven US recessions since the Second World War have been *preceded* six to twelve months earlier by a major oil price spike,[7] a fact that is easily verifiable through published data. He then identifies the three possible explanations for this correlation. *Hypothesis I, the correlation is a coincidence*: the factors truly responsible for the recessions occurred by chance at about the same time as the oil price increases. *Hypothesis II, the correlation results from an endogenous explanatory variable*: there is some third set of factors that caused both the oil price increases and the recessions. *Hypothesis III, at least some of the recessions were causally influenced by an exogenous oil price increase*. Which is true?

Hamilton first discards hypothesis I through simple probability analysis – the correlation would be just too much of a coincidence. He then discards hypothesis II by looking at the underlying drivers of each oil price increase. The list is dominated by factors specific to the oil industry, such as the Iranian nationalization, the OPEC embargo, the Suez crisis and the Iran–Iraq war. It is hard to argue that these types of event would lead to US recessions through any other route than the oil price.[8] Hence, Hamilton concludes that hypothesis III is the only possible answer, i.e. that there is a causality link. This means that oil prices have been a contributing factor (not the only factor, for sure) to the recessions, a link that would be very hard to believe if the importance of oil lay only in its contribution of a few per cent to US GDP.

Together, these results suggest we should think of energy and resources as the third big input factor into economic growth, next to labour and capital. That economic growth continues to be highly correlated with increased resource use is well known (see for instance Figure 2.1 from the International Resource Panel) but these results also show the opposite: that resources, productively used, drive growth.

There are several important consequences. First, economic policy-makers should spend much more effort on energy and other natural resources, and how productively they are used. Resource productivity is a major source of wealth. These questions certainly exist today, but, in our experience, there are in order of magnitude more seminars and research on labour and capital than on natural resources. When did you last attend a seminar on how to deploy more (clean) energy into the economy, or hear of an international resource attraction strategy?

Also, these conclusions challenge the common economics presumption that growth will continue indefinitely, independent of natural resources. A common economics argument for postponing environmental action is that our children and grandchildren will be much richer than we are (since the economy will continue to grow) and therefore it is economically rational to leave the clean-up to them. If energy and resources are important, and are struggling with a number of major 'full planet' challenges we will look at in the next chapter, it is not obvious that growth will automatically continue.

Material use highly correlated with economic development

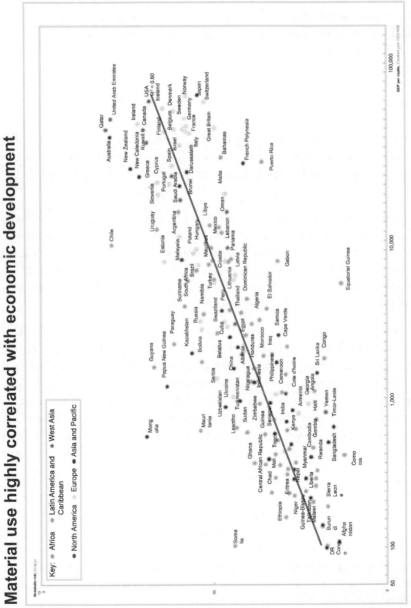

SOURCE: UNEP (2011)

Fig. 2.1

Chapter 3

Borrowed – a growth of liabilities

Neither a borrower nor a lender be,
For loan oft loses both itself and friend,
And borrowing dulls the edge of husbandry.

Shakespeare, *Hamlet* Act 1

Our addiction to GDP growth is in principle no problem, if the global economy could count on growth continuing, and if the growth itself is beneficial. But as this chapter will show, neither of those requirements are true in today's set-ups and a major part of the last decades' global economic growth was actually borrowed from the future – in very different forms. Borrowing not only took the form of financial borrowing but also borrowing from the planet and from society at large. In all cases, the promise of repayment is low and, in any event, only achievable if the underlying asset is subjected to massive strain. This level of indebtedness has increased massively in a bid to fend off the new realities: demographic challenges, weaker productivity growth and uncontrolled volatility. We have grown both accustomed and addicted to post-war levels of growth and want to sustain what we perceive as its desired 'natural' rate. To achieve that, we are borrowing constantly, moving from cyclical deficits to structural deficits. While borrowing can often be beneficial (a house mortgage, for instance), we hope to convince you in this chapter that the borrowing that is currently going on is far from sound. Globally, we have started trading the long term for the short term. Sometimes this takes the form of tacit collective choices; sometimes it takes the form of grand strategy. And sometimes it is pure ignorance of just how much we are borrowing.

3.1 Planetary borrowing – leaving safe operating space

At the time of writing in the autumn of 2015, Indonesia is on fire.

Across Sumatra, Kalimantan and Papua, large expanses of peat and forest – 3.8 million hectares, an area the size of Taiwan – are burning. NASA satellite pictures show a dense haze across the archipelago. Up to November 2015, 600,000 people had been treated in hospital for respiratory diseases, and Singapore had repeatedly declared a state of emergency. Total greenhouse gas emissions associated with peat and forest fires in 2015 amounted to 700 million tons CO_2 equivalents, which is the yearly fossil fuel CO_2 emission from the UK and Brazil combined. Even using the most conservative estimates, the peat fires were the largest discrete event affecting our climate during 2015. In Indonesia, after recent legislative changes, peatlands are not legally protected. While the fires are to an extent the result of a massive drought associated with 2015's super El Nino (the strongest since 1950), they are often started deliberately so that farmers can expand into new agricultural land. Many regional governors welcome the trend and are keen to see new land available for development. Accordingly, government counter-action is weak and, to date, has had little impact.

The fires are turning some of the world's richest ecosystems and most effective carbon storages into fragile arable land and into a gigantic carbon source. The economic benefits from any newly established agriculture, mostly palm oil, are borrowed – from neighbouring countries which are affected by the haze, from a global community increasingly exposed to the effects of climate change and from future generations of Indonesians who have to live without the many advantages that well-kept peatland can provide in terms of water storage, flood protection, tourism income, biodiversity and plain natural beauty.

Today's generation has already been left with less than 80 per cent of the rainforest and less than 50 per cent of the forested peatlands that existed in 1990. Instead they are stuck with vast expanses of unproductive land and industrial plantations.[1,2] When driving through Kalimantan, this wasteland is the only passing view for hour after hour. Land that was dense with rainforests only ten or twenty years ago is today infertile and covered with alang-alang grass. Farmers abandon the wasteland soon after claiming it and move on deeper into the remaining forests. Careless forest clearing is borrowed growth, and is among the more graphic examples of how planetary debt levels are pushed out and transgressed in search of short-term economic growth.

The Indonesia story is one of many that can be told about environmental degradation. Readers know them too well. This book is not about repeating the history of environmental destruction, which has been such a steady companion of human development. Instead, this book wants to raise the issue of systemic failure of our current global economic engine. That failure has resulted in environmental degradation at a scale and speed previously unknown, and one that has accelerated dramatically the last thirty years alone. It is no longer a failure of local governance or personal malpractice. It is the inescapable consequence of a global economic model that, on the one hand, rides on the assumption of open-ended, abundant resources, and on the other assumes unlimited 'sinks' for the disposal of post-use carbon, household waste or nutrient run-off. Over the last few decades, we have taken a historic and unprecedented step from a spacious to a full planet, from the Holocene to the Anthropocene, from nature as the norm to nature as an exception. Eighty-three per cent of the global land area has now been altered by man: we changed the surface, the vegetation or the flow of water.[3] And humans consume 17 per cent of what the biosphere produces in a year.[4] No animal ever claimed such a high share of the Earth's production. The predominance of humans as a shaping planetary force changes everything. It makes the discussion of how we use natural resources to create wealth economically relevant, politically urgent and morally imminent.

All of this happened for good reasons and in the legitimate attempt to provide for families, grow local economies, protect our communities and allow for better lifestyles. In many ways it reflects the best and not the worst of mankind: our understanding of nature, our science and engineering prowess, the ability to form complex institutions and relationships, divide labour and share the benefits of joint work. A more dramatic view is that on the back of a resource-intensive model of growth we have been led towards a historically unprecedented predicament – one where progress destroys its very foundations.

The Global Footprint Network is an Oakland-based not-for-profit organization founded in 2003 with the vision of providing tools and data that help countries to thrive in a resource-constrained world. The Network has established the concept of the 'ecological footprint': the hectares of biologically productive land and water that are required to produce the goods and services we use, and to absorb the waste we generate, using today's technology and resource management practices.[5] It is a broad and relatively well-accepted way of measuring the total environmental impact of all our human activities. Dramatically, the Network found that, with current technology and economic practices, the hectare requirement surpasses the limit available on planet earth. Globally, we required the equivalent of 1.6 planets in 2015. Under business-as-usual growth, this requirement will increase to two planets by 2030. In order to visualize the fact that we have started to massively overuse our planet's resources, the Global Footprint Network launched the Earth Overshoot Day, the day of the year when humanity has used up that year's resources. In 1970, we went into debt for the first time. Since then the debt day moved forward year after year – all the way to 13 August in 2015 (see Figure 3.1).[6] Numerous reports from the UN, the World Bank, the World Resource Institute, the Pentagon and lately the papal encyclical *Laudato Sí*[7] have all come to the same conclusion: on the current global development path, despite all efforts, we are losing the battle for a healthy and enjoyable planet.

Despite all efforts, the overuse of our planet's resources is growing worse, not better

Earth Overshoot Day from 1970-2015

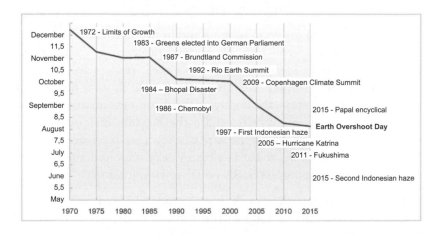

SOURCE: Global Footprint Network (2016) and authors' analysis

Fig. 3.1

Since 1750, demand, extraction and consumption of almost any resource has exploded (see Figure 3.2). Johan Rockström from the Stockholm Resilience Center has analysed the effect of massive consumption on earth systems and defined a 'safe operating space' for humanity, described along nine resource systems.[8] These are systems that are vital to the productivity of the earth, as well as human well-being, and that will shift suddenly in response to one critical control variable, such as greenhouse gas concentrations. For four of them – atmospheric CO_2 concentrations, biodiversity, land use and the phosphorus and nitrogen cycle – we have already passed the threshold and are close to a potentially irreversible tipping point. For two further systems, we are swiftly approaching that threshold and may soon be leaving what the twenty-eight scientists of the 'Planetary Boundaries' working group call the safe operating space. Let's zoom in on a few of these boundaries:

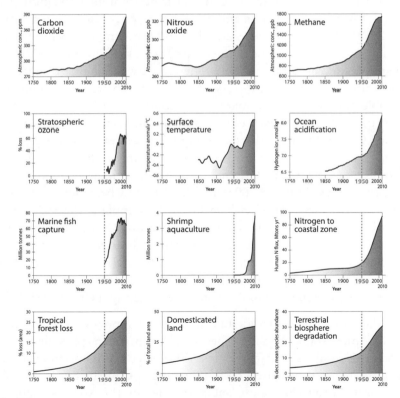

Fig. 3.2

Freshwater use. At first sight, water looks like the ultimate, abundant resource. And we are still on the right side of the planetary boundary globally. Yet, we are stepping over the line locally in increasingly dramatic ways. There is ample evidence today how water scarcity and pollution suffocate economic growth, harm livelihoods and provoke conflict. Within a few decades, water will turn into the ultimate scarce resource in the full world.

Despite being the blue planet: We have 1.3 billion km^2 of water on our planet. Of this, 96.5 per cent is seawater, 1.8 per cent is deep groundwater and 1.7 per cent is bound in glaciers and ice shields. Freshwater available for human use in rivers, lakes, soils or wetlands is far less: only 0.03 per cent of our total water.[9]

The competition for that water is getting fiercer by the day. We see it along the banks of the river Jordan, on the headwaters of the Indus, the Irtysh River between China and Kazakhstan, or in the Mekong basin. By 2030, 40 per cent of the water demand (growing at 2 per cent p.a.) will go unmet. That is one of the findings of a report published by the Water Resources Group in 2009. The report was the first to quantify total supply: the amount of water that is renewable, sustainable, reliable and accessible to mankind is about 4,500 km^3.[10] Expanding that quantity comes with either massive financial or environmental costs. One example is the $25 billion 'man-made river', a pipeline that channels 6 million m^3 from the Nubian sandstone aquifer to Libya's coast every day. Original projections estimated the duration of that flow as close to 5,000 years; this has now been downgraded to only 30–50 years.[11] Another breathtaking example is the $62 billion South-to-North Water Diversion Project linking China's Yangtze river with the arid and industrialized north through three canal systems; or Jordan's Red–Dead Sea canal, which will channel water from the Red Sea into the Dead Sea which has been losing a metre of water level every year since the Jordan River stopped reaching its historic sink.[12,13]

In other cases, the search for additional water supplies takes countries far beyond sustainable yields. These can be seen on an epic scale at Lake Aral in Central Asia which has lost 90 per cent of its original size as a consequence of intensive cotton farming within the Syr Darya and the Amu Darya basin. Saudi Arabia provides another striking example.

Ever since the inception of the national wheat programme in the 1970s, the country's aquifers – estimated then at 2,000 billion cubic metres – have lost 20 billion cubic metres per year in the production of 4 million tons of wheat, which is five times the amount needed to meet local consumption. The rest was exported to Kuwait, the Emirates, Qatar, Bahrain, Yemen or Oman, or left to rot. This strategy is leaving the country with only half of its original water reserves and some aquifers with a depletion time of less than 20–30 years. There is no plan B for Saudi Arabia; even desalination is unable to fill the gap.[14] For the first time we are witnessing the ultimate economic, political, social and environmental exposure facing a country as it transgresses safe water yields.

The battle for water runs even deeper. It extends beyond the 'blue' water that hits a river or a groundwater reservoir. A part of that water evaporates via the surface or through plants: so-called green water. We need it for the production of our food. Today, we use 7,800 km^3/year for food production. Per head of our global population, that amounts to 1,200 m^3 or 1.2 million litres per year. A US citizen is consuming 2.4 million litres of 'virtual' water per year, a European 1.7 million litres and an Indian 0.5 million litres. The major reason for the dramatic difference is the amount and type of meat consumed in different countries. Beef requires 16,000 litres of water per kilogram, four times more than a kilogram of chicken, and twelve times more than a kilogram of grain. By 2050, we will require almost 13,900 km^3 of green water per annum to eradicate hunger and allow 3 billion middle-class consumers to have 'modern' diets.[15] Water it seems – irrespective of whether it is delivered to us fresh or hidden in the products we consume – is the ultimate currency of a constrained planet. And it is in need of a management approach that reflects its ultimate importance.

Pollution through novel entities. According to the Planetary Boundaries research team, the release of substances and materials into the biosphere that were not designed for such environmental release will very soon start to destabilize earth systems, too. No other experience is more telling than that of polychlorinated biphenyls (PCBs), a group of chemicals produced since the 1930s, and used in everything from appliances to some types of paper. Even if banned today, they continue to accumulate in the ocean with massive harm to the marine biology. Other persistent and bioaccumulative substances are still in use, from phthalates via flame retardants such as hexabromocyclododecane, to perfluorinated alkylate substances (PFASs). A 2015 report authored by experts from Harvard Chan School of Public Health documented that this widely used industrial chemical, which is linked to cancer and immune system interference, is transferred to babies through breast milk. For every month of breastfeeding, concentrations in baby tissue increase by 20–30 per cent.[16] Mothers unknowingly and unintentionally intoxicate their children.

Polymers, while far less harmful in their own right, are also novel entities. Plastics are the workhorse material of the modern economy and for good reason: they are cheap, durable, strong, light and extremely versatile. At the same time, however, they are the epitome of a single-use material. Plastic production has exploded over the past fifty years, from 15 million tons per year to 311 million tons, a figure that is projected to double again in the next two decades. Eight to 12 million metric tons end up in the ocean every year. By 2025, the oceans will contain one ton of plastics for every three ton of edible fish in a business-as-usual scenario; by 2050, they will contain more plastics than fish. In the marine environment, the plastic debris – largely originating from packaging material – disintegrates into particles through oxidation, UV-light and wave motion, dissipates into the water column and finally integrates into animals: 86 per cent of sea turtles, 44 per cent of seabirds and 43 per cent of fish carry plastic in their bodies.[17,18]

This background pollution has already started to affect the bioproductivity of the ocean ecosystem that enables the global fishing industry to supply 15 per cent of global protein intake.[19] UNEP estimates the annual damage of plastics to marine ecosystems at $13 billion per year; the Asia-Pacific Economic Cooperation (APEC) forum calculated the costs to the fishing, tourism and shipping industries at $1.3 billion in Asia alone.[20] Even in Europe, where leakage is relatively limited, costs for coastal and beach cleaning alone could reach €630 million per year.[21] Photographs of albatross skeletons with their bellies stuffed with plastic debris are demonstrating a much deeper predicament: that we have, with today's model of production and consumption, departed from the very design principles of nature and got away with it for quite some time. However, on a full planet, we are no longer getting away with it.

Land system change. It is the land that will have to provide us with food and the biomass we increasingly need for energy and materials. Our calorific intake alone is expected to grow by more than 69 per cent between 2010 and 2050. The demand for grain is expected to grow 1.5 times, that for milk and meat products is expected to double.[22] These are significant numbers, especially in the face of three worrisome trends. First, in 2010 the increase in grain yields was surpassed by population growth for the first time on record.[23] Over the last fifty years we have observed that agricultural productivity is flattening. In the 1970s, hectare productivity increases were around 2.7 per cent a year; now they are down to 0.9 per cent,[24] a pattern that is consistent across all major production regions with the exception of the Middle East and Northern Africa.[25] This decline is happening despite the massive increase in agricultural inputs: usage of pesticides, fertilizer and liquid fuels has grown by around 2 per cent a year.[26,27,28] Despite the use of ever more plentiful and powerful inputs, soil exhaustion is one of the most dramatic, far-reaching and least understood economic riddles of our days. Part of the answer lies in the incomplete absorption of inputs into plants, which manifests itself in the wholesale run-off of nutrients from fields into rivers, lakes and seas, where they eventually generate 'dead zones'. In the European Union, 95 kilograms of nitrate per hectare are washed off fields into rivers every year (exceeding the 80 kilograms permissible at present).[29]

Second, we are losing arable land. Globally, 3 billion hectares of land are degraded often due to large-scale soil erosion. Seven tons of soil per hectare of agricultural land is lost every year, as a global average. Over the past 150 years, 50 per cent of global topsoil has been lost. Rebuilding 2.5 cm of topsoil takes 500–1,000 years. At that rate we will lose all our topsoil –the source of 95 per cent of our food – in only sixty years. For some countries this is a reality today: Kazakhstan has lost more than 50 per cent of its arable land since 1990.

Third and lastly, flat productivities and land degradation are pushing us to claim new land, approximately 200 million hectares by 2030. While land reserves exist, this will continue to increase pressure particularly on primary forests in the tropics, of which we have lost more than 10 per cent since 1990 according to FAO. Much of today's agricultural success story already seems 'borrowed' indeed.

Biosphere integrity. Our sphere of life and the diversity it hosts are degrading faster than ever before. In a 2015 research paper 'Accelerated Modern Human–induced Species Losses', a group of scientists measured the current rate of species loss and compared it with previous mass extinctions. The 'natural' rate of extinction, the researchers concluded, predicts two species to become extinct per 10,000 species in 100 years. Today, we are losing species at 8 to 100 times that rate.[30] Since 1900, for example, we have lost 477 vertebrates, including the Bali and Caspian tigers, the passenger pigeon and, in 2015, the Northern white rhino. The 'natural' rate would have been nine. Even in the scientists' most conservative estimates, the extinction rate is higher than that of the previous five mass extinctions. Dramatically, another study carried out by Ripple in 2014 estimated that 60–75 per cent of large carnivores are at risk of extinction, including many 'familiar' large animals.[31]

This is a loss of beauty, grandeur and genetic optionality. But there is also an economic opportunity cost. The loss of regenerative capacity of wild fisheries is a case in point. In our oceans over the last decade, we have just about been able to maintain the entire catch of wild fish at stable levels. Many might celebrate that. However, a second look reveals that such stability came at a price. A study carried out by Watson in 2012 reveals that between 1950 and 2005, fleet capacities have increased tenfold, growing fivefold since 1975 alone,[32] yet the catch per unit capacity has declined by a dramatic 83 per cent. That means more vessels, more days at sea and more diesel burnt. In some fisheries, the decline of stock is even more dramatic. In the Philippines the catch per unit of effort went down from 36 kg in 1950 to only 3 kg in 2000. The amount of animal protein available to local communities decreased by 35 per cent at a moment when population growth continues to be high. The massive explosion of effort required to land a ton of fish reflects the depletion of stocks: 40 per cent of global stocks are fully exploited and another 50 per cent are overexploited or even collapsed.[33]

Climate change. While the threats through water scarcity, land degradation, pollution and biodiversity loss are hard to ignore, climate change has been subject to an epic controversy – at least among citizens. The 2010 Gallup Global Warming worldwide survey across

111 countries showed that 48 per cent believe in man-made global warming while 14 per cent reject it and 38 per cent are unaware or uncertain. Different in science: out of 4,014 peer-reviewed scientific arcticles that take a position on climate change written between 1991–2011, 97 per cent endorse man-made global warming, while only 2 per cent reject it ('Quantifying the consensus on anthropogenic global warming in the scientific literature', J. Cook et al., 2013). The report of the Intergovernmental Panel on Climate Change summarizes science's position as follows: 'Scientific evidence for warming of the climate system is unequivocal.' Evidence and facts today are well documented and easily available as through NASA's eye-opening website. What's more, the expected effects are happening at a faster speed and a bigger scale than expected, especially in Antarctica and Greenland. A recent example, the record melt of the Greenland icesheet in spring of 2016, left scientists from the Danish Meteorological Institute incredulous. They – like their profession at large – feel caught between jumping to conclusions on a complex issue and failing to ring the alarm bells on time.

Climate change may well turn out to be the most important boundary condition for our economic model at large. The 2006 Stern report was the first to draw conclusions from climate change science in the cold language of economics. The stabilization of greenhouse gases would be made possible by investing approximately 1 per cent of global annual GDP into mitigation through 2050.[34] Nine years later and equipped with a much better understanding of the physics of climate change, with graphic examples of extreme weather impact, with more trust in improved power generation technology and with civil society and global business claiming a voice, the Paris conference had a different outcome than its predecessors in Copenhagen, Cancún, Durban, Doha, Warsaw and Lima. The historic spectacular agreement brokered under French leadership and signed by 195 nations is a recognition that the costs of climate change are real.

That completes our tour of the main earth systems. The important conclusion is not that there is environmental degradation – that is old news – but that the degradation is so pervasive, has gone so far, and continues to accelerate. For the first time, almost all major earth systems are under strain.

We knew it for a while – we are borrowing our way into the future by overexploiting the planet. However, reviewing the factbase, we must conclude that our play with the planet has reached a new level. Says United Nations Secretary-General Ban Ki Moon, 'we stand at a crucial crossroads in history'.[35] We believe that the challenge is different and more grave for three fundamental reasons. First, the *challenges are connected*, and the buffer that different earth systems could provide for each other is getting less effective. Historically, less arable land could be compensated for by additional irrigation; ambitions to reduce greenhouse gas emissions could be met through bio-ethanol programmes. But now these buffers are starting to disappear: irrigation water is embattled, as is land for biofuels (see Figure 3.3). Nowhere else is the link between two resource systems clearer than between water and energy. In recent years the energy intensity of a water system has increased massively, as has the water intensity of our energy system. The abstraction and treatment of freshwater historically required less than 0.3 kWh per cubic metre. Desalination – needed when freshwater is getting scarce – requires 4 kWh per cubic metre, even when the most

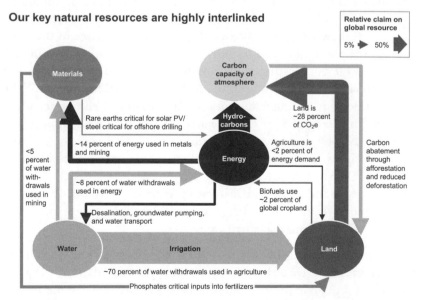

Our key natural resources are highly interlinked

Relative claim on global resource
5% ➤ 50%

Materials

Carbon capacity of atmosphere

Hydro-carbons

Rare earths critical for solar PV/ steel critical for offshore drilling

Land is ~28 percent of CO₂e

Energy

~14 percent of energy used in metals and mining

Agriculture is <2 percent of energy demand

<5 percent of water with-drawals used in mining

~8 percent of water withdrawals used in energy

Carbon abatement through afforestation and reduced deforestation

Desalination, groundwater pumping, and water transport

Biofuels use ~2 percent of global cropland

Water

Irrigation

Land

~70 percent of water withdrawals used in agriculture

Phosphates critical inputs into fertilizers

SOURCE: McKinsey analysis

Fig. 3.3

modern technology (reverse osmosis) is applied. And within the energy system, the production of one terajoule of natural gas (or oil) required a maximum of seven (or 70) cubic metres of water. Unconventional sources of fuel require up to 1,000 times as much: oil sands up to 1,800 m³, enhanced oil recovery up to 9,000 m³ and bioethanol up to 380,000 m³.[36] Not only are our resource systems failing to buffer each other, but their depletion is also mutually reinforcing. The lack of rainfall as a result of climate change requires more fossil fuel combustion in desalination plants. The higher winter temperatures caused by climate change require artificial snowing in winter resorts, which in turn creates a major strain on water resources and causes excessive energy consumption, still provided through fossil fuels. The world of abundance has turned into a blanket that is both too short and too narrow.

Second, *the problem is our industrial model at large*, not the type of energy we use to power it. This may sound counterintuitive. Particularly in the context of the climate change debate, energy use has been seen as the

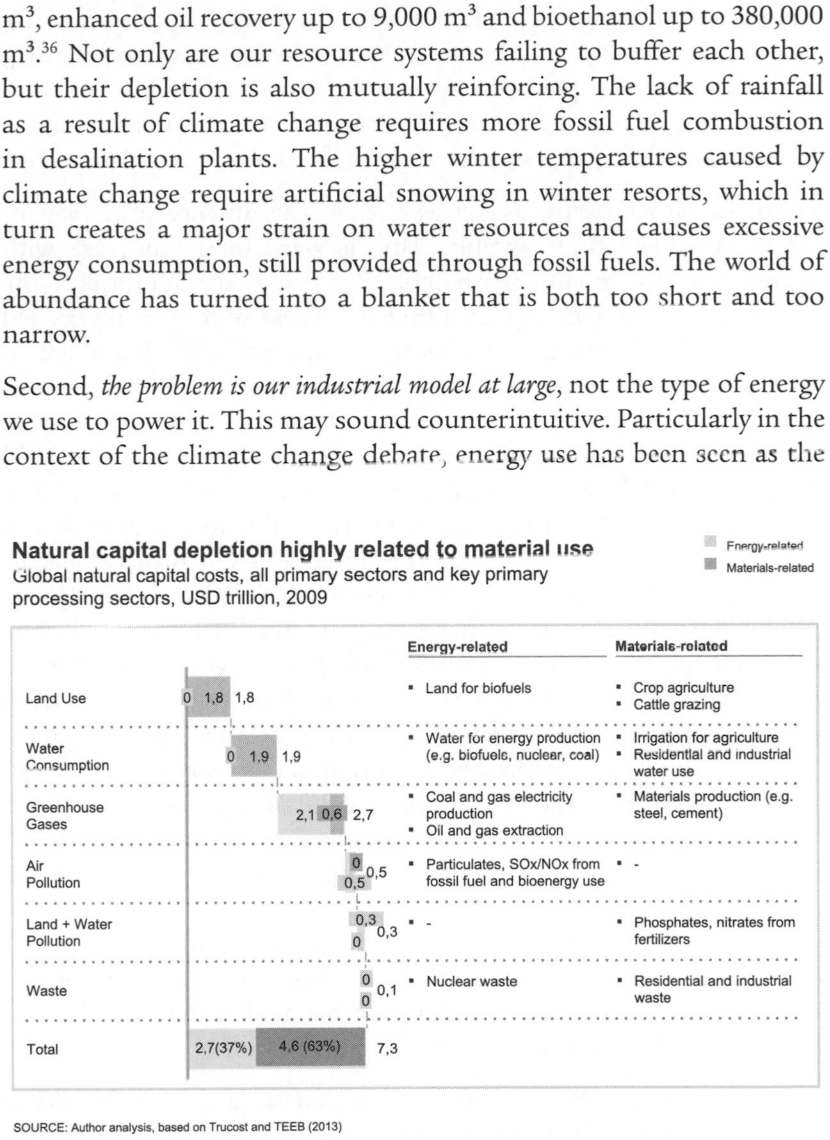

Natural capital depletion highly related to material use
Global natural capital costs, all primary sectors and key primary processing sectors, USD trillion, 2009

■ Energy-related
■ Materials-related

		Energy-related	Materials-related
Land Use	0 1,8 1,8	• Land for biofuels	• Crop agriculture • Cattle grazing
Water Consumption	0 1,9 1,9	• Water for energy production (e.g. biofuels, nuclear, coal)	• Irrigation for agriculture • Residential and industrial water use
Greenhouse Gases	2,1 0,6 2,7	• Coal and gas electricity production • Oil and gas extraction	• Materials production (e.g. steel, cement)
Air Pollution	0 0,5 0,5	• Particulates, SOx/NOx from fossil fuel and bioenergy use	• -
Land + Water Pollution	0,3 0 0,3	• -	• Phosphates, nitrates from fertilizers
Waste	0 0 0,1	• Nuclear waste	• Residential and industrial waste
Total	2,7(37%) 4,6 (63%) 7,3		

SOURCE: Author analysis, based on Trucost and TEEB (2013)

Fig. 3.4

key driver of degradation, through global warming and the massive land, water and materials consumption associated with our global energy chains. There is a way to turn this argument around. Material use is the underlying issue for its primary effects on water, land and atmospheric resources, but also because it is our material-intensive industrial economy that is driving our loss of energy demand. The $7.3 trillion of natural capital depletion highlighted by the Trucost/TEEB analysis[37] found that two-thirds (63 per cent) are related to material use and only one-third (37 per cent) to energy consumption (see Figure 3.4).

Third, *we do not have a deleveraging plan*. The absence of a plan of action is evident and tangible. This is particularly the case with reference to two recent occurrences. The first is the approval of the Sustainable Development Goals (SDGs). These were formally signed by 193 heads of state in New York on 26 September 2015, and are an attempt to define progress beyond the narrow notion of economic growth. Instead, seventeen objectives – from gender equality to clean oceans – were singled out as measures of human progress. They hold governments in both developed and – different from the Millenium Development Goals – developing countries liable to a joint vision of how we want to live. The UN and the signatories stated that the goals are a 'set of integrated and indivisible goals which balance three crucial dimensions: the economic, the social and the environmental'. The goals call for life outside poverty for all (goal 1), good standards for nutrition (goal 2), health (goal 3), education (goal 4), water access (goal 6), employment (goal 8) for all. At the same time, they call for a halt to climate change (goal 13), the destruction of the terrestrial (goal 15) and marine ecosystems (goal 14).[38] Peace Nobel Prize laureate Muhammad Yunus says in the interview later in this book: 'Even if we attained all SDGs on time without changing the engine more deeply, we would relapse in a day. The issue is the very model of wealth generation.' If we adhere to today's model of production and consumption, the SDGs are a complete list of incompatible objectives. One of the aims of this book is to contribute to the exploration for models that will allow us to reconcile SDGs with the use of planetary resources.

The lack of a map also manifests when revisiting 'sustainable development'. This was the ultimate conclusion of the Rio Earth Summit in 1992 and stands at the heart of many national strategic growth plans. Often, however, 'greening' is taken to mean becoming more like, say, Denmark. This is a fatal assumption, because the resource requirements of allegedly 'green economies' such as Denmark, Sweden, Switzerland or Germany are all deeply unviable. All of them are borrowers. Denmark, a poster-child country of modernism, diversity, digitization, wind power and bike riding, is emitting 7.2 tons of CO_2 per capita. Danes require 20 tons of materials per capita per year to sustain their lifestyle and produce 750 kg waste, out of which 400 kg are incinerated. If we all lived by Danish standards the world would require three planets, moving Earth Overshoot Day to the beginning of May.[39,40,41,42] Denmark is more agile and provident than many other OECD countries, but it remains a massive borrower.

In conclusion, planetary borrowing seems to be directly linked to a frame of thinking that sees a vast planet with regenerative capacity that is both infinitely elastic and physically inexhaustible. In reality, we have transitioned to a new paradigm: that of a fully utilized planet. The full planet has to deal with a world where humans dominate: today, more than 70 per cent of the global nitrogen cycle is for human use and 67 per cent of all greenwater reserves are being used by humans.[43] This unprecedented dominance of one species over other shaping forces of the environment has led Eugene Stoermer, and later Paul Crutzen,[44] to proclaim a new geological age: the Anthropocene. It is a remarkable moment in science when one of the most conservative groupings of all, the International Commission on Stratigraphy, an institution accustomed to think in millions of years, has created a 37-member Anthropocene Working Group and put forward a proposal to recognize the Anthropocene as a stratigraphic age, only 11,600 years into the Holocene – a blink in history. 'The evidence of human earth system intervention', their president, geologist Jan Zalasiewicz summarized, 'is just overbearing.'[45]

3.2 Financial borrowing – the new default

Never has the stock of global financial debt been higher. According to a report by the McKinsey Global Institute, it amounted in 2014 to $199 trillion up from $87 trillion in the year 2000.[46] The ambition to maintain inherited levels of growth has taken us deep into a debt crisis. The crisis manifests itself in many ways: massive government deficit spending, more corporate borrowing and – in many countries – excessive consumer debt. All of these trends have been driven by forceful monetary and fiscal incentives, and few countries have resisted the temptation of providing them. We acknowledge that the debate about benefits and risks of budget deficits is as old as John Maynard Keynes's early academic papers, and discussing the arguments is beyond the scope of this book. However, what this book aims to do is to highlight that our addiction to an old vision of growth, paired with an old, resource-intensive and scale-driven industrial system to deliver the growth we want, is luring us to trade the long term for the short term.

In companies, many businesses leaders are optimizing for the short term in ways that are leaving all constituents, shareholders included, exposed. In government, leaders are overly inclined to borrow their way out of slow growth and through structural barriers. And lastly, in the consumer sector, excessive borrowing is happening for goods that are then hardly utilized and are not delivering the benefits consumers expect or deserve. All three factors have one thing in common: they are trying to perpetuate an old vision of growth based on a traditional engine of production and consumption.

Short-term capitalism. The value of corporate borrowing is undisputed and has been well established by academics. While the recent financial crisis has provided evidence that some industries, particularly the financial sector, are in need of deleveraging, overall there seems little reason to criticize our established corporate funding model. The real drama, however, is playing out at a different level.

Companies are borrowing short-term returns against long-term health. Dominic Barton, the managing director of McKinsey, called out this inconsistency. While 70–90 per cent of share prices are a reflection of cashflows three years and more out, 'management is preoccupied with what's reportable three months from now, then capitalism has a problem'. This 'myopia' is manifest: the average tenure of CEOs has decreased from ten to six years since 1995, at a time when the size and complexity of companies require more rather than less familiarity and immersion. Bonuses and incentives are overly tied to short-term bottom-line performance, leading to little motivation for long-term change: only 43 per cent of non-executive directors of public companies consider themselves in a position to influence strategy. Stockholding periods are down from seven years to seven months, and 70 per cent of US stock trading is now executed by hyperspeed traders who are holding stocks for a few seconds only.[47] These traders exert pressure on CEOs and management teams who are predominantly occupied in delivering quarterly earnings. Business consultants are today largely employed in order to drive large-scale performance programmes that deliver within eighteen months, while in the past many of their analytical powers were deployed to provide strategic foresight. This behaviour happens in spite of substantial evidence that large corporate success – even in the recent past – is associated with through-cycle behaviour and patience: Apple, Tesla, GE, or the German family-owned *Mittelstand* are good examples.

These examples show that myopia comes at a price. Long-term projects and game-changing plans are not receiving the funds they require, valuable business initiatives are not given the time to take off and important expertise is lost in down cycles. More fundamentally, there is growing antagonism and friction between business and society. Annual surveys show that the level of trust in business, particularly large corporations, is at a historic low. In two-thirds of the twenty-seven markets covered it has been declining and has fallen below 50 per cent in fourteen countries, the lowest value since 2008.[48] Occupy Wall Street is only the tip of the iceberg; mistrust runs deep in living rooms around the world. Critics from politics, civil society and from business itself have long called for a reversal of that trend, a reinstitution of long-term capitalism and a generation of managers who act like owners. This will require new rules and conventions: long-term performance metrics, managers at risk, for example with one or two annual salaries, more empowered non-executive directors and restricted voting rights for short-term stockholders. However, none of this will fix the deeper challenge expressed by the CEO of a leading packaged goods company: 'In today's system of revenue and profit generation, managers are caught in a trap. We have to convince our customers to consume beyond the point that is good for them or society. We have a vision of what good products would look like. But we do not have the time to develop these offerings, nor business models that allow us to benefit. In the meantime and under the short-term regime, I see company and consumer interests diverge.' Comments like this – coming straight from the boardrooms of a leading consumer goods corporation – are remarkable, and an acknowledgement of the need to rethink our model of growth from one where massive societal costs are accepted to one where they are designed out in the first place. It is such a model that we will be proposing in this book.

Public debt and structural deficits. Public deficits started to build up in the 1970s, in response to the oil shock and the subsequent recession. Anti-cyclical government spending, as recommended by John Maynard Keynes, was increasingly accepted as a cure for economic downturn. In hindsight, the emotional debate that dominated the 1970s and 1980s seems innocent and off the point. The fierce discussion evolved around the best way to tame the cyclic growth engine. At no point did either of the sides – Keynesians or supply-side economists – argue that deficit spending be substituted for underlying long-term growth. It was taken for granted that, despite any ups and downs, an economy would grow. But now the growth engine is stuttering. In his 2014 paper, Robert Gordon predicted a slowdown of real per capita GDP growth in the US from the 2 per cent enjoyed between 1891 and 2007. Gordon predicted that in the 25–40 years after 2007, GDP per capita will grow at only 0.9 per cent and real income at 0.4 per cent. He identified six powerful headwinds that the US and other advanced economies will be facing: demography, inequality, global competition, education, environment and public debt.[49] To close that gap, governments in the US and around the world are providing stimulus on an ongoing basis, but it comes at the high price of massive sovereign debt. Between 2000 and 2014 alone, such debt levels soared from $22 trillion to $58 trillion, an astounding 7.5 per cent year-on-year growth rate. Across the OECD gross debt-to-GDP ratio has increased from 73 per cent to 111 per cent between 2007 and 2013. It is not only European crisis-hit countries like Greece that will be unable to repay such debts.

While public borrowing is often done for good reasons, it also increases the lock-in to an industrial system that, as we argue in this book, requires major redesign. First, it obstructs future growth, as debt repayments ultimately require higher taxes and lower transfer payments, which in turn reduces growth in its own right. For the US, Gordon estimates that 0.2 per cent of the lower growth in the future will be due to this effect. What started as a way to close the growth gap is turning into a boomerang. Second, the interest burden is crowding out the investments that are urgently needed for economic renewal. A study of US government spending showed that between 2008 and 2014 the share of government spending for the 'future' has come down by 12 index points,[50] whereas non-discretionary commitments such as pensions instead increased. We are losing our freedom to shape our future.

Consumers in debt. Households, too, are borrowing against the future. We should remember that it was household debt that triggered the 2008 financial crisis. Never have consumer debt levels been higher, now standing at $40 trillion and double the amount of the year 2000. In advanced economies in particular, the debt-to-income ratio has reached very high levels: over 200 per cent in countries like Denmark, Netherlands or Norway, or levels of 100 per cent of household income in the US, UK, Canada, Korea or Australia. Most of that is mortgage debt, which is a reflection of tight real estate markets in urban environments.[51]

This is important in a number of ways. It is a telling reflection of stagnating real incomes and is associated with massive pressure on families and lost autonomy over their lives. This is particularly true for urban families whose income has been outpaced by the costs of housing. It is also the foreboding of weaker growth in the future, as highlighted by a 2015 research paper on US consumer debt and GDP.[52] Most importantly, it indicates how households continue to be pushed into unproductive assets. Around 34 per cent of household spending is on real estate, cars and household durables – analysis that we will elaborate later in the book shows that service or sharing models are able to provide the benefits of cars, washing machine, power tools, white goods, consumer electronics or sports equipment at significantly lower cost to the user. It appears that the ownership of largely underutilized durables is placing additional strain on disposable household income and exposing families to greater financial risk.

In summary, we observe increasing and often excessive levels of debt on all levels, capital stuck in unproductive assets, accumulating systemic risk and a lack of funding for long-term investments and projects. Our addiction to conventional growth, in conjunction with the demands of the twentieth-century industrial engine, makes us prone to crisis and unprepared for the system-level change that we urgently need.

3.3 Social borrowing – losing the glue

We are borrowing from society too. Never in recent history has that been more evident than in the last few years. Across the West, the calls for economic protectionism and de-globalization are getting stronger. They reveal anxiety, a deep skepticism of the current economic wealth engine and a loss of social glue at large. At the same time, the need for social glue is increasing exponentially in an increasingly interconnected economy. In 2012, philosopher Jürgen Habermas provoked his listeners when he talked about solidarity as a scarce resource within the capitalist society.[53] His point was that paradoxically, many of the efforts to strengthen economic growth in fact causes the glue to get unstuck, eroding an important prerequisite for further growth.

The economic importance of social capital had long been neglected. This started to change in 1995, when Robert D. Putnam published an article entitled 'Bowling Alone: America's Declining Social Capital' in the *Journal of Democracy*. For more than twenty years, Putnam had analysed different towns in southern and northern Italy. For decades, the communities in northern Italy – many of them famed as industrial clusters – had been prospering and demonstrating resilience to the economic ups and downs. Their southern counterparts, on the other hand, were performing poorly, with lower incomes, higher exposure to external shocks, and fewer, smaller and more vulnerable companies. Formally, there had been no difference between the governments of the north and the south, but their effectiveness varied massively.[54] The northern Italian communities flourished as a result of very high levels of civic engagement, which Putnam measured in terms of newspaper readership, voter turnout, and membership in choral societies and football clubs. Southern Italian towns were trailing their northern counterparts along all of these dimensions. Putnam concluded that it was the social capital that made the difference. He defined it as the networks and the norms of reciprocity and trust, which make life easier and economic success more likely. Putnam's article struck a chord with social scientists, who had found a way to link social development to economic, and could demonstrate that one does not work without the other. And it resonated, too, with a broader US readership, because it provided an explanation for the degradation of many US communities where social cohesion had been measurably in decline, leaving card tables deserted and bowling alleys empty. American citizens, Putnam could show, had been withdrawing from their communities for more than three decades. In the meantime, many studies have confirmed similar trends in other regions of the world. On the other hand, those countries particularly well endowed with social capital – such as the Scandinavian countries – also score high in terms of economic productivity and wealth.

Since the financial crisis in 2008, and with the rise of populist movements in mature democracies the interest in social capital has been reignited. Many researchers and political observers suggest that the crisis was another culmination point of a latent degeneration of social capital, one which is leaving societies more vulnerable and economies less vibrant.

The erosion of trust. The global financial crisis has shaken many lives, eradicated jobs, caused companies to default, and driven countries into debt and austerity. For many, it is also a crisis of trust that is far from over. Trust, they argue, has been abused by carelessly deregulating governments, reckless banks or an unholy coalition of the two.[55] Others argue that the blame lies with a new hedonist culture nourished by forces of consumerism. But even before the trauma of the crisis, there had been signs of disintegrating trust. And after the crisis, investigations from around the world are coming to the same conclusion – that trust and social cohesion are evaporating. For the last fifteen years Edelman, a marketing firm, has performed annual surveys and asked thousands of respondents who they trust, including peers, government, business, NGOs and the media. While their surveys do not capture all aspects of societal trust, Edelman's longitudinal data set created over the years tells a story of trust erosion, redirection and contraction.[56]

Trust erosion has been observed across all countries since 2001. The total trust index[57] indicates that the number of countries with high index values ('trusters') has declined, while the number of distrusters has grown. In addition, countries do not 'grow into trust', nor is the composition of 'trusters' correlated to any medium-term growth trajectory that a country has taken. A second finding was that business and media have lost more trust than government. And importantly, the circle of trust is drawn closer: peers are seen as more trustworthy than distant institutional leaders, and local institutions are more trusted than national ones. The narrowing perimeter of trust towards the closest circle of friends and family has been a consistent observation for many years. This is affecting our ability to convene around a shared challenge at a very critical juncture.

The trust index and other related studies also offer a glimpse into what it takes to build or erode trust. Leadership integrity is important. Commonality of purpose is another pivotal driver of trust: the 2002 floods along Germany's Elbe river reignited trust and collaboration and eventually secured Chancellor Gerhard Schröder's re-election in reward for his caring (and wellington-prone) management of the crisis.[58] After 11 September 2001, Putnam observed a measurable increase of community-minded Americans: higher levels of civic engagement, more volunteering and more interest in political affairs. The 9/11 trauma not only created the generation that built the momentum for the Obama campaigns, it also – Putnam speculates – reversed some of the civic decline characterized by empty bowling alleys.[59]

Putnam and other scholars[60] have provided ample evidence that economic growth needs trust but today it does not automatically produce it. Instead of creating a cycle of mutual enforcement, short-term growth seems to erode trust when it splits society and when it is unable to provide a shared sense of direction. So, we are not growing in terms of trust and thus creating a more productive, liveable fabric of society. In fact, over the last ten years, evidence is accruing that we are, with the current model of wealth creation, growing out of it.

The erosion of equality. Few intellectuals have recorded a faster rise to celebrity status than Thomas Piketty, the French author and economist. His 2014 treatise *Capital in the Twenty-First Century* essentially argues that income inequality in many Western countries has risen to levels not seen in the last hundred years, something Piketty attributes to diverging rates of return to capital and the growth rate of the economy, and also to continued downward pressure on wages in a global race for the cheapest hour.[61] It was in the same year that Oxfam made the headlines by reporting that the world's 62 wealthiest individuals had a combined wealth equal to that of the bottom 50 per cent of the world's population, which equates to about 3.5 billion people, and suggesting that by 2016, the richest 1 per cent would have more combined wealth than the other 99 per cent of the population – a prediction that materialized one year ahead of time.[62] Klaus Schwab, the World Economic Forum's founder, consequently opened that day's plenary session with the words: 'I want Davos members to take a history lesson and realize that capitalism cannot survive if income and wealth become concentrated in too few hands.' In the same vein, a Davos attendant, moving on to lunch afterwards through deep Alpine snow, picked it up this way: 'This takes us back to the income concentration levels of 1910, the year when my entire village in Bohemia set off for America.'

With a strong sense of history, Piketty used literature to illustrate what the pre-1910 world of impermeable, patrimonial capitalism looked like. In *Pride and Prejudice*, Jane Austen explained the nineteenth-century wisdom that a decent life (then requiring £1,000 a year) could never be attained through hard work, law degrees or book writing, but through marriage alone. While Piketty's methodology and exact results have been passionately debated, and also criticized, the basic observation of a less inclusive society and diverging incomes remains largely uncontested. Piketty does not analyse the effects of inequality at any length but hints at the massive price we are paying: income inequality is not only divisive but also stifles growth in the long term. Economists widely agree that consumer spending is higher for low-income brackets than for top earners.

Inequality is undermining society. Today, there are some US states where 15 per cent of Walmart employees live on foodstamps.[63] While no single company is to blame, we seem to have turned around the Fordian creed ('Every employee must be able to buy our cars') into one that is uniformly focused on the supply side and cost. While this may be individually prudent, it has collectively undermined our ability to prosper. It is time to recognize that the wedge being driven through most major societies is now calling raucous voices on stage and populist and isolationist agendas into the political mainstream. It will require massive political resolve, investment and courage to correct that.

The possible erosion of generosity. Increasingly, we are seeing that the inherited model of growth, our resource dependency and the doctrine of scarcity are limiting our ability to embrace the new realities: a planet of close to eight billion people and a more immediate exposure to a diverse and torn global community (as witnessed in Europe during the Syrian refugee crisis). Under these circumstances, the premise of rivalry of goods is breeding rejection, undermining our social norms and limiting our ability to adapt and accommodate. Again, we are borrowing from the future.

Generosity is measured in donations, volunteering, or the willingness to help a stranger.[64] When measured for individuals, companies and governments, all of these parameters remain high. But in developed countries in particular they are stagnating at a relatively constant constant level of around 0.2 per cent of GDP in Europe in the past ten years. Beyond individual catastrophes such as the Haiti earthquake, they are developing in parallel to any other consumptive spending item. Giving, it seems, is a mature market. The real concept of generosity, however, is broader than that of giving. It describes our behaviours in our daily exchanges. To understand why generosity may be at risk under the current paradigm, it helps to understand two essential determinants: scarcity and dissociation.

A group of scientists analysed how farmers in Mufindi in the lowlands of Southern Tanzania share the water with which they irrigate their crops. Today this is done without any defined rules; the practice is a result of the villagers' sense of rivalry and generosity. The researchers asked the villagers to rank their neighbours in social status (high/low) and to choose how much water they would – under different conditions of flow – share with neighbours or keep for themselves. In the test, they were promised rewards both for high yields on their fields but also for sharing. The result is as unsurprising as it is stark. During times of abundance, villagers are generous and share, even if grabbing more water would further improve the yields on their own fields. This changes during times of scarcity. Now the farmers become greedy, and divert as much water as possible to their own fields. They are rating their crop higher than the rewards for sharing. A different pattern appeared for high status individuals. Influential men were self-serving even during times of abundance. They felt sufficiently dissociated from the community and knew that downstream neighbours would not dare to stand up against them. Influential women continued to supply downstream neighbours during times of drought, because women generally were expected to abide by the norms.[65]

Thus, in the absence of strong rules, generosity seems to flourish only if resources are seen as accessible and abundant. In a paradigm of finite resources and a resource-intense model of value creation, our generosity is at risk of being engulfed by the increasing 'boat-is-full' rhetoric. In mathematics, a proof is valuable if assumptions are widely applicable. Such a solution is valid in similar cases 'without loss of generality'.[66] In the economy, the search is on for a model that works for ten billion people 'without loss of generosity'.

It is clear that our addiction to growth has created massive debt levels – ecological, financial and social. The borrowing has reached levels that are hard to repay, and if it goes on much further, will be impossible to repay. Borrowing our way out of structural stagnation is increasingly a dead end, with fewer options, and fewer buffers against shocks. And it is massively degrading our natural world, making it less productive and benign, and with far less beauty. Therefore a broad movement that feeds from academic disciplines – or sometimes ideological sources – has started to question growth more fundamentally, arguing that the world needs a completely different concept of growth. Ideas are emerging but remain contradictory, incomplete and untested. There are three broad schools of thought for what is needed: zero growth, more growth 'down the Kuznets curve' or a new and transformationally different kind of growth. In the next chapter, we will explore these three avenues.

Chapter 4

Lost – the great divergence

Doublethink means the power of holding two contradictory beliefs in one's mind simultaneously, and accepting both of them.

George Orwell

The borrowing we described in the last chapter took us up to here. But not much further, as we'll show in this chapter. On the one hand, because it's ineffective in driving real long-term growth, and on the other hand, because we increasingly understand that the old conception of GDP growth is not giving us the outcomes we want. We continue to be addicted to growth, but at the same time we start realizing that it is only partly correlated with the progress we want. Both notions coexist and right now, we are doublethinkers.

On one level the growth engine is stuttering. Plainly, growth rates in mature economies such as the US, Germany or France are coming down (see Figure 4.1). There might be many reasons for that, such as demography, or fewer working hours per employee. Partly, however, it also reflects a slowdown in productivity growth. Robert Gordon[1] shows how growth in US output per worker dropped over the century. Between 1891 and 1972 it grew by 2.3 per cent, then by 1.4 per cent until 2004, and only 1.3 per cent between 2004 and 2012. This was in spite of the most dramatic acceleration of technology, particularly the wholesale introduction of computing power into services and industry. 'We should feel fortunate if we will have half the growth that we had in the past', says Gordon.[2]

And something else is different this time: monetary instruments seem blunt. Even the most expansive monetary policy and an unprecedented negative-interest rate regime were unable to revive meaningful growth. Also fiscal stimulus and excessive budget deficit spending have been unable to return growth to its previous levels.

Whatever the reasons and cures, many economists would agree that growth has slowed in a way that does not appear to be cyclical; it is more unequal, increasingly jobless and less easily stimulated by public intervention. There is reason to believe that the effort required to get the old growth engine running at the old steam will be higher and not lower in the future. The world seems faced with a new, inconvenient reality: that the growth engine that served us so well in the past might be much less powerful in the future.

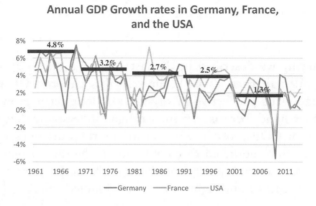

SOURCE: Insee, Statistisches Bundesamt, U.S. Bureau of Economic Analysis

Fig. 4.1

The second inconvenient reality is that the growth engine has stopped delivering the outcomes we want, at least partially. We will look at facts that suggest we might already have entered a zone of uneconomic growth, at least in some countries. As an initial example, an analysis for the New Climate Economy Commission concludes that the average negative health and mortality effects of air pollution in the fifteen countries that emit most greenhouse gases are running at a full 4.4 per cent of GDP; in China the burden is more than 10 per cent of GDP.[3] For the first time, GDP growth and societal progress may move in altogether different directions in some countries. We call it the 'great divergence', a mismatch for the first time strong enough to rethink altogether the growth aspiration and the indicator cockpit for our economy (see Figure 4.2).

4.1 Rethinking GDP – our cockpit for growth

Nicolas Sarkozy is not known for sentimentality. So when France's centre-right president announced in 2009 that he had commissioned a group of experts to find alternatives to GDP for measuring economic and societal progress, the news travelled fast. Sarkozy is one of several political leaders who believe that GDP growth is only one of many metrics needed to describe and measure human development and societal progress, and that the myopic focus on GDP is increasingly misleading. It is some years since Robert Kennedy said of GDP that 'it measures everything, in short, except that which makes life worthwhile'.

Sarkozy did not leave it to the amateurs. The commission was headed by Nobel laureate Joseph Stiglitz and comprised fellow laureates Daniel Kahnemann, Kenneth Arrow and Amartya Sen, as well as Lord Nicholas Stern and nineteen other economists. The results of the Stiglitz–Sen–Fitoussi commission were published in 2010, under the title of 'Mismeasuring Our Lives'.[4]

The Commission called for a complete revamp of how we think of and measure economic and social progress, and emphasized the many limitations of GDP as a lead indicator of such progress. By design and intent, GDP only measures the economic value-add of a country; it does not look at its environment, health, inclusiveness, social cohesion, education or other areas crucial to our well-being. It also fails to measure how a country's assets develop – be it natural capital or infrastructure – and consequently it does not say anything about how a country is trading

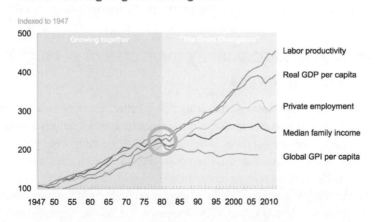

We are seeing a 'great divergence'

Indexed to 1947

SOURCE: Federal Reserve Bank of St. Louis, Brynjolfsson and McAfee , Kubiszewski et al. (2013)

Fig. 4.2

short-term consumption off against long-term economic, social and environmental sustainability. The Commission suggested broadening the measurements of progress. First, they argued, the measurements of how our societies are doing 'here and now' must include the key determinants of people's perceived quality of life: material living standards but also health, education, political agency, environment, equality and security. Second, measures of sustainability need to be included, specifically measures that look at how the stock of financial and natural assets develop.

Since the 1970s, scientists have been working on a new and improved compass for progress. Initially, welfare indices were proposed as a new measure for human well-being, such as the Index of Sustainable Economic Welfare (ISEW), which starts from GDP but then also looks at additional sources of income (e.g. volunteering or household work), hidden costs (e.g. pollution clean-up and remediation) and capital depletion (e.g. loss of ecosystems). In 1989 ISEW was replaced by the Genuine Progress Indicator (GPI). It clearly has – like GDP – methodological limitations and yet it has been widely adopted as an alternative measure to GDP for long-term welfare creation. Another measure is the Human Development Index (HDI), which was developed by the United Nations. There is also the Inclusive Wealth Index (IWI), which takes into account the contributions of human capital, produced capital and natural capital.[5] And finally, Life Satisfaction metrics measure the subjective well-being as indicated by respondents in representative surveys. Together these analytical approaches make up for many of the inadequacies of GDP.

Fact box: Complementary measures of economic and social progress

Genuine Progress Indicator – measuring flows, better. The 'genuine progress indicator', or GPI, is a metric that has been put forward to supplement GDP as a measure of development. The GPI calculation starts from GDP, but then also takes into account environmental and social factors which are not measured by GDP, such as environmental depletion, unpaid work, education and inequality. As such, GPI is still a flow-based metric but remains a much more comprehensive one than GDP. However, it is sometimes criticized for lacking transparency.

Inclusive Wealth Index (IWI) – measuring capital stocks. The IWI measures changes in wealth as part of the development of a country's total capital stock, including manufactured, natural and human capital (with a number of sub-categories for each). It argues that if this 'productive base' develops positively – specifically in per capita terms – then a country is on a path of sustainable development. IWI was developed by a group of prominent economists with support of the UN.[6] 'In inclusive wealth, sustainability is defined as positive change in human well-being. A country's inclusive wealth is the social value (not dollar price) of all its capital assets, including natural capital, human capital and produced capital. If inclusive wealth is positive, then well-being across generations is positive.'[7]

Human Development Index (HDI) – measuring social progress. HDI is the flagship metric of the United Nations Development Programme, and is also used extensively by other development organizations. HDI is defined as the geometric average of indices for life expectancy, education and income per capita. Recently, the income per capita calculation has been adjusted to account for inequality. Notably, HDI does not include any considerations of natural capital development.

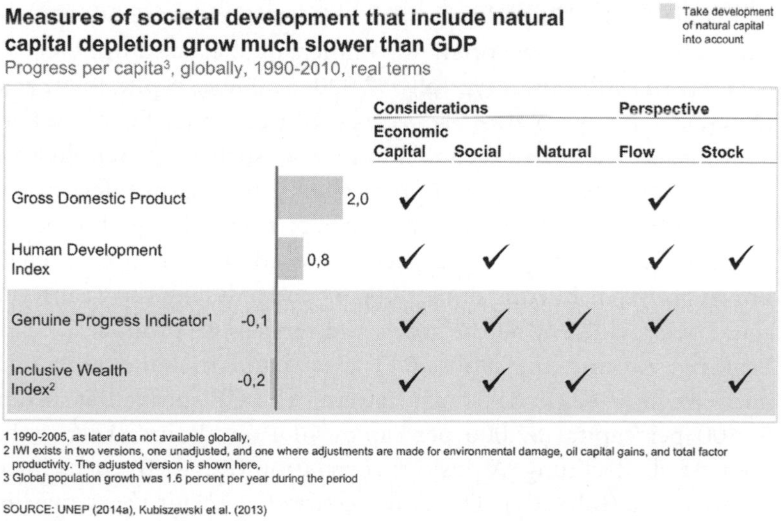

Measures of societal development that include natural capital depletion grow much slower than GDP

Take development of natural capital into account

Progress per capita[3], globally, 1990-2010, real terms

		Considerations			Perspective	
		Economic Capital	Social	Natural	Flow	Stock
Gross Domestic Product	2,0	✓			✓	
Human Development Index	0,8	✓	✓		✓	✓
Genuine Progress Indicator[1]	-0,1	✓	✓	✓	✓	
Inclusive Wealth Index[2]	-0,2	✓	✓	✓		✓

1 1990-2005, as later data not available globally,
2 IWI exists in two versions, one unadjusted, and one where adjustments are made for environmental damage, oil capital gains, and total factor productivity. The adjusted version is shown here,
3 Global population growth was 1.6 percent per year during the period

SOURCE: UNEP (2014a), Kubiszewski et al. (2013)

Fig. 4.3

So what do these alternative approaches say about growth and progress? Disturbingly, all of them report much slower progress than GDP. Look at Figure 4.3, which presents how the four most commonly used metrics developed globally between 1990 and 2010, in per capita terms. GDP growth was at 2 per cent per year, HDI growth at 0.8 per cent per year, less than half the growth of GDP. Perhaps, most strikingly, both the metrics that include the development of natural capital report no growth at all in per capita terms.

Researching the same question, in 2013, a team of academics reviewed the development of all these measures (except IWI which had only just been published) since 1950 and compared them to the development of GDP (Figure 4.4). All of these indices are taking a specific perspective and rate different aspects of long-term welfare creation,[8] and all of them have obvious shortcomings. Yet, strikingly, since the early to mid-1980s, all of them show a visibly different trajectory than GDP. While post-war GDP increased threefold, GPI only doubled. If GPI represents welfare, then welfare was massively outpaced by GDP. The extensive meta-study reviewed seventeen countries around the world and delivered a number of findings which were largely in line with the Stiglitz commission.[9,10]

- **Welfare losses**: Even during times when GPI and GDP are correlated, GPI trails GDP. While the reconciliation of GPI and GDP is tricky and subject to many, often incommensurable, assumptions, the data returns GPI values typically $2,000–3,500 per capita lower than the GDP. This is noteworthy because GPI accounts for all welfare-creating activities – market and non-market, such as household work, childcare or subsistence food production. And yet the effect of cost for pollution clean-up or natural asset depletion (mining of resources, deterioration of soil) are outpacing the additional income effect. Brown growth is hurting our well-being and reducing the wealth that could be provided by all the goods and services we produce.
- **Peaking**: Around the globe, GPI grew hand in hand with GDP until about 1980. In 1980–85, however, the GPI peaked at around $3,500 per capita ($7,000 per capita GDP) and since then it has been slowly declining. A positive correlation (R2=0,98) turns into a negative one (R2=0,61). The peak occurred at about the same time that the ecological footprint exceeded the biocapacity of the earth.

Since then, capital has been lost, negatively affecting GPI. In the mid-1970s, the Satisfaction Index also happened to stall.[11]

• **Pathways**: While the peak in the 1970s can be observed in a very wide array of countries (EU, US, China), country pathways differ a lot. In some countries, GPI continues to trend in the same direction as GDP (Japan being very efficient; the UK is transitioning to a very successful service economy). In others, GPI and GDP are more visibly decoupled, due in some part to increasingly unequal income distribution (Germany, Belgium, Australia), and in some part to the massive expansion of the ecological footprint and the reduction of biocapacity per person (China due to massive consumption growth; India due to population growth).

• **Uneconomic growth**: Some countries find themselves in a zone of 'uneconomic growth' where the disutility of growth exceeds the utility of growth.[12] This is indicated by a declining GPI – here interpreted as a decline in welfare – in parallel to GDP growth. While the environmental cost is highest in countries like China or India, low-growth countries like Belgium or Australia can also easily flip into uneconomic growth due to the costs of environmental degradation and inequality.

• **Growth resistance in a full world**: Finally, there are indications that GPI is peaking at lower GDP levels in China and India. While this is far from affirmative, those countries that have to plan for their economic ascent in a 'full world' are facing higher costs, more resource stress and stronger resistance to growth than the industrial powerhouses of the twentieth century – at least, if they follow the same model of resource-intensive growth.

The IWI was not part of the meta-study quoted above, but their conclusions are similar; looking at the 1990–2010 time horizon and assessing 140 countries, they found average global IWI growth was 32 per cent, compared to a GDP growth of 187 per cent. This implies an annual IWI growth of 1.6 per cent. In per capita terms, annual IWI growth was 0 per cent, as population grew as fast as IWI. Finally, the 'adjusted' IWI per capita, where natural capital is not only impacted by resource extraction but also by direct environmental damage such as climate change, was actually negative at -0.2 per cent annually. This is the metric IWI considers most important, as it measures whether countries face issues in sustaining current consumption patterns.[13]

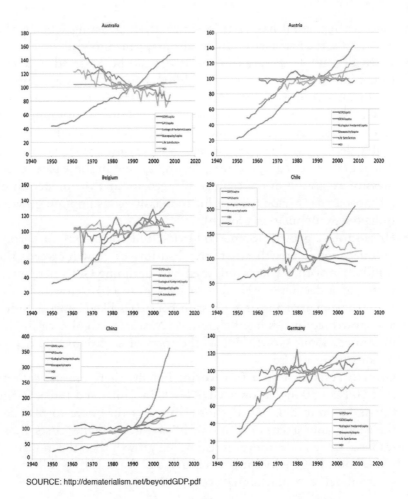

SOURCE: http://dematerialism.net/beyondGDP.pdf

Fig 4.4 GDP and alternative measures of human progress 1950–2003

It is becoming well known that GDP is inadequate as a measure of welfare and societal progress. But to us, there is something deeply disturbing in the massive differences between GDP and *all* the alternative metrics. This raises questions about the success of our current economic engine, in addition to underlining how crucial it is to complement GDP with other metrics. Joseph Stiglitz summarized his commission's work with a very obvious point: that GDP was never from the start designed to measure economic well-being. It was chosen to guide US government efforts to recover industrial production after the Great Depression. The inventor of GDP, the economist Simon Kuznets, himself made this clear when he presented his GDP analysis to Congress:

> Distinctions must be kept in mind between quantity and quality of growth, between costs and returns, and between the short and long run. Goals for more growth should specify more growth of what and for what.[14]

4.2 Externalities – the dark matter of growth[15]

In physics, 'dark matter' is believed to make up for the majority of all matter in our universe, but so far it is not fully understood, and it eludes our current detection systems. We often call externalities the 'dark matter of growth' for the very same reasons: they are often bigger – sometimes much bigger – than the economic activities recorded; they are not well understood; and they go largely undetected by economic measurement systems.

To start at the beginning, economists define an externality as 'a consequence from an economic activity that is experienced by unrelated third parties'.[16] When the founding fathers of economics wrote their papers, externalities were considered a marginal phenomenon. In Adam Smith's world, most trade took place in a village market, and the consequences for anyone except the buyer and the seller were negligible. Surprisingly, this view is still prevailing in a lot of economics literature and in many economic policy debates: externalities, when they are discussed, are seen as exceptions, and not of a scale to influence industries or economies. Look at any economics textbook, and you are likely to see externalities described in a separate sub-chapter, with few implications for the big picture.

Today, the reality is very different, at least for the product and resource systems that this book is most concerned with. With a global economy now approximately 400 times[17] bigger than in Adam Smith's day, major externalities are the norm rather than the exception, and they are often worth much more than the monetized transaction value.[18]

In 2012, economic consultancy Trucost,[19] on behalf of The Economics of Ecosystems and Biodiversity (TEEB), took on the Herculean task of estimating the total global unpriced environmental externalities (the 'natural capital cost', in Trucost's language) – to our knowledge the first time anyone has carried out such a comprehensive assessment. In more detail, they looked at all primary production sectors (agriculture, forestry, fisheries, mining, oil and gas exploration, utilities) and the primary processing sectors with the largest environmental footprint (cement, steel, pulp and paper, petrochemicals), and estimated the economic cost of the environmental degradation caused by these sectors. They did this for the six most important types of environmental impacts (greenhouse gas emissions, water use, waste, air pollution, land and water pollution, and land use) and across world regions (capturing local contexts such as local freshwater availability).

Their results both fascinate and terrify. The total global natural capital cost amounted to $7.3 trillion for 2009, the last year for which complete data was available. This corresponds to a full 13 per cent of global GDP in 2009, or to approximately half of US GDP in that same year. The total cost if all industries were included would be even bigger – the housing and transport sectors, for instance, are known to cause major environmental externalities but were outside Trucost's scope.

If one considers that the primary production and processing industries that were in scope represent only a small share of the global economy, the conclusion becomes even more interesting: at today's market prices, *the natural capital cost is higher than the total revenue of these sectors.* This result held true also when double-clicking on individual business sectors in individual regions: among the top 100 such region-sectors (which together represented 65 per cent of the total environmental costs), there were only five where revenues were higher than natural capital cost. In profit terms, most of these industries would go into the red if they had to carry their natural capital costs – see Figure 4.5 for a comparison between the profit margin before and after natural capital costs for a selected set of industries.

We find agriculture particularly striking. Often, the natural capital cost from overuse of water or clearing of land is an order-of-magnitude higher than the associated revenue. In severely water-stressed Pakistan,

Negative profit margins in most of the world's raw material industries if natural capital costs are included

Profit margin (EBIT) before and after natural capital costs, based on top-2 companies in each Morgan Stanley Composite Index category, Percent, 2012

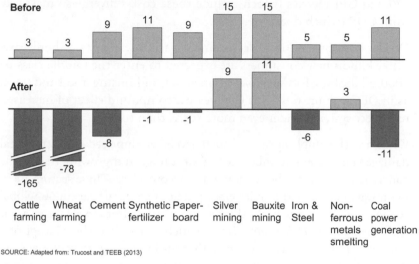

SOURCE: Adapted from: Trucost and TEEB (2013)

Fig 4.5

the natural capital cost of growing water-intense cotton is a full 120 times higher than the revenues generated.

Disaggregating instead into different types of natural capital costs, greenhouse gas emissions account for 38 per cent, water use 25 per cent, land use 24 per cent, air pollution 7 per cent, land and water pollution 5 per cent, and waste 1 per cent.

While Trucost's report is the most comprehensive we've seen on the topic, their results for individual externalities build heavily on the large body of research that now exists on many of the environmental issues concerned. For instance, a report titled 'Hidden Costs of Energy' published by the US National Research Council of the National Academies in 2010, estimated the cost of US coal combustion to human health at $53 billion per year, compared with US coal industry revenues of $25 billion.[20] So externalities were twice as big as the revenues – and this study did not even include greenhouse gas emissions as an externality. In a recent report we authored, the externality cost of inner-city car traffic was valued at €0.19 per car kilometre. Again, the negative externalities were of the same order of magnitude as the monetized costs. These huge and largely undetected (in economic measurement systems) environmental costs give an important explanation why the IWI and GPI metrics (which include these costs) diverge so massively from GDP (which doesn't).

On our current economic development path, these costs will only rise. Three billion new consumers are expected to enter the middle class by 2030, all looking forward to the same levels of housing, food and travel as in OECD countries. This will create a compound effect of increased use of ecosystems under even more stress than today.

What are the implications of such levels of unpriced environmental damage? First, these numbers represent a huge and growing risk to the concerned sectors, to the economy, and to ourselves. These sectors are in many ways crucial to our well-being, and lie at the very heart of our global economy. A few years back, the Carbon Tracker Initiative caused a stir with their report *Unburnable Carbon* which introduced the concept of a 'carbon bubble'.[21] The report argued that the market capitalizations of oil, gas and coal companies were too high, since a big share of their reserves would have to stay in the ground as 'stranded assets'. It led to seventy major pension funds collectively asking oil and gas companies in an open letter how they were managing these risks,[22] resulting in some investors reducing their exposure to these sectors. In a way, it was the first real sign of a perception shift – that fossil fuel assets are risky for an investor.

Now consider this: the total environment bubble described above is *three times* larger than the carbon bubble, as carbon is only about a third of the total natural capital costs. If these sectors had to carry all their costs, the first order approximation is that their market value would be *zero* or *negative*. Of course, this is an oversimplification: if natural capital costs were imposed, some of the costs would flow through to consumers as price increases, and some of them would lead to technology shifts – luckily the cost to avoid environmental damage is often (but far from always) much lower than the value of the harm done to ecosystems. So the net impact on market capitalization would be smaller, but still represent a massive risk to investors.

Second, if the large product and resource sectors had to take care of the environmental damage they cause, they would look very different from how they do today. Resources would be managed and reused in a completely different way, new technologies introduced and ecosystems protected.

Third, it is disturbing to us how little of this debate has penetrated into mainstream economics. Sure, many economic debates underline the seriousness of environmental issues, and pricing externalities is an evergreen proposal. But once this has been stated, the implicit assumption in most economic and industry debates is still that the monetized market prices and market capitalizations are more or less 'correct' and 'optimized', and a lot of economic modelling, even in resource-related sectors, all but disregards externalities. If the numbers in this section were new to you, it is a symptom that something is quite wrong with how we look at our economy, pay out subsidies, levy taxes, define our accounting standards and measure value.

4.3 Where from here – no-growth, Kuznets or deep transformation

What are our fundamental options to respond to the massive systemic failure that these numbers so conspicuously reveal? There are three fundamentally different propositions to escape this ever more intractable trade-off: not to grow, to massively grow 'down the Kuznets curve' towards greener outcomes, or to transform the underlying operating system of our economy altogether. Let's explore each of them.

The no-growth economy. In 2013, the German psychologist Harald Welzer, in a rage over his own inconsistent consumption patterns, wrote a book that hit a nerve with readers. *Selbstdenken* [Think yourself] is a radical critique of modern consumerism. He describes resource depletion and climate change as the 'perfectly unsolvable problem' within a framework of a growth economy and 'extractivism'. He calls for a radical shift from 'growth' to 'cultivation'.[23] The book forms one of the latest – and intentionally populist – incarnations of a deeper debate about non-growth. The conversation about the end of growth has a tradition and comes with different language: steady-state economies (1973) or 'decroissance' (2002).[24,25] Given the deep entrenchment of the growth assumption into our lives and societies outlined in Chapter 1.3, this is a major blasphemy.

This school of thought is rooted partly in the environmental movement, partly in economic analysis of demographics and productivity. The German economist Reinhard Miegel made the argument back in the 1970s. He stressed the link between labour and growth. Economic growth has virtually been absent between Charlemagne and Napoleon.[26] Over a millennium, the annual growth rate did not exceed 0.07 per cent. It took the economy a thousand years to double output. Only with the start of industrialization did population and economic growth start their spectacular surge. In turn, Miegel sees that demography – a dramatic drop in available labour hours and massive rise in average age – will come in the way of growth.

The other line of argument is based on the observation that resources and 'sinks' for the deposition of post-use waste are finite. Surprisingly, this is the older argument. And even more surprisingly, this concern was raised by one of the most liberal and utilitarian thinkers of all, John Stuart Mill, in the mid-nineteenth century when industrialization was in its infancy. Mill came to the conclusion that 'stationary states of capital and wealth' were preferable to the destruction of the environment and the reduced quality of life that come with unlimited growth. He wrote:

> With every rood of land brought into cultivation, every hedgerow or superfluous tree rooted out, every flowery waste or dell ploughed up, there is not much satisfaction in contemplating the world with nothing left to the spontaneous activity of nature. If the earth must lose that great portion of its pleasantness – which it owes to things that the unlimited increase of wealth and population would extirpate from it for the mere purpose of enabling it to support a larger, but not a better or a happier population – I sincerely hope, for the sake of posterity, that we humans will be content to be stationary, long before necessity compels us to it.[27]

When Mill wrote this in 1848, the global population amounted to 980 million and the world's first regular timetabled railway passenger services, from Liverpool to Manchester, had been in operation for less than twenty years. Even then he was clear about a circumstance which has only most recently started to return to our awareness: that we moved from a spacious world without resource constraints into a full world where the economy is a sub-system of a finite biosphere. This, the no-growth proponents argue, is the big shift in paradigm.[28] Like the surrounding world, any economy must eventually and asymptotically converge towards a steady state, a dynamic equilibrium where birth rates and deaths, production rates and depreciation rates, growth and decay balance. Like a forest and any ecosystem, the economy in this view moves from growth efficiency (maximum gross stock production per unit of effort) to maintenance efficiency (maintaining existing stock with minimum effort).

It took 150 years of explosive growth for Mill to be rediscovered. His environmental wake-up call was earlier, different, more fundamental and more optimistic than that of the much-quoted Thomas Robert Malthus. Malthus believed food supply would finally get in the way of growth and capitalism.[29] Mill did not believe that capitalism always required growth. So, with inconceivable providence and based on what feels like a very modern view on the reality of natural resources, two leading thinkers were rehearsing in the late nineteenth century a fierce debate that is now reignited well into the twenty-first century: whether capitalism, as some academics like Jackson[30] or Ekins[31] believe, could sustain itself as a no-growth system; or whether 'capitalism, green or otherwise, is ecological suicide', as Smith and others argue.[32] Mill against Malthus, still counting.

The Kuznets economy. When Indira Gandhi visited the first UN conference on the environment in Stockholm 1972, her key message was short: poverty is the biggest polluter.[33] A population in need of essentials, and with poor infrastructure and the lack of legal mechanisms, are circumstances that a society needs to grow out of. Gandhi's view reflects the historic experience of European countries. In 1858, a session in the House of Commons in London had to be cancelled because MPs could not withstand the piercing smell of dying fish emanating from the River Thames. The neglect and degradation continued, and a hundred years later the Thames was declared biologically dead. Today, after massive investment in sewage treatment and the introduction of effluent standards, 125 species of fish are back in London's river – a remarkable rebound, however incomplete. Or take air pollution. Throughout the nineteenth century London homes were heated by coal or wood. Later, industrial pollution was added to the mix. In 1952 the Great Smog caused an estimated 4,500 deaths in the capital. And yet, today Hyde Park joggers enjoy much cleaner air on their morning run and all Londoners can enjoy their sunrise. The same happened in Manchester, Paris, and the Ruhr industrial area. That experience went deep: grow first, clean up later. Consequently 'Less CO_2 needs more growth'[34] is the slogan of a German pro-business lobbying group.

The idea of growth as a remedy for resource overuse is best captured by the Kuznets curve, which plots resource intensity as a function of prosperity. Take plastics (see Figure 4.6): India with a GDP per capita of $1600 is consuming 10 kg of plastic per person and year.[35] As incomes per capita grow, that amount massively rises, to well beyond 100 kg per person. But then, plastic intensity peaks at a GDP level of around $15,000 per capita, through the introduction of return systems, larger purchases or consumer awareness. Similarly energy: US GDP growth per capita between 1986 and 2011 amounted to 2.5 per cent while

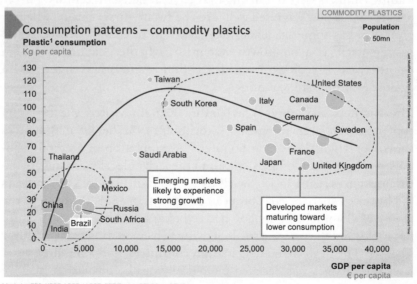

Fig 4.6

energy use per capita fell 0.17 per cent per annum during that era.[36] One 1 kg of CO_2 was needed in the US to generate 1 of GDP in 1980; in 2006 this number was down to 770 grams per dollar.[37] The UK energy peak occurred in 1973;[38] in Germany it was 1979.[39] Since then total consumption has been – however slowly – in decline.

That must be celebrated. And yet, there are problems with the conventional grow-green view. First, not all resources are following the Kuznets curve. Their resource intensity is rising, not falling. The global per capita consumption for cement, bauxite and iron ore is rising, not falling – largely due to the massive infrastructure investments in the BRIC nations. Second, the Kuznets effect is often local and the result of global offshoring. London banished the furnaces to the suburbs and neighbouring counties. Europe is shifting a good share of its industrial production to Asia. Out of the 14 gigatons by which emerging economies have increased annual CO_2 emissions per year since 2000, at least 2 gigatons are directly linked to exports.[40]

And most importantly, growing green is happening at the wrong speed. We have a Kuznets gap! China has doubled its CO_2 emissions over the last eight years, at a moment where we operate well outside safe planetary boundaries already. Our total nitrogen consumption for fertilizer is increasing by 1.4 per cent per year, whereas we should decrease by 4.6 per cent to meet our commitments.[41] The amount of plastic debris entering the ocean is growing by 5 per cent every year, while it should be decreasing by 10 per cent to stop leakage by 2025 as proposed in the 'Stemming the Tide' report by Ocean Conservancy and McKinsey.[42] Our total resource consumption and disposal continues to grow despite the Kuznets effect. And we have not taken the right turn. If we wanted to halve the emissions caused by deforestation by 2030, we would have to slow deforestation by 4.5 per cent per year – doable if following the example of Brazil, which halved emissions between 2004 and 2009, but not accounting for rising deforestation in Indonesia in the past years.

The point that GDP growth is the best predictor of progress towards a sustainable economic model is – as outlined above – hard ground to defend. The reverse remains true: GDP growth continues to be the best predictor for energy and resource use. If GDP grows by 3 per cent in New Zealand, CO_2 emissions increase by 1.5 per cent. If the

Fig 4.7

economy grows by 10 per cent in China, emissions increase by 6.3 per cent.[43] In India, GDP and CO_2 emissions rise at the same pace, recently at 6.5 per cent. In Italy, if the economy grows by 1 per cent, emissions remain constant. For now, we are not growing green, but only less brown.

The transformed economy. None of the previous solutions is attractive. We are caught between a rock and hard place. The rock of Mill's steady-state economy offers the hope that we escape the path of massive environmental destruction, but it comes with huge implications: for social systems that need to be funded out of lower incomes and taxes; for entrepreneurs who need to take risk in the expectation of winning a part of a smaller pie; or for education that thrives on the promise to its students that there is more, rather than less, to be gained. We have economically, politically and mentally locked ourselves into a model that needs to grow. But beyond the lock-in that will be so hard to overcome, there are three reasons to believe that **zero growth is a demand-side impossibility**. First, the resource effect of a zero-growth agenda would be minimal on a global scale if mature,

Western, post-materialistic societies with 'six pairs of shoes' were to go into zero-growth mode. Between 2020 and 2030, more than 45 per cent of additional GDP will originate from China, India, Brazil, Mexico, Russia, Turkey and Indonesia alone.[44] By comparison, eight of the world's twenty biggest economies in 2030 will be economies with today less than half of the per capita income of an OECD country.[45,46] Any Western growth abstention will not translate into a levelling of resource demand in any meaningful way. Second, there is neither a politically realistic nor a legitimate position suggesting that pre-take-off countries such as the BRIC states will abstain from growth. These countries will aspire to the same level of wealth, defined in living standards or 'utility', as their Western role models: passenger miles travelled, hours of light, calories a day, hours of indoor heating or showers per day. And lastly, we cannot congregate society around a minus-vision with less wealth or 'utility'. For that reason, abstention is – for all practical purposes – not a viable position.

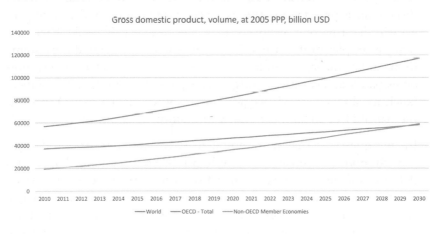

Gross domestic product, volume, at 2005 PPP, billion USD

SOURCE: OECD (2013)

Fig 4.8

So we turn to the other option: Kuznets-type and (too slow) Kuznets-speed greening. It is the 'hard place' and will – as we argued before – lead to explosive risks and a massive backlash in the form of global warming, water scarcity, clean-up costs, soil depletion, etc. The economy will be exposed to rapidly diminishing returns of natural systems and huge increases in the cost of resources, as illustrated in previous chapters. Even if the hopes of many politicians, industry leaders, environmentalists and economists rest on this option, **naturally growing green is a supply-side impossibility**. They believe that gradual energy efficiency improvements, a switch from coal to gas and cleaner combustion engines will do the trick. Having reviewed the numbers in the previous chapters and realizing a 3–10x gap between the provided and required speed of change, this belief can be demasked. Twenty-three years after the Rio Earth Summit, we have to admit that growing green is a broken promise with a view on the past and a dangerous drug with a view to the future. Volume growth has outpaced efficiencies for almost any resource.

So the solution cannot be no-growth nor relying on the Kuznetz effect. Instead, it is a territory of massive, step-change improvement in resource productivity and regenerative capacity of the earth through system-level redesign and a transformationally new way to run our economy. A new group of transformative thinkers from across several academic disciplines is propagating this new way with an ever louder voice, and we will describe our version of it in the rest of this book. There are many examples of it at the micro level (such as integrated biosystems in Brazilian villages) for individual companies (such as Desso), technologies (such as Ecovative's fungi-based packaging material), products (such as sludge-derived plastic) and resources (such as CO_2-derived methanol). But so far, they mostly remain niche applications.

In our quest for that new capital-accretive and resource-productive growth model, we looked at the system-level waste contained in today's delivery systems and made a major discovery. While product level waste is often very low and largely optimized, system-level performance reserves are massive. More and more we saw the massive opportunity opening up as we move from item level to system level. Seeing the systemic failure very concretely helps define the changes necessary to make economic and ecological ends meet.

Chapter 5

Wasted – system waste as a new resource

The behaviour of a system cannot be known just by knowing the elements of which the system is made.

Ancient Sufi proverb

In failing to recognize the importance of resources and planetary health for the growth of our economies, we have over the last two centuries built an economic system that is massively wasteful. In this chapter we would like to open your eyes to that historic mission, and the ensuing opportunity. Europe, for instance, still loses 95 per cent of the value of all raw materials after one use cycle, in spite of all its recycling efforts. And the utilization of cars – a major infrastructure category with big resource implications – is only about 2 per cent in the US and in Europe. More than 30 per cent of all food produced globally never reaches a mouth; it is instead wasted along the supply chain. So much waste in our largest value chains is perhaps surprising, since we often think of these value chains as mature and optimized. But we show below how a combination of historic reasons and inadequate public governance has led to a situation where the components of these systems (the products themselves) are improving at a good pace, but where the systems are stuck in an inefficient structure. The results are huge economic and environmental losses.

5.1 Waste, waste everywhere[1]

As part of the research for this book, we diagnosed how Europe is using resources. We picked Europe because the European Commission developed its 'Circular Economy' policy during the second term of the Barroso Commission under environmental commissioner Janez Potočnik and finally announced it in December 2015, and because

Europe is already at the forefront of global resource productivity, so that European solutions are likely to be valid also for other parts of the world.[2] We assume as much system-level waste exists across all economies and the opportunity is at least as formidable. We conducted in-depth investigations of the mobility, food and housing value chains. Together these value chains cover 70–80 per cent of Europe's resource use, and they represent more than 60 per cent of the average European household budget. So these value chains go far beyond examples: if the resource use in these value chains alone could be addressed, it would bring the world much closer to sustainable economic development.

In 2012, the average European directly used 13.5 metric tons of materials.[3] This is 16 per cent less than the 16 tons used in 2005 but still represents a full 260 kilograms per person each week – a very high amount.[4] Once used, a full 60 per cent of materials were either landfilled or incinerated, while only 40 per cent were recycled or reused as materials. Even so, this does not mean Europe has come 40 per cent of the way towards a 'closed loop' economy where materials that can be reused are reused. In value terms, Europe loses a full 95 per cent of the material and energy value after one use cycle, while material recycling and waste-based energy recovery represents only 5 per cent of the original raw material value.[5] Even recycling success stories like steel, PET and paper lose 30–75 per cent of material value in the first-use cycle. Partly, this is because only a share of the volumes is actually recycled. But more importantly, the value of the material is severely reduced because it is mixed with so many other materials that it can only be reused in low-value applications. For instance, the high-quality virgin steel used in cars is primarily reused as low-value construction steel (armouring rods), since it gets mixed with other metals, paints and pollutants in the scrapping process.

Aluminium is another interesting case. It is largely recycled – in Europe at a rate of 90–95 per cent.[6] And yet there is an important secret hidden behind these numbers. Collected aluminium is typically contaminated with foreign metals such as iron, nickel or chromium. These elements massively affect material properties and are costly to eliminate from the melt. So to ensure the aluminium performs to standard, a major proportion of virgin aluminium must be added back. US aluminium sheet giant Novelis has to cap the use of recycled aluminum at a mere 40 per cent. The indium used for smartphone screens, as another example, is largely lost because fewer than 20 per cent of phones are returned for recycling. And if they are, only 48–64 per cent of the 25 per cent metals is extracted.[7] 'Spice metals' dissipate and are lost, as does the phosphorus and organic matter from food waste. In Jardim Gramacho – Rio's infamous dumpsite where Vic Muniz produced his heartening movie *Wasteland* and which was shut down in 2012 – there was enough nutrient-rich food waste to warrant waste pickers reselling it in the dumpsite; this waste rots, produces hazardous methane, spreads infections and degrades the value of other materials even further. The plastic packaging that wraps our food and our consumer goods similarly turns into waste in today's system. Out of the 45.9 million tons of plastic produced annually in Europe, only 25 per cent is recycled – typically into low-value applications, 35 per cent is incinerated, often in conjunction with dioxin-generating PVC, and the rest is dumped or littered.[8] In China, the collection rate for plastic is as low as 40 per cent; the rest is deposited close to waterways and on non-sanitary landfills and too often washed into the sea.[9] Eight to 12 million tons of plastic leak into the ocean every year and are starting to clog one of our most indispensible ecosystems.[10] Within the linear system we have to replace a large part of the annual material requirement with virgin resources and at the same time fight the costs of pollution.

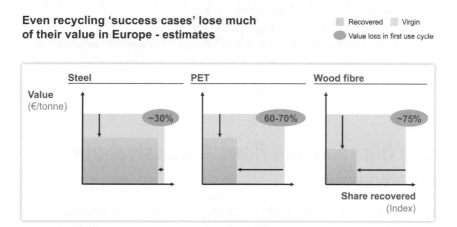

Even recycling 'success cases' lose much of their value in Europe - estimates

Recovered · Virgin · Value loss in first use cycle

Steel · PET · Wood fibre

Value (€/tonne)

~30% · 60-70% · ~75%

Share recovered (Index)

SOURCE: Expert interviews

Fig 5.1

Also during their productive lives, it is questionable how well we use products: the average manufactured asset lasts only nine years (twenty-eight years if buildings are included), and the lifespan of many product categories (e.g. consumer electronics, electrical appliances) is actually *decreasing*, not increasing.[11] And utilization is very low in many product categories, as we show below for mobility, food and housing.

So in summary, we overuse the planet's resources in a major way, to produce products that we underutilize and discard after an average nine years, and then, despite all our recycling efforts, 95 per cent of the material value is gone. Not our finest hour. (See Figure 5.2)

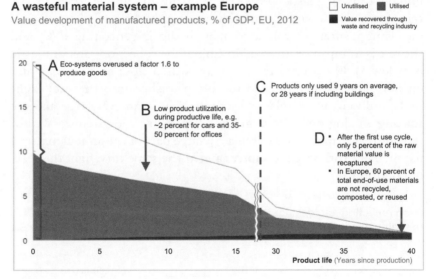

A wasteful material system – example Europe
Value development of manufactured products, % of GDP, EU, 2012

☐ Unutilised   ■ Utilised
■ Value recovered through waste and recycling industry

A — Eco-systems overused a factor 1.6 to produce goods

B — Low product utilization during productive life, e.g. ~2 percent for cars and 35-50 percent for offices

C — Products only used 9 years on average, or 28 years if including buildings

D — • After the first use cycle, only 5 percent of the raw material value is recaptured
• In Europe, 60 percent of total end-of-use materials are not recycled, composted, or reused

Product life (Years since production)

SOURCE: McKinsey Center for Business and Environment, Ellen MacArthur Foundation & SUN (2015)

Fig 5.2

5.2 Our resource flows – massive, and one-way[12]

In June 2015, our team had the chance to present our analysis to the European Commission in Brussels. We took them through it, and subsequent speeches showed that the numbers left an impression. Even our most mature sectors are highly wasteful.

Mobility – one man, one car, 2 per cent utilization. Let's turn to *mobility*, for which capable car manufacturers have optimized products for a century. In total, mobility captures 15 per cent of the average European household's spending, so it is a very large value chain.

The average European car is parked 92 per cent of the time – often on valuable inner-city land (See Figure 5.3). Another 3 per cent of the time is lost to congestion and looking for parking, so the car is only driven productively about 5 per cent of the time. And then only 1.5 of its 5 seats is occupied. Multiplying these figures, we reach a utilization of less than 2 per cent from a capital point of view. And remember that many families have one or more years of disposable income tied up in their car, so this is a very low utilization for a very large infrastructure category. Let's look now at the car from an energy point of view. The average deadweight ratio is about 12:1 – 1.2 tons of car is used to transport 100 kilograms of human, and less than 20 per cent of the total chemical petroleum energy in the tank is translated into kinetic energy for the car. Multiplying the two numbers, less than 2 per cent of the chemical energy of the petroleum in the tank actually ends up transporting people; the remaining 98 per cent gets lost along the way.

Next, let's look at the land perspective. Approximately 50 per cent of inner-city land is devoted to road mobility, if one includes both roads and parking spaces. But even at rush hour – typically 5–10 per cent of the time – cars cover only 10 per cent of the average city street. Again a very low utilization – this time of 0.5–1 per cent – yet congestion cost approaches 2 per cent of GDP in cities like Stuttgart and Paris. Finally, today's mobility system causes many accidents, health issues and environmental problems. Similar research has been done for the US, and shows very similar results. All in all, these numbers indicate a tremendous opportunity to get much more economic value out of our existing infrastructure and products, in one of our economy's biggest value chains. As we will show in Parts II and III of this book, new capital-accretive ways of doing business married to new technology and business models are available to achieve a substantially better utilization and avoid unhealthy outcomes upfront.

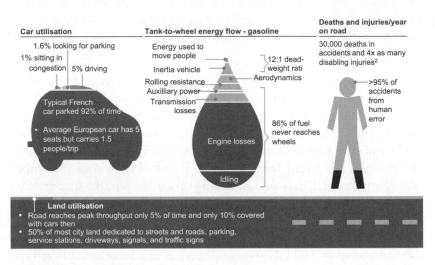

Major structural waste in the mobility system

SOURCE: McKinsey Center for Business and Environment, Ellen MacArthur Foundation & SUN (2015)

Fig 5.3

Food – don't bite the hand that feeds you. We see the same patterns of major system waste also in food. This value chain accounts for 19 per cent of average household spend in Europe. But a full 31 per cent of European food goes to waste along the value chain, according to research by the United Nation's Food and Agriculture Organization (UN FAO). Globally, the UN FAO estimates that 1.3 billion tons of food is wasted every year, about a third of all food produced. Categories such as fruit and vegetables lose as much as 46 per cent of their edible mass in Europe.[13] Most of the waste occurs at the farm (about 9 percentage points out of the 31 total) and at the consumer (11 percentage points), with the remaining share lost during processing and transport. Several ambitious research efforts have identified what share of this waste is avoidable. For instance, a recent report of UK charity WRAP estimates that 60–77 per cent of UK food waste is unnecessary.[14]

Key resources for producing food are also wasted. Look at fertilizers:[15] crops absorb only 30–50 per cent of applied fertilizer and use almost 25 per cent of that amount to create the non-edible parts of crops, which in today's model are mostly discarded as waste (while they could have been brought back to the fields). Also taking into account the share of food wasted as presented above, and that the human body does not absorb all the nutrients, this means 95 per cent of the fertilizer applied never gets used as nutrients for humans – a significant loss, since fertilizers are one of the major inputs in agriculture, and since there are approaches to drastically reduce this waste (more about this in Part III).

Another major input is irrigation water. Agricultural activities account for almost 70 per cent of global water withdrawals, and a quarter of Europe's withdrawals. Twenty-five per cent of this amount is lost in conveyance, and crops today absorb less than 35 per cent of the water applied to the field. The compound effect is that people consume only 20 per cent of all water withdrawn (considering again the food wasted along the value chain). Meanwhile, 23 per cent of the European surface area is water-scarce during the summer, a figure that is expected to increase to 45 per cent by 2030.

A second major type of waste, after the economic waste discussed above, is that our current agricultural practices are destroying the preconditions for future agriculture at a quick pace – borrowed growth par excellence.[16] This massive issue has been overshadowed by climate change in the environmental debate of the last 5–10 years, but it is in many ways just as serious. Today, for instance, more nitrogen is fixed synthetically in fertilizers than fixed naturally in all terrestrial ecosystems combined. Nitrogen is one of the most important nutrients in the global ecosystem, so it is deeply disturbing that more of the nitrogen fixation into soils and water now comes from synthetic fertilizers than from biological sources. Phosphorus flows have tripled compared to pre-industrial levels, causing both eutrophication and a geopolitical exposure for most countries of the world (80 per cent of global fossil phosphorus reserves are located in politically unstable Northern Africa).[17] The fertilizer run-off into rivers, lakes and oceans creates a breeding ground for algae that cause eutrophication, depleting stocks of fish and other species. This has created more than 400 dead zones or low-oxygen zones in oceans and lakes around the world. Today's intense agricultural practices also lead to topsoil erosion. Studies estimate that soil degradation affects 60–160 million hectares in Europe[18] – high numbers compared to the total agricultural area of 185 million hectares in the EU in 2012. On a global scale, continuing current rates of degradation would mean losing all of the world's topsoil within sixty years. As the saying goes, we are biting the hand that feeds us.

While these numbers are alarming, they also offer major opportunities for improvement and growth. With the world's population expected to reach 11 billion by 2100 (recent forecasts have revised the number up from 9–10 billion), and a dietary shift towards more protein, the food system will need to produce at least 70 per cent more food calories in 2050 than at the beginning of the century. This growth must happen at the same time as dealing with a scarcity of natural resources, climate change, and a system that faces declining productivity gains. This could be the time to take a new path. Many of the solutions and

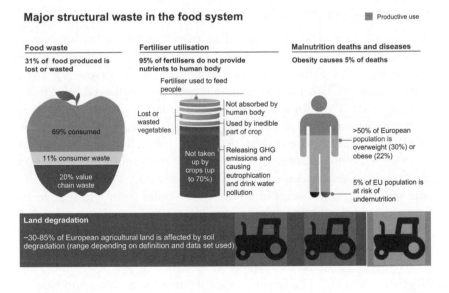

Major structural waste in the food system   ■ Productive use

Food waste

31% of food produced is lost or wasted

69% consumed

11% consumer waste

20% value chain waste

Fertiliser utilisation

95% of fertilisers do not provide nutrients to human body

Fertiliser used to feed people

Lost or wasted vegetables

Not taken up by crops (up to 70%)

Not absorbed by human body

Used by inedible part of crop

Releasing GHG emissions and causing eutrophication and drink water pollution

Malnutrition deaths and diseases

Obesity causes 5% of deaths

>50% of European population is overweight (30%) or obese (22%)

5% of EU population is at risk of undernutrition

Land degradation

~30-85% of European agricultural land is affected by soil degradation (range depending on definition and data set used)

SOURCE: McKinsey Center for Business and Environment, Ellen MacArthur Foundation & SUN (2015)

Fig 5.4

technologies are now available, as we'll show later in this book, but they need to be scaled up massively.

Housing – amazing space. The future of housing and urban planning are crucial topics for countries across the world. Housing is the largest direct expense for European households, with an average annual cost per household of €9,600, or 27 per cent of direct annual spend.[19] What's more, construction is one of the largest economic sectors of the European economy, representing 8.8 per cent of GDP and almost 14 million jobs. Housing and construction are largely urban phenomena, as 80 per cent of Europe's population is expected to live in cities and suburbs by 2020.

Although recent decades have seen great progress in improving the energy efficiency of buildings and the liveability of cities, this value chain remains wasteful in four ways:

First, productivity development is weak. Over the last twenty-five years, the US and Germany, two of the world's largest economies, have seen a labour productivity development in the construction sector of close to zero, while productivity in the rest of the economy increased 50 per cent. Many other countries face similar productivity stagnation. Root causes vary from country to country, but they often include a

Major structural waste in housing

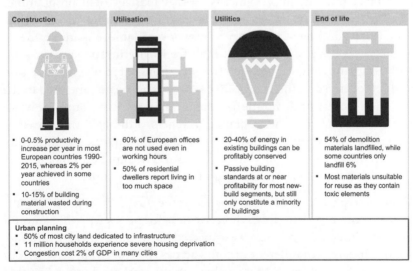

Construction	Utilisation	Utilities	End of life
• 0-0.5% productivity increase per year in most European countries 1990-2015, whereas 2% per year achieved in some countries • 10-15% of building material wasted during construction	• 60% of European offices are not used even in working hours • 50% of residential dwellers report living in too much space	• 20-40% of energy in existing buildings can be profitably conserved • Passive building standards at or near profitability for most new-build segments, but still only constitute a minority of buildings	• 54% of demolition materials landfilled, while some countries only landfill 6% • Most materials unsuitable for reuse as they contain toxic elements

Urban planning
- 50% of most city land dedicated to infrastructure
- 11 million households experience severe housing deprivation
- Congestion cost 2% of GDP in many cities

SOURCE: McKinsey Center for Business and Environment, Ellen MacArthur Foundation & SUN (2015)

Fig 5.5

fragmented industry structure with many small firms, a conservative attitude towards new construction practices, a large share of informal work, and stifling building codes. Estimates of how much material is wasted on site are often around 10 per cent. These barriers are not impossible to overcome, as the examples of Belgium and Austria show. Both have seen productivity increases of 2 per cent per annum over the last fifteen years. In total, this means the customer gets 35 per cent more house for his money in either of these two countries compared to fifteen years ago, in contrast to 0 per cent in the US or Germany.

Second, utilization is often low. For instance, even during working hours, only 35–40 per cent of European offices are used, despite high prices for space on expensive inner-city land, while 49 per cent of owner-occupied homes in the UK are 'underoccupied' (at least two bedrooms more than stated need, according to a recent *English Housing Survey*). In the UK about 33 per cent of people over 60 would like a smaller residence, but only 10 per cent actually downsize. Better optimized utilization would reduce costs for companies and households.

Third, energy consumption remains much higher than necessary. Buildings continue to use enormous amounts of energy, despite the availability of many improvements. Energy management programmes often reduce energy consumption in existing buildings by 20–40 per cent. Passive and zero-net-energy houses are available in many segments of the market – and are often profitable from a lifetime perspective – but still constitute only a minority of new buildings. Finally, construction and demolition account for 25–30 per cent of all waste generated in the EU, and recovery of demolition waste is unattractive because the waste is often contaminated with paints, fasteners, adhesives, wall-covering materials, insulation and dirt. Current demolition waste comes from old buildings torn down yesterday and today, but buildings erected now may well cause the same issues in thirty years' time.

Taking a step back, we have now looked at the three largest product value chains of our economy. In all three, we have found a surprising amount of waste, much more than we expected from such big and mature sectors. It comes in different flavours across the three value chains, but there are also common themes: low utilization, products optimized for low sales cost rather than for total lifetime costs, untapped system optimization opportunities, and practices that disregard tomorrow. Since mobility, food and housing together consume 60 per cent of the average household budget, reducing such waste offers a tremendous opportunity to improve living standards, consumer choices and the environment.[20] In short, today's use of resources does not match today's possibilities.

5.3 System-level waste – fuelling the next economy

Given the huge amounts of structural waste in our economy, an interesting question is: are we addressing the waste? Do the collective efforts of companies, policy-makers, civil society and other stakeholders add up to a reasonably effective strategy to address the waste? Hence, if our economy continues on its current trajectory, and we were to conduct the same waste analysis ten years from now, would we see a major difference?

The simplest answer to these questions is 'no – we are by and large not addressing the waste'. A more nuanced answer is that some parts of the waste are indeed being addressed effectively – primarily through product-level improvements – whereas most parts are not effectively addressed. This is an important insight – *our economy is, on the current trajectory, not about to capture the huge system waste and corresponding value pools that exist within our current economic system* – so let us go into some detail to explain, and let's use the three usual value chains to make it concrete.

For *mobility*, let's look back to the waste chart (Figure 5.3) and ask ourselves which of the major sources of waste are being addressed. The focus of most countries and companies is on fuel efficiency, alternative powertrains, emission requirements and road safety. Many cities are also working on improving public transport, with varying degrees of success. But most of the other sources of waste are not being addressed:

- Take the <2 per cent utilization of cars. Of course, in some countries there are fuel and vehicle taxes that indirectly push to increase utilization, but these taxes are primarily designed to improve fuel efficiency and are not very effective in increasing utilization. The most obvious utilization lever is car sharing, but very few cities or countries actively support car sharing, even though there are plenty of arguments for doing so, and plenty of viable policy options. For instance, cities could reserve attractive parking space for shared cars, an action that is easy to motivate as shared cars are on average parked so much less. When the city of Paris reserved parking spaces for car-sharing company AutoLib (and others) around the city centre, it became a key selling point for car-sharing services that customers always know there is a space waiting when they arrive – no more circling around looking for parking. But few cities are doing this on a big scale. And if anything, Uber and its competitors are seen as a threat, and hindered rather than helped. Countries could be proactive in solving the issues around taxation and driver certification that are holding back peer-to-peer taxi businesses around the world, but few countries have yet taken action. Sharing business models are growing in any case, but they could grow much faster and be better integrated into transport systems with suitable support.

- Interconnected cars are another interesting example: this can increase the capacity of roads many times over, through dramatically decreasing the safe distance between cars. And the technology largely exists; several high-end cars now have such technology as standard, and there are companies who even retrofit interconnection equipment in existing cars. If a substantial proportion of cars had interconnectivity technology, it would work wonders on congested cities and road authority budgets. But how many cities are actively pursuing it, for instance by lowering congestion charges or reducing parking fees for cars that have this technology? None, to our knowledge.

- Access parking, i.e. parking space close to public transport to make cars a last-mile solution, is a powerful lever to reduce congestion, and does not rely on any advanced technology. Still, it is rare compared to the opportunity, perhaps because the huge congestion costs are 'externalities' that don't appear in any public budgets. In Europe more than 80 per cent of car commuting is single-mode.[21]

- Comparatively few cities still have congestion charging, in spite of congestion being an obvious externality that commuters are painfully aware of every morning.

So our conclusion is that beyond product-level improvements, we are not addressing waste in the mobility system effectively.

The story is largely the same for *food,* but with more of an environmental angle. Each actor along the value chain is improving its own efficiency, and new technology under the umbrella name of 'precision agriculture' has come to help. But since the key externalities in the food value chain are either not priced at all, or priced far below their real value, the efforts to address the major negative externalities remain underwhelming. A key example is anaerobic digestion of wastewater and food waste. It is an excellent way to produce biogas for energy, while returning phosphorus and nitrogen to the fields as bio-fertilizer, and reducing remaining waste volumes. But currently there is only capacity to digest 0.5 per cent of the world's organic waste.[22] And the pick-up of key resource-efficient agricultural techniques, such as no-till agriculture and sub-surface drip irrigation – both of which have substantial environmental benefits and in many cases carry no extra cost – remains slow.

Finally for *housing,* most developed countries are trying to improve energy efficiency in buildings. However, one can speculate how ambitious those efforts are: the energy efficiency of buildings is improving at approximately the same pace as it has for the last 100 years and has even slowed between 1990–2010, in spite of the recent push on energy efficiency – an estimated $80 billion is being invested annually in energy efficiency measures.[23,24] Most of the other sources of waste are currently not being ambitiously addressed: house sharing – for instance through Airbnb – is growing fast, but could be a much bigger phenomenon if governments made it a priority and realized the tax issues are very possible to resolve. Office sharing is happening, but could progress much faster.

The point of this section is not to be negative about all the commendable efforts to reduce system waste that are being undertaken by companies and policy-makers around the world. But we need to be sober about the size and speed of those efforts. Put in positive terms, better addressing this waste is a massive economic and environmental opportunity.

Next question: How come we are so wasteful, and that we don't go after the waste? What 'should' these waste numbers be in the future? No one knows, of course, and to some extent they represent a market optimization between owning your own car and having access to one when you need it, between using virgin materials and recycled, and so on. Yet, there are several strong arguments to say that these waste numbers should be much lower in the future than they are today, and that the current state of affairs represents a major economic loss in addition to an environmental one.

- First, we are not used to thinking and talking about our economy in this way, so by and large we do not 'see' these opportunities. The type of waste numbers we show above are not regularly measured in the way GDP and employment numbers are. There are no targets for waste, as there often are for unemployment, emissions, education, and other aspects of our economy. As a result, we rarely discuss the topic, there is no way of knowing whether a certain country is doing well or less well compared to other countries, and there is not much knowledge of which waste reduction policies work and which don't work. Compared to the economic opportunity (just think of the potential in getting car utilization from 2 to 4 per cent) it seems to us a very undermanaged aspect of our economy. There is also an important custom-and-habit effect at play. Both consumers and business executives have grown up in a 'one family, one house, one car' world, and simply don't have the same intuition for these improvement opportunities as they do for more traditional areas such as product cost cutting. 'Lean' manufacturing is a useful analogy for industry: when this new view of supply chains grew popular in the 1980s and 1990s, managers suddenly discovered 'new' profit improvement opportunities[25] that had of course long existed, but that only became 'visible' to business leaders when they looked at their operations from a waste perspective. On the consumer side, research shows a yawning gap between intentions and actions. According to a 2014 survey, almost all Europeans (96 per cent) think that Europe should use resources more efficiently, but only 21 per cent have leased or rented a product instead of buying it, and only 27 per cent have used sharing schemes.[26]
- Second, our fiscal system is not helping, perhaps because we do not 'see' the opportunity in reducing system waste. As we discussed in the previous chapter, damaging the environment of others is largely for free, and if these 'externalities' were priced, our big resource-intense

sectors would look very different. But also, taxation systems focus on labour and capital, and resources make up only a minor share of taxation. This is in spite of the fact that governments across the world want to increase employment but decrease resource use. Figure 5.6 shows the situation in Europe, where resource taxes constitute a mere 6 per cent of the total tax base, and are decreasing as a share of GDP.

- Third, untapped technology. Rapidly falling technology costs are creating major opportunities to reduce waste that have yet to achieve wide adoption. For example, the huge drops in the transaction cost of sharing and virtualization business models enabled by smartphones (e.g. car sharing and house sharing) are just starting to permeate the market. The internet of things can keep track of valuable products and materials much more cheaply than in the past, radically increasing opportunities to recover them, and waste management technology is progressing quickly.

Summing up, we hope to have convinced you in this chapter that reducing system waste is a huge economic and environmental opportunity – and one which countries and companies around the world should pursue with a much higher ambition level than today.

Environmental and resource taxes constitute a small and decreasing minority of all taxation - example Europe

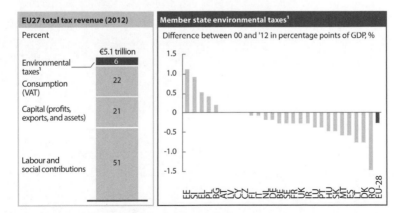

1 Environmental taxes include taxes on energy, transport, pollution, and resource extraction

SOURCE: The En'tax Project et al. New era New plan. Fiscal reforms for an inclusive circular economy. Case study the Netherlands, 2014; Eurostat, Taxation trends in the European Union, 2014.

Fig 5.6

Chapter 6

Broken – the unfulfilled sustainability dream

Being less bad is no good.

Michael Braungart and William McDonough, *Cradle to Cradle –
Remaking the Way We Make Things*

Against the backdrop of the scope and urgency of the resource challenge
and the systemic nature of the failure we have described, the sustainability journey needs a restart. That journey started already in 1711.
Back then, Hans Carl von Carlowitz's main issue was wood, or rather
the lack of it. As the newly appointed director of mining at the court of
Kursachsen in Saxony, it was his job to ensure a good supply of timber
to the silver mines and silver smelting that were a main source of tax
revenue for the court, and provided income for thousands of families.
All the nearby forests had already been cleared to keep the mines
going. Next, the local Erzgebirge river systems had been engineered to
allow timber to be transported from more distant forests, but these
were also quickly depleting. Carlowitz's response was to develop and
publish the *Sylvicultura Oeconomica*, a set of integrated principles for
sustainable forest management, in 1713. It described for the first time
how the local economy was dependent on its surrounding ecosystem,
how to calculate sustainable yield levels and contained principles for
harvesting, replanting and timber logistics. Carlowitz's book is widely
seen as the first example of integrated sustainability thinking, and he
is often referred to as the father of sustainability. Unfortunately, most
evidence suggests Carlowitz's advice was ignored (he died the following
year). Forest clearing continued, prices for the scarce remaining timber
soared to levels the mines could not afford and many of the local silver
mines went into bankruptcy.[1] An early premonition perhaps of what
was to come.

With the industrialization of the 1800s came the first environmental
protection laws. The UK passed the Alkali Act in 1863 to regulate air

pollution from soda ash production, and the Sea Birds Preservation Act was passed in 1869. Industrialization also led to the first environmental organizations: the UK's Commons Preservation Society was set up in 1865, the Sierra Club was founded in San Francisco in 1892 and the Coal Smoke Abatement Society in London in 1898 (today's Environmental Protection UK). Under Woodrow Wilson, the US National Park Service was set up in 1916, and in 1919, Britain's Forestry Commission was established to protect and expand UK forests. Britain's Clean Air Act was passed in 1956 in response to the 1952 Great Smog in London, and is often seen as the first example of modern environmental legislation.[2]

But it wasn't until the 1960s and early 1970s that the environmental movement became a major public and political phenomenon. In 1962, Rachel Carson published *Silent Spring*, documenting the devastating effects of DDT and other pesticides on birds and whole ecosystems. She criticized the pervasive use of such chemicals when their consequences were not fully understood. She also accused the chemical industry of knowing many of the side-effects their products would have, and she accused public officials of not standing up to the industry. The public concern caused by the book eventually led to the ban of DDT in 1972.[3] In 1969, the Cuyahoga River, flowing into Lake Erie, caught fire. The absurdity of a river catching fire stirred media attention, and led to a public outcry against the dumping of industrial chemicals and sewage water that caused the fire. Then in 1972, NASA released its Blue Marble photo, showing the earth as seen from Apollo 17. It became one of the most reproduced photos in history, and for many it became a symbol of the frailty and isolation of our planet, and created a sense that we need to take care of our common home.[4,5]

All of these events, underpinned by increased consumerism and the revolutionary mood of the day, together made the modern environmental movement take off. It was also during this period that many of today's most vocal environmental organizations were founded: the World Wildlife Fund in 1961, Friends of the Earth in 1969 and Greenpeace in 1971.

Crucially, the focus of the early legislation and influencing groups was environmental *conservation*, through protecting land areas or species, or through banning dangerous substances. Since then, the conservation approach has scored many victories: controlled use of lead and mercury, banning of many dangerous chemical substances, improved sewage treatment and improved waste management, among many others. Most of the issues were local, or at most national, and for businesses, environmental protection largely became a question of staying away from a set of black-listed substances and business practices.

During the 1980s and 1990s, it became clear that the conservation approach, for all its great achievements, was insufficient to tackle the environmental issues of the day: the first signs of climate change, water acidification, desertification, the ozone hole, city smog and defor-estation. Many of these issues were international, and many of them related to overuse of a resource or a business practice that was not bad per se. Increased resource use was also in many ways desirable, as it helped industrialize poor countries.[6]

The UN's Brundtland Commission[7] attracted global attention for its framing of the issues: it described societal development and the surrounding environment as deeply intertwined, whereby real progress on one dimension cannot be achieved without the other. The Commission popularized the term *sustainable development* as development that meets the needs of the present generation without compromising the ability of future generations to meet theirs. As a consequence of this shift in perspective, the global environmental strategy broadly shifted focus from *conservation* to *eco-efficiency*. It was no longer enough to protect particularly important forests, lakes or species, or to ban particularly dangerous substances. In addition, the entire economy had to use natural resources as efficiently as possible. In a way, environmental protection started to be everyone's business, and all companies, countries and consumers were expected to be eco-efficient. Energy efficiency, light-weighting, water efficiency, land productivity – all these major efforts are expressions of the same underlying idea, that natural resources should be used as efficiently as possible. Eco-efficiency was also one of the key outcomes of the UN's Rio de Janeiro Earth Summit in 1992, and later the World Business Council for Sustainable Development (WBCSD) was formed with the idea of eco-efficiency at its heart.[8]

Eco-efficiency is still the dominant global environmental strategy. Most advanced economies have a long string of environmental regulation that sets eco-efficiency standards for different sectors: fuel standards for vehicles, energy efficiency standards for buildings and electrical equipment, water efficiency standards for appliances, compulsory consumer labelling to show the relative eco-efficiency of different products. Many of these have been in place for decades. They come in different flavours: some are static performance standards, others stipulate an improvement trajectory over time (for instance Europe's carbon emission standards for cars) and yet others use a front-runner logic where the best-performing product in the market sets the standard for everyone else (for instance Japan's appliance regulation).[9,10]

'What about environmental and resource taxes?' someone might say. Surely they are also an important part of the global environmental strategy? Unfortunately not as a global average. As Chapter 4.2 on Externalities showed, the untaxed environmental damages correspond to a whopping 13 per cent of global GDP, a number that is growing fast. In Chapter 5, we showed that even in Europe, with its tradition of high taxes and high environmental ambitions, resource taxes stand at only 6 per cent of total taxation, or approximately 3 per cent of GDP, and are on a declining trend. If one looks at subsidies as the flip side of taxation, clean energy received about $121 billion globally in 2013, whereas fossil fuels received more than 4 times that amount.[11,12] These observations are not meant to take anything away from the many commendable efforts to introduce taxes on harmful resource use. But the sobering global conclusion remains that current taxation harms as much as it helps.

Unfortunately, eco-efficiency, for all its good intentions and achievements (the world is a much better place as a result of these efforts), has now also proven inadequate as a response to current global environmental challenges. That might sound harsh, but eco-efficiency has now been the strategy of choice for 20–25 years, for companies and countries alike, and still we are observing an *accelerating* global environmental deterioration, not a stable or declining one. The Earth Overshoot Day – one often-used indicator – is not even settled in August, it is moving earlier and earlier each year (see Figure 3.1). The core problem is that the incremental efficiency improvements achieved by most industries and countries are dwarfed by the sheer volume growth resulting from economic growth and from the rebound effect described above. The net effect is that all the curves on absolute resource use – which is what matters to our global environmental issues – keep growing, not declining. Between 1995 (when eco-efficiency had been broadly established) and 2010, global freshwater withdrawals increased by 18 per cent,[13] iron production by 81 per cent, plastic output by 83 per cent, fossil fuel carbon emissions by 48 per cent[14] and fossil phosphorus extraction (the vast majority of which ultimately ends up overfertilizing lakes and oceans) by 30 per cent,[15] to take just a few examples. Also in the rich part of the world, there is a flat or slowly growing use of most major resources, and no real evidence of a Kuznets effect or decoupling. So the sad truth is that the planet is far worse off today than 20–25 years ago when we embarked on the eco-efficiency strategy. Aiming to be 'less bad' is not good enough, it seems, as Michael Braungart and William McDonough provocatively formulated it in their seminal book *Cradle to Cradle*.

Looking forward, the same story seems to be playing out. Even though the financial crisis has let some of the steam out of the resource boom, almost all forecasts suggest natural resource overuse will continue to grow, not decline. Freshwater withdrawals, for example, are expected to grow by 41 per cent from 2010 to 2030. Nitrogen fertilizer use is expected to increase by 30 per cent until 2030, agricultural land by 11–14 per cent, and so on.[16,17]

Global car emissions provide an interesting case in point. On one hand, many major economies have set very aggressive goals for increasing fuel efficiency. The Obama administration's fleetwide standards for car makers is targeting 54.5 miles per gallon (mpg) in 2025 compared to 30 mpg today, the European Union is aiming at 60.6 and China at 50.1. But on the other hand, the number of cars worldwide is expected to double during the same time period, from about one billion today to two billion by 2030.[18] The net effect is an *increase* in global greenhouse gas emissions from cars, even if auto manufacturers manage to reach the aggressive mpg targets – something one cannot be sure about. So in a way we are actively planning for further environmental deterioration.

But it is only a matter of time, goes another argument. When all the populous countries are developed, the curves will start to point downwards: the famous Kuznets effect. That might be true, but it doesn't help much; by the time it happens, many of the planet's crucial ecosystems will already be irreversibly downgraded.

So in spite of all the achievements of eco-efficiency, it seems we are again coming to the end of an era in environmentalism, and we are in great need of a new paradigm, one that allow us to combine a good life for potentially 10–11 billion inhabitants with a planet that is at least healthy enough to allow us to sustain that modern lifestyle. We will argue that the vision we outline in Part II comes close to the answer we are looking for. It is an economic growth paradigm that empha-sizes getting more out of what we have, through attacking the huge amount of system waste in our largest resource-intense value chains, in combination with designing products that are actually positive for the environment (as opposed to 'less bad'), and creating a circular material system whereby materials are used over and over again. It is an excellent way to make the current amount of virgin resource extraction economically obsolete, and therefore resolve many of the world's resource issues not by ban and control, but by economic development.

So to sum up, our current growth is very far from what it should be – in fact one can argue whether there is any real growth at all, if borrowing effects are excluded. But its broad direction is still seen by academics, policy-makers and corporate leaders as 'rational' or even 'optimal' because of the deeply-held belief that markets are always right, and because the massive externalities that exist are not part of mainstream models or mainstream measurement systems. With that framing, the key question on economists' and policy-makers' minds since 2008 has been how to get the economy 'back on track'. We hope to have shown in this first part of the book that getting growth 'back on track' is not the right question. Growth has not been 'on track' for at least three decades, and if we use the standard theories, we will at best get back to the wrong track. Instead, we need to recognize we are living on a full planet in resource terms, and use the ongoing technology revolution to get growth onto the right track. That is the exploration during the rest of this book.

PART II: TOWARDS A GROWTH MODEL FIT FOR THE TWENTY-FIRST CENTURY

We hope Part I stirred you a bit. The most important message we tried to convey was that our environmental issues are much more important – both to the planet and to our economy – than the public debate reflects; they are related to materials as much as energy, and our current resolution strategy is deeply insufficient. Resource-wise, our current growth model has become a victim of its own success, and needs a deep rethink.

In Part II, we will lay out our vision for what an alternative could look like, one that will make the ongoing disruption a good one. Given the scope, it is a sketch more than a blueprint. We will first describe the pillars of a better resource economy, then discuss why we think a 'net-positive' norm needs to replace the current eco-efficiency norm and what it could mean for companies and countries, and finally we will describe a European case example and what the new growth model would mean for its GDP, employment and environmental footprint.

We are aware that putting on paper a vision for a better growth model can open us up to accusations of both naivety and arrogance. After all, isn't it both unrealistic and cynical to suggest deep changes to an economic model that has in many ways served us so well over the last decades, and into which we are so massively invested? We will stick our necks out and provide this alternative vision anyway, because it is so clear to us that tinkering around the edges of the current growth model will not get us anywhere close to where we need to go. When it comes to the resource-related parts of our economy, we need a deep redesign, not of the principles of the market-based economy, but of its wasteful set-up for energy, materials and systems. In Part II, we will describe the vision itself, in Part III we discuss the enabling conditions that are coming into place, and then in Part IV we will discuss how to achieve it.

What to call this new economy?

'A dear child has many names', goes an old saying. There are several different terms in use to describe the attractive future economy we outline in this book, each with support from different stakeholder groups, and each with its benefits and limitations. We – the authors have great sympathy for the circular economy concept and worked hard in recent years to analyze and communicate the benefits. We have experienced first-hand the excitement and engagement that the circular economy framework sparks. However, we have decided not to exclude other concepts that span a comparable scope nor to coin yet another term for the future economy. We did that because we feel that the mobilization around the 'good disruption' cannot afford to exclude any serious school of thought – it must be inclusive and accretive itself.

Below we give a short overview of the main terms in use, and how we see them relating to our vision:

- *Circular economy.* This is a name we have often used ourselves. We like it because it is concrete, increasingly well underpinned and it captures a lot of what is new with the future economy we envision, for instance the focus on making material flows circular, and making assets intelligent. And many proponents of a circular economy may rightfully say that what we are describing in this book is nothing but a fully circular economy. Alongside the strong reference to material flows, we acknowledge that sizeable opportunities reside in new energy systems, virtualization and integrated system design.

- *Sustainable development,* or *green growth.* In many ways, sustainable development is the incumbent term, used in countless reports and debates since the Brundtland Commission popularized it in 1987. Sustainable development covers everything, but it is an aspiration statement rather than a description, and it does not give any real hint of what such a future economy should look like. Also, a key point in this book is that a major departure is needed from the reductionist way sustainability is currently pursued.

- *Resource productive economy.* This is the most comfortable term to many economists. But this term also says very little about what the future economy should look like, and to many it also implies a 'more of the same' sustainability approach and resource strategy, rather than a departure from our current practices.

- *Cradle-to-cradle.* Cradle-to-cradle can take substantial credit for much of the novel thinking that is starting to supplant a conventional conception of sustainability. The idea emphasizes that materials and products should be designed and used so that they don't lose their value but instead can be the basis for the next use phase, and that 'good' is the right ambition level (as opposed to 'less bad'). Perhaps this is also the term most likely to touch consumers' hearts. We use this thinking extensively in our book but, to many, it talks primarily about products, and less about the overall economy.

There are many other related terms: performance economy, bio-mimicry, third industrial revolution, natural capitalism, shared value – each one contributing one or more exciting aspects of the new economy.

We chose instead to frame the challenge as one of making the ongoing disruption a good disruption, since technology is so crucial to many of the changes we want to see, since disruption is already on every decision-maker's mind these days, and since it is so clearly undermanaged, to the detriment of us all. When we describe the future economy we're aspiring to, we alternate between the terms 'circular', 'net-positive' and 'accretive' depending on whether it is the material, the business or the economic aspect we want to emphasize.

Chapter 7

Three pillars of a better growth model

It always seems impossible until it's done.

Nelson Mandela

In November 2015, the foundation of world record sailor Ellen MacArthur convened leading innovators from all fields to celebrate their Disruptive Innovation Festival. This is a three-week web event that convenes designers, entrepreneurs, industry, visionaries, learners and doers to co-create the next economy. The contributions could not be richer: sludge that turns into plastic, apparel from upcycled super-fibres, at-home manufacturing, high-tech borrowed from dragonflies, LED lights that replace pesticides, a life with 3 kilos of plastic, remanu-facturing megafactories, biologically decomposing shoes, biologics enabling precision medicine, user-engaged design, eternal coffee machines or clean water through green roofs. The diversity and sheer upside of each idea left the online audience breathless and created a mosaic of what a more benign next-generation economy could look like. And yet these innovations remain product-level solutions. They are additive, and even though their implementation would be a great success and bring great benefits, they won't get us to the required new levels of system performance.

So what would? We believe a simple but powerful way to think about the new growth model we need to create to make the ongoing disruption a good disruption is in terms of three physical pillars: 1) abundant clean energy, acknowledging that clean energy inputs are important drivers of growth; 2) a cradle-to-cradle material bank, where materials are circulated many times instead of just used once; and 3) regenerative high-productivity systems for all the largest value chains of our economy: mobility, housing, food, health, leisure and communication. All this underpinned by a new 'net-positive' norm that sets a higher bar for companies and countries in terms of what constitutes acceptable performance and behaviour, and all enabled by the technology disruption that is anyway changing our economy so fast. This framework is nourished by our findings that we are using products and materials in a wasteful way today and that this is the root cause of many of our environmental problems. It is our attempt to structure a discussion about how the economy can take the next steps beyond eco-efficiency, to a level that is high enough to be comprehensive, yet concrete enough to be meaningful and guide real change. It aspires to link the technology disruption, resource economics and systems thinking.

The framework perhaps looks 'simple' compared to the challenges we painted in Part I. But compare it with today's situation: the world is only going after the first pillar – clean energy – in an ambitious way today. Pillars two and three are not ambitiously addressed, and the underlying norm is one of 'eco-efficiency', or less bad. So something like this vision would make an enormous difference.

Vision for an economy that reconciles planet and prosperity

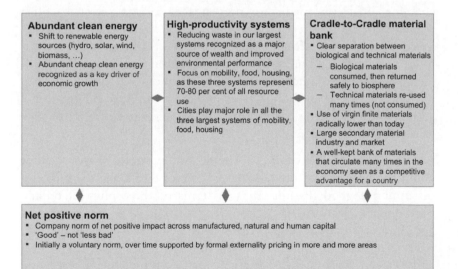

Abundant clean energy
- Shift to renewable energy sources (hydro, solar, wind, biomass, …)
- Abundant cheap clean energy recognized as a key driver of economic growth

High-productivity systems
- Reducing waste in our largest systems recognized as a major source of wealth and improved environmental performance
- Focus on mobility, food, housing, as these three systems represent 70-80 per cent of all resource use
- Cities play major role in all the three largest systems of mobility, food, housing

Cradle-to-Cradle material bank
- Clear separation between biological and technical materials
  - Biological materials consumed, then returned safely to biosphere
  - Technical materials re-used many times (not consumed)
- Use of virgin finite materials radically lower than today
- Large secondary material industry and market
- A well-kept bank of materials that circulate many times in the economy seen as a competitive advantage for a country

Net positive norm
- Company norm of net positive impact across manufactured, natural and human capital
- 'Good' – not 'less bad'
- Initially a voluntary norm, over time supported by formal externality pricing in more and more areas

Fig 7.1

7.1 Abundant clean energy – conversion unlimited

'The Stone Age did not end for lack of stone, and the Oil Age will end long before the world runs out of oil.' This was the message of Sheikh Zaki Yamani, at that time the Saudi Arabian oil minister, in *The Economist* in 2003. Thirteen years later, it looks like he might have been right, and that the fossil fuel age will end because new renewable energy sources are coming into the money and becoming more commercially attractive than burning oil, coal and gas. One of the major reasons why a 'good disruption' and an economy that stays within planetary boundaries are realistic ambitions is the perspective that – if we get it right – abundant renewable cheap energy will be available to us already within 10–20 years.

This has the potential to change everything. As we saw in Part I, the first, and particularly the second, industrial era were characterized by enormous increases in energy use. We looked at research that suggests this increased energy use can explain a major part of the observed historic economic growth. Some historians even liken all human history to a story of energy. New fuels (biomass, coal, oil and gas) and new ways to convert energy (horses, water wheels, steam engines, steam and gas turbines) are the backdrop against which human civilization evolved. But since the nineteenth century, that energy was largely fossil-based and came at a price: global warming, massive geopolitical dependencies, polluted cities and deep scars on our landscapes.

Now that the prospect of abundant cheap clean energy is becoming more real with each passing year, there is every reason to become excited. It will allow us – like nature itself – to use its very building blocks to rebuild and recombine the products we need for living. With abundant cheap clean energy, there are no limits on converting water into hydrogen, CO_2 into polymers, seawater into freshwater, hydrogels and photopolymers into printed nano-structures, or just old glass into new glass.

This creates an exciting dual, and perhaps mutually reinforcing, dynamic. The costs of renewable power generation and storage are declining in parallel to the costs of new conversion technologies – producing an upward spiral, and so the potential for a race to the top.

The energy revolution is now unfolding at a pace deemed unthinkable only ten years ago. In the summer of 2015, Nevada Power sought approval for two 100 megawatt (MW) solar PV facilities. That was no big deal in the electricity industry, but when the prices it had secured became known, it raised eyebrows throughout the industry. It turned out that Nevada Power will be paying $46 per MWh for SunPower's Boulder Solar plant, and a mere $38.7 per MWh for First Solar Inc's Playa Solar plant. Austin Energy in Texas reported earlier in summer 2015 that it had received firm bids to build a 600 MW solar PV plant for less than $40 per MWh.

Nevada and Texas are both sunny states, but the fact that new installations of solar PV are so cheap is nonetheless a remarkable development. The cost-per-watt capacity has dropped more than 70 per cent over the last ten years alone. And solar PV are winning similar victories around the world.[1] In total, global solar installations are at about 175 GW today, and the International Energy Agency expects the figure to be around 400 GW by 2020.

There is no reason to believe that this development will stop any time soon. In fact, even the most efficient solar panels only transform 20–25 per cent of the incoming solar energy to electricity, and, every month, one can read about new technology breakthroughs. Researchers are working on layering different types of solar cells on top of each other to capture energy from different wavelengths, on better semiconductor alloys and on super-thin solar cells that can be laminated onto walls and roofs, to mention just a few examples. And on top of the technology improvements, there are all the 'ordinary' savings that come from scaling up and professionalizing an industry that was very small until just a few years ago.

A similar development, but somewhat less dramatic, can be observed with wind power. It started to scale before the solar industry, and already has an installed base of around 300 GW globally. By 2020, the IEA expects that number to double to around 600 GW. Costs per MWh have dropped by 30–50 per cent over the last five years, and are also expected to continue to decrease, although less sharply than those of solar PV. As Figure 7.2 shows, the revolution is also unfolding much faster than forecasted: the actual installed capacity of solar PV in 2015 was a factor 9.3 higher than the IEA forecasted as late as 2006, and the 2030 forecast has been revised upwards by a factor of 8.4.

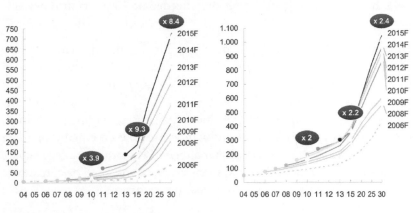

Global growth of solar and wind has been much faster than forecasted
International Energy Agency's forecasts for global cumulative capacity, gigawatts

SOURCE: IEA World Energy Outlook (2006, 2008-15)

Fig 7.2

In 2014, development reached an historic tipping point. For the first time, total global investments in renewable electricity generation – at $340 billion – were larger than those in fossil fuel-based generation. In total, until 2040, Bloomberg New Energy Finance expects renewable energy investments to be almost twice as big as fossil fuel ones: $6.1 trillion versus $2.6 trillion.[2]

In parallel, the cost of batteries is also plummeting, and investment levels are surging (such as Tesla's 'Gigafactory' in Nevada). This is crucial not only for the transport sector, where BMW, Tesla, GM, Nissan, Mitsubishi and others are now proving that electric vehicles are an interesting alternative for big customer segments. It is also crucial for the power system, where the issue of back-up capacity to weather-dependent renewable energy sources has long been seen as a major issue. Most data points now indicate that the issue is much smaller than first believed. It turns out there are many cheap ways to compensate: paying large industrial users to temporarily reduce consumption, using hydro dams as energy batteries, importing from neighbouring regions, firing up old gas-based power plants and using power from car batteries (many electric vehicles have enough battery capacity to cover the electricity needs of an apartment for weeks). Boris Schucht, the CEO of German transmission company 50 Hertz, has said that in Germany, storage is 'only needed at 70 per cent renewable penetration'.[3]

Incumbents in crisis. This development is already shaking the electricity industry to its core. A conservative industry with notoriously long asset lifetimes, the electricity industry has always thought of coal, gas, nuclear and large-scale hydro as the workhorses of any power system, with wind and solar at best providing additional marginal capacity. That solar and wind can now be equally or more cost-competitive than conventional alternatives, provide a large share of the electricity required and, in many cases, be installed by consumers themselves, is nothing short of an energy revolution.

This has already taken much of the attractiveness out of the old industry. The coal industry is a case in point: in Europe and the US, demand for coal has been declining for the last decade.[4] Even in China, coal use has actually decreased over the last two years. Estimates about China's future coal use vary, but most forecasts say China either has reached 'peak coal' already, or will do so before 2020. The only big global exception is India, where coal demand is expected to double until 2025.[5]

As a result, global market prices for coal have plummeted in recent years, from a level of $75–85 per ton in 2011 to $46 per ton on 1 December 2015. The tipping point logic was evident: cheap shale gas took market share from coal in the US electricity system and at the same time China's growth slowed. Growth of Western coal mining turned negative, and the effect on pricing, profitability and valuations was disproportionate. The Stowe global coal index – which summarizes the market capitalization of the world's biggest traded coal companies – lost 75 per cent of its value from 1 January 2013 to October 2015. In comparison, the NEX index of clean energy companies instead *increased* by 43 per cent during the same period. Interestingly, the same phenomenon has even started to play out on a large scale in China: the country's benchmark coal price fell 27 per cent during the first nine months of 2015 and in Shanxi, the largest coal-producing region, the number of mines has fallen by two-thirds since 2008.[6]

The way forward. Even though there is much to be excited about in the energy revolution, much work still remains – 81 per cent of the world's primary energy still comes from fossil fuels.[7] In addition to continuing to provide incentives to renewable energy technologies, we see three other priorities for maintaining the momentum. First, increase research into energy technologies. Annual investment in energy research in the US is still only about $6 billion per year, whereas investment in medical research, for instance, is (rightfully) $30 billion.[8] Second, take advantage of the low current market prices for fossil fuels to phase out fossil fuel subsidies (which today stand at approximately $600 billion annually worldwide compared to $100 billion in renewable energy subsidies). Third, once the energy system has been cleaned up, acknowledge the economic importance of energy abundance for growth and prosperity.

7.2 A cradle-to-cradle material bank – the 'best after' revolution

Today, 10.6 tons of resources from the earth are needed to support the annual consumption of one human being: coal, oil, aluminium, indium, phosphorus, wood, grain, grass.[9] We are using it to produce heat, power, vehicles, mobile phones, buildings, clothing and break-fasts. That in its own right is unproblematic. Elephants extract 100 tons of biomass per head every year. And ants in total use three times more biomass than humans.[10] There is one fundamental difference: in nature, nutrients circulate in safe, bio-compatible metabolisms. Waste is food for the subsequent use cycle, and materials never cease to be nutrients. Not so in the linear industrial system. Here instead, the vast majority of materials are used once, and altered in ways to make them either useless or much less valuable for the next generation of users. We saw in Chapter 5 that even in Europe, 95 per cent of all material value is lost after one use cycle, and even for recycling 'success cases' like steel, aluminum or PET, a majority of the value is lost.

This one-way material use is deeply problematic: it causes a majority of our global environmental issues, huge economic losses and massive geopolitical risks. Europe, for instance, imports fuels and minerals worth

€760 billion a year,[11] and is hugely dependent on many unstable parts of the world: Middle East (oil), Russia (gas), China (rare earth elements), Congo (copper), Morocco (phosphorus), to name just a few.

There is a fundamentally better alternative available: we need to mimic nature and make materials fit for reuse in a circular material system. Buildings, cars, industrial equipment, household goods would be elements of a gigantic material bank. Imagine what an advantage it would be for a country to have a steady supply of clean high-performing materials circulating in its economy. A well-run material bank would be a pillar of competitiveness for a country in the same way as a strong logistic infrastructure or an effective labour market is today, and – increasingly – an important warrant for national security. Given the obvious advantages, such a shift has been discussed for decades. What's new is that technology is now making it a feasible and attractive reality. Let us first describe the principles of such a system, and then why it is now getting realistic.

One of the most important principles for building such a material bank is to recognize the fundamental difference between biological and technical materials (see Figure 7.3):

- Consumables should largely consist of biological materials (see left side of Figure 7.3) such as food and paper. They are inherently renewable and can be *consumed* as long as they are safely returned to the biosphere without any contamination and in ways that regenerate biological systems. Waste becomes food. The most practical and urgent application of this principle is to keep as much organic matter as possible out of landfills and incinerators. Instead, in bio-refineries bacteria and enzymes can convert biomass into fibres, sugars and proteins, and later into plastics, medicines or fuels. Bio-refinery technology is advancing quickly, and its implementation would make a major contribution to solving the nitrogen and phosphorus issues that threaten the future of global food production.
- Durables consist of technical materials (see right side of Figure 7.3) such as minerals, they should be *used* rather than consumed. This means keeping them in a state whereby they can circulate at high value many times in the economy: either as products (through reuse, refurbishment and remanufacturing) when this is the most

Outline of a circular economy system

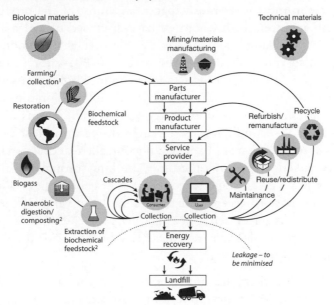

Fig 7.3

cost-efficient solution; or as materials, through different types of recycling systems. Recycling is the technology of last resort. Once ample clean energy is available and materials are easily recovered, material recycling may become the standard.

Getting to such a circular material bank starts with a new design brief: a simple but very different set of principles on how to make a product. Products should be designed to keep biological and technical materials apart (so that biological materials can be safely returned to the biosphere, whereas technical materials will be reused again and again), not to use additives that reduce material properties and to facilitate disassembly (so that materials and components can cheaply be recovered after the first use, e.g. by not welding or glueing together different materials). Behind it all is the idea that products should not be designed for *one use cycle*, but instead for *multiple use cycles*, or for safely returning to the biosphere.

Respecting such design principles might initially appear ambitious, but consider the massive design and development changes most product categories have been through during the last twenty years. They are in most cases much bigger, and most of the product development engineers with whom we have discussed this idea agree that such design changes are entirely feasible over a few product design cycles. Also think about the alternative: in 2014, for instance, 311 million tons of plastic products were produced globally without any real post-use strategy. The result? From the 100 million tons of plastics consumed in coastal regions, a staggering 32 million tons, a third!, are littered and 8–12 million tons end up in the oceans. Close to all of the rest is burned as waste or hauled to uncontrolled landfills – with a huge energy and entropy loss as a result.[12] Thinking through the after-life in the design phase is simply a requirement of good design. Why should customers have to accept that the second-hand value of the product they bought is zero when it does not need to be, if only designers had gone the extra mile? Why not make this brief part of the innovation that is already happening?

Already today, there are products designed this way: the non-profit Cradle-to-Cradle Products Innovation Institute based in California, for instance, has certified 400 products, 65 of these with a gold certificate. Products range from detergents, carpets, concrete additives, yarn, seating cloth, packaging materials, furniture, flooring and turn-key wood-houses. All these products have demonstrated that they keep their material value intact or increasing. They can be reutilized and have been produced in ways that do not negatively affect natural capital. These products mark significant progress and create confidence in the viability of superior designs without sacrificing customer performance, convenience or consumer appeal.

In many cases, such a shift in design and business models is profitable. A study by the Ellen MacArthur Foundation and McKinsey demonstrated the significant economic and environmental advantages of such a transition for five very concrete examples: mobile phones, smartphones, light commercial vehicles, washing machines and power tools. For all five categories, the study showed the total cost to the user could be substantially reduced by better design, and by capturing the value of that better design through new business models. In the case of a washing machine, moving from a sold low-end machine built for 2,000 wash cycles to a leased high-end 'design-to-last' machine that safely

Leasing high-end equipment instead of buying low-end equipment often profitable for customers – example washing machines

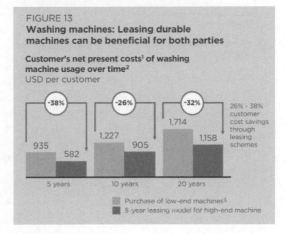

FIGURE 13
Washing machines: Leasing durable machines can be beneficial for both parties

Customer's net present costs[1] of washing machine usage over time[2]
USD per customer

-38%   -26%   -32%   26% - 38% customer cost savings through leasing schemes

935 582   1,227 905   1,714 1,158

5 years   10 years   20 years

■ Purchase of low-end machines[3]
■ 5-year leasing model for high-end machine

SOURCE: Ellen MacArthur Foundation (2013)

Fig 7.4

delivers well over 10,000 cycles created massive value: it reduced the cost of a wash cycle to the customer by up to 38 per cent, and increased profits to the manufacturer by 35 per cent: a win–win that no conventional efficiency programme would ever attain.[13] (See Figure 7.4.)

Different circular solutions will be found for different types of products and materials. Let us offer Figure 7.5 as a framework for thinking about the 'end-state' of different product categories. Items where much of the recovery value lies in the product itself, and where the relative take-back cost is low, will likely get circulated as products or components. This is already happening today for high-value products such as high-end medical equipment or jet engines, but is likely to happen for many more equipment categories in the future (e.g. washing machines). At the other end of the spectrum, if the recovery value lies primarily in the material rather than the product, or if the take-back cost for a company is high, the product should likely end up in a public recycling system (think of a glass bottle), but then the material specification should be such that the material can be reused at high value. Finally there are fractions where incineration for energy is probably the best option today, but where biorefineries are quickly becoming a realistic option.

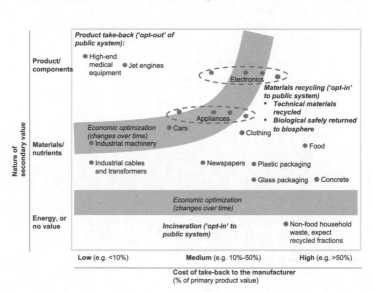

A differentiated circular material system

SOURCE: Authors' analysis

Fig 7.5

What looks like a beneficial side-effect might be the most pivotal advantage of cradle-to-cradle design: health. All over the industrialized world, the rates of cancer, asthma, allergies and hormonal diseases are increasing. Most toxicologists believe this is because of the increasing chemical stresses we are exposed to: while each single chemical exposure might be below the regulator's threshold, the combined effect is clearly not healthy, in addition to destroying material properties for the next use cycle. So there is an important health argument for cleaning up our material use, in addition to the environmental and economic arguments.

Policy to set the right direction

Today, many companies already have plenty of attractive circular opportunities. Some of these opportunities they pursue, but many are not pursued because managers and designers have grown up with a different mindset (compare the 'lean operations' analogy we gave in the 'A new narrative emerging' section). But there is also a wide set of opportunities where the end state is attractive, but getting there requires policy changes to align incentives. An example: much plastic packaging could be taken back and reused many times over, retaining the plastic's quality and value. But this does not happen today, because effective standards and markets are not in place, and there isn't enough volume and business certainty for any single company to take a bet on building a high-value secondary material market.

Let us offer one idea for a policy framework that could take us a big step towards a material bank: a **take-back scheme**. What if European (or any other) policy-makers decided in 2016 that from 2030 onwards, manufacturers selling physical products in the European Union had a choice between two options:

a) Either they choose to take back their products into a *proprietary material bank* and take responsibility themselves for the next life of the product, for instance through reuse, remanufacturing, or through safely disposing of biological materials. In this option, manufacturers would have the same degree of freedom as today in designing products and materials, as long as they take care of the after-life themselves.

b) Alternatively, manufacturers can choose to use the *public material bank*, but then they need to comply with rules that allow the public system to circulate materials at high value and low cost. This means observing the design rules above (separate technical and biological materials, materials standards, design for cheap disassembly).

Of course, manufacturers could also make a hybrid choice, whereby they take back their products, reuse the components and materials that make economic sense for them and then comply with the public material bank rules for the remaining components.

If policy-makers decided that such straightforward, dependable, regulation would take effect 10–15 years from today – enough notice to give manufacturers time to readjust – we believe it would unleash a massive amount of innovation, whereby manufacturers would redeploy some of their development engineers to figure out which components and materials to reuse in what way, and would use their sourcing departments to calculate the cheapest way to get their products back. Industry associations would devise standards and collaboration schemes to pool volumes and reduce take-back costs, and today's waste industry would be replaced by a much more sophisticated secondary material industry. It would not surprise us if most of the changes were achieved within the next five years, rather than the 10–15 years allowed.

Such a system would accelerate the transition towards a cradle-to-cradle material bank in several ways: it would increase the volumes and sophistication of secondary materials markets tremendously; reduce the demand for primary materials substantially; and incentivize manufacturers to only use additives when the economic value is greater than the material degradation costs. It would also create a wave of renewal and innovation opportunities for many industries – we will discuss this more in Chapter 13.

One level of the resource backbone will likely be especially important: cities. As the urbanization rate of the global population is surging from 50 per cent now to 70 per cent expected for 2050, more and more resources will be circling into and then repeatedly through cities.[14] Cities will be the resource aggregators of the modern economy. Organics will have to be channelled as pure and high value flows in and out of the city back to the field. Some resources will be concentrated and prepared for global transhipment. The majority however – such as polymers, glass, construction material – will remain in the city. The quality of the resource markets will be an important determinant of city productivity and liveability.

7.3 High-productivity regenerative systems – reducing system waste

Given the huge amounts of system waste we identified in Part I, it should come as no surprise that we believe better system integration holds a huge economic and environmental opportunity, and that optimized physical value chains are a crucial third pillar of a net-positive economy.

We will describe below our visions for our economy's three largest physical value chains: mobility, food and housing. These visions have been extensively tested and discussed with experts from each sector. In spite of the great uncertainty always involved when thinking about a future ten or twenty years out, we find these scenarios useful to get a sense of the direction and speed of change.

Note how different the visions are from how these value chains operate today, and from their current development path. If captured, the compound effect of new technologies, materials, product ideas, business models and infrastructure is huge, able to redefine the way we travel, live and eat, and powerful enough to decouple our well-being from resource use.

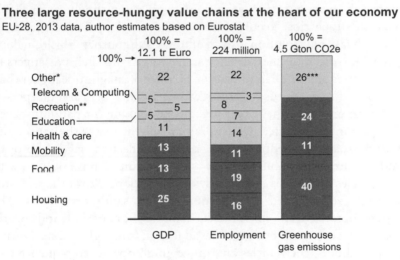

Three large resource-hungry value chains at the heart of our economy
EU-28, 2013 data, author estimates based on Eurostat

* Clothing, public administration (excluding health and education), other consumption goods
** Sports, media, other recreation
*** Split-up not available

SOURCE: Eurostat, EEA, authors' analysis

Fig 7.6

Mobility – towards a shared, integrated, electric system

Mobility – a mega-market of $10 trillion according to Morgan Stanley – is a case in point.[15] It is being hit by several concurrent major technology shifts: electric vehicles are being produced on a big scale, lightweight materials such as carbon fibre and aluminum are entering the market and autonomous vehicles could be launched in only a few years. The speed of development is breathtaking, and we will come back to it in Part III.

Even so, the real opportunity does not lie with these 'supercars', but at the system level. The real revolution comes through the emergence of shared vehicle platforms and new business models, as represented by Car2Go, Uber, BlaBlaCar, Lyft and many other fast-growing new global players, and by the improved system integration that they offer.

Imagine a system where a major share of cars is owned by central fleet managers and summoned by consumers on a smartphone, or available in ample supply close to public transport connections. They are predominantly a last-mile solution instead of today's all-journey vehicle, making many journeys multimodal. They arrive to pick up their passengers in five minutes or less. Their utilization is order-of-magnitude higher than the current 2 per cent use of privately owned cars. They carry one person at a time or many. They don't waste time looking for parking spaces. They are interconnected, which dramatically increases the capacity of existing roads and reduces traffic jams. The fleet manager who owns and operates this mobility service is in constant communication with the vehicles in the fleet. A central system is responsible for the real-time dispatch, routing and optimization of thousands of vehicles. The system monitors traffic and predicts demand ahead of time, and ensures sufficient supply of vehicles is available in the right place. During off-peak hours, the vehicles are routed in an optimized sequence to a depot for servicing, cleaning and battery charging. Components with a statistically significant probability of failure are exchanged as part of a predictive maintenance programme. Cars could consequently have a useful life of 0.5–1 million kilometres as opposed to 0.2–0.4 today. As they approach their end of life, 30–40 per cent of the components could be reused and remanufactured in the next-generation vehicle. The cost and availability of mobility would be much better than today, and the environmental footprint a fraction of today's.

This might sound like a idealistic far-out vision, but think through the individual technologies and business models mentioned above: all of them – with the possible exception of fully autonomous cars – are being launched on a big scale today or in the next few years. The vision is in fact fully feasible in a 10–20-year perspective if cities and countries were to pursue it.

Contrast this vision with the direction we are heading in today: mobility systems in most cities develop much slower than car technology, so, on the current development path, fast-changing technology will lure even more people to buy a car, further choking inner cities and motorways, increasing average commuting times, and resulting in more roads and higher pollution.

The difference between the two scenarios is massive, with the first one being much better from almost any perspective imaginable. Compared to this opportunity, we would argue that almost all cities and countries are vastly undermanaging this system.

Food

The global food system also illustrates the opportunity in improved system integration. This has become increasingly specialized over recent decades, with farmers, food processing companies, retailers and waste managers each focusing on optimizing their own business, with the usual 3–5-year planning horizon. The result has been increased efficiency but also an overexploitation of soils, major irrigation needs, massive nutrient leakage into lakes and oceans, and waste – very serious problems for the future global food supply, and for the broader environment, as we laid out in Part I.

With a systems view, these nutrient loops would be closed. Imagine a world where food waste is separated from other waste and put through an anaerobic digestion process. This produces biogas – a renewable energy source – and bio-fertilizer that can be brought back to the fields. In Appendix 2 there is a case example of how the city of Stockholm uses food waste to fuel local buses, with a whole range of benefits for cost, employment, CO_2 emissions, local air pollution, fertilization and eutrophication. Second, imagine if the 31 per cent of food waste throughout the value chain were reduced. As a simple example, some large retailers like Intermarché have begun to sell fruit and vegetables outside the size and shape norms at a discount, instead of discarding them, with a very good response from consumers. Finally, imagine if farming practices were transformed to the much more resource-efficient and regenerative technologies and practices that are now available, for instance precision agriculture and no-till farming (these are further described in Part III).

This vision perhaps looks like a smaller change than the one outlined for mobility above, but it would mean a dramatically better and healthier food system, with much less need for irrigation, fossil fertilizers and pesticides. Any extra short-term cost (it is much debated whether there are in fact extra costs, and there are many examples to the contrary) would look small in comparison to longer-term productivity gains as soils recover, and to risk reduction for future food supply and the environment. In a 5–10-year horizon, economic gains would outweigh any extra upfront costs. And again, all the technology to realize this vision exists today.

So are we heading towards this vision? Rather the opposite: we are increasing fossil fertilizer use to compensate for depleting soil, separation of food waste remains a marginal phenomenon, and there are few signs that food waste along the value chain is decreasing.

Housing

The story is similar for housing: a specialized value chain with architects, urban planners, construction companies, real estate providers, users, demolition companies, all optimizing their own business (as they should). But with a systems view, the sub-optimization becomes obvious: energy consumption is much higher than necessary, since upfront construction costs are optimized rather than lifetime costs. Houses are not built to last, as the demolition time and its consequences are far beyond anyone's planning horizon. And insufficient resources are spent on urban planning, in spite of its huge long-term impact. Perhaps most surprisingly, the productivity of the construction sector itself has stagnated in many Western countries: in Germany and the US, for instance, it has essentially stood still for the last twenty-five years.

That could easily change, with massive benefits to the economy in three major areas. Buildings themselves can be built much more cheaply and with much better performance thanks to new technology and construction practices. Energy-positive houses are already in the money in many situations. Modular building technologies are also allowing construction times and costs to be slashed. Huge 3D printers for concrete have been developed, allowing the building envelope to be erected in a fraction of the time. Chinese company WinSun recently constructed the envelopes of ten single-family houses, each of 195 square metres, in 24 hours using only a handful of construction workers.[16] Next, utilization of offices and hospitality offer an enormous sharing opportunity, as visualized by the staggering success of Airbnb. The unutilized residential space is in many cities much larger than the total professional hospitality space. Lastly, urban planning is back. A better built environment would reclaim the inner-city land unlocked by a better mobility system to create high-quality spaces where people would live and work. The system would integrate green infrastructure (e.g. parks) with durable, mixed-use buildings designed in a modular way and constructed with looped and non-toxic materials. In total, this could lead to a reduction in the cost per square metre of more than 30 per cent compared to today. It could turn the sector's currently highly negative environmental impact into a net-positive one. And it could make our buildings healthier and more attractive to live in. These three systems alone represent huge changes to our lives, our economy and our environment.

In summary, it is striking how attractive these visions are – and not only in commercial terms. Wouldn't you like to live in such a world? This is not because we have been overly optimistic in our technology assumptions – they are in fact quite conservative. Instead, the reality is that our current systems are so wasteful – for all the historical reasons we explored in previous chapters – and technology has now come so far, that we have a real option to create systems that are just profoundly better, from whichever angle you want to look at it. Acknowledging that, and addressing the huge improvement potential, represents a massive improvement opportunity, especially now that the disruption is starting to sweep through these value chains, and there is a real chance to influence their development.

Chapter 8

The 'net-positive' norm –
accretive, productive, healthy

We cannot solve our problems with the same thinking we used when we created them.

Albert Einstein

An executive of a world-leading packaged goods company put it succinctly during one of our recent conversations: 'We have a problem. We are selling bad conscience with every product we sell. Our customers know our products don't do anything good for them or the environment. Improving a little bit every year will make that more visible, not less. In the long run, it will be a hard sell.'

In their 2002 book *Cradle to Cradle: Remaking the Way We Make Things*, Michael Braungart and William McDonough ask the simple but provocative question: why shouldn't products be made in a way that is truly good for us, and good for the environment? Or put the other way, why should we accept products that are harmful to ourselves, or to the environment we live in and depend on? How can it be a valid marketing argument that a company's product causes a little bit less damage than last year, or a little bit less damage than competitors' products? Should it not be a very basic quality requirement of the products we buy that they are at least not harmful? As outlined in Chapter 6, this is about more than eco-efficiency. Energy-efficient vacuum cleaners, low-tenside detergents, lightweight plastic packaging, PET bottles partly sourced from plants – all of these efforts are commendable, but so far they have not won the hearts of consumers and have been collectively unable to turn the tide. Braungart concludes: 'There is only one way out – products good by design.' For him, that is the ultimate design and quality revolution.

We described what we call the 'net-positive' principle already in the 'A new narrative emerging' section, and we defined it simply as the net effect of an economic activity being positive across manufactured capital, human capital and natural capital. We also suggested that this principle needs to replace eco-efficiency as the bar for companies. This chapter describes how the net-positive principle translates to concrete decision criteria, for companies and for governments. It is not a complete description – specifically for countries, such definitions are highly technical and go far beyond the purpose of this book – but instead is intended to give an overview of this concept.

8.1 A new way of doing business – managing for good

Let's first look at *companies*. Most of them do not have the luxury or ability to think about the long-term stock of different types of natural capital. Companies live off income, and most of them have a planning horizon of a few years at most. For them, net positive needs to be used as an aspiration and a norm – this will already make a major difference, as outlined in the 'A new narrative emerging' section – and it needs to be translated to company-relevant decision criteria that can be used at many different levels: for product development, supplier selection, business development, reuse/remanufacturing and so on. Working a net-positive principle into such decisions will take time, but eventually the net-positive principle could get as intuitive as the profitability principle is today.

In technical terms, companies should incorporate shadow prices for the main externality costs into their everyday business decisions, using a lifetime perspective (including the after-life for materials and key components). The exact externality set will vary by company, but in our experience, four or five externalities are usually enough to reach a very good understanding of net positive. Carbon emissions, freshwater use, health impacts from air pollution, impacts from waste treatment (or the lack thereof) will be common externalities. There are plenty of sophisticated tools available such as InVEST from the Natural Capital Project. They make it possible to estimate costs for these externalities, and with a relatively modest effort companies can already today triangulate costs relevant to their situation. These estimates are not perfect, and there will be grey zones where it is debatable where the company's responsibility ends. But this is often the case already today, for instance when it comes to unethical business practices by suppliers and sub-suppliers. And, in a few years, imagine if national environmental agencies or national statistics offices published proposed shadow prices for the key externalities on an annual basis, depending on the local context (freshwater externalities, as an example, will vary hugely by location and over time). This would make net-positive calculations straightforward, and it would start to set a common bar for the companies active in that country.

The two calculation approaches – with externality shadow prices and without – would coexist, also for the long term. We hope that more and more of the key externalities will be awarded formal prices, along the lines of those the European Trading Scheme established for European CO_2 emissions, but this will take time, and we doubt that all relevant externalities will ever be formally priced. So the two types of calculation will need to coexist, rather as a cash-flow statement and a profit-loss statement do today. After a few years, when managers and financial controllers have become familiar with the net-positive way of looking at their business, and when investors and customers start asking about it, we believe the calculation without externalities will seem more and more partial and hard to defend.

This is not dramatically different from how some sustainability departments of advanced companies make big investment decisions today. But we know of very few companies that make such numbers a substantive part of their overall decision-making. Some do not translate natural capital and health impacts to a common currency through externalities costing, some only do this for the very largest decisions, some don't invest in creating the required knowledge throughout the organization, and very few apply a net-positive principle as the bar to reach. So in reality, the difference between today's practices and a net-positive approach could not be bigger. The closest analogy in use today is that some companies define a shadow price for CO_2 even in jurisdictions where they are not obliged to, and look at investment cases both with and without CO_2 costs.

But isn't it naïve, some people have asked us, to assume companies would voluntarily start to use a net-positive principle, if it does not fully coincide with profitability? We don't think so, over a decade or two. Think about issues such a gender equality, diversity, child labour, or corruption. Practices – implicit and explicit – that were commonplace just a decade or two ago are today unimaginable for most large corporations. That does not mean we think it will be easy. For instance, there are competitiveness trade-offs to manage in many industries, and it is often difficult to influence the behaviours of suppliers and sub-suppliers. And there are industries where technology is simply not available yet, and companies in reality have little choice between continuing to use net negative business practices and going out of business (global shipping for instance). But for the broad set of industries, the technology disruption is now quickly making net positive an economically and technologically viable vision over the next 5–15 years.

Also, what is the alternative? Business-as-usual clearly is not, as we've shown at great length in this book. Waiting for formal environmental legislation (be it through bans, taxes, emissions pricing) will be a wait too long, even though this also needs to be a major part of the future solution.

8.2 A toolbox – in support of real life decisions

To test how the three-pillar framework and the new norm could play out at the industry level, we translated it into a set of action areas for companies and industries, together with the ReSOLVE framework (see Figure 8.1). In different ways, these action areas all contribute to the vision we laid out above. None of the action areas guarantees that an economic activity becomes net-positive, but they all help substantially:[1]

- **Regenerate**. Shift from finite to renewable energy and materials; restore the health of ecosystems to get a better economic return. The massive renewable energy trend falls into this category, and so do land and forest restoration efforts around the world.
- **Share**. Get more economic value out of products and infrastructure by sharing them. Major car-sharing schemes like Uber, Car2Go, Lyft and BlaBlaCar fall into this category, as do house-sharing schemes like Airbnb. For example, the BlaBlaCar car-sharing scheme is

growing 200 per cent a year and has 20 million registered users in nineteen countries. Airbnb has more than one million spaces for rent in more than 34,000 cities across more than 190 countries.

- **Optimize**. Increase performance/efficiency of a product; remove waste in production and the supply chain (from sourcing and logistics to production, use and end-of-use collection); leverage big data, automation, remote sensing and steering. A good example of this is the Lean Operations philosophy made famous by Toyota.
- **Loop**. Keep components and materials in closed loops, to extract maximum value from them. For finite materials, this means reusing, remanufacturing and recycling components and materials, as Caterpillar, Michelin, Rolls Royce and Renault are doing. For renewable materials, it means bringing nutrients back to the fields, anaerobic digestion and extracting biochemicals from organic waste.
- **Virtualize**. Dematerialize resource use by delivering utility virtually: books, music, online shopping, virtual offices, online banking, remote physical examinations, remote security. The list of products and services that can be virtualized is long, often resulting in dramatically less material consumption, as well as less travel and better service.
- **Exchange**. Replace old materials with advanced materials; apply new technologies (e.g. 3D printing, electric vehicles); choose new products and services (e.g. multimodal transport).

Each action area represents a major business opportunity in itself, and there are many examples of global leaders who have built their success on only one of these action areas, as Figure 8.1 illustrates. We often use this toolbox in company workshops to generate growth and innovation ideas, and in our experience, it resonates well with executives – there are very few companies who cannot identify several attractive improvement initiatives from this toolbox. Each action reinforces and accelerates the performance of the other actions, creating a strong compound effect.

The attractiveness of this toolbox also says something important about how much has happened over the last 10–15 years, and about the reality of getting to net positive for most industries. A number of crucial factors have come together to make a net-positive model not only possible but highly beneficial for a broad range of products and services. First, clean energy has over the last decade become

ReSOLVE – a menu of business actions for a better economy

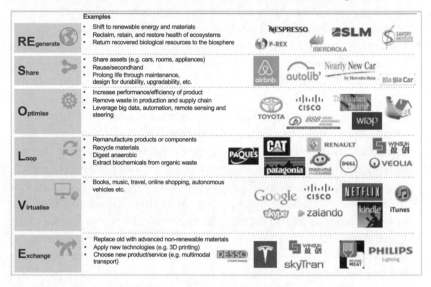

SOURCE: McKinsey Center for Business and Environment, Ellen MacArthur Foundation & SUN (2015)

Fig 8.1

cost-competitive in most countries across the world. This changes everything, as fossil energy accounts for a significant share of the negative side of the net-positive equation. Second, a circular material system is now within reach, since we can cheaply keep track of products and materials, and waste separation technology has taken many steps forward over recent years. This addresses the second major 'negative' in the net-positive equation. Third, digital technology advancements have made sharing and virtualization much more attractive over the last decade, massively increasing the positive side of the equation, since they allow a much better utilization of products. Fourth, digitization is also increasing transparency and accountability at a fast pace – it is quickly becoming harder for companies to get away with unethical practices, even on the other side of the world. So all of the crucial components of the net-positive equation have been turned upside-down in the new millennium.

Let's look at a few product categories to see how a net-positive principle and the ReSOLVE framework would work out:

- *Cars.* A lot of car use is defendable against a net-positive principle already today, since the economic and social value is so high that it compensates for the natural capital damages, whereas some other car use is not. But imagine the compound effect if the car was propelled by clean energy, materials were reused many times over and utilization increased substantially from today's 2 per cent. These changes massively reduce the natural capital and health damages, and in parallel increase the economic and social value of the car many times over. A car like that, and the materials it contains, would clearly add to our common capital stock. Realistic? Not for all car companies tomorrow, but there are already shared car companies with all-electric vehicles that run very successfully on completely commercial terms and are growing fast. Paris-based AutoLib is one such company, and is further presented in the final chapter.
- *Cotton clothing.* Fashion in the future could work with new and homogeneous fibres that can easily be upcycled, produced from renewable energy, with dyes that are bio-benign and with glues so that garments can be easily dismantled. Take-back or recycling would be the norm rather than incineration. Cotton itself will be sourced from biological farms that manage their water resources and soil differently from today's industry norm.
- *Paper napkins.* If paper napkins (and other consumables) are produced from renewable resources, using clean energy and designed in a way that they can be safely returned to the biosphere (i.e they do not contain toxins or non-biological materials, which would stop sewage sludge from producing high quality fertilizer), then they will have caused no natural capital depletion and they clearly have a value as a part of our manufactured capital.

So for all of these product groups – which are mainstream products and not outliers – there is a visible path to net positive, and plenty of in-the-money first steps. And remember, these are just the opportunities that are visible today. Whenever incentives and ambition coincided in the past, human ingenuity was able to develop the unexpected, often within breathtakingly short time frames: the man-to-the-moon mission, the Manhattan project, or the renewable energy revolution, to name a few examples.

8.3 A programme for accretive growth – a country's compass

Companies changing voluntary norms and metrics will not in itself be enough to challenge the massive vested interests in the old resource economy, but it is a very important step and crucially, this new way of looking at the world is a prerequisite for political leaders to be able to introduce formal externalities pricing, that is, for countries to start to manage their natural resources.

What does 'accretive growth' then mean for countries? Primarily it means looking at their economies, and the performance of those economies, in very different ways. We described the limitations of GDP as the lead metric in Chapter 4, and discussed a number of alternatives, among them the Inclusive Wealth Index ('IWI'). IWI comes very close to how we define net-positive growth: it looks at the value of a country's capital stock, and it uses a broad definition of capital, including manufactured, natural and human capital. It then defines growth as an increase in that broad capital stock. We sometimes also talk about 'accretive' growth, to emphasize even further that it is a growth that builds capital. The only reservations we have regarding IWI is that its definition of natural capital damages is relatively limited, and does not include some of the crucial impacts like water shortage, nutrient flows and biodiversity. Negative health impacts from environmental hazards (e.g. particle pollution from fossil fuels) are also not included, so even though IWI is already reporting growth numbers far below those of GDP, it is still underestimating the depletive aspects of our current growth model. But IWI is still a nascent initiative, and its reports state clearly that it is working on expanding its methodology.

If countries started to measure and publish growth in IWI (or a similar metric) in parallel to GDP, we believe it would create a very healthy debate. People would start to compare the two growth numbers, researchers would dissect why IWI growth is so much lower than GDP growth, and the debate would soon focus on what can be done to close the gap between the two growth numbers. Crucially, it would also start to challenge the widely held belief that GDP is the only objective and rational way to look at economic progress.

Countries could also start publishing recommended shadow prices for companies to use for key natural resources and start asking for such calculations in public tenders and other interactions with companies, creating an informal expectation that companies start taking such shadow prices into account.

All this would make it substantially easier for political leaders to then impose formal regulation of natural capital damages.

Readers with a sustainability background will notice that what we are suggesting is a version of 'weak' sustainability for companies (whereby impacts on different types of natural capital and other types of capital are balanced against each other through one common currency, with an implicit mindset that one type of capital can be substituted for another). Countries, on the other hand, need to adopt a mindset of 'strong' sustainability (where no substitution between different types of resources is implied), even though the actual IWI metric summarizes all natural capital and health impacts in one number. We believe this is the right split of responsibility: companies cannot realistically be asked to understand and take responsibility for a country's environmental situation, and they must be allowed to trade off different forms of impact against each other. Countries, on the other hand, need to manage natural resources such as freshwater – to take an important example – so that total use does not outweigh sustainable supply.

Chapter 9

A European case example – positive for economy and environment

A profound transformation of the way our entire economy works. By rethinking the way we produce, work and buy, we can generate new opportunities and create new jobs.

Frans Timmermans, First Vice-President of the European Union, at the launch of the EU's circular economy package, December 2015

Could a three-pillar model work in practice? And how would it change the economy and employment at large? To test this theory, we quantified some of the visionary scenarios described previously.

First, we modelled the systems individually, to understand the cost and performance implications. For each system we looked at the 'good disruption' scenario described above, and also at a 'current trajectory' scenario, which anticipates where we will end up if we pursued the current set of policies. In the 'current trajectory' scenario, primarily product-level improvements are implemented; in the 'good disruption' scenario, the full set of new technologies and new business models are compounded.

Second, we studied the economy-wide implications of the two scenarios using a general equilibrium model. For the modelling, we used the services of a well-regarded academic macroeconomic modelling team, using the European Union as a test region. We believe other economies with less optimized resource systems and higher degrees of freedom might benefit even more than Europe.

The results were astonishing and the opportunities exceeded our expectations. The 'good disruption' scenario was significantly more attractive for economic growth, for natural capital impact, and for equality. For employment, no formal modelling was done, but the literature study we conducted as part of the research suggested a positive impact. In short, we got encouragement that the vision above could in fact address many of the ailments we described in Part I.

9.1 More for less – a pay rise for all Europeans[1]

Looking first at the value chain level, the analysis shows that, over time, these improvements could reduce the total household cost of mobility by as much as 60–80 per cent, food by 25–40 per cent and housing by 25–35 per cent, all in real terms (see Figure 9.1). These are huge numbers for sectors of this size and maturity, and they would effectively act as a major 'wage increase' for European households, a proportionally larger wage increase for low- and middle-income households. To be clear: we do not believe all of the improvement opportunity would be captured as cost savings; some of it might well instead be captured as better food, more convenient cars, more floor space and so on. But the opportunities for total cost savings give a sense of the size of the changes ahead.

Cost-reduction potential in the three value chains
Total annual cash-out costs per household; EU average 2012, €
Improvement potential for 2050[1]

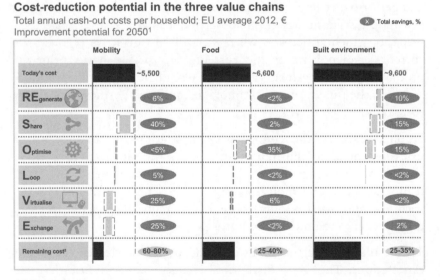

SOURCE: McKinsey Center for Business and Environment, Ellen MacArthur Foundation & SUN (2015)

Fig 9.1

At the macroeconomic level, the modelling shows a dramatic positive impact as a result of pursuing a 'good disruption' strategy. Both of the scenarios show a positive impact compared to today – which is very logical, since both assume rapid technological improvements – but the net-positive pathway leads to better outcomes on all the key performance dimensions: GDP, employment, greenhouse gas emissions, and resource consumption (see Figure 9.2).

Let's look first at GDP. The 'good disruption' scenario could increase European GDP by as much as 11 per cent by 2030, seven percentage points more than the 'current trajectory' scenario, or half a percentage point per year. This is a very large impact – a size that is rarely seen when doing economic modelling – and such results need to be taken with a pinch of salt. Equilibrium models are the standard economics tools available for this type of quantification, but their accuracy decreases when modelling scenarios that are far from 'business as usual'. But intuitively, the results make a lot of sense: if one can use new technology and smarter policy to radically reduce the system waste inherent in our largest economic sectors, and do so at a comparatively low additional cost, that should have a major positive impact. Effectively, we would get much more economic value out of our existing infrastructure and investments, at a low extra cost. Critics might say we are assuming 'manna from heaven', but we showed in Chapter 5 that today's situation is highly wasteful, we demonstrated that system waste is not effectively addressed today and we will argue in Part III that new relevant technology is developing at breakneck speed. So while the exact size of the economic growth benefit is certainly debatable, the direction is clear and the underlying economic strategy of extracting more value from existing products, materials and infrastructures certainly seems a very sensible one.

What about employment? The *Growth Within* research included an academic meta-study of how employment would be affected by a shift to the type of economy described above. After reviewing 65 academic studies, the authors from Mannheim University concluded that the existing state of academic knowledge suggests a positive employment effect: more job creation than job destruction. Why? First, because secondary production is generally more labour-intensive than primary; the recycling sector is more labour-intensive than the raw material sector; industrial remanufacturing is relatively more labour-intensive than primary, and so on. For example, waste disposal generates only 0.1 jobs per 1,000 tons, while recycling processing creates two jobs per 1,000 tons. Second, spending should increase across sectors as prices fall, creating an important indirect employment effect. Third, and most important, a large number of markets and types of jobs would either be created or massively scaled-up: vehicle disassembly and recovery, shared vehicle fleet managers, rare earth metal aggregators, mobility system integration consultants, large-scale shared office provisioning, bio-fertilizer production, material toxicity reduction managers, secondary component sourcing, net-positive product designers, secondary building material providers, material consultants, soil biologists, energy contracting agents, energy storage aggregators, implant greenhouse operators, nitrogen certificate traders, rental fashion coaches, do-it-yourself coaches, traffic contingency operators, energy data analysts, to mention just a few.

The type of innovation involved in the shift to a three-pillar 'net-positive' economy is one that Clayton Christensen of Harvard – the doyen of innovation academics – identifies as employment- and growth-creating. His research identifies three broad types of innovation: *substitution innovation* (for instance, where a better car model replaces another), *efficiency innovation* (for instance, where Walmart's large-scale and efficient business system allows it to deliver the same goods cheaper than competitors) and *market-creating innovations* (where a *new need* is being serviced, for instance, instant navigation services through a smartphone, large-scale energy storage, etc.).

While all three types of innovation are required in a competitive market economy, according to Christensen's research, it is only market-creating innovation that can really create new growth and employment: substitution innovation by definition replaces earlier products and production, and efficiency innovations are overwhelmingly aimed at reducing labour. His research gives many examples of how market-creating innovation has led to growth and employment in the past, and criticizes how much policy-maker effort and public resources (for instance, in the form of development aid) nonetheless goes into stimu-lating the first two types of innovation.[2]

In our case, many large new needs would be serviced – with a myriad of smaller needs – and the corresponding markets would be created: the need to bring back food nutrients to fields, the need to maintain value in our material bank, the need to better optimize our large physical value chains and the need to clean up our energy systems.

9.2 Resources in balance – from Achilles' heel to strength

Turning to resources, a 'good disruption' strategy could be a powerful decoupling force between economic growth and environmental impact. Across the three systems, CO_2 emissions in the 'good disruption' scenario drop as much as 48 per cent by 2030 and 83 per cent by 2050, compared with 2012 levels. Primary material consumption drops as much as 32 per cent by 2030 and 53 per cent by 2050 (see Figure 9.2). These numbers would mean Europe – and the world, if other regions follow suit – would be well on track to meet the 'well below 2 degrees' target for climate change established by the Paris agreement, and address many of the other environmental issues as well. If these numbers are anywhere close to correct – and we certainly believe they are – it means that addressing system waste in our big physical value chains is a powerful recipe for combining increased growth and prosperity with an order-of-magnitude lower environmental footprint. But there are also many other benefits to reap: Europe – the world's largest resource importer – would be much less dependent on volatile international resource markets, and face fewer security-of-supply issues of scarce materials, and therefore fewer economic and geopolitical risks.

One important difference between Europe and fast-growing developing economies is that in Europe, supply of secondary material could be a significant share of the total demand in many categories if properly handled, whereas in industrializing economies demand far outweighs secondary material supply. So the opportunity to reduce material consumption is lower in developing countries.

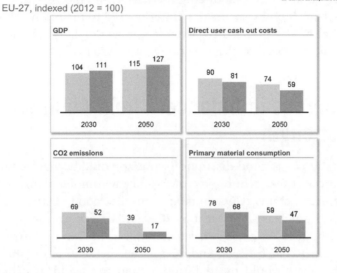

Better economic and environmental outcomes

EU-27, indexed (2012 = 100)

☐ Current development scenario ■ Good disruption scenario

SOURCE: McKinsey Center for Business and Environment, Ellen MacArthur Foundation & SUN (2015)

Fig 9.2

Impact on the climate. All three pillars above can provide important contributions to the fight against climate change. But this is not well recognized in the climate change debate and negotiations, which tend to focus on renewable energy, energy efficiency (including transport and buildings), land use and agriculture. A cradle-to-cradle material bank, and high-productivity systems, when they are mentioned, are typically well down the list. That is a mistake – and a lost opportunity – for three reasons.

First, it will be near impossible to reach the 2 degrees target without big steps towards a cradle-to-cradle material bank. The production of raw materials accounts for 19 per cent of global greenhouse gas emissions, and the waste sector represents another 3 per cent. Switching to renewable energy and improving energy efficiency in the production process will help reduce these emissions, but we find it difficult to imagine that it would be sufficient to cut emissions at the 90–95 per cent level needed.[3] The volume of raw material production must also be reduced.

Second, many circular opportunities can be addressed profitably already in today's market, and many more with appropriate incentives. In our recently published report *Growth Within: A Circular Economy Vision for a Competitive Europe*, we identified more than 100 measures that are already cost-effective, many of which are additional to those that were the focus of the climate discussions.

Third, many of these opportunities will not be captured by a carbon price (or tax) or by the other actions in the climate debate's focus. The mechanisms of a circular system are simply different. In the cases of steel and plastics, for example, keeping the material value high would require actions such as better recovery, tracking and recycling systems, improved secondary material markets, bans on certain toxins and perhaps extended producer responsibilities.

If you find these arguments convincing, then what should be done? Most importantly, a cradle-to-cradle material bank should be recognized as one of the key pillars in the transition to a low-carbon society. Similar areas, such as energy efficiency and deforestation, have benefitted hugely from such recognition in the past decade, in terms of financing, policy development, knowledge investments and concrete on-the-ground results. The thinking on circular material systems is still in its infancy, and would benefit immensely from a similar development. In our collective battle against climate change, we have already made good progress in shifting the direction of the energy system. Now we need to address the material flows that underlie our industrial engine. Circular material flows could be the missing vector needed to meet the Paris climate ambitions.

Impact on the water cycle.[4] As for climate change, there is an increasing recognition that our global water crisis calls for a radical rethink, and that circular principles could lead the way. Clearly, much of the water predicament is due to dysfunctional political systems and ill-defined markets. But the real issue is a very linear model of using our most precious resource, which gets successively more polluted as it travels through the system, and eventually turns into a worthless trickle, creating high costs for subsequent users and society in general.

We could instead close the water loop by applying some basic rules: for water that will be released back into the water cycle, we have to ensure no hormones, toxic inks (as found on poor-quality toilet paper) or textile dyes are added that cannot be recovered at low cost. This simple rule would stop us from creating 9 million tons of contaminated sludge every year in Europe alone.[5] There are fantastic new technologies available that allow energy and nutrients to be extracted from wastewater and for water to be reused altogether, as practised by Singapore's utility which has made bottled NEWater a brand name against the odds. Or water can be treated as a durable, and kept in a closed loop under zero-liquid-discharge conditions. This is the right choice whenever it is too costly to dispose of the solvents or to recreate them – for example, when water contains very specific water-borne solvents, electroplating baths, acids, and alkaline solutions used in heavy-duty cleaning.

At the country level, water can take the form of a finite stock or a renewable flow. Aquifer water, as applied to Saudi agriculture for instance, is a finite stock and should only be used to the extent it can be replenished through aquifer recharge programmes. Other water sources are luckily flow systems – rivers or naturally replenishing aquifers. Their water can be abstracted as long as the volume taken does not exceed the amount of flow required to keep the ecosystem healthy.

Finally, we can interpret water as an infrastructure system: our global water networks and treatment plants are worth approximately $140 billion. Following the net-positive principle, we should maximize the benefits from these assets. They could be used for more services, for instance using the pipes for telecommunication fibre or for aggregating food waste. Or start selling performance, not water: instead of charging by the cubic metre, utilities could pay consumers for curbing use and then sell the conserved volume – termed 'nega water' – back to the system. Or we could optimize resource efficiency and use utilities as a source of green power. There are many examples where anaerobic digestion of sludge alone produces biogas that covers more than 60 per cent of energy consumed at wastewater treatment plants.

Accretive principles provide the guidelines needed to move resource systems such as carbon or water from a massive source of waste into systems that provide major benefit with no or positive effect on the natural environment. Readers will have noticed that there is a striking difference between a conventional sustainability-derived perspective and net-positive framing.

9.3 Accretive investments – already at work

Also from an investment point of view, there are strong indications that a double dividend of improved returns and improved environmental performance is possible, at least until financial markets have caught up and absorbed the reality of sustainability risks. A major 2014 meta-study of sustainable investment by Oxford University and financial firm Arabesque reviewed over 200 academic studies and found strong evidence that 'it is in the best economic interest for corporate managers and investors to incorporate sustainability considerations into decision-making processes'. Their explanation of the seeming paradox that limiting investment options can yield higher economic returns is as follows. Lack of sustainability eventually catches up with companies, as consumers, media or policy-makers eventually discover and react to worker exploitation, misuse of natural resources and other major sustainability issues. This in turn punishes the share price. These risks are overlooked in the stock market today, explaining how asset managers who avoid the risks can beat its relevant comparison index.[6]

Al Gore's Generation Investment might be the best-known example of an asset management firm using this strategy today, and very successfully. In its first ten years of operation, it has significantly outperformed its peer group, yielding an average return in the period 2005–15 of 12.1 per cent annually, compared to 7.0 per cent for the MSCI World Index. According to a recent survey by London-based financial analyst firm Mercer, this places Generation in second place in a list of 200 global equity managers.[7]

Balkissoon and Heaps (2014) arrived at similar results in an academic study. They looked at Standard & Poor's 500 data for the period

2008–14 and compared the risk and return of different low-carbon equity portfolios with the return of similar carbon-indifferent portfolios. They concluded that for several common investment strategies (such as minimum variance or maximum diversification), picking low-carbon equities yielded moderately better results across many of the success metrics used by fund managers.[8] Their conclusion was that fund managers in a wide range of situations can viably choose low-carbon equity portfolios and still observe their fiduciary responsibilities to maximize risk-adjusted returns.[9]

The broader field of 'impact investing' is still a small share of total investments ($12.2 billion are expected to be committed to impact investing in 2015, according to the Global Impact Investment Network) but it is growing at 15 per cent per year. BlackRock – one of the world's largest asset managers with total assets of $4.5 trillion under management – recently launched their Impact US Equity Fund, and Goldman Sachs recently acquired impact-investing specialist firm Imprint Capital. The growth is expected to continue, as more than $40 trillion of wealth is shifted from baby-boomers to millennials in the next decades.[10]

This is a big deal. The investment community seems to be catching on to the fact that in a world of quickly increasing sustainability risks, and quickly decreasing costs of clean technology costs, the old trade-off of returns versus sustainability no longer applies. Competent companies and clever investors can in many cases have both.

PART III: THE BIG DISRUPTION – TAMING THE BEAST

Our economy is changing in front of our eyes and shaking the very foundations of our inherited industrial model. The world's largest shop does not have stores (Alibaba), the largest taxi company does not have cars (Uber), the largest lodging provider does not have rooms (Airbnb), the largest media company does not provide content (Facebook), the largest movie house does not have a cinema (Netflix), the fastest growing car manufacturer is a Silicon Valley-based battery factory-cum-component assembly (Tesla), the largest phone company does not own wire (Skype) and the largest charity does not have projects (Justgiving). In such an economy, can and will the entire resource equation be redefined? And will formerly intractable concepts – such as externalities, free-riding and overuse – finally be addressed?

In Part III, we will look at the disruptions currently shaping the global economy: the technology disruption that is sweeping from sector to sector and changing them in ways few could imagine twenty years ago; the massive migration to cities that is taking place all over the world; and the demographic development that will turn many deeply held beliefs on their head. Crucially, we will show how the technology disruption, which has so far had most impact in information businesses like entertainment and publishing, will hit the physical industries with full force over the next 10–20 years, and how this raises the stakes for both the economy and the environment. We will give you an update from the frontlines of change, and (hopefully) inspire you with many examples of the fantastic development. And we will argue that the disruption provides us with the capabilities to build a a much better economy, one that is planet-compatible, and one that can address the social borrowing we described in Part I.

But we also bring a sobering message: for all their benefits, the megatrends we observe will not by themselves solve the serious issues related to our industrial model that we laid out in Part I, and might instead make them worse. For advanced economies, there is even a question of how positive the total effects of the technology disruption will be, if one adds up all the expected effects on growth, natural capital depletion, employment and inequality.

Finally, Chapter 13 will show that innovation and technology development are not the unpredictable and ungovernable forces that many believe. Innovation today is not driven by random sparks of genius from individual inventors, if it ever was. Instead, as we will show, the broad patterns of new technology development are in many ways predictable, determined by market forces, policy and government investments. This adds another important strand to our argument: as a society, we will over time get the innovations we ask for, and we have an opportunity to steer our innovation engine to create a much better outcome than we are currently heading for. An undoubtedly good disruption.

Chapter 10

Disruptive trends – the world at a turning point

We are at a point where we can digitize just about everything.

The Second Machine Age, Erik Brynjolfsson and Andrew McAfee

10.1 From C40 to C440 – the age of urbanization

When the global city cooperation organization C40 was created in 2005, forty cities around the world were considered 'megacities', and those forty were the ones that C40 wanted to organize. By 2015, a lot had already happened: C40 counted eighty members, 80 per cent of global GDP was created in cities and 70 per cent of global energy-related GHG emissions were generated in cities.[1,2] Cities have truly become the centres of global economic activity.

But we have only seen the beginning. By 2030, C40 might have to count a full 440 members: according to McKinsey's Urban World initiative, close to half of all global economic growth between 2010 and 2025 will happen in 440 cities, each with a population of more than a million. Currently, a staggering 1.4 million people move from the countryside to cities across the world every week. By 2050, an additional 2.5 billion people will have moved to cities, making two-thirds of the global population urbanites.[3] In China alone, the government expects 100 million people to move to cities in the next five years, meaning 60 per cent of the population will be urban by 2020.[4]

The reason is simple: cities are where a modern lifestyle is available. Good housing, well-paid jobs, public services, entertainment, career development – all of these cornerstones of a modern lifestyle are associated with cities in most parts of the world. From an economic point of view, urbanization is not just a matter of moving economic activity from one place to another. Throughout the centuries, cities have acted as engines of economic growth, since they allow for labour specialization, lower the transaction cost for trade, create knowledge spillovers and (recently) allow for two careers in a family. It is also much cheaper to provide basic infrastructure, such as roads and water access, for a city population than for a rural one. But perhaps most importantly, cities act as innovation and talent hubs – intense social interaction seems to be a good breeding ground for new ideas, in business as well as in science and the arts.

So urbanization matters hugely, for our economy, for our quality of life, and for our planet. And the city structures we build now will be there for hundreds of years. Famously, Napoleon masterminded much of the current layout of central Paris more than two centuries ago. The Global Commission on the Economy and Climate gives a thought-provoking example of what's at stake: Barcelona, with its dense city structure, houses 5.33 million people on an urban area of 162 square kilometres, and its transport systems emit a total of 0.7 tons of CO_2 per person per year. Atlanta, with 5.25 million people, sprawls over 4,280 square kilometres, and its transport systems emit 7.5 tons of CO_2 per person per year – a factor 15 times higher CO_2 emission per person. The Commission also estimates that excess urban sprawl costs the US $400 billion per year in the form of higher infrastructure investments, higher cost of providing public services and accident and pollution damages. Chinese research of 261 Chinese cities suggests that labour productivity would rise 8.8 per cent if employment density doubled.[5] So enormous economic and environmental values are at stake.

The contrast between the importance of urban planning and how it happens in reality could not be starker. Most city growth is based on rudimentary planning, and most cities come nowhere close to having the analytic resources for sophisticated urban planning. In a 2013 report, the World Bank estimated that only about 20 per cent of the world's 150 largest cities had even basic tools for low-carbon planning in place. Financing is another massive issue: in the developing world, only 4 per cent of the 500 largest cities have a credit rating of BBB or higher (i.e. deemed credit-worthy), and hence developing world cities by and large do not have access to international capital markets.[6]

What does this mean for the arguments in this book? It means that the stakes for economy and environment are high and increasing, that urbanization could in principle be a strong enabler of a net-positive economy, but also that on the current trajectory, cities are growing into 'more of the old' rather than the infrastructure of a new better economy.

10.2 Digitization – of just about everything

In Bangladesh in late 2004, sixth-grader Nadia failed her upper-secondary school entrance test in mathematics. Having none of it, her mother called in cousin Sal, living in the US, and known in the family for having a head for numbers. Cousin Sal – or Salman Khan, to give him his full name– was happy to help. Using Yahoo!'s Doodle notepad tool, he worked remotely with Nadia, and helped her to pass the test with flying colours. The word of Sal's magic got around in the family, and soon the requests for his help far outgrew the few hours of spare time his job as a hedge fund manager allowed him. He started to automate the process by recording YouTube videos in which he explained key mathematics concepts while simultaneously drawing equations and calculations. The pick-up was instant. A man with a new-found mission, Salman Khan left his job and started Khan Academy, a not-for-profit organization aiming to bring 'a free world-class education for anyone anywhere'. Since those early days, Khan Academy has grown explosively. In 2015 it had 15 million students every month who had collectively solved more than 3 billion problems. In 2015, a total of more than 5,000 courses in everything from mathematics to physics, chemistry, languages, history and art are now available free of charge in 23 languages (some courses up to 65 languages).[7] The course material is also used in more than 20,000 classrooms around the world.

The success has allowed Khan to attract high-profile donors such as Bill Gates, Google and Carlos Slim, allowing him to scale even further. 'The numbers get really crazy when you look at the impact per dollar [...] We have a $7 million operating budget and we are reaching, over the course of a year, about 10 million students in a meaningful way',

Khan said in 2012. That is less than 1 dollar per student, and less than 1 cent per problem solved.[8,9]

Fascinating as the Khan Academy story is, it is of course only one out of an array of examples of how new technology is disrupting our economy. Many books have been written about this already, and most of us literally see the development at our fingertips every day as we discover new apps for our smartphones, with functionality we did not even dream about until we saw it. So our only ambitions with this section are to inspire you, make the point that we seem to be approaching a tipping point and discuss what this means for our argument of an accretive, three-pillar economy.

In *The Second Machine Age*,[10] Erik Brynjolfsson and Andrew McAfee argue that development has now reached a point where 'just about everything' can be digitized, and that the global economy is at the cusp of a fundamental digital shift. They – and many others – argue this will lead to a very different economy. Since the new digital technologies are general purpose, with a very wide applicability across our economy, they argue that the impacts will be as big as those of the steam engine or electrification.

Let's look at the education sector again. At university level, one of the online pioneers was Stanford professor Sebastian Thrun. In 2011, he started to offer his course on Artificial Intelligence (AI) online. Instead of the normal 200 students, by the time the course was due to start, a staggering 160,000 students had signed up from all over the world. 'It absolutely blew my mind', said Thrun. Even more impressive, a total of 23,000 of the students eventually completed the demanding course – another record.[11] And with 23,000 graduating students, the cost per student was close to nothing, even at a world-class institution such as Stanford.[12] Since then, Massive Open Online Courses (MOOCs) has become an established term, and many world-leading universities have followed suit in one way or another. Harvard and MIT were part of founding edX, a non-profit organization aiming to bring excellent online education to the world, and Princeton and Stanford are part of Coursera, with a similar purpose. In total edX reports 5 million students enrolled in more than 800 courses and Coursera has 15 million students choosing from 1,100 courses.[13,14,15,16]

Online education will certainly not be a panacea for all the issues plaguing the education sector, such as low motivation among some student groups, and perhaps won't bring all the benefits of a 'physical' education. But already today, close-to-free education at all levels and on thousands of topics, offered by some of the world's best professors and universities, is available to billions of students all over the world. When compared to the old system, which in 2012 cost $4.5 trillion globally,[17] and where a higher education comes at $50,000 a year, it is easy to believe that tomorrow's education system will be vastly different.

Or look at lawyers. Sifting through documentation is a big part of commercial legal work. For large corporate cases, millions of documents need to be screened, keeping a busload of junior lawyers busy for months. Now, eDiscovery software is available to do the same task, but instead of junior lawyers, it uses AI to sift through the documents in search of specific formulations, cost estimates, arguments or proof that a client was aware or not aware of certain information at a specific point in time. The cost is a very small fraction of that of manual labour, the software is much more accurate – even eager lawyers fresh out of law school get tired – and the lead time is dramatically shorter. Mike Lynch, the CEO of software company Autonomy, estimates that for document review, one lawyer equipped with his software package can now get as much work done as 500 without it.[18]

Or look at mathematics and engineering. Advanced mathematical software and Computer Aided Design (CAD) is nothing new, but in many areas, the software has now become so user-friendly that many construction tasks start to feel like building a virtual Lego. Another fun example: MicroBlink's *PhotoMath* now allows maths students to simply point their smartphone camera at an equation, and PhotoMath will instantly solve it for them. Not only that, PhotoMath will also explain the key intermediate steps involved in solving the equation. As of 2015, PhotoMath is only available up to high-school mathematics, but it is not hard to imagine how it will quickly be upgraded to solve ever more complicated problems.

So we're already far beyond automation of simple repetitive tasks, and are now automating knowledge work at a fast pace. At the research frontier, machine-learning approaches – where the system itself develops new strategies by observing and analysing its surroundings – are becoming more practical by the day. In March 2016, Google's 'AlphaGo' system beat human Go champion Lee Sedol in what was seen as a landmark victory for AI. Go is far too complex for the sort of 'brute force' calculation of millions of combinations that have allowed chess programs to beat humans since the 1990s. So instead AlphaGo has been programmed to figure out its own Go strategy by observing other games and players – apparently very successfully. Add to this the encyclopedic knowledge that IBM's 'Watson' showed when it thoroughly beat long-standing human Jeopardy champion Ken Jennings in 2011, and it gets difficult to come up with any human endeavour that is completely out of reach for computers.[19]

In the not-too-distant future, robots might also play a big role in helping us to translate computer-generated insight and knowledge into intelligent and versatile action. Did you know there are already robots that can cooperate to put together IKEA furniture? Or that in RoboCup, the annual world soccer cup for robots, robots can now dribble, pass, shoot and interact with each other. There are drones designed to follow action sports, and a hotel in Nagasaki, Japan staffed by robots.

While robotics has been slower to materialize than the science fiction movies of the 1960s predicted – the total global robot market is still only ~200,000 units per year[20] – researchers can now start to see how and when robots could be part of our everyday lives. In the words of Daniela Rus, director of MIT's Computer Science and Artificial Intelligence Lab: 'Creating a world of pervasive, customized robots is a major challenge, but its scope is not unlike that of the problem computer scientists faced nearly three decades ago, when they dreamed of a world where computers would become integral parts of human societies [...] It has become possible to imagine the leap from the personal computer to the personal robot.'[21]

Let us stop the list of examples there, and just make the final point that these new technologies are also adopted at record speed. The radio, with broadcasting starting in the 1920s, took thirty-eight years to reach 50 million users. For TV, reaching the same number of users took thirteen years, for the iPod four years, for the internet three years and for Facebook a mere year.[22] By 2014, a total of 1.2 million apps had been created for the iPhone and iPad, and the total number of downloads was 75 billion, approximately 10 per person globally.[23]

12 highest-impact technology areas according to the McKinsey Global Institute

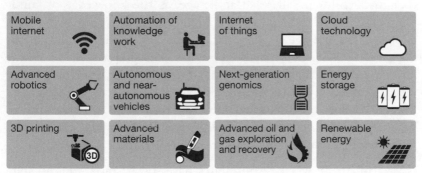

SOURCE: Manyika et al (2013)

Fig 10.1

10.3 Demographics – a world of 11 billion?

We are likely heading towards a world of 11 billion people by 2100. That was the startling conclusion of the UN's global population review published in 2015.[24]

Taking a step back: ever since the UN's last major population report in 2004, the conventional wisdom has been that we are heading towards 9 billion people.[25] In the last decade, many reports have been written about how to feed 9 billion, how the 9 billion will all want modern lifestyles and how to fit the 9 billion into the planet's carbon budget. The tone of many of these reports has been that providing a good life for 9 billion without destroying the planet is a real stretch but will be possible. Now changing 9 billion to 11 billion turns everything on its head, and makes the global resource equation even more difficult to balance. Compared to today's 7.3 billion people, the new forecast essentially doubles the amount of additional farmland, freshwater, housing, transport and energy that will need to be provided.

In Africa, children matter. That is the upshot of why the forecast has changed – Africa explains almost all of the global increase from 9 to 11 billion. The pattern in most parts of the world is that when societies advance, fertility rates quickly decrease, as parents can start to trust that their children will reach adult age, as the knowledge of family planning improves and as children are not the only retirement scheme. Globally, the average woman today has 2.5 children, only half as many as 1960–65, and in many countries demographers have seen the fertility rates quickly decrease from 4–6 children per woman to 2–3 in just a decade or two. In countries like Nepal, Myanmar, Azerbaijan and Mexico, fertility rates are today around 2.3. And many rich countries have the problem of too low fertility rates. In Germany, the US and Japan, for instance, fertility rates are at 1.4, 1.9 and 1.4 respectively.[26,27]

Not so in Africa, where fertility rates have so far stayed high in spite of economic development. Nobody quite knows why, espically given that women state they want small families. So theories include gender roles and other cultural phenomena and also – luckily – HIV/AIDS has claimed fewer victims than assumed in 2004. The UN now forecasts that 4.4 billion people will call Africa home by 2100. This is an increase of more than 2 billion from the previous forecast, and a quadrupling compared to today's African population of 1.2 billion. If the forecast is right, it means Africa will grow to be almost as populous as Asia, and four times more populous than Europe and North America put together.

In parallel, the advanced economies of the world are coming to an important turning point already in 2016. For the first time since 1950, their population between 18 and 65 (wrongly called working-age population) will shrink, not only as a proportion of the total population but in absolute numbers. By 2050 it will have shrunk by 5 per cent on average, but the shrinking is much bigger in many of today's advanced economies: in Germany and Italy 23 per cent, in Japan 28 per cent, in China 21 per cent. The only exception among the world's largest economies is the US, where the working population is expected to grow 10 per cent in absolute terms until 2050, but still decrease as a share of the total population.[28]

Demographic changes are often thought of as slow, predictable and therefore manageable. But these shifts are dramatic, and the implications will be far-reaching. For our story, they mean an even higher importance of shifting to a net-positive growth model, and a higher importance of getting growth right in Africa.

Chapter 11

Digitizing the physical world – the next revolution

Our intuition about the future is linear. But the reality of information technology is exponential, and that makes a profound difference. If I take 30 steps linearly, I get to 30. If I take 30 steps exponentially, I get to a billion.

The Singularity is Near, Ray Kurzweil

Mobility, nutrition and housing are next in line to be disrupted. Having looked through these huge product value chains in detail during the last year, it is hard for us to come to any other conclusion. For almost every large segment in these value chains, there is not only one but several blockbuster technologies and business models that are commercially attractive or close to it, and that look to have a profound impact over the coming 5–10 years.

This future disruption is even more important for our society than the previously digitized industries (primarily information and trans-action industries such as banking, photography, entertainment, retail, publishing), since these value chains are so large, so close to the core of our human needs and so crucial for our economy and environment. To give one headline number: $60 trillion will be invested in public infrastructure in these three value chains during the next ten years.[1,2]

This chapter will use the value chains of mobility, food and housing to paint the somewhat schizophrenic picture of amazing progress on the one hand, but which on the other hand is currently leading us in a doubtful direction due to lack of steering.

11.1 Next generation mobility – beyond the car ride

Let's look first at mobility. Sharing, electrification and interconnectivity are all massively important trends that are already scaling, and autonomous vehicles could soon be a commercial reality. Higher utilization of cars in sharing schemes, in turn, will make lighter materials like aluminium and carbon fibre more attractive, and challenge steel as the 'obvious' material choice for many car components. Each one of these new technologies could individually have a disruptive impact on the car industry, and in fact there are many global leaders, such as Uber or Tesla, which have built their success on just one of these levers. Together, the trends make for a landslide, which could lower the cost per passenger-kilometre in cars by up to 80 per cent over the next decades. This, is turn, will mean a very different mobility system, since cars account for the vast majority of motorized ground transport in most countries (more than 80 per cent in Europe, for instance).[3] And as we saw in the waste chapter, there is no shortage of inefficiencies to attack in our transport system.

Let us give some key examples and figures for the biggest trends to show the size of what is happening.

Sharing. Car-sharing businesses are thriving across the world, thanks to smartphones, big data and an increased acceptance of sharing among a new generation of consumers. In Europe, for instance, car sharing grew 40 per cent per year between 2010 and 2013, and in the US 24 per cent between 2012 and 2013.[4] It is amazing to see the many flavours of this simple concept that are emerging:

- Uber, Lyft, Hailo and Kabbee are all promoting e-hailing services – on-demand hiring of a private or shared-occupancy car via a service that matches passengers and drivers.
- Car sharing through a fleet operator offers on-demand, short-term rentals of cars owned and managed by the fleet operator. This is growing so fast that even car manufacturers have decided to invest, in spite of the risk of cannibalizing on their own car sales: well-known examples are AutoLib collaborating with Renault, DriveNow owned by BMW/Sixt, Quicar owned by Volkswagen, and Car2Go owned by Mercedes-Benz.

- Peer-to-peer car sharing such as Drivy is a variation on the fleet model. Users share individually-owned vehicles on an online platform.
- App-enabled car-pooling, such as BlaBlaCar, links a non-professional driver with passengers to fill empty seats.
- Finally, sharing models are also popping up in transit transport, with shuttle bus services such as Via, Chariot, RidePal and Summon.

Given that today's car fleet utilization is a meagre 2 per cent, it is not difficult to imagine that these businesses will continue their rapid growth for quite some time. Longer term, it will be interesting to see if they will be primarily a city phenomenon, or if they can also be successful in suburbs and rural areas, and whether large consumer segments are willing to give up the freedom – and, to some, status – of an individually-owned car.[5]

Electrification. Electric vehicles (EV) today cost more upfront than cars with an internal combustion engine (ICE), but EV prices are falling rapidly due to major improvements in battery costs (the main cost item of EVs). Once bought, EVs often cost 50–80 per cent less to operate, since electricity is most often cheaper than petrol, electric powertrains are several times more efficient and EVs have far fewer components that require maintenance. All this means that EVs have lower lifetime costs than ICEs now have for many segments, and this cost advantage will only grow. As an example, Tesla revealed in early April 2016 that it plans mass production of its Model 3 by 2017. At a starting price of about US $30,000,[6] the Model 3 would have a range of 340 km, and thus be price-competitive with many ICE cars even on upfront sticker price, and much more cost-competitive over its lifetime. And as anyone who has owned a good EV knows, they are fun to drive, spacious, convenient, and many expect them to last much longer as they have fewer wear-and-tear components. Tesla is of course not alone: most major car manufacturers now have all-electric models, or have stated that they will release such models in the next 1–2 years. Imagine what a change this will be for the car industry, as well as for the oil industry.

Autonomous driving. Once the stuff of science-fiction novels, self-driving vehicles are now quickly becoming a reality. Google's self-driving car may be the most famous, having logged more than

1.5 million miles at time of writing,[7] and they are aiming to launch a commercial product by 2017, but Google is far from the only player in the game. Tesla's Model S now has functionality that makes it close to autonomous on highways. Audi, Mercedes-Benz, BMW and Volvo are likely to introduce fully automated models to the market around 2020. And the cost is dropping fast. Today, a 70 per cent autonomous Mercedes-Benz with active blind spot assistance, lane maintenance and collision prevention commands a price premium of only €2,500.[8] With sufficient penetration, autonomous vehicles will improve the mobility system dramatically. They have optimal acceleration and deceleration and can convoy with other autonomous vehicles, which could reduce congestion by more than 50 per cent by closing the space between cars (1.5 metres versus 3–4 car lengths today) and at the same time improve energy efficiency. They can cut accidents by 90 per cent – saving lives and reducing insurance costs.[9] Google's driverless cars have logged only eleven minor accidents[10] – most of them caused by human error – over 1.5 million miles. In fact, technology outperforms human drivers so much that it begs the question: how long will humans be allowed to drive around and cause serious accidents? Driverless cars will also open up individualized mobility to segments that today don't have good access to it: the young, the old, the disabled. And perhaps most important of all, people will be able to use their transit time productively. Even the shorter step to semi-autonomous and interconnected cars would deliver many of the above benefits.

New materials, and looped. BMW i3 and others are using carbon fibre to create lightweight vehicles with better aerodynamics and much longer life. Renault's disassembly and remanufacturing plant at Choisy le Roi is the company's most profitable industrial site. It reuses 43 per cent of carcasses and recycles 48 per cent in foundries to produce new parts. Both are examples of new and recycled materials coming into play in ways enabled by the trends above: when cars last much longer and are utilized more, expensive lightweight materials become more attractive, which in turn increases incentives for remanufacturing and recycling.

Taken together, how will these mobility trends play out? They will reduce the cost per passenger-kilometre drastically, maybe by as much as 80 per cent according to our modelling, and in parallel reduce the environmental footprint dramatically. New cars employing the technologies described above could very realistically be net-positive. And they should at the same time substantially increase convenience, for instance allowing you to catch up on emails while your car is driving you to work, or through speedier access to a taxi service. Everything else being equal, this will make individualized transport much more attractive and increase demand: people will be willing to commute longer distances, there will be a shift from public to individualized transport and underserved segments will travel more. If historic correlations between price decreases and demand increases hold, decreasing the price of individualized transport will substantially increase demand.

At first sight, this could be a good thing, since there are certainly unmet needs for convenient and cheap individualized transport. But given that most of this demand increase would happen in larger cities, where congestion, land shortage and urban sprawl are already major problems, this would in practice negate many of the benefits. Even a traffic increase of just 10–20 per cent would have major congestion implications in many big cities.

The challenge for cities and countries, then, is to promote the new beneficial technologies and business models, but at the same time hinder the negative system effects. The key to this, is of course, better system integration: public transport systems should be upgraded in tandem with cars, modal integration should be improved so that the car becomes only a 'last-mile' solution, road systems should be adapted and traffic volumes should in many cases be controlled through congestion charging or other means.

These measures are all possible, but judging by history, improvements in car technology will be achieved much faster than system integration improvements, which require political majorities and public budgets. In the *Growth Within* report, we modelled the impact of the current development trajectory, based on historic demand elasticities and traffic modelling experience. The results indeed showed many of the initial benefits were negated by system effects.

11.2 New nutrition – every hectare counts

Let's now turn to the nutrition system. This is also plagued by waste and environmental degradation on an enormous scale, as we saw in Chapter 4. Topsoil is eroding at an alarmingly high rate globally, and the global flows of nitrogen and phosphorus are seriously disturbed.[11] With the world's population potentially growing towards 11 billion, this is an alarming situation.

Luckily, there are new technologies and agricultural practices available that could change this in important ways, turning the food value chain net-positive. Our conclusion after reviewing a fair number of these novelties is that the food value chain is not heading towards the same all-will-be-different transformation as city mobility, but many parts of the food value chain are changing fast, and it is fair to say that the tools required to address the major problems are now known and available. Let's review a few of the most important ones:

Precision agriculture. The tractor slowly pulls BlueRivers' lettuce robot over the vast field of seedlings. It is time to cull, ensuring every remaining lettuce head gets enough space and sunlight. Just a few years back, this would have meant busloads of manual workers, but no longer. The robot's cameras photograph each seedling it passes over. Its image processing software determines which of the seedlings within the allotted space are healthiest by looking at their individual size, colour and dark spots. It measures the distance between the healthiest seedlings, determines which seedlings should be weeded out, and does so. It also senses nutrient levels, and dispatches the appropriate amount of fertilizer to each individual seedling. A microcosm of an agricultural revolution that has just started to bite. 'Precision agriculture', as it is called, applies robotics, big data, remote sensing, drones and satellite positioning data to make agriculture a science, whereby each plant and square metre is treated individually and advanced statistics are used to determine the best treatment. These technologies simultaneously increase yields and reduce inputs of fertilizer and water, often substantially.

Today, 70–80 per cent of new farm equipment sold includes some precision agriculture component, and the 'smartness' is increasing fast.[12] Other technological solutions could further increase resource efficiency. For example, vapour-transfer irrigation systems enable saltwater irrigation by using low-cost plastic tubes so water vapour, but not water or solutes, can pass.[13]

This is all very promising, but – you guessed it – these efficiencies are unlikely to be enough: global use of synthetic fertilizer increased 20 per cent from 2000 to 2010. In our modelling, even taking the new technology into account, on the current development path it will continue to grow. Volume growth beats efficiencies.

Organic farming is growing – in Europe by 6 per cent per year – but still only represents a minor fraction of all land under cultivation.

Closing nutrient loops. At the other end of the food value chain, an enormous amount of nutrients and energy is released as food waste, organic industrial waste, human and animal waste. The potential to extract valuable biochemicals, nutrients and energy from these waste streams is huge. But as a global average, most of these waste streams are burned for energy, the ashes used as fillers or put on landfills. There is momentum to capture a larger share of the nutrients and the value in parts of the world: for example, phosphorus recovered from waste in Europe amounts to almost 30 per cent of its use of synthetic phosphorus fertilizer.[14] And in the UK, 66 per cent of sewage sludge is treated in 146 anaerobic digestion plants to produce biogas, while another 175 plants produce bio-energy from solid waste.[15] But overall, we are not heading for anything like the bio-economy vision laid out in Part II – this is a turn in direction that still lies ahead.

Even better is to not generate any waste in the first place. To address the 20 per cent of food wasted from farm to retail, companies have started to leverage big data and IT to take inventory management to the next level. Tesco's weather team better forecasts local sales and required stock levels using local weather forecasts. SAP's dynamic consumer pricing system changes item prices in real time, based on availability and expiration date of the product. The Co-op supermarket chain in the UK has automated its replenishment system for fresh food.[16] Consumers waste a further 11 per cent of food in Europe. Organizations like WRAP in the UK have invested a lot of effort in reducing consumer food waste, and estimate that their various local campaigns and other interventions have reduced food waste by 15–80 per cent.[17] Several companies have also developed closed-loop systems that use by-products or the waste from one process as input for other processes. *The Plant* in Chicago has created a carefully balanced system whereby a production mix of carefully selected tilapia, vegetables, beer and kombucha tea exactly balance waste and feedstock needs. Combined with a commercial kitchen and an anaerobic digestion chamber to convert remaining waste into power and steam, this is a fully closed-loop, zero-waste system.[18] So inspirational and far-reaching solutions exist, but so far, they represent a very small share of the total market.

Restoration of natural capital. There is an enormous amount of degraded land available globally, between 1 and 3 billion hectares depending on how one defines 'degraded'. By comparison, the total amount of land under cultivation globally is 1.7 billion hectares. Restoration of large, damaged ecosystems is possible. The most famous example is probably the Loess plateau in China, where 1.5 million hectares of degraded land were restored. This project lifted more than 2.5 million people out of poverty, almost tripling their income, by replacing low-value agricultural commodities from low-productivity land with high-value products from high-productivity land. The shift increased per capita grain output 60 per cent, doubled the perennial vegetation cover from 17 to 34 per cent, increased employment from 70 to 87 per cent, reduced flooding risk and increased the availability of water, biodiversity and carbon absorption.[19] The Loess plateau was a government-led programme, but there is also a small but growing set of companies that make a business out of restoration: SLM Partners, for instance, acquires and manages rural land on behalf of institutional investors and delivers financial returns and environmental benefits by scaling up regenerative, ecological farming systems. And the Land Life Company provides low-cost, biodegradable products to improve the ecological and aesthetic value of land as part of large restoration and landscaping projects in dry climates like Spain. So again, the potential is huge for increased food supply, carbon absorption and better local ecosystems, but it is not being captured.

In summary, where do all these trends leave us, and what development should we expect from the global food system? To us, it is again a schizophrenic picture where fantastic technologies and approaches are available, more than capable of getting the food-value chain to net-positive, but still the sheer demand growth and desire to get the last kilogram of output from every hectare every year lead towards ever more intense one-way agricultural practices. Precision agriculture and digital supply chains will reduce synthetic fertilizer use per unit of food produced, and will reduce food waste. But given the population increase and better living conditions, absolute volumes of irrigation water and fertilizers are still likely to increase. And the efforts to recover nutrients, stop topsoil depletion and restore degraded ecosystems remain embryonic. So in total, in spite of the opportunities, the global food system remains on a highly unsustainable development trajectory, which is a major problem.

11.3 Housing – another brick in the wall

When they came home from work, the neighbours could hardly believe their eyes. Ten new houses had been erected in less than 24 hours, and the construction crew had already moved on to the next construction site. This happened in April 2014 in Suzhou, China, and it was Chinese construction company WinSun which had used its giant 3D printers to print and assemble the ten houses, each of about 195 square metres, at a cost of less than €5,000 per house.[20] The 'ink' they use for their 3D printers is a mixture of dry cement and construction waste, which uses 30–60 per cent less virgin material than traditional construction – an enormous environmental gain – and the 3D printed sections come with prepared cavities for electric wiring, plumbing and insulation. WinSun is growing fast, and plans to open 100 recycling factories in China to transform waste into cost-efficient building material. This is just one example that the technology disruption has now reached the construction and housing value chain. In total, we have identified five major developments that will reshape this value chain fundamentally over the next decades:

Sharing and virtualization rapidly increasing utilization and decreasing demand for new construction. Online house-sharing company Airbnb now has more than one million spaces listed in more than 34,000 cities across more than 190 countries. On New Year's Eve 2014, over 0.5 million people stayed in Airbnb spaces – 4 per cent of total global hotel capacity. The list of Airbnb spaces grew 90 per cent a year between July 2011 and the end of 2014. At that rate, Airbnb listings would overtake the total number of hotel rooms worldwide in four or five years, and spell major trouble for the traditional hotel industry.[21] Perhaps reflecting the shift, Airbnb's valuation at over €9 billion also makes it worth more than incumbent leaders such as Wyndham and Hyatt. A similar development can be observed for office space: flexible seating, desk-sharing, office hotelling, tele-working and audio and video conferencing are all major trends in the real estate marketplace. As an example, a full 39 per cent of IBM's 300,000 staff members worldwide work in a remote environment, and the staff-to-desk ratio has increased to an average of 12:1, providing global real estate savings of around €1 billion over the last ten years.[22] This trend is developing rapidly and could accelerate in the coming years. In a 2012 survey of 500 construction and building management CEOs, they predicted a 55 per cent reduction in average office space per employee within five years, thanks to tele-working and office sharing. Imagine what this could do to the construction industry, especially in mature markets where growth is feeble in the first place.

Industrial production and 3D printing. Moving construction towards factory-based industrial processes is already helping companies cut costs by 30 per cent or more, and shorten delivery times by 40 per cent.[23] While not a new idea, industrialization has much untapped potential, and the 3D printing process with its extreme versatility might well be what is required to move industrialization to a tipping point. Consider the Broad Group. Off-site production of modules in a factory (up to 93 per cent of construction hours off-site) enabled this Chinese company to erect a 30-storey hotel in 15 days, after only six months of industrial activity. The cost was low: €900–1,100 per square metre, or 10–30 per cent less than conventional construction, with no sacrifice in quality (resistance to a magnitude-9 earthquake and five times higher energy efficiency than average buildings).

Modularity and durability. A big part of getting buildings to net-positive is to make building envelopes last longer, as this is where most of the material and embedded energy lies. This, in turn, requires more interior flexibility, as tenant needs change over the decades. Durability and modularity often go hand-in-hand. Modular design typically reuses and refurbishes some 80 per cent of the components in the envelope of a building that can stand for 100 years or more, infusing life into unattractive buildings and avoiding demolition. This is particularly relevant in the developed world: 80 per cent of Europeans, for instance, live in buildings that are at least 30 years old.

Energy-positive buildings. While buildings have historically been one of the largest energy-using sectors, radically better energy management solutions combined with local energy production now makes energy-positive buildings a very real opportunity for new construction in many contexts. Often better building design can achieve heating and cooling energy savings of up to 90 per cent, with an average upfront investment of only 10 per cent more than traditional construction (which is often more than paid back over the lifetime of the building). Yet still only a small minority of all buildings globally are built to energy-positive standards globally. Retrofitting an existing building into an energy-positive one is more difficult, but solutions to reduce energy consumption by 20–40 per cent in existing houses, such as better insulation and better HVAC (Heating, Ventilation, Air Conditioning) systems, are becoming more prevalent.[24] Energy management tools (smart meters and connected devices, lighting controls, smart thermostats) are growing at an annual rate of 20 per cent. Water consumption is moving in a similar direction. Green roofs, for instance, can capture and filter rainwater, which is then used to flush toilets or for outdoor purposes.

Urban planning. Changes such as shifting land-use patterns, taking advantage of inner-city vacant land, and promoting compact urban growth can reduce land use by as much as 75 per cent, compared with a sprawl scenario.[25] Barcelona offers an example. Its compact growth shaped by smart urban planning makes its CO_2 emissions 10 times lower and its land consumption 26 times lower than the city of Atlanta, which has a similar population of five million people.[26] But in spite of this enormous potential, only about 20 per cent of all cities have access to even basic low-carbon planning tools, according to the World Bank.[27]

So buildings also can clearly become net-positive, through a combination of positive energy, better utilization, longer life, better urban planning and reused building materials. And most of these actions are profitable today, over the lifetime of the building. But again, we see a picture where many attractive opportunities are left underexploited, and where the value chain overall develops in a direction that is far from optimal.

This completes our tour of the three largest physical value chains. There are several common denominators: a huge current environmental footprint, disruptive technologies, and business models that could change this under economically attractive conditions, but primarily the product-level innovations have momentum, and the total development of the value chains points towards increased resource use rather than the opposite.

Chapter 12

Disrupted – for better or for worse?

'Would you tell me, please, which way I ought to go from here?'
'That depends a good deal on where you want to get to,' said the Cat.
'I don't much care where –' said Alice.
'Then it doesn't matter which way you go,' said the Cat.

Lewis Carroll, *Alice's Adventures in Wonderland*

Let's lift ourselves a few levels now and look at what overall impact the technology disruption could have on our economy and societies. Let's review what impact it could have on economic growth, employment, income equality and resource demand. Each of these topics is the subject of endless dissertations, books and reports, so we'll only provide an overview. But we believe this overview is already enough to lead to an important conclusion: that the technology disruption is a beast in need of taming.

12.1 Waiting for tailwind – technology for future growth

The impact of technology on economic growth is a hotly debated topic. On the face of it, history seems to be in favour of those who argue that the technology impact on growth will be no bigger than in the past. In the US for instance, the average output per worker grew by 2.3 per cent per annum from 1891 to 1972, only to then slow down to 1.4 per cent per annum from 1972 to 1996. For eight years until 2004 it then jumped up to 2.5 per cent per annum, only to again slow to 1.3 per cent per annum from 2004 to 2012.[1] So a slowing trend, in spite of ever more accumulated knowledge, ever more university graduates and ever more investments into research and development. This would suggest that today's innovations are actually *less* impactful than yesterday's.

Technology optimists have several explanations for why these numbers don't reflect reality. First, GDP statistics do not account well for the huge value created by free services such as digital entertainment and information, nor do they capture well the huge consumer surplus[2] of new technologies, which have become more important over recent decades. For instance, consumers might have been willing to pay as much or more for email as for physical mail, but since email services are often provided for free, their value does not get captured in GDP. The same is true for much of the services of Google, Facebook, Skype, Spotify, Instagram and many others. And there are of course also many new services that are paid, but where the real willingness to pay might have been much higher (new medical treatments for instance). Second, optimists claim there is a time lag: while the technologies themselves develop at breakneck speed, companies, industries and consumers need time to integrate them. Once consumers and companies get used to the novelties, we will see a compound positive effect.

On the other side of this debate, there is a group of technology sceptics. They argue that the innovations of today, impressive as they are, have much less importance for our everyday lives and our economy than the innovations of the 1900s. In 'Same As It Ever Was', Martin Wolf (2015) lists some of the groundbreaking technologies of the past century, such as refrigerators, vaccines, motor vehicles, telephones, flushing toilets, electric lighting and radio. Next to such innovations, he asks, 'who cares about Facebook or the iPad?'[3] Technology sceptics acknowledge that consumer surplus is not captured in GDP statistics but argue that this is nothing new – the consumer surpluses created from fresh food (enabled by refrigerators) or good lighting (enabled by electrification) were probably at least as important, and were also not captured in the GDP statistics of the 1900s. Robert Gordon, one of the leading sceptics, argues that since 2000, when computers and the internet were already mainstream, there have been no fundamental changes to either labour productivity or standard of living.[4]

Gordon quotes a thought experiment he often uses to illustrate the importance of the innovations of yesterday compared to those of today:

> You are required to make a choice between option A and option B. With option A you are allowed to keep 2002 electronic technology,

including your Windows 98 laptop accessing Amazon, and you can keep running water and indoor toilets, but you can't use anything invented since 2002. Option B is that you get everything invented in the past decade right up to Facebook, Twitter, and the iPad, but you have to give up running water and indoor toilets. You have to haul the water into your dwelling and carry out the waste. Even at 3 a.m. on a rainy night, your only toilet option is a wet and perhaps muddy walk to the outhouse. Which option do you choose? I have posed this imaginary choice to several audiences in speeches, and the usual reaction is a guffaw, a chuckle, because the preference for Option A is so obvious. The audience realizes that it has been trapped into recognition that *just one* of the many late nineteenth-century inventions is more important than the portable electronic devices of the past decade on which they have become so dependent.

The debate will probably rage for a long time. Our view is that the evidence of long-term declining growth rates in the developed world is so convincing that it takes a real leap of faith to believe that technology, on its current trajectory, will help restore growth to historic levels. This is also consistent with the modelling of the largest value chains that we presented in Part II. There, technology, left to its own devices, had only a marginal positive impact on growth, and it was only when combined with active measures to integrate it well that the benefits materialized.

12.2 Employment and equality – headwinds ahead

On employment, there is less ambiguity: there is reasonable agreement that the technology disruption will lead to a major destruction of today's jobs. Look at taxi drivers: there are approximately 250,000 in the US alone. When driverless cars become a reality, what will happen to them? In the meantime, the Ubers and Lyfts of this world are already putting immense pressure on incumbent drivers, as their protests around the world show. Or look at bus and truck drivers, another 2.5 million of the US workforce, or at retail cashiers, another 3.5 million. A traditional mom-and-pop store typically has a turnover of $145,000 per employee.[5] Walmart is at $220,000 and Amazon at $400 million, more than a thousand times higher. A similar development is unfolding in many industries, and it is not difficult to construct a scenario where hundreds of millions of jobs are at stake.

In an ambitious 2013 study,[6] researchers at the Oxford Martin School estimated what share of US 2010 employment is at risk of computerization, through assessing 702 detailed occupations. Their startling conclusion was that 47 per cent of total US employment is at risk. Less surprisingly perhaps, they also found a correlation that less qualified and lower-paid jobs are in general at higher risk of being automated, even though many categories of knowledge work are also at risk. One exception was that many middle-income manufacturing jobs were at higher risk than low-income service jobs.

What is more contested is whether these jobs will be replaced with new ones, when, and by what types of work. On one side, people say this debate is a red herring – 'end of work' concerns have been around at least since the days of the first industrial revolution, and have never materialized. As old industries have died off, new ones have sprung up, and been able to absorb the workforce: 1.1 billion new non-farm jobs have been created in the past thirty years alone. And in most advanced economies, the population is ageing, as we discussed in Chapter 11, which means both more elderly people to take care of, and fewer young people to keep employed.

But what is different this time, the other side argues, is the scale and pace of change. It used to take a generation to roll out a new technology across the world, but today it takes only a few years. And what happens when machines that are a hundred or a thousand times faster appear not only in one or a few major industries at a time, but in dozens? Even previous transitions were often painful, and many employees never found new positions, even though the labour market overall adapted and was eventually able to accommodate the same amount of workers or more.

Perhaps the two sides are not contradictory, and what we will see is a historically big and fast transition, probably painful for some industries and occupational groups but a new equilibrium eventually arising.

The European electricity industry offers an interesting example of how quick and dramatic the transition can be. Known for its long-lived assets and stable demand, many incumbent companies argued it would take decades before new renewable technologies like wind and solar PV reached significant market share, and therefore many of them carried on with their 'old' business model. The argument was true (and still is), but it completely missed the point: the additions of renewable energy were much faster than the overall market growth. This turned the growth of incumbent technologies negative and caused overcapacity, which in turn had dramatic implications for electricity market prices, growth prospects of incumbents and share prices. The market capitalization of RWE and E.ON – two incumbents – has fallen almost 80 per cent compared to 2008.[7] Other factors have also contributed, such as the decrease in CO_2 prices and the economic recession, but the fundamental reason why other shares have fared much better than those of electric utilities is that the utilities' growth prospects are now very bleak.

Could the same happen in the automotive industry? Absolutely. One does not need to make overly aggressive assumptions for car sharing to turn sales growth of new cars negative in many parts of the world. As with electricity, this would lead to overcapacity, price wars with marginal cost pricing, and lowered share prices (as both profitability and growth take a simultaneous hit). Similarly for hotels, one does not need to assume many more years of very fast growth for Airbnb and other sharing platforms to turn the growth of the incumbent hotel industry negative in many countries. Nor for office buildings: if (when?) sharing takes off, a trend of increased utilization could quickly wipe out the growth of underlying office building construction in many parts of the world, with dramatic consequences for real estate owners and for the construction industry. So while large 'new' attractive business models are growing fast, the attractiveness of the 'old' industry models will in parallel decrease, potentially very quickly. Transition at work.

Now turning to the technology disruption's impact on income equality, that impact is less contested: most researchers seem to agree that the forces at work contribute to labour market polarization. Some even talk about a 'super-star' economy, where those individuals who are able to develop successful new technologies and companies, not least online ones, see the value of those innovations explode, since they can now quickly be scaled globally at a very low cost. Google and Facebook, for instance, had market capitalizations of $522 billion and $296 billion dollars at the end of 2015, and were founded in 1998 and 2004 respectively.[8] These are of course extreme examples, but there is also a broader trend that the highly skilled can use new technology to increase their reach, and increasingly outcompete the semi-skilled. Automation is eating into semi-qualified knowledge jobs all over the world.

We all know the results: the richest sixty-two individuals having the same combined wealth as the poorest half of the global population,[9] a middle class that is shrinking in many advanced economies and an income distribution not dissimilar to that of the early 1900s. Technology is not the only culprit, but there is plenty of research to say it is an important explanation factor.[10]

12.3 Resource demand – waiting for Kuznets

Since the technology disruptions seem to hold so much promise for the physical value chains, will they solve our resource problems? Is the best strategy for policy-makers to just let these new technologies run their course? You have probably already guessed the answer: if left alone, they will solve a part of the issue but far from the whole problem. This is for three main reasons:

First, as we saw above, primarily product-level improvements will materialize by themselves, and then only to a part of their potential. System-level opportunities such as a better integrated mobility system, circular material flows and bringing nutrients back to the fields instead of into the oceans, all require interventions to materialize. But also product-level improvements often require support to achieve their full potential, such as reserved parking spaces for shared vehicles, clear taxation and safety rules for Uber-type services, and so on.

Second, most of the new technologies in resource-related sectors reduce resource needs, sometimes dramatically. The total effect, however, is lower than one might believe, because of demand elasticity (what is sometimes called the *rebound* effect). Put simply, when resource efficiency increases, this decreases consumer costs, which in turn increases demand, and eliminates part of the original resource savings. Once consumers have installed LED lighting, for instance, leaving the lights on for another hour costs very little, and people tend to do so. The rebound effect has been extensively studied in energy efficiency, and many studies estimate that it negates 25–40 per cent of the original savings. Similarly in transport and food, if relative prices decrease by 10 per cent, research suggest demand will increase by about 5 per cent (but with wide variation depending on the situation). In buildings, the effect is even stronger: a demand increase of up to 9 per cent if relative prices decrease by 10 per cent. So there is a major unmet need for more and better food, housing and mobility that will negate a considerable share of the original savings if not managed. The total volume effect is hard to anticipate since the changes are so big (who knows how much further people would be willing to commute if they could do so in individualized driverless vehicles?). But we can be quite sure the volume increases would be significant. At first sight, most economists would say this is good news: consumer benefits increase, and the economy grows.

Third, the combined effect of population growth and wealth increase creates strong headwinds for efforts to reduce resource needs. To get a sense for how big these headwinds are, consider the following approximate global resource equation through 2050. It is broad-brushed, but we only need to get to the right orders of magnitude:

- Population increase with a factor 1:4. As we saw in Chapter 11, the UN's latest global population forecast is 10 billion by 2050, up from 7.3 today, representing an increase of nearly 40 per cent. And by 2100 we could be headed for 11 billion.
- Increase in real GDP per capita with a factor 2.0 until 2050 assuming a real GDP per capita increase of 2 percent per year on average.
- In parallel, the ecological footprint needs to be reduced from 1.6 planets today to the one planet we have – a reduction of about 38 per cent.

Multiplied together, these factors mean the world economy needs to get a factor ~4.5 more resource-productive until 2050. In our modelling of the effects for the three most important human needs in Europe (where both population growth and economic growth are comparatively low), the conclusion was that left alone, the new technologies would achieve about half of the total opportunity, and not take us onto the required improvement path. But fully exploited, as laid out in Part II, they would come a very long way towards where we need to go.

Chapter 13

Turning innovation into a force of good

Needs drive the evolution of technology every bit as much as the possibilities for fresh combination and the unearthing of phenomena. Without the presence of unmet needs, nothing novel would appear in technology.

Brian Arthur, *The Nature of Technology*

We don't need to look at technology and innovation as unpredictable forces of nature that gush over our economy with (good and bad) implications we cannot control. Instead, as a society we often get what we ask for in terms of innovation. If the right direction was set for innovation in resource-related areas, there is every reason to believe that we could see fantastic progress over the next decades, and that we could get to net-positive growth. We will argue that setting direction for the technology disruption is one of the most crucial tasks for environmental and business policy-makers in the next decade.

Those are the key points we will try to convince you of in this chapter. Then in Part IV, we will get more practical and describe how we think policy-makers and business leaders could go about this.

13.1 Net-negative versus net-positive innovation

First question: Why is the total result of all our collective innovation work so doubtful? When literally tens of millions of clever people around the world are hard at work on innovation, why are the results not undoubtedly good?

For the physical value chains this book is most concerned with, a big part of the answer lies in the type of innovation pursued. In Figure 13.1, we have illustrated the innovation mechanisms at work in many product markets.

Our current downward product innovation cycle

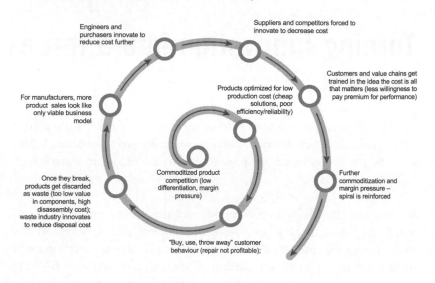

SOURCE: Authors' analysis

Fig 13.1

In most product markets, the largest segment is one of commoditized competition. The differentiation between companies is limited, and hence there is intense margin pressure. This, in turn, leads companies to design products that are optimized for production cost, not performance, since the sticker price is a more important purchasing decision criterion for many customers than the total lifecycle cost. Cheap materials and solutions are used, often compromising reliability, efficiency and product lifetime. This in turn makes single-use ownership the most viable business model. Why should customers repair a product that didn't cost much in the first place, and that is anyway likely to break down again soon anyway? And from the company's point of view, why try to develop sharing, leasing or recovery business models for a low-value product? So after the first use cycle, the product may simply be discarded as waste, since the value of its materials and components is too low for recovery, and the product has not been designed for easy disassembly. Often, different materials have been glued or welded together and toxic additives been used, making the residual value of the product zero or negative. After a full cycle, the market will be even more commoditized, and even more dominated by cheap one-time products.

Now think about the innovation – intended and unintended – that happens in the different parts of this cycle. Strategy and business development departments will think about how to increase primary sales volumes even further. Engineering and purchasing departments will try to come up with new ways of pushing down production costs. This, in turn, will force competitors and suppliers to decrease their production costs. Customers will get used to the idea that products don't last and are not worth repairing, and their willingness to pay a quality premium next time will certainly not increase. The whole reuse and recycling value chain will not develop much; what could have been secondary production, where materials and components are reused or remanufactured, instead becomes waste management, with the objective function of disposal at the lowest cost per ton, rather than capture of as much material value as possible.

This competition dynamic is of course not at work in all markets, and we have simplified a bit, but in our experience, many product markets are dominated by a large commodity segment where one can observe much of this dynamic. And of course, there are a lot of things to say about this innovation as well: it makes products cheaper, and allows consumers to afford more.

The issue of cheap products that quickly end up in the bin is of course not a new one, so why do we bring it up? The point we want to make is this: a large part of current global innovation investments is locked into such a downward spiral. If this is how we spend our enormous innovation investments, we should not be surprised that what we get is ever more cheap products, that product flows continue to be one-way, and that natural capital costs keep soaring.

Now contrast this with the dynamics at work in the positive innovation cycle below. If companies compete on lifetime cost and performance, that is where innovation resources will be deployed. Customers will feel they have custody of a valuable product, will get it repaired when it breaks down and will expect it to have a second-hand value after a use cycle. Sharing and leasing business models will be much more attractive to explore, since they will pay off much better. Engineering departments will spend time thinking about how to increase the repairability of a product, and how an even bigger part of the product value can be retained at the end of a use cycle, through better design choices. Marketing departments will spend their resources convincing customers to try out new business models, and promoting the durability and high performance of their products. Finally, the waste management industry will transform into a secondary material industry, which competes on secondary material sales, rather than waste disposal at lowest cost.

A positive product innovation cycle

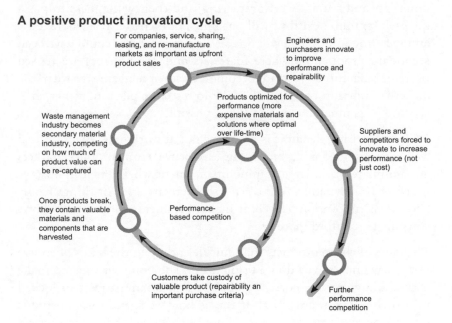

For companies, service, sharing, leasing, and re-manufacture markets as important as upfront product sales

Engineers and purchasers innovate to improve performance and repairability

Products optimized for performance (more expensive materials and solutions where optimal over life-time)

Waste management industry becomes secondary material industry, competing on how much of product value can be re-captured

Suppliers and competitors forced to innovate to increase performance (not just cost)

Once products break, they contain valuable materials and components that are harvested

Performance-based competition

Customers take custody of valuable product (repairability an important purchase criteria)

Further performance competition

Fig 13.2

It is easy to see how different the innovation investments and innovation results are in the two cycles, and how the myriad of innovation decisions in the two cycles reinforce each other to create a downward or upward spiral. The downward version creates an ever stronger lock-in towards increased material use and one-way products. The upward version creates innovation investments towards highly utilized products that are optimized for performance, and a circular material system. Net-positive innovation, in our language.

Of course, getting from one dynamic to another is far from easy. We will discuss this matter more below, but let us for now conclude how important it is to get into the right type of innovation dynamic.

13.2 Innovation – can it be steered?

The romantic view of innovation is still pervasive in the public debate and in policymaking. We are born and raised with stories of lonely geniuses and eccentric entrepreneurs, and their amazing ability to create new products and industries out of thin air. And what's not to admire about the Wright brothers, Marie Curie, Thomas Edison or their modern counterparts such as Steve Jobs, Bill Gates and Elon Musk. The best society can do to have more of their great innovations, the thinking goes, is to create fertile ground in the form of adequate IP protection, a good financing system and a well-educated workforce. In short, society can create enabling conditions, but innovation itself is seen as unpredictable and unmanageable, and by implication, so is the overall direction of technology and innovation.

This romantic view of innovation is less and less true, if it ever was. Great innovations almost never come out of thin air. Instead, argues technology guru W. Brian Arthur[1] and many other technology researchers, they arise from combining existing technologies and business models in novel ways. Once the underlying technologies have matured enough, it is often only a matter of time until some individual or company will figure out a way to combine them to meet an existing or new customer need. Once digital mobile telephony and the internet had matured enough, for example, it was only a matter of time until they would be combined to create mobile internet devices. And once touchscreen and Global Positioning System (GPS) technology had matured, it was once again only a matter of time until companies would find a way to integrate them into mobile internet devices. Voilà the iPhone. The same story could have been told of laptops, modern combustion engines, submarines, or any other major technology area.

This is not to take anything away from the many fantastic achievements of Apple – they were certainly the first to combine all of these technologies in an appealing and user-friendly bundle and get the app-development industry going, and by doing so they revolutionized the mobile telephony industry. But it offers a quite different explanation for how innovation comes about: it is about adding one technology building block to the next. If the underlying blocks are not there, the technology won't mature, but if they are (and there is a customer need), then it is often just a matter of time until a product is developed.

This is important, because it means technology development can to a significant extent be steered. If there had not been investments in the touchscreen and GPS, there would not be an iPhone. If we want a circular material bank or high productivity delivery systems, we need to identify the required technologies to get us there, and the building blocks of those technologies in turn, and make sure there is momentum in developing those technologies.

Let us review some other key findings of modern technology and innovation research, and then discuss what it means for the argument in this book. Most important technologies consist of myriad different sub-technologies, which in turn consist of further sub-technologies. Some of these are competing, some complementary, and there are often many different engineering solutions to the same problem. Look at Figure 13.3, showing all the main solar PV technologies being worked on around the world. In total, 10–15 alternative technologies are being pursued in earnest, each with their different strengths and challenges. Double-clicking on each one of the alternatives would in turn reveal a whole new set of detailed alternatives on wafer thickness, layering, material chemistry, and production approaches. So even though Figure 13.3 is graphically complex, it still vastly underplays the real complexity of the myriad technology development initiatives going on around the world. In total, thousands of research teams are pursuing different aspects of solar PV – competing, but also borrowing from each other. These technology systems are often compared to ecosystems, and it is not a bad analogy: a Darwin-type evolution is certainly at work, both between companies, technologies, individual sub-technologies and production approaches. And there is plenty of diversity in both systems, with interdependence, complementarity and cross-pollination.

This diversity of approaches and research teams is important, because it makes overall progress much more robust and predictable. Progress often does not depend on whether or not any single sub-technology breaks through, nor on the success of any individual firm. In the same way that a skilled evolutionary biologist can triangulate approximately how long it should take for living organisms to develop certain skills and features, a skilled research team and their development manager can predict approximately how fast a certain technology will mature (this is indeed an important consideration when technology firms develop their research programmes).

The resilience of new technology areas also grows over time. When researchers, entrepreneurs and investors have devoted their careers and their wealth to a certain technology, it takes a lot for them to let go of this technology and move elsewhere. Vested interests are built up, and this translates to both resilience and political influencing ability. Look at renewable energy, for instance. Many believed that its progress would stall when fossil fuel prices dropped after the financial crisis. But enough time had passed, and enough resilience built up by the renewable energy ecosystem, that progress has continued at a very high pace.

Technology development rarely depends on a single breakthrough – example solar PV

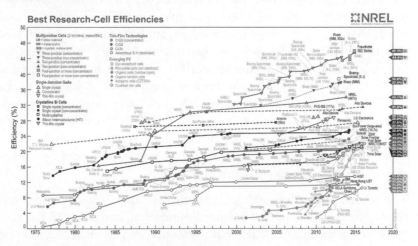

SOURCE: Courtesy of the National Renewable Energy Laboratory, Golden, CO.

Fig 13.3

And then there is Moore's law. Famously, Gordon Moore – a co-founder of Intel – observed in 1965 that the capacity of integrated circuits had doubled every year since the integrated circuit was invented, and he predicted that the same trend would continue for the foreseeable future.[2] His prediction turned out to be quite accurate, and over time it has become generally accepted as a rule of thumb in the semiconductor industry. It captured something fundamentally important about technology development: if enough companies believe fast progress is necessary to stay in business and prosper, they will invest research and development resources accordingly. These investments, in turn, are what keeps the innovation pace high – a self-fulfilling prophecy. The same phenomenon has now spread to many other industries; current examples include battery technology, memory storage and solar PV.

The role of government

Government often plays a major, but underestimated, role in the development of new technology. And the more groundbreaking and novel the technology, the bigger the role of government is likely to be. Those are the key messages in *The Entrepreneurial State,* a 2011 book by Mariana Mazzucato, a Professor of Economics and Technology at the University of Sussex, which rightfully attracted a lot of attention when it was published. Take the iPhone example again. The touchscreen and the HTML protocol were developed in publicly funded universities. The US Defense had a key role in developing GPS, voice controls, microelectronics and the internet itself (together with publicly funded researchers at CERN). And the Finnish state played a big role in the development of mobile telephony. So the Apple story most people have in their minds – that of Steve Jobs and Steve Wozniak, two lonely geniuses who beat all the odds – should also be complemented with an acknowledgement of the huge role of the state in developing the key technologies that enable Apple's products.

The search algorithm behind Google's success, for instance, was funded by the US National Science Foundation, and a full 75 per cent of all new molecular entities that were approved by the US Food and Drug Administration between 1993 and 2004 were based on original research conducted at publicly funded National Institutes of Health

(NIH) labs in the US. Other examples of state-funded breakthroughs include satellites, jet engines and nuclear power.[3]

The reason states are so important is, of course, that the risk in betting on major breakthrough projects like the GPS is too big for private companies, the rewards are often spread over many sectors and stake-holders, and the timelines involved are too long.

Interestingly, when looking at the list of state-funded technology breakthroughs, a striking number have been funded by the US state, and arguably, the single biggest innovation engines over the last decades have been the US Defense Advanced Research Projects Agency (DARPA) and the NIHs. Mazzucato argues that the technological pre-eminence of the US is not only owed to its successful entrepreneurs and venture capitalists in Silicon Valley, but is perhaps owed in equal measure to the successful civil servants in its research agencies. It should also be noted that in most of the breakthrough examples above, the government did not just provide funding through basic research grants. Instead, many were 'man to the moon' type missions, where the government decided what new technological capabilities they were after, designed the huge research and technology programmes to get there and eventually achieved their goal. In other words, the state played an active, technology-picking role, not the laissez-faire 'let the market decide the best solution' role that is so often touted as the only viable common ground between the public and private sectors. At the same time, of course, one should be aware that there are also endless examples of publicly-funded technology efforts that have gone nowhere.

Is the important role of states just an interesting academic curiosity, or does it have real-world implications? The latter. Innovation is crucial for economic growth and improved living standards. Without DARPA, the digital revolution would be decades behind where it is today, and its enormous consumer benefits would not have materialized. But in many countries, the state is often discussed as a hindrance to innovation rather than a help. This leads policy-makers to reduce the role of the state as much as possible, often to that of pure funding of basic research. In many countries, it is completely unthinkable that the government would set 'man to the moon' type innovation ambitions and design research programmes to get there, even when the budgets are available. As Martin Wolf succinctly put it when he reviewed *The Entrepreneurial State* in the *Financial Times*: 'The failure to recognise the role of the government in driving innovation may well be the greatest threat to rising prosperity.'[4] As we will discuss in the next chapter, there are a number of suitable man-to-the-moon type of innovation missions that are highly relevant for the economic turnaround mission in front of us, where it would be highly relevant for states to engage.

Defense Advanced Research Projects Agency – a key global innovation engine

On 4 October 1957, the Soviet Union launched Sputnik, the world's first manned space travel, and scored a major win in the Cold War's arms and technology race. The Pentagon's response was to create the Defense Advanced Research Projects Agency[5] (DARPA) in 1958, with the objective to ensure future US technological leadership. The key idea was to provide a bridge between universities' basic research – with its long timelines and sometimes unclear applications – and the product development work of commercial firms. In practice, DARPA earmarks a certain part of US Defense R&D spending to more advanced, novel, longer-term projects. A key source of inspiration was the Manhattan project, which in a few short years had managed to translate nuclear physics – then a very theoretical field of physics with few applications outside universities – to an all-too-concrete product. The Manhattan project had also shown it was crucial for governments to understand the latest scientific research, and its military and commercial possibilities.

DARPA was much discussed in policy debates in the 1970s and 1980s (and often mentioned in science fiction novels), but seems to attract less attention today. That is a pity, since there are many lessons to learn. What is most interesting about DARPA is the combination of its remarkable successes, and that it operates in a way that contradicts much of the conventional wisdom about how governments should deal with innovation. Far from just providing 'enabling' conditions, such as basic financing and strong IP protection, DARPA has consistently taken a very active role in managing innovation. To start with, it has actually 'picked winners' in the sense of decided what technologies it wants to see developed. Second, it has actively developed and managed long-term research and development programmes to get there. For instance, its grant-making is very strategic, funding sub-technologies and research topics that are needed for the big programme to succeed, and acting as broker between industrial companies, universities, venture capitalists and government departments – all in the spirit of effective information exchange and quick identification of winning approaches and dead ends. It also funded prototype labs for new semiconductors and computer science departments at US universities.

Crucially, DARPA has a high degree of independence, even though it is funded by the federal government, and cooperates with the Department of Defense and many other government departments. It recruits highly capable programme managers, and has managed to create a non-bureaucratic, flexible organization. It has a permanent staff of about 220 and a budget of about $3 billion per year.[6] This approach has led to successes such as the internet (together with CERN), the GPS system, speech recognition, parts of the semiconductor industry and the touchscreen. All in all, many of the crucial building blocks of the digital economy can trace their roots back to a DARPA programme.

Of course, the US is the largest economy in the world, and not all countries could achieve what DARPA has. But a few billion dollars is much smaller than the total research funding of most of the world's top economies, and this is about reallocating funds more than increasing them, so size might be much less of an issue than it appears at first sight.

Summing up

What have we learned? That in some many product markets, innovation is in a downward spiral where the economy is actually innovating itself further away from net-positive products. But also that innovation and technology development is much more predictable and 'manageable' than public belief has it. Companies invest innovation resources based on their beliefs about how future markets will develop, and how much they think others are investing. And we have learned that states have historically taken an active role in many of the most groundbreaking technological achievements.

So what should states do? In the words of Mazzucato, 'a core lesson [...] is the need to develop a new industrial policy which learns from the past experiences in which the state has played a leading, entrepreneurial role in achieving innovation-led growth [...] The assumption that the public sector can at best incentivise private sector led innovation (through subsidies, tax reductions, carbon pricing, green investment banks and so on) [...] fails to account for the many examples in which the leading entrepreneurial force came from the state rather than from the private sector.'[7]

This is a very optimistic message. In brief, public policy-makers have an important role to play in setting the direction for technology development, presumably to help create the future society we want. As a society, if we get our act together, we do not need to regard technology as an untameable beast.

13.3 Innovation and renewal – the untapped source

The economic and environmental benefits of a net-positive economy are massive, as described in Part II. The single biggest transition benefit, however, could be the spark that such a new paradigm could provide to innovation, and to societal renewal at large, particularly at a moment of widespread disenchantment with new technology as a driver of productivity and growth. While the notion of 'sustainability' has started to induce fatigue and disappointment in ways ironically similar to the underlying industrial system that called for sustainability in the first place, innovation towards a future economy that works has not. Students and companies flock to conferences and speeches about planet-benign innovation. They light up when they are exposed to net-positive thinking, cradle-to-cradle product design, digitized business models and systems thinking. We are hungry for innovation and change that is positive, meaningful (as opposed to a doctrine that makes technology an objective in its own right) and sufficiently different ('disruptive'). And when we see such innovation (be it in the form of Tesla, Beyond Meat, Uber, Airbnb) we leave our old ways behind without much sentimentality.

The innovation opportunity inherent in a transition to a net-positive, three-pillar economy is massive. And it is largely a very positive one: consumers will benefit from more durable products with a better secondary value, and have access to more capital goods through shared and digitized business models. Companies will escape the 'less bad' trap and genuinely be able to communicate that they are doing good, all things considered. And policy-makers will reject the age-old economy versus environment debate and support innovation that is good for both.

Does this sound overly optimistic? Read through the list of innovation areas below, and see if you don't agree with us that most of them are huge, and very compelling. And in many of them, an entrepreneurial state could certainly play an important role.

Innovation to establish a cradle-to-cradle material bank

Think first of the sizeable and sophisticated **secondary material industry**: supply chains and markets that channel materials to the highest value uses with speed and at industrial scale. Today's waste sector – opaque, crime-ridden, with massive health standard violations – would morph into a modern, vibrant, technology-driven sector. Today's secondary markets for glass, aluminium, scrap metal and cardboard will be dwarfed by the upcoming markets for highly defined polymer grades, high-quality metals, textile fibres, second-hand clothing, warranty mobile phone parts or high-value sludge. Some of these new markets will be discrete and project-based (waste heat, effluents), some will be peer-to-peer (vintage car parts), some will be captive (return of high-end, non-standard equipment), some will be local and physical (wood chips), and others global and web-based (smartphone antennae).

A cradle-to-cradle material bank would also likely include '**product IDs**'. This concept has long been proposed by pioneers, but now the internet of things and electronic tagging has made it technically feasible and affordable. Product IDs contain all the information needed to ensure a car, a powertool, a handbag or a summer shirt remains at the highest value at all times, also after the first use cycle. It reveals the biography of the product, the producer, the materials (referencing to the nutrient database) and components, the history of use, the post-use options. It gives products identity, producers accountability, users assurance and post-users valorization options. And it gives governments the ability to act – reward performance and sanction any trespassers. As an example, consumer electronics with sales of $390 billion annually are today losing almost the complete value during the first use cycle.[8] Through tagging, a system of tradeable warranted goods could be created which will significantly reduce the costs of connectivity and the environmental burden, an opportunity that both Google and Oracle are pursuing. It is about building the second and missing half of the supply chain and empowering it through big data.

The whole **bio-economy** is another exciting innovation area. Microbes can be used at industrial scale to generate fuels and neutralize effluents. Bio-refineries promise to recover valuable organics which are today just burned. Soil and plant science and management will be a significant industry involving the use of biologics, recovery of organic matter and biological pest control. Chemical markers will allow companies to trace materials, condition, lease and insure them.

Well-designed net-positive products will mean a completely different innovation focus, as the upward and downward spirals showed. We will enter a real product-performance competition in which the lifetime performance (not the lowest purchase price) is the key selling point. This will reduce costs to the user through longer lifetimes and easier repair which in turn creates readiness to enter long-term performance contracts. With those, more products can be returned to the producer, helping to reduce costs through easy disassembly, component harvesting and reuse. This allows industry to offer even better deals, deepen customer relationships, increase take-back volumes and lower recovery unit costs. With better customer relationships and insights, companies can make a more personalized offer and adjust functionalities fit-for-use – a self-reinforcing innovation engine, and a race to the top.

Novel ecosystem services. We have a new ability to monitor environmental performance such as the aggregate health of river systems or ocean patches, the sequestration capacity of forests or soils, or the environmental footprints of mines. This opens up a new opportunity to create and manage entirely new markets for novel services such as CO_2 sequestration, fishstock regeneration, or biodiversity. The most prominent example is the new technology that has more or less stopped deforestation in Brazil (see Appendix 2). With the tailwind of the Paris agreement promoting 'results-based payments', such markets can become an important element of our international resource management regime. They could be revolutionary in providing income particularly to low-income countries for conserving rather than extracting their resources.

Innovation to get to high-productivity delivery systems

On a systems level, too – in the mobility sector, say – innovation will accelerate and provide more benefits to all constituents. Where currently most innovation effort is focused on the development of the most advanced and luxurious car, the innovation spark would leap to the platform level. Within the system, an open-access data pool on vehicle movements would allow the creation of most value, because vehicle flows can be optimized. Uber-type data managers and service brokers would emerge, using data streams to optimize flows and ensure mobility services best match individual needs. Those services would improve utilization of the assets in use and increase incentives to all asset operators to join the platform. With more customers and operators joining, leading to critical volumes, some players will start optimizing the connections between different transport modes. Now, cities have ways to influence the quality of mobility services, by setting up inter-modal platforms, regulating third party access to data and ensuring a safe handover between rail, tram, bike and shared vehicle fleets. This will trigger competition between cities for the best mobility offering.

Big data brokers. Data trading, brokerage and analysis are a huge and growing profession that is changing many industries by allowing them to predict consumer behaviour, assess commodity markets, steer marketing campaigns and optimize complex operations. Thanks to the increasing ability of data on primary and secondary resources, there is huge scope to harness the power of data on behalf of more effective resource markets.

Abundant energy. A positive cycle of innovation will emerge between the material and the energy world. As materials get easier and more attractive to recover, their use cycle might accelerate and more customer value can be created out of every unit. Each time energy is needed it will become cheaper, which will in turn create more beneficial goods from the stock of materials.

In summary, this would create a wave of innovation, growth and economic renewal – a Schumpeterian wave of creative destruction with shifts between companies, sectors and national economies. Any company and sector – even mining – could win if they find the right strategic answers on time. In the end, it will be a contest between the fast and adaptive on the one hand, and the laggards on the other. Compare this with the entrepreneurship and creativity released by the market liberalizations of the 1990s and 2000s. Or in Europe, compare it with the innovation and efficiency effects unlocked when the internal European market was created as a result of the Single European Act in 1993. The size and importance of the change certainly makes these comparisons fair.

PART IV: THE GREAT RECONCILIATION – HOW TO CROSS THE CHASM

Improvement must here be understood in a wide sense, including not only new industrial inventions, but improvements in institutions, education, opinions, and human affairs generally.

John Stuart Mill (1848)

The evidence provided so far describes an old system in crisis as mankind has started a bank run on our planet's resources. This results from our collective attempt to drive economic growth in a way that worked well during the nineteenth and early twentieth centuries – at the time with a global population of 1.5 billion and a resource extraction of 4.6 tons per person per year. But those premises have been overtaken by the new realities – a world with a population approaching 10 billion by 2050 and with 10.6 tons of resource extraction required to support our lifestyle.[1] Under these new circumstances the old model of wealth creation is a dead end and more and more people feel it. Already today, our growth engine is stuttering, much of the growth is borrowed and many of its underlying economic premises no longer hold. Part I of the book provided many datapoints: we moved from a spacious planet to a full one, at least by the standards of today's resource requirements. And on a full planet many of the most fundamental economic assumptions have to be subjected to review.

Between a doctrine of 'decroissance' and continued destructive growth, is there a viable model, the third way to prosper within the capacity of the planet? We think the answer is yes. We described such a model of accretive, net-positive growth in Part II. We need to go there because our efficiency drive and the attempts to correct today's model around the fringes have so far been dwarfed by the hunger for more resources which, in turn, is driven by population and economic growth. We describe the principles which will allow us to depart from the path of resource-intensive industrialization, mass production and fossil fuel-based growth – to build a positive, net-positive economy, not just one that is 'less bad'. This is an economy that is able to generate wealth in abundance while natural systems thrive. Part III of this book has introduced us to the breathtaking trends that take over our economy, not only to the speed of change but also to its pervasive and disruptive nature. There is no doubt that we are at the start of a new economic era. That era is dominated by new digital capabilities, new forms of energy, new business models, enlightened consumers and overhauled markets. It is a unique opportunity. At the same time we try to show that these new capabilities are essential but insufficient. We are not innovating ourselves out of borrowed growth. In fact, much of the innovation is taking the wrong turn. Three-dimensional printing may massively increase household waste, Uber may increase the number of journeys, and thinner, multilayer plastic may be too cheap to be picked up.

To move from the 'great divergence' to what we call the 'great reconciliation', more than technology is needed. It requires new economic thinking to inform foresighted political decision-makers, who in turn feel encouraged by successful pioneering businesses. And these innovative businesses must thrive on the superior value they deliver to their ever more loyal customers. These again favourably support the political agenda that makes us more positive, net-positive and planet-benign. It requires an upward spiral, entering what we call system-level change. This is the focus of Part IV of this book.

Can we cross the chasm from an economic tradition that depletes our capital stock to one that is accretive? We have collectively failed on less ambitious transitions and in the face of a global governance and geopolitical environment that is deteriorating rather than improving – so how can we believe that such a fundamental shift will succeed? We are seeing a disruption not only in the way the economy will work but also in the way we can navigate and steer system-level change. There are reasons for optimism: first we have a burning platform that is harder to ignore. We see a new world view, a different paradigm in the making. We are seeing the power of a digitally-enabled citizenry. We are witnessing the birth of a third economy, the meso-economy, which is much more prone to shift systems than either transactional markets or the state. And finally, there is a powerful new segment of long-term investors seeking to derisk their portfolios and to channel funds into new directions. Taken together, it could be the perfect storm.

Chapter 14

Ten years that matter – the case for change

Nothing is more powerful than an idea whose time has come.

Victor Hugo

For the last thirty years, ever since the mid-1980s, we have steered a course that has massively reduced and finally reversed the benefits of economic growth. We have entered a phase of uneconomic growth. The next thirty years will be about returning to a model of growth that is not depleting capital at the same time. Whether that rebound will succeed will be decided in the next ten years; in retrospect they could well be remembered as the *D-cade*. We have ten years to enter a different trajectory, to correct some of the massive deficiencies in our ailing prosperity engine. And then, we have twenty years to take it mainstream. To avert the loss of bioproductivity and unknown cost to our economy. And of course to stabilize our natural capital, avoid climate change, ocean acidification and pollution, to protect our major carbon sinks in South America and Asia, our signature habitats and flagship species. And to use the wave of innovation and investment in ways to build the technology backbone for the twenty-first century. Why ten years?

14.1 Moving beyond the planet – in praise of the alarmist

Within the next ten years, we *will* hit boundaries. Today we have – as outlined in chapter [1.2.1.] – already trespassed the planetary boundaries of four vital natural resource systems: the phosphorus and nitrogen cycle as well as biodiversity, climate and land-use change. For two further resource systems (aerosols and novel substances) our level of overuse is hard to determine; we might well stand in the red zone. For two categories (ocean acidity and freshwater) we are approaching the limits fast, and might – based on today's model of use – transgress the boundaries very soon. For climate change and under the assumption of a 2-degree threshold, these dynamics are particularly well understood.[1] Over the next fifteen years, primary energy demand will rise by 25 per cent,[2] demand for water by 41 per cent,[3] for cropland by 11–14 per cent and for meat by 9 per cent.[4] The rally has only just started. Around the earth, we are seeing what might happen if we transgress boundaries. South Africa – the economic beacon on the continent – is riddled by power outages. California has introduced strict laws and huge investment programmes to handle its water crisis; in 2014, Governor Jerry Brown signed off a $687 million drought plan that included funding for water recycling projects as well as immediate aid such as drinking water for communities facing dire shortages and food and housing assistance.[5] Bolivia's Lake Poopó, the country's second biggest, has disappeared as the temperature has risen by 0.9 degrees Celsius, destroying thousands of livelihoods.[6] Madagascar's president was ousted in the attempt to close a land deal with Korea, a country in need of more agricultural land.[7]

Are we exaggerating and derailing a debate that deserves more rational composure? Environmentalism has long been charged with alarmism and bias. Rightly so? From experienced firefighters we learn that when a fire hits a cinema or a theatre it is not panic or stampede that causes the highest death toll, it is people's tendency to stay in their seats for too long and to react too little and too late to the first signs of fire. When they finally move it is often too late to escape to safety and – yes – panic becomes an additional threat. Let's look at history. One important case of purported eco-alarmism is the forest dieback in Germany – the 'Waldsterben'. In 1981 the magazine *Spiegel* reported on the enigmatic loss of needles and leaves in central European forests. It had affected all important endemic trees: oak, beech, spruce, fir and elm. The speed of deterioration was so high that forestry experts speculated about a complete demise of forest landscapes in Central Europe. The *Spiegel* report was filled with alarming statistics on soil acidification, pest proliferation and vitality loss. Immediately, acid rain caused through oxides of nitrogen and sulphur (NOx and SOx) made the headlines. It was the central agenda of TV debates, student protest ('First it's the forest, then it's us') and elections. An evening programme was launched on TV, the postal service issued a stamp 'Save our Forests' with a ticking clock, catalysts were introduced and a green party was elected into parliament. Today, German forests are in good shape again. The German agricultural ministry declared in 2003 that the forest threat is over and the total area covered by forests in Germany is growing. A hoax and hyperbolic eco-alarmism, many have concluded. Let's look at the facts. In 1983, a new generation of emission rules for NOx and SOx was approved by the German parliament.[8] In 1987, the Helsinki accord on sulphur oxides reduction took effect. Between 1980 and 2010, the emissions of unified Germany dropped massively from 7.5 million tons in 1980 to 0.4 million tons in 2010 – a reduction of 95 per cent (see Figure 14.1). Clearly, today the enabling conditions for the massive dieback of the early 1980s are much better understood: nitrogen oxides, sulphur oxides, heavy metals, two extreme summers in the late 1970s and an obsolete practice of overstocking spruce trees. And yet, the resolved set of actions on all levels was linked to a changed frame of reference: the recognition that the very existence of forests could be at stake if emissions were not controlled.

German emissions of Sulphur dioxide have decreased dramatically since the 1990s

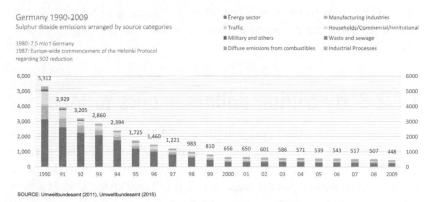

Fig 14.1

But at what cost? Business and other opinion leaders continue to alert politicians to the detrimental effects of environmental legislation, especially during phases when growth and employment seem weak. It is the jobs-versus-environment argument that continues in many debates, from the 2015/16 US primaries to the reception of the EU Circular Economy package in 2014 with which we started this book. More surprising are the results of an independent study published in 2014 by the OECD. This analysed the environmental laws, both explicit and implicit, of twenty-four OECD countries from 1990 to 2012 and concluded that 'an increase in stringency of environmental policies does not harm productivity growth'.[9] Another 2014 paper, from the Grantham Research Institute at the London School of Economics, summarizes the broadest literature research so far on environmental legislation. It concluded that the effects of environmental legislation on 'employment and productivity [...] appear to be small and transitory [...] the estimated effects [...] on trade and investment location so far are negligible'. Even more so, 'The benefits of environmental regulations often vastly outweigh the costs'.[10]

Alarmism exists – it can be ideological and biased. And yet, often wake-up calls are legitimate and effective, but discarded as alarmist. A prominent example is the Club of Rome's historic warning of 'The Limits of Growth'. In hindsight, that report might receive late recognition for the start of decoupling and resource awareness. Its failure – the prediction of an immediate resource crisis that never happened – might turn out to have been the report's biggest achievement. In the face of the evidence provided in this book: when is the right moment to hit the alarm button?

14.2 Sixty trillion dollars – ours to lose

Over the next ten years we will invest $200–270 trillion into our economy:[11] into industrial assets, housing, different kinds of infrastructure, and other assets. $60 trillion will be invested in transport, energy and water infrastructure, most of it in large cities: US$6 trillion every year. This estimate – provided by the New Climate Economy Commission – applies to the business-as-usual development path. The study found that the number would be only insignificantly higher (by $270 billion per year, or less than 5 per cent) if we were to migrate towards a low-carbon development path, and at the same time the infrastructure operating costs would be significantly reduced. This is typical of a low-carbon technology like photovoltaic solar, wind or geothermal which requires upfront investments but no feedstock later on. With those numbers comes the commission's very important message: that investments in a low-carbon economy are a compulsory but at the same time profitable insurance against climate change and its costly consequences. But equally importantly, that we have the chance to invest the $200–$270 trillion into the next economy, or the old one. If we lock into old resource-intensive infrastructures, we will have wasted the biggest, most urgent opportunity for renewal available to us. It is ours to lose. Not only infrastructure but every industrial investment, every house, every piece of agricultural equipment, every low orbit satellite will be part of the resource-productive new platform – or not, if we waste the opportunity. Those investments will keep operating well into the twenty-first century: a coal power plant typically operates for fifty years, an automotive manufacturing plant for twenty years, an incinerator for thirty years, a mine for forty years. Aeroplanes are typically in use for more than thirty years, trains forty years, heavy duty vehicles ten years, agricultural tractors for six years, and even washing machines (for eight years) and television sets (seven years),[12] stay with us for a while. If we miss the opportunity to instal assets that are part of higher performing, benign and resource-productive systems, we will create an unprecedented lock-in for bad. We will continue to generate stranded assets in the trillions. And we have been warned.

A *Rolling Stone* article from 2012 was first to alert us to the 'carbon bubble' – the fact that out of the known 2,800 billion tons of fossil fuels only 600 billion tons can be burnt within the remaining carbon budget until 2050 without leaving the politically agreed 2 degrees centigrade corridor.[13] Dramatically, the valuation of fossil fuel companies is based on known reserves, and we are faced with a massive overvaluation. CitiBank estimates the loss in value of the fossil fuel companies of $100 trillion over the next two decades due to tighter rules and growing competition from the renewables industry.[14] The UK's Committee on Climate Change foresees the emergence of stranded assets on a historic scale and has alerted government that the overvaluation of fossil fuel companies constitutes a serious threat to the economy.[15] The effect on market evaluations remains unclear, but fossil fuel majors concede that other effects are beginning to show, especially on the recruiting market.

The looming carbon bubble is one reason why, over the next years, significant capital flows are available to be channelled into the new economy. The broader reason is the general oversupply of capital – Credit Suisse estimates that global wealth has doubled between 2000 and 2015 from $117 trillion to $263 trillion.[16] This vast supply of savings is facing limited opportunities for investment. And more capital than ever before is made available for 'impact' – social or environmental. Impact capital funds are growing by a staggering 37 per cent per annum.[17] Some of these funds are linked to bold ambitions such as the Breakthrough Energy Coalition announced in November 2015, a joint effort between billionaires Bill Gates, Jeff Bezos, Richard Branson, Vinod Khosla, Jack Ma, Ratan Tata and others. However, the new economy is not yet ready to absorb these capital flows. Investors complain about a dearth of projects.[18] Given the systemic nature of the change, the reliance on new rules, political arrangements, joint industrial action or investor endorsement, it is not good enough to wait for the market to pick up.

14.3 Peak child – a new generation

In 1960 there were 1 billion children under 15 years old. Today there are 1.9 billion and the number is not expected to grow. Nor is it expected to shrink before 2050, but the share of children in the total population will drop from 27 to 20 per cent.[19] Our behaviour, our consumption patterns and the resource intensity of our lifestyles are all shaped in the years before our fifteenth birthday, so for that reason the following ten years are critical. If in ten years' time all 15-year-olds were to embrace a more compatible lifestyle based on new business models and new technology and subsequently hand over the new ways to the next generation, 655 billion human years out of the 875 billion human years that will be lived in this century (that is 75 per cent) will be lived in net-positive ways, or ways that take us closer to that vision. If we gave ourselves twenty more years to achieve the same level of change, that figure would be little more than 50 per cent.

Reaching the peak child generation would help spread the new values and behaviours fast. Not only would the young change posterity, they would change their parents' generation, too. The young can teach the old. Singapore's late founder and long-term president Lee Kuan Yew once shared a key idea of the country's fast ascent in front of an audience of international McKinsey partners. 'Some of our challenges', he related, 'were so pressing that we did not have time for the parents to teach their children. We had to do it the other way round.' At school, children learnt about the existential importance of water for the newly independent country and ways to save this resource. At home, water-saving behaviour became a social standard, with children pulling their parents along. The 'no waste' story has significant appeal to children and young students, as educators can vividly recount. Something similar seems to happen globally around climate change. The recognition that end-of-life products are simply bad design and burning fossil fuels seems awkward comes very naturally to a child's mind. And yet, environmental education quintessentially follows the old paradigm of human guilt, abstention and the need for incremental repair – a harder lesson to embrace for a child's mind than the story of waste equals food.

The disruptive power of a young generation is tangible. Take the unstoppable Malala who, after surviving an assassination attempt by the Taliban, persisted in promoting human rights and was eventually honoured with the Nobel Peace Prize, becoming the youngest recipient ever. Or the seventeen-year-old Felix Finkbeiner who started an initiative at the age of nine, leading to already more than 14 billion trees being planted. And there are countless children's and youth initiatives around the globe with millions of members mostly below the age of twenty-five, such as DoSomething.org, a platform where young people encourage each other to make a change for the good by using various channels like Snapchat and Twitter. The millennials are more connected than ever and they appear to share more beliefs than ever.[20,21] Beliefs in the past seemed to be related to culture and background, but today feel more a product of age. The readiness to share, virtualize, return, lend and borrow is significantly higher with the millennials. They are making new trends. Even in Germany, the heartland of the automobile, car ownership rates are down by 10 per cent among young people, as is the share of twenty-year-olds that hold a driving licence.[22,23] No economic model – despite any theoretical advantage – will ever stand a chance if it does not appeal to the millennials and if it does not turn this generation into evangelists of a 'benign' model of production, usage and consumption.

14.4 The quest is on – the Paris tailwind

'We fought for a long time and today we've reached a solid agreement. It is a historic turning point', Barbara Hendricks, the German environment minister, said.[24] Only history will tell whether the Paris climate accord from 12 December 2015 marks mere lip service on the way towards an ever less hospitable planet, or a turning point towards rapid decarbonization and economic transformation. The deal constitutes the single biggest leap of faith – or predicament, some may say – that the global community has ever signed up to. The global agreement was to curb global warming to 'well below' 2°C, which many have interpreted as aiming for a maximum of 1.5°C warming. This requires global greenhouse gas emissions to be close to 'net-zero' by 2050 or 2060. However, the national climate plans[25] submitted to the Paris climate negotiations add up to 59 gigatons of CO_2-equivalent emissions by 2030, well above the required maximum of 42 gigatons that most modelling say is necessary to be on a pathway towards 'net zero' by 2050–60 . The current emission forecasts are taking us onto a 4° trajectory.[26,27,28] A UBS research paper from December 2015 summarized: 'It's not a gap, it's a chasm.'[29]

Looking at the Paris agreement in positive terms, one could instead call out the enormity of 195 nation states agreeing that climate change is a material threat, that warming must remain below 2°C, that we need to enter a net-zero emission economy after 2050, and that all countries must contribute.

We are convinced Paris was a fork in the road and a date that will be remembered. First, because history shows that non-binding agreements can provide much-needed convergence points for decision-making, such as the Helsinki Accords. These Accords created clarity of direction and mutual trust. Second, because the Paris agreement is hitting the world stage at a moment where – as elaborated in Part I of this book – no incumbent development theory is owning the high ground. Six years after the financial crisis, with the economics profession in disarray, with growth rates down, with the BRIC locomotive stuttering, with the productivity paradox ever more evident and with huge anxiety within bedrock industrial sectors such as energy, automotive or banking, the vision of building a low-carbon economy will receive its share of attention. There is anxiety particularly in middle-income countries. Out of 100 countries that were called middle-income 100 years ago, only thirteen attained high-income status.[30] Staying ahead of the demands of their increasing populations proved to be daunting. Polluted and congested cities and inadequate infrastructure were the result.

So, economic catch-up to OECD standards did not prove to be an automatism, and bearing in mind some of the new environmental costs and constraints, that journey seems even more insecure. Particularly with regard to Africa which will experience massive population growth, but also for other emerging economies, there is a lively discussion about how to leapfrog Western economies and enter into next-generation, dematerialized modes of production and consumption: off-grid solar instead of large-scale utilities, mobile phones instead of fixed lines, 3D printing instead of loaded material supply chains, ride sharing instead of car ownership, urban farming instead of packaged goods from mass production. This model seems less centralized, less infrastructure-dependent, less size-dependent – a better fit, some argue, for emerging economies. Paris hit at a moment where a window is wide open for a new growth model to win the attention and ultimately the hearts of all those who have a promise to keep to their electorate.

Chapter 15

An intuition reset – structure of a good revolution

If we did all the things we are capable of, we would literally astound ourselves.

Thomas A. Edison

The great transformation that we are outlining in this book requires us to stretch our beliefs in what is possible. Our inability to do that in the past is no measure for the likelihood of such a shift in the future. That, too, is a reason for optimism.

Why have we not seen more momentum and mainstreaming of planet-positive solutions? Much of the new system exists on paper, in lab scale, in niche products and markets. Like David, circular 'benign' businesses and concepts seem unable to win out against an ever-accelerating Goliath-size linear economy with shortening life cycles, pressure on production costs and ample incentives to externalize costs. The incremental improvements of the old design have started to become the enemy of the new design. Improving, optimizing and repairing are our strongest disciplines, system-level change is not. During the late days of the old second industrial model, the competition between an improved status quo and real system-level shift will become the epic theme. The shift towards a net-positive model of growth from within will not be achieved through the gravitational force of history alone. We are too locked into old legal, mental and physical givens to escape them with ease. We have to create the new system and perceive it as a societal option; it is ours to choose and ours to lose. To avoid stalemate, we need to call out the cognitive dissonance that took possession of us, reframe the fundamental choices and manage the tipping points. It is important to remember that the starting point is different from that of 1970s and 1980s environmentalism: the target solution, if systemically implemented, is very well in the money.

15.1 A fable of inaction – psychology of stagnation

As we write this book, an avalanche of 60 million cubic metres of mineral-laden mud is rolling down Brazil's 'Sweet River' after a dam burst. The mud released from the Samarco Mineração iron ore mine has killed nineteen people and devastated the ecosystems of the Rio Doce for over 500 km, from the rainforests to the beaches of Espirito Santo with their famous turtle populations. The sheer amount of hardening mud is likely to change agriculture and shift watersheds. And there is fear of toxicity from the avalanche. While the mining company reports that the mud is not poisonous, state authorities have ordered people who came in contact with it to wash diligently and carefully dispose of clothes. Also, there is evidence that the mud contains significant amounts of ether amine compounds which are broadly used in Brazilian mines. Ether amines, according to the internet website of Air Products, a company that produces them, 'are not readily biodegradable and have high toxicity to aquatic organisms'.[1] It will likely take generations to recover some of Rio Doce's original productivity and beauty.

The price for our resource dependence is high, and yet we seem unable to imagine a world without resource extraction and continued degradation. We understand the appeal and the logic of a system shift towards using existing resources indefinitely and in full circular ways, but feel it is unattainable. We are holding incompatible beliefs about the desirability of change and the possibility of achieving it, and as a result we are discarding the opportunity. We are acting like the fox in Aesop's fable:[2,3]

> *The fox who longed for grapes, beholds with pain*
> *The tempting clusters were too high to gain;*
> *Grieved in his heart he forced a careless smile,*
> *And cried, 'They're sharp and hardly worth my while'.*

Aesop presents a fox that tries to eat sweet grapes from a high-hanging vine but cannot reach them. Rather than admitting defeat, the fox despises the grapes: 'They're sharp and hardly worth my while'. The fox convinces himself that life without the grapes is a preferred state. His strategy to overcome the pain of cognitive dissonance and two irreconcilable ideas is what psychologists call 'adaptive preference formation'. The easier option wins, the harder one is discarded, despised, or ridiculed.

We are right at that point. Like the fox and the grapes, we cannot move ourselves to try something different. We look up at the vines, see the sweet grapes but turn away in disbelief and convince ourselves that the old model can be fixed once more. The price for not going after the grapes is high as environmental degradation, financial debt and social division escalate. This book has provided ample evidence that shifting towards a new model is now a real option. An economy decoupled from finite resources has long been described by philosophers, environmentalists and selected resource economists. We increasingly sense there is an attractive, available and affordable alternative. New technology is creating 'Tesla moments' – disruptors taking share from incumbents that felt invincible, such as power giants E.ON or RWE – and the Paris accord is providing a convergence point. Are we on the journey? What does it take for a disruption to become a revolution?

If we look for acts of cognitive dissonance, we find them everywhere. We own three combustion-drive family cars and are concerned about climate change. We are articulate about conventional agriculture's risks to soil, water, landscape, food quality and farm communities and hop in for a fast burger on our way home. We send our employees to circular economy conferences and launch the next generation of low-value, single-use products because the markets want it. The level of cognitive dissonance – always accompanied by bad conscience and cynicism – is overbearing. To escape it we do not innovate our lifestyle or business model; instead we reinterpret our cognitions to fit our behaviour ('nothing would change if I stop owning a car'), add new cognitions ('my new car will be cleaner') or reject information ('the link between emissions and climate is unproven').[4] It would be worth the social scientists' sweat to analyse which of these is the true barrier to change: rejected information or manipulated cognitions. Is it the fact that many people don't share the problem statement developed in Part I of this book, or the disbelief or lack of understanding that we have new capabilities at our fingertips? Or are we failing to act because individual movement is deemed to be too insignificant?

Whatever the deeper reason, psychologists are pointing to a way out. They found that dissonance can lead to realignment of behaviours with cognitions, which then becomes the precursor of learning and change. In fact, this approach is used actively in constructivist education. Students who have been exposed to conflicting cognitions[5] were more able and ready for directed conceptual change.[6] The current anxiety within large parts of society may prove to be the much-needed seeding ground for transformational change.

15.2 Filling the imagination gap – historic precedents

Departing from a resource-intensive, net-negative model of growth towards a new one will not be the first system shift for mankind, and as before, the choice will seem trivial in hindsight. The abolition of slavery had been refuted for decades by reputable men before it happened. They pointed to the catastrophic effects for the overall economy – as did Temple Luttrell in a speech to the House of Commons 1777. If Britain did not engage in the slave trade, then others would. Commercial rivals such as the Dutch and the French would fill the gap and African slaves would be worse off. Child labour was a recognized pillar of the Victorian economy and prevailed well into twentieth-century Europe and America. And those readers who entered school before 1980 may have been sitting in classrooms with teachers smoking; prohibiting it was preceded by long debates. From women's rights to mandatory safety belts, the transition took years – from an old social standard towards a conflict of beliefs, a social struggle over short-term realism towards a new social contract. Over 200 years elapsed between slavery being raised as a public concern and its eventual abolition, and more than 60 years from the first campaigns for women's rights in the UK to the establishment of equal voting rights in 1928. DDT was banned ten years after Rachel Carson's book *Silent Spring*.[7] Safety belts were first proposed in the 1930s and took until the 1970s to became mandatory in all jurisdictions.[8] FinnAir was the first airline to ban smoking on its planes in 1969.[9] Nineteen years later, in 1988, smoking on airplanes was forbidden altogether.[10]

Every transition has been an episode of cognitive dissonance that only faded as the new standard became legal and social practice. During the interim, issues had been raised and arguments aired, but each transition had to wrestle with short-term realism and seemingly well-reasoned concerns.

Taking a longer-term historical perspective is one way to reframe our current predicament and to open up to systemic change. An effective way to reframe our choices is to assume the hindsight view and ask how our current set of actions will be perceived once a new standard has come into place: the entry of millions of tons of plastic onto markets without any after-use infrastructure; the expansion of oil, coal and gas extractive capacity; the application of nitrates and phosphate in agriculture without any mechanisms in place to retain them in soil or biomass; the production of 90 million motor vehicles globally which are only fit for crude and rudimentary resource recovery. In 2015, these practices seemed obvious, as Thomas Kuhn's famous duck did. Until we started seeing the rabbit. It is what we call a paradigm shift.

15.3 Duck or rabbit – paradigm crisis

Scientific books are a hard sell. But Thomas Kuhn sold his 1962 book *The Structure of Scientific Revolutions* 1.4 million times. Miraculously, the number of copies sold remains remarkably robust fifty years after its first publication.[11] Kuhn's powerful account of shifting paradigms is still hitting a nerve and appealing to the minds of the millennials. Kuhn observed that scientific communities work, debate and progress within established frames of reference provided by a scientific theory such as Einstein's relativity theory or Bohr's atomic model. Most experimentation serves to confirm and refine this existing body of theory. This is 'normal science' until anomalies occur that cannot be explained by normal science. Initially, scientists will attempt to assimilate the unsuspected phenomenon into the existing paradigm, but as these observations abound the fundamental incommensurability becomes obvious, sending the old paradigm into crisis. Some scientists will attempt to find new ways to explain what they observe and articulate a competing paradigm. Paradigm wars start until – typically much later – allegiances tip towards the new paradigm. The more scientists convert and opponents demise, the more they are invested into old theory and the less ready they will be.

Kuhn's interpretation of scientific progress overturned the view that science is progressing in a linear and additive fashion by taking the concept of the paradigm shift mainstream and providing insights into the episodes of a transition. The transition itself happens late and only in the presence of overwhelming evidence. At its heart is a 'gestalt shift' – the moment when we see the rabbit where before we saw a duck. The old gestalt is one of an economy that must be fed with resources, where scarcity governs, where deterioration is the unavoidable condition for human prospering, and where 'less bad' is already an achievement. From that perspective, an economy which revitalizes our natural environment, generates abundance and leaves behind more productive ecosystems for future generations seems unattainable. It is a set of outcomes which runs against experience and convictions.[12]

Fifty years after Kuhn's groundbreaking analysis, mass psychologists have provided remarkably concrete descriptions of how old paradigms tip, and the necessary prerequisites. Many systems tip, they found, when 10 per cent share a new belief. This insight comes from a very unlikely source: the Social Cognitive Network Academic Research Center, created and funded by the US Army. A key objective of SCNARC has been to understand how insurgency and counterinsurgency operations are able to control or influence populations, based on the core belief that 'the decisive battle is for the people's minds'.[13] In 2011, SCNARC published a paper in the *Physical Review* with the innocent title 'Social Consensus Through the Influence of Committed Minorities'.[14] The team had used complex computer models to identify the tipping point where a minority belief shifts to become the majority opinion. SCNARC director Boleslaw Szymanski summarized the findings: 'When the number of committed opinion holders is below 10 per cent, there is no visible progress in the spread of ideas [...] Once that number grows above 10 per cent, the idea spreads like flame.'[15] The authors also refer to historical precedents such as the suffragette movement in the UK, or the Arab Spring in Tunisia and Egypt. Prior to SCNARC's work other scientists had proposed higher activation thresholds. Much will depend on the influencing power of the minority: Malcolm Gladwell identified connectors, mavens and salesmen in his popular book *The Tipping Point* as prerequisites for the fast proliferation of a new idea.[16] SCNARC's research found that the level of conviction of 'committed opinion holders' mattered more than the type of network in which the influencers were working. Every time, the threshold number turned out to be 10 per cent regardless of where that opinion started to spread. The speed of infection Gladwell emphasizes is a function of group size. The epidemic power of ideas is strongest in groups of up to 150 people (known as Dunbar's number).[17] It will be even higher if these groups comprise individuals who reside over deadlocks, such as employer and employee representatives, opposing politicians or social activists. Circularity and regeneration have been proven to possess the power to open the solution space, to reframe a discussion and to re-engage parties to explore common ground.

Why is the new model not becoming an epidemic – despite the evident malaise of today's growth engine and the popular support for a development model that is bio-benign, more affordable and more equitable? Despite the bedrock of 'committed opinion holders' (the green consumer, likely in the 10 per cent range)? And what is needed to tip it?

15.4 Managing tipping points – creating the Tesla moment

We find it hard to convince ourselves that massive change is possible. This is against our own historic experience. As we are standing on the verge of a major economic shift, there is value in reminding ourselves of the disbelief that has preceded massive change in the past. Each time we felt unable to grasp the new reality.

- In 1873, the appointed Surgeon-Extraordinary to Queen Victoria said: 'The abdomen, the chest, and the brain will forever be shut from the intrusion of the wise and humane surgeon.'
- In 1895 the Scottish mathematician and physicist Lord Kelvin asserted in front of students that 'heavier than air flying is simply impossible'.

- In the early twentieth century, the population of the Swiss canton of Appenzell was reported to have thrown stones at the railway, believing it to be devilish.
- In 1957, the editor in charge of business books for Prentice Hall told his colleagues: 'I have travelled the length and breadth of this country and talked with the best people, and I can assure you that data processing is a fad that won't last out the year.'
- Fred Smith received this reaction to his idea of a reliable overnight delivery service from his Yale University management professor: 'The concept is interesting and well-formed, but in order to earn better than a "C", the idea must be feasible.' Then he went on to found FedEx.
- In August 1968, *Business Week* reported: 'With over 50 foreign cars already on sale here, the Japanese auto industry isn't likely to carve out a big slice of the U.S. market.'
- 'There will not be a woman prime minister in my lifetime', is a famous line attributed to Margaret Thatcher, delivered five years prior to her election.

In hindsight, and having gone through massive social, economic and technological disruptions, we are shaking our heads over the incipient disbelief. But there are more recent examples, too. The renewable energy revolution is a case in point. Unsettled by the prospect of devastating climate change, the quest was on for renewable sources of energy. For most companies, a dramatic cost disadvantage of more than 50 cents per kilowatt hour seemed insurmountable and a reason not to get started. A few early renewable-energy pioneers invested heavily in photovoltaics and wind in the early 2000s. They read the signals – from high market prices, regulators and academia – differently and told the story of a clean energy system. They set in motion a Moore's law of energy and a massive and increasingly predictable reduction of generation costs. The improvement pace became a self-fulfilling prophecy and a rule of the game. Companies needed to make major research and development investments to keep pace, and these investments of course further accelerated the speed of development. Then a watershed was reached: a broadly held industry belief shared outside the pioneer camp that the future would be clean and resource-productive, and that these would be survival criteria for companies.

Research and development investments shifted quickly, and fantastic technology stories started to emerge in solar PV, battery technology, electric cars and many other areas. Today, renewables are heading safely towards grid parity and starting to show their disruptive force to incumbent power producers. In 2000, renewable energy seemed like a fool's bet. Costs of generation, economies of scale, vested interests and company mindsets all suggested fossil fuels were here to stay. How wrong.

Where will we witness the next revolution? Many see mobility as the upcoming arena for such a dramatic shift. On the one hand, this is owing to the superior customer value that the new mobility system delivers, as comprehensively discussed in Part II of this book. On the other, this expectation is nourished by the sudden reversal of customer perceptions in the face of a new product – the Tesla. While the future of this automotive start-up remains unclear – and clearly it is not planet-positive – its appearance still marks a turning point in the automotive industry: *a Tesla moment*. The traditional paradigm implies that green comes with self-restraint and abstention. The Tesla offers prestige, a new experience of connected driving and a software-driven product philosophy. The entire green movement has, from its very beginning, carried a social stigma and found itself subjected to ridicule, but not for much longer. Driving a Tesla, or operating the apartment through a Nest application earns the modern urbanite prestige and a new sense of cool. The net-positive revolution might only be a few Tesla moments away.

Chapter 16

Shaping, not gaping – government's new role

A thriving American innovation ecosystem requires not only visionary and risk-taking entrepreneurs and companies, but also the foundational 'building blocks' of innovation in which the Federal government invests.

The White House, Office of the Press Secretary, released on 21 October 2015 – the unofficial celebration of the date to which Marty McFly travelled 30 years into the future in *Back to the Future Part II.*

Economists would claim that there is an easy way out of our planetary crisis: we have to price externalities. Once companies and consumers feel the costs of pollution or social exploitation, they will automatically develop better answers. And yet this is exactly what we have not observed in the recent past. In a global context of massive price competition, governments feel unable to impose higher costs onto the economy. In fear of a backlash on competitiveness, growth and ultimately employment, they are caught in a seemingly unresolved trade-off between providing clean energy, healthy products, liveable cities and shared prosperity on the one hand, and short-term growth and employment on the other. Their room to manoeuvre seems minimal, and their macro- and micro-economic instruments increasingly blunt. They are caught in a race to the bottom.

More recently there have been indications that the tide might be turning. There is reason for optimism. Beijing and Brussels have – however imperfectly – entered a new round of competition. But this time it is a positive competition. Both countries are jockeying for position in the circular economy. China has adopted circular economy rules with its thirteenth five-year plan. The management and recovery of scarce resources is gaining significant political status. China has discovered that today's level of pollution will not allow it to rise to the aspired and deserved economic status, and also that its current levels of resource productivity will limit its capacity to grow in very tangible ways. Today, China emits 3.5 times more CO_2 per dollar of GDP than Germany and 2.5 times more than the US.[1] Recycling rates for plastic are at 11 per cent compared to Europe's 35 per cent.[2] But resource performance is improving – as is China's green energy production which has added a breathtaking 30 GW of solar PV within less than five years.[3] At the same time, Europe has also entered the race for the resource productivity crown. After intense debates within the Commission and with industry representatives in 2014, the Commission decided to develop an ambitious circular economy package that will help Europe, step by step, to escape its massive resource dependency, lower costs and provide impetus for innovation. The new resource productivity race is creating two winners: Europe can regain some of its value-add lost to China, China can leverage its labour cost position more effectively, and both can escape resource dependency and environmental degradation.

That economic strategy – however incipient and incomplete – will give the economies a new dynamism. In a good way, both regions have the chance to repeat a mechanism of the first and second industrial revolutions which were driven by the explosion in labour productivity. Labour markets allowed higher productivities to be translated into higher wages, which in turn provided incentives to entrepreneurs to increase labour productivity further. Between 1900 and 2000, labour productivity increased eightfold (in the US), creating unprecedented wealth.[4] A resource productivity spiral could trigger a similar dynamic. And it can – once defined as a target with the same unambiguousness as existed for labour productivity – become a self-fulfilling prophecy, rather like Moore's law. In the same way that our economy came to assume constant labour productivity progress, the IT industry takes Moore's law for granted as quasi-scientific reality that will roll on. Therefore business models are built around this fundamental interpretation of that law: chip producers have roadmaps with performance increases built in according to Moore's law, even if the necessary basic technologies for the performance leaps are not yet available; software developers assume continuous performance increases; and IT product and service providers assume a continuous pressure on margins unless they innovate at high speed. What can a government do to enter that positive, self-fulfilling and self-stabilizing pathway for resource productivity?

Once governments recognize the competitive opportunity that resides in resource productive systems, they can bring their classic instruments into use: macroeconomic policy instruments such as taxation or cutting harmful resources (estimated at $1.1 trillion for resource extraction and use[5]) or microeconomic instruments designed to 'make markets'. To boost integrated systems, governments should shift the tax burden from labour to (depletable) resources. As outlined in Chapter 5.3 , there is an uneven playing field between labour and resources in general, and between depletable (89 per cent of resource use in the EU) and renewable resources (11 per cent of resource use in the EU) more concretely. Labour taxes amount to 52 per cent of the EU tax burden, green taxes only 6 per cent, thereof only 4 per cent on resources (which means an effective resource tax of a mere 0.3 per cent). The share of green taxes has been decreasing since 1999. Many initiatives and policy-makers are battling for a shift. They envisage more resource productivity, higher employment and smaller shadow economies as the immediate results. And they have prominent support, for example from the IMF, which in a 2015 report emphasized that 'large efficiency gains could be achieved by shifting the tax burden away from labour, and towards consumption and capital income'.[6] The opportunity of resource taxes is significant; at the same time, this is a very controversial, complex and slow-moving agenda, and time is running out. In the meantime governments should turn to the micro- and meso-economy in order to transform the system.

16.1 Market makers – rediscovering the art of market design

Compared to the position of a group of economists who call themselves ordo-liberals, much of the discussion between neoliberals and market sceptics we've heard in the 1980s, and then again in the aftermath of the 2008 financial crisis, seems crudely out of date and strangely behind the nuance of the discussions of the 1950s and 1960s. The core idea of the ordo-liberals that markets need to operate within a well-defined and regulated perimeter to ensure its forces work on behalf of our society feels very modern indeed. The wisdom with which economists like Walter Eucken and Wilhelm Roepke synthesized the historical experience of unbridled markets in the 1920s and 1930s and state interventionism in the 1940s, which created the underpinning for much of the economic miracle in Germany and Europe, deserves more attention from both right and left of the political spectrum today. They were cultural economists in Max Weber's tradition, with a natural scepticism against materialism and the erosion of values. The main group, the so-called Freiburg School, teaches us that perfect competition is impossible, that uncontrolled markets do not build humane societies, that the power of private enterprise and principled market regulation have to go hand-in-hand. There is value in uncovering many of their insights: a well-protected company law, a liability principle for all stakeholders, independent currency banks committed to price stability, progressive tax, balanced budgets, monopoly control, autonomous settlement of wages between the parties and minimum wages for the needy.

Their work particularly deserves revisiting in the context of the economic revolution needed to free our economy from its crippling resource dependency. Already, in the 1950s, Wilhelm Roepke identified the environment as one area that will not be delivered without state support. The most effective way to shape society, Roepke deeply believed, was to create, shape and transform markets. Governments have to be market makers and define the order ('ordo') and regulation that markets need to deliver the right outcomes. Ironically, a mid-twentieth-century economist has to remind us that we should work on large-scale market design not small-scale intervention. For the big transformation, we need to design and define markets to shift from resource-based growth towards 'accretive growth'.

In order to build the accretive economy, we have to entirely rethink the concept of resource markets. Building the energy and resource market is an effort at least as big and as deserving as the (incomplete) restructuring of financial markets after the 2008 crisis. The required design of future energy markets is becoming increasingly clear: it requires a level playing field for renewable energy (and often some production incentives, a mechanism to ensure back-up capacity when weather-dependent renewables are not available – a capacity market or a so-called strategic reserve) and a well-functioning wholesale market accessible to new entrants. The market requirements for building a high-performing material bank are less clear. Here are eight concrete market rules that could revolutionize resource markets: some are post-use materials ('comply or collect', phasing out of landfills), in-use markets (positive lists, defined use, sharing) and new factor markets. All eight measures are effective but many are uncharted terrain for the regulator.

- **'Comply or collect'**: There is one single root cause underlying most of today's waste issues. Everyone is allowed to dump almost everything into our common waste systems. We all pay for the clean-up and the dirtiest fraction defines the cost. All incentives are in favour of the ugliest dumper. That has to change, and it can. The current system has to give way to a new 'comply or collect' system. Producers of goods are only allowed to enter their post-use materials into public material streams ('public material bank') if they are compliant with content requirements: they must have nutrient value, be non-contaminating and ideally traceable. Essentially all materials, metals, paper, glass, chemicals and organics have to be designed for a defined post-use and must not reduce the value of any other material collected in the same stream. Plastics must not have additives that constrain future use, metals must be pure or of the same alloy, paper must not be contaminated by toxic inks, effluents must not be carrying chemicals that could stand in the way of nutrient recovery. All materials that do not meet the standard have to be recovered by the producer into a captive take-back scheme ('proprietary material bank'). Take-back is the new all-encompassing standard for non-compliant materials. Producers can transfer the obligation to third parties but only if they valorize the materials. There will be a public domain recovery system for to-standard materials, and a private domain for non-compliant materials. Both the cost of proprietary post-use recovery systems and incentives to produce compliant materials will be very high.

- **Defined use**: The loss of more than 95 per cent of value during the first use cycle of any material and the massive external costs that we elaborated in this book are the result of poor design. In the future, products that enter the market have to come with a defined use, a defined use period and a defined pathway, as outlined in McDonough and Braungart's cradle-to-cradle design concept.[7] All three goals are revolutionary – but quite achievable. Producers will have to define whether a product will circulate in the technosphere in multiple reuse cycles, or whether it will enter the biosphere eventually after use. In that case the product must not contain substances that are toxic, carcinogenic, teratogenic, endocrine-disruptive, bioaccumulative, ozone-depleting or persistent. Beyond use and pathway, the period of use also needs to be defined. Defined periods of use must be agreed upon between producers and users. Imagine the new LIAM process announced by Apple. The 29-armed recycling robot will be able to disassemble the iPhone 6S in only 11 seconds to return parts and materials.[8] This is a massive improvement over today, when even the most sophisticated smartphone recycling is only returning nine out of forty-one elements and typically not the rarest ones.[9] Such a sophisticated system as envisaged by Apple can only be built if use periods for any product are defined. Every assembly run is correlated with the disassembly a number of defined years later. Returning the product after the disassembly programme has terminated with not only kill the post-use value, it will also stand in the way of innovation.

- **Positive lists**: Building the material bank requires a further paradigm shift. We need to shift from negative to positive lists and end the failing race of forbidding substances which we cannot win. Greenpeace's 'Detox my fashion' campaign identified more than 200 harmful substances such as perfluorinated compounds (PFCs) that should be phased out and gained commitment from thirty-five global brands to ultimately eradicate these chemicals. In an industry that uses 17,000 chemicals, these might soon be replaced by new and more complex ones.[10] We will always be a step behind, as Michael Braungart points out in our interview (see Appendix 1). But the list of substances that are healthy, biodegradable and benign is a huge opportunity for the industry to agree on these positive lists. The set of benign substances is the currency of the circular economy which will allow the value chain to collaborate without suffering value loss and leakage at any point. The attempts of the plastic packaging industry to develop something like a plastic protocol with substances that permit standard treatment is such a first step.

- **Zero landfill**: Globally, 44 per cent of all materials still ends up in landfill.[11] In Europe it is 40 per cent, ranging from less than 3 per cent (Germany) to more than 98 per cent (Bulgaria).[12] The wastefulness of this system and the toll on land use, groundwater and health risks is unspeakable, as is the economic loss that comes with landfilling. Governments must recognize that the phase-out of landfilling is a straightforward instrument to create markets that grow the economy. Landfills should be reserved only for selected inert residues, as energetic use must be reserved ultimately for bio-based feedstocks. The phase-out of landfilling and the introduction of sizeable gate fees has proved to be a very effective mechanism to keep materials in the loop. Clearly different countries are at different points of their journey. In Europe some countries have effectively phased out landfilling and the key challenge is to pull the others along. In the Philippines, sanitary landfills are rare and would represent an improvement on the huge amount of littering and unorganized burning of waste, particularly if they were managed in ways that will allow effective mining in the future, once better recovery technology is at hand.[13] Better policing of littering and roadside dumping of collected waste, in conjunction with the stricter landfill regime (sanitary standards, gate fees) could massively accelerate the build-up of a closed-loop economy with higher recovery rates, higher value recycling and eventually the development of cradle-to-cradle products.

- **Sharing**: In this book we have gone a long way to analyse and explain the benefits of sharing. Sharing is a new and powerful source of prosperity. And yet that is not reflected by today's discussions about Uber and Airbnb revolving around two aspects of sharing: the risks of a skewed playing field, and the benefits of sharing economics. Many governments are caught and paralysed between protesting taxi drivers and hoteliers. Governments have to provide a level playing field for incumbent, asset-based players and the sharing economy disruptors in terms of social and environmental standards, insurance requirements or reporting responsibilities. But once the same rules apply to all players, there is no reason for pro-growth governments to stand in the way of sharing. In fact, governments should actively promote the sharing of infrastructure, industrial equipment or even consumer goods. In California, Uber has reduced the traditional taxi business by 50 per cent but at the same time has created a fivefold growth in the total mobility business by mobilizing new demand, according to Prof. Stefan Heck of Stanford University. Governments should start to see sharing as an opportunity and help create fair and effective markets.

- **New factor markets**: Importantly, governments should create new market places. Congestion fees, emission trading, habitat banking, collateralization of ecosystem services, water rights, licensing requirements (e.g. for days at sea, entry permits into sensitive habitat, exploration rights) are not only massively impactful drivers of resource productivity but also constitute the boundary conditions for the twenty-first-century markets which in turn will create economic activity where today there is none. In this way creating markets generates economic activity, income and growth: three examples of how governments could create mega-markets that are non-existent today.

- **Ecosystem services markets**: Ecosystems have value in their own right. However, they also provide vital services with a significant economic value: forests or peatland store water, and run-off peaks in a way that provides dependable flood protection; forests sequester CO_2 (worth \$3.7 trillion per annum) and swamps are highly effective biological treatment plants for certain effluents; bees and other insects provide fertilization services for orchards (generating \$213 million in Switzerland alone).[14] Countryside in general provides leisure and recreational opportunity. The value matters. It can be monetized and provide income and protection for vital ecosystems at a moment really is would otherwise be at risk of being converted. Pioneers such as the Nature Conservancy have provided impressive numbers: more than 700 million people in the world's 100 largest cities such as Bogotá or Cape Town would benefit from these ecosystem services. In these cities they are essentially 'in the money' and cheaper than the second-best alternative (often grey infrastructure).[15] The ecosystem services market that the International Union for Conservation of Nature estimates to be worth \$16–64 trillion today[16] only translates into real market worth of \$100–150 billion.[17] Governments have the opportunity to close that gap by creating ecosystem services markets and removing the obstacles. They must allow collateralizing of the services, provide infrastructure like satellite monitoring, provide securities for long tail risks, etc. These are numbers that would automatically translate into growth, by GDP, not only by GPI definitions.

- **Road space**: Congestion is a huge issue, with massive costs in terms of unproductive time and devalued inner-city assets. London, Stockholm and Singapore have successfully introduced congestion pricing and significantly unchoked their cities. Congestion charging can do more: in the recent *Growth Within*[18] work, its economic impact was modelled by looking at how much idle labour time it could free up. The modelling predicted a decrease in unemployment rate of 0.2 per cent, an increase in the average disposable income of households of 2.3 per cent, and GDP of 1.4 per cent – what the report called a double dividend.

Creating markets for rational use of resources is a particularly promising agenda for governments. These markets will be as natural or as artificial as the financial markets of today. The discussion around market regulation and deregulation misses the point that any modern markets – particularly those mature markets we looked at in detail: mobility, housing, food – are highly regulated today. Shaping markets to provide better outcomes reconnects us with ordo-liberal economic policy. It comes as a surprise (or not!) that Wilhelm Roepke, the economic father of the German *Wirtschaftswunder*, provided – in his own words – a definition of natural capital half a century ahead of the pack: 'Specialized agricultural production, if it is to be carried out rationally, requires an agrarian technique which maintains the fertility of the soil, a factor of particular importance today when even in Europe erosion is more endangering this fertility.'[19]

16.2 Market creating innovation – focusing on growth

There is broad agreement on the importance of innovation: 'Today, innovation performance is a crucial determinant of competitiveness and national progress. Moreover, innovation is important to help address global challenges, such as climate change and sustainable development' writes the OECD.[20] And yet, innovation comes in different forms and with different benefits to society. Harvard's Clayton Christensen differentiates three different types of innovation.[21] **Substitution innovation** relates to the replacement of old products with new higher-performing ones. The iPhone 5 replaces the iPhone 4, the new 3 series BMW replaces its predecessor, fashion stores are swept for a new assortment. **Efficiency innovations** allow companies to provide their goods and services at a lower cost – by introducing robots on the shop floor, merging retail space better, or selling through the internet. In both instances the innovations address the same demand with a renewed or lower cost offering. Therefore their growth and employment effects are small. **Market-creating innovation** is different. It addresses new demand or a new segment. Market-creating innovation is essentially competing against non-consumption, and not against existing consumption. Christensen offers a few examples: Kenya's M-Pesa service, which took the share of Kenyans using banking services from 20 to 80 per cent; South Africa's MTN, which boosted cell phone use across Africa by introducing cheap devices; the Aravind Eye Hospital in India, which made low-cost eye surgery available to 'non-consumers'.

Governments should view the net-positive transition as a market-creating innovation with positive effects for growth and employment. The recovery, recycling, refurbishment or reuse are effectively competing with non-consumption. This is why closing the loops is so beneficial for economic development. In 2012, South Africa introduced new legislation to mandate the recovery of used tyres through a system managed by a new recycling company. In the past tyres had been burned in open fires in order to recover some of the steel wire, with no health protection in place. Three years after the introduction of the new scheme, 70 per cent of tyres were collected. Recycling capacity increased from 8,000 to 60,000 metric tons. This system is essentially competing with non-consumption and therefore the economic benefits are substantial. By 2020 the system is expected to create 1,900 jobs, contribute $8 million to the economy and substantially reduce pollution and CO_2 emissions.[22] Phosphorus recovery, anaerobic digestion, mobile phone disassembly, land rehabilitation, CO_2 recycling, urban-garden agriculture are essentially competing with non-consumption. They create jobs and growth, replenish our capital, mobilize demand internally and lay the foundations for further industrial international expansion. This is exactly the pattern that Japan, Korea and Taiwan were following, and that Honda, Embraer and Chile's agricultural sector successfully pursued. They were all net positive to the economy.

Too much of our public investment – from governments, the World Bank or the International Monetary Fund – is directed at replacement or efficiency innovation and it fails to develop the economy, often in infrastructure or in extractive industries. With the concept of market-creating innovation in mind, governments have the opportunity to refocus their capital, their market regulation, and business education towards those innovations that are net-positive. Developing economies in particular should reverse today's patterns of providing low-cost manufacturing of existing products for international markets and look out for market-creating domestic opportunities, and then take their products, experience and brands global.

16.3 The rise of the meso-economy – spin doctors' magic

In 2004, Dopfer, Foster and Potts[23] wrote: 'The domain of change in an evolutionary process is neither micro nor macro but meso.' To them the economy is not just the interplay of rational, utility maximizing actors (micro) that collectively strive towards general equilibrium (macro) but a complex, interactive and holistic living system of rules and institutional relationships. Linkages are relational and not transactional. What they imply in their very own lingua comes as good news to governments. At a time when most of the classic economic instruments such as lending rates are blunt, they point at a new playing field between the microeconomy (e.g. sector and industrial policy) and the macroeconomy (e.g. fiscal and monetary policy) that is opening up: aligning institutions and groups around a new set of system rules, and reinforcing all motions into new directions. In an era of systemic change, governments can act as spin doctors. They can help trigger a perfect chain reaction and escape the current stalemate which imprisons us in an economy that is so evidently built for the twentieth century. This in turn can reinforce the knock-on effects between different players of the economy. Rather than waiting in paralysis for the other party to move, we could see synchronous action and steady advance. Here's what a perfect storm towards the establishment of a new economic norm could look like:

- If businesses feel that the net-positive economy is an emerging new norm, they would invest in new materials, through-cycle products and business models. They would regain control of their chains, agree on better standards and protocols all the way down the value chain. Rather than communicating to consumers how the products are 'less bad', they would commit to a clear roadmap towards 'good' products and define visible milestones on the way.
- Governments pick up these signals and change the way in which success is measured: from GDP flow-based towards capital-based. The total amount of externalities is made transparent and debated, the reduction is seen as reinforcement and stimulus. Investments are increasingly channelled into building the infrastructure of a regenerative circular economy. Market-creating innovation is fostered and the direct employment effect of new markets (such as post-use treatment) to becomes visible.
- Research institutions and academia are investing massively into accretive e-technologies, such as new materials, material tracing, regenerated energy or soil management, in order to stay attractive for business and government. For some disciplines, turning towards the positive economy can be transformative and the stimulus stronger than experienced in decades: architecture, agriculture, chemistry or marketing.
- Financial institutions will be able to benefit from other actors' moves if they provide long-term capital, take activist positions to accelerate the shift or invest into enabling infrastructure. They

will increasingly move to long-term valuation, take a different view on risks and enforce transparency standards such as the Carbon Disclosure Project.

- Customers will feel encouraged to rediscover quality over quantity and access over ownership. They will demand more transparency and better data on the products they use. Very often they are prosumers rather than consumers – for energy, content, intellectual property and increasingly for physical products themselves. The relationship to companies changes: it will be more long-term, more service-driven and more individual. In a more intimate relationship, the question about the planet-positive character of the service delivered will be ever more important.

- Trade unions will embrace the emergence of new markets and segments and the associated employment opportunity. They will promote new technology as an enabler (rather than killer) of new employment and help pave the way for new skill profiles and training paths. Much of their support has its roots in the levelling of international competition. Accretive economies are more self-sustained and localize more labour than the extreme version of a global economy.

Clearly there are many more constituents in this play: industry associations, tax authorities, patent offices, schools, cooperatives, energy providers, NGOs, etc. And we could have started the list with any actor. What matters is the reinforcement across different institutional camps of the economy, the ability of governments to amplify signals and ultimately take us beyond a systems threshold, from net negative to net positive.

Chapter 17

More is different – the unstoppable crowd

I'm relieved to say there's been a positive resolution to the situation.

Senior Ferrero officer after an online revolt concerning its
flagship product Nutella

Evidently the internet is another reason for optimism that an accretive economy can become a reality. On the one hand, it is providing the very technology for sharing, tracking, reselling, or reconditioning of products or infrastructure. On the other hand, it is the technology agent for change itself. It provides the peer-to-peer, many-to-many medium that is needed to shape our collective dialogue, to convene critical groups of pioneers or to move businesses to action. There is no way to mobilize group action, to trigger innovation or to build the trust needed to unleash funding without the web. The internet has transformed our lives and unnerved economists. Perhaps the real transformative task still lies ahead for the internet.

17.1 Revolution of expressive power – forming the new normal

On 11 July 2013 six female Greenpeace activists landed a coup by scaling up the landmark Shard tower in central London. The campaign was in protest against Shell's drilling activities in the Arctic and took the web and social media by storm. For years Greenpeace had defined the standard for bold media campaigns, but the Shard marked a new highlight.[1] What had taken tens of thousands of protesters in the past took the bravery of six activists this time round, plus amplification through the web. Campaigners and web activists are increasingly keeping the upper hand, building digital roadblocks the way they built physical ones in the past. Corporations struggle to develop adequate responses in time. Blaming has become more effective, piercing and inescapable. For building a net-positive economy, that is not good enough.

Secondly, the web mobilizes for action. After the 2008 earthquake which left 69,225 dead, Chinese parents who mourned their only child took on public authorities for lax building standards which they felt caused so many schools to collapse.[2] Mobilization through the internet triggered such a wave of support that officials publicly surrendered and self-flagellatingly knelt in front of the protesters. Many of them were suspended and convicted – an act without precedence in China.[3] A similar story occured in Indonesia, where rainforest destruction has slowed under the eye of the web community. International and on-the-ground activists are now powerfully connected through global mobilization (e.g. through the crowdsourcing platform 'Tomnod') and local verification through smartphone photographs, blogs or realtime fire alerts.[4]

Thirdly, it paves the way for a new set of norms. Big game hunting will never regain respectability since the storm that hailed a Minnesota dentist after killing a lion named Cecil just outside Zimbabwe's Hwange National Park (for right or wrong). That storm has established a new norm that will not stop big game hunting, but will stop it from playing out in the public domain.[5] It is easily conceivable that a new ethics of accretion, regeneration and circularity which fundamentally challenges industries as they dispose of or emit waste could thrive in the same digital medium. In the same way that gay and lesbian rights were embraced by the web community, a vegan diet became a viable choice or the fashion for body painting returned, a zero-waste standard could take hold more easily, faster and with more consequence through the web.

17.2 Everyone's data – the new transparency

The biggest free ride in economic history, the overuse of unpriced resources can be largely linked to incomplete information. We never knew how much our 'cows are grazing of the commons' – now we do. We can literally count – at a very low cost – the caloric intake, the movement patterns, the litres of milk and the tons of dung. We had no understanding of volumes and composition of effluents that entered public sewage systems from individual companies and homes – now we do, through remote sensing and at negligible cost. We could not track a car's consumption of peak- and low-time roadspace – an ability that every one of the 1.75 billion smartphones provides.[6] We were blind to the origin of harmful chloride-bearing plastic in an otherwise high-grade feedstock – now we can trace it to the source. And we did not know which of the vessels on the high seas outside the 200-mile zone had, on its long journey, trespassed marine protected areas or economic exclusive zones – now we can track them on the internet (www.globalfishingwatch.org). Big data is a double-edged sword. In the public domain, deployed information can be a critical enabler for an accretive economy and a historic opportunity to overcome the elusiveness of resources and natural capital to property rights, accountability, quantification and sanctions. It essentially moves the boundary from unquantified to quantified and from unpriced to priced. Through this, it allows us in a unique and unprecedented way to turn externalities into internalities.

17.3 Crowdfunding and blockchains – the trust revolution

The regenerative, positive economy is essentially a business model revolution in need of substantial and innovative forms of funding. Through crowdfunding a completely new source of capital has been made available to start-up entrepreneurs, particularly those with unconventional ideas at the systems boundary. Crowdfunding today is a $34.4 billion investment market[7] and some pioneering environmental start-ups such as Mosaic and Open Utility have been funded through the crowd. Perhaps the more pervasive innovation, for both funding and enabling net-positive businesses, is the blockchain. This revolutionizes digital transactions and makes it unnecessary for central authorities to verify and clear transactions.

A blockchain is a distributed cryptographic or encoded ledger database with a digital log of transactions which is hosted on a shared, open-source network. It removes the need to check every transaction, with a counterparty saving in the billions. *The Economist* has described it as 'a trust machine'.[8] Banks and other corporations are starting to understand the sheer unlimited opportunity of that new technology. Twenty-five banks have recently joined forces to found a blockchain startup by the name of R3 CEV. We are only beginning to understand the opportunity that trusted transactions offer to the new agenda. Examples are replete. Component trading is very important to keep resources in circulation within the technosphere. So far their quality and former users could not be guaranteed. However if they are identifiable and the blockchain ledger exists on the string of former users and uses, the value can be warranted in the future. Honduras and Greece are currently testing the blockchain for land registries.[9] The so-called 'tragedy of the Commons', i.e. the mismanagement of some of our most important environmental assets because no one has responsibility for them, could be resolved through better property rights which in turn can be warranted by blockchain-based ledgers. What's more, and in even more straighforward terms, blockchain provides a safe mechanism for micropayments and could be a key enabler of the shareconomy as well as of the performance economy with their small and frequent payments. We could go on.

Trusted, ample, distributed information and access to many-to-many social media are the quintessential infrastructure for the new economy we describe. Most importantly, because they provide visibility and accountability in the resource space where data has been poor, they allow the trade of intangibles and they allow groups to convene around a common interest.

Chapter 18

The new capitalist – the rise of long-term entrepreneurism

I am absolutely sure: if we wait until consumption is a socially undesirable term we are too late to rescue our businesses.

Board member, global consumer goods company

Most corporations and CEOs find themselves in a triple squeeze, and are looking for ways out. First, competition has intensified, efficiency reserves are exhausted and time horizons have shortened. Then, they have to reconnect with their customers and reconfirm that they are truly acting in their best interest. And finally, they have to mitigate the massive and accumulating risk which has been observed to destroy value in the billions and centuries of tradition in the blink of an eye (see Volkswagen, British Petroleum, but also Nestlé, Coca-Cola, etc.). Within those lines of tension, the time of muddling through is running out. Companies need to reset themselves more fundamentally. Net positive and the radical and simultaneous redesign of products, supply chains and business models are increasingly perceived as a way out.

Diminishing returns: Most industries are competing in cut-throat markets and feed from razor-thin margins. Globally, margins had massively increased between 1980 and 2010 but are now stagnating and bound to decrease. McKinsey Global Institute is expecting corporate profits to decrease between 2015 and 2025 from 9.8 to 7.9 per cent of global GDP.[1] This is the result of intensified competition as entry barriers crumble, market volatility and slow growth – an overall shift towards idea-intensive sectors that produce big winners.

Social meaning of the brand: Most established businesses have manoeuvred themselves into conflict with no less than their own customers. While global advertising spend is exploding to $540 billion in 2015,[2] at the same time companies are essentially telling their customers that consuming more is not in their and the planet's best

Global corporate profits may fall as a share of GDP in the next decade, despite a jump in revenue

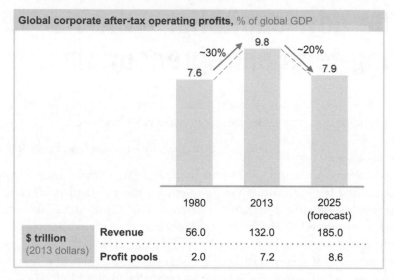

Global corporate after-tax operating profits, % of global GDP

		1980	2013	2025 (forecast)
$ trillion (2013 dollars)	**Revenue**	56.0	132.0	185.0
	Profit pools	2.0	7.2	8.6

SOURCE: Adapted from McKinsey Global Institute (2015)

Fig 18.1

interest. Sustainability reports are replete with explanations of how the level of social harm and environmental damage that comes with consuming products is slowly decreasing, but remaining. The message that companies are sending their customers is what psychologists call 'dissonant'. It is a proposition that is hard to maintain in the long term and executives feel it. And they express it behind closed doors. Companies need to move from 'less bad' to 'good', as Michael Braungart describes it,[3] and redefine the social meaning of their brand.

Systemic risk: Companies operate under mounting systemic risk. Many of these risks are correlated with the amount of resources required and subsequently returned into public systems and the environment. Volkswagen, British Petroleum, Exxon or Vale have made this risk blatantly clear. Moving towards healthy, planetary benign products and zero waste can be seen as a very reliable and affordable insurance.

Clearly there are no easy answers for how to manage such a field of tension. And yet we believe that the economy outlined in the course of this book represents a viable pathway to mitigate the pressures and risks felt by CEOs and managers around the world. And a new generation of investors and CEOs is starting to see the allure of the new model. That, too, is reason for optimism.

18.1 Embracing the new rules – out of the trenches

From Michael Porter to Gary Hamel to Clayton Christensen, it is hard to find management thinkers that would not recommend playing an innovation game ahead of market requirements, customer demand and legal requirements. A changing business environment is viewed as an opportunity for differentiation, arbitraging and premium risk-taking. A resource productivity play as outlined in this book is such an opportunity. Heck and Rogers call it 'the biggest business opportunity in a century'.[4] The transition towards a positive, resilient, high-quality, service-driven industry should be embraced, but typically is not. New standards and market rules are rejected, often against good evidence. Very often, industry opposed environmental legislation, drawing a picture of lost competitiveness, bankruptcy and massive job loss. While these cases might have occurred and should caution policy-makers, an empirical study of the twelve major and most controversial environmental bills of the US performed by Hart Hodges reveals that costs have – without exception – been significantly lower than advertised during the legislative debate, partly by a factor of ten or more.[5] Stopping benzene pollution was estimated to generate costs of $350,000 per plant and turned out to be neutral. EPA's 1980 Coke Ovens emissions bill was advertised to create extra costs of $4 billion but turned out to have generated costs of $250–400 million. Limiting vinyl chloride emission to meet the 1 parts per million permissible exposure limit was expected to generate $109 million cost per year and put the 'industry on a collision course with economic disaster',[6] yet according to a retrospective study by the Wharton School of Business, the actual costs turned out to be $20 million per year, without any impacts on industry performance. The reason for actual costs being significantly lower than estimates might be an overstatement to some extent. More likely, however, it is an underestimation of the cost decline of clean technology and the positive effect on production efficiencies. Most examples indicate that early adopters have benefitted from embracing new competitive rules.

Cost of complying with environmental regulation almost always much lower than expected upfront

Cost of Control			
Pollutant	Ex-Ante Estimate	Ex-Post or Revised Ex- Anle Estimate	Overestimation as a Percent of Actual Cost
Asbestos	$150 million (total for mfg. and insulation sectors)	$75 million	-
Benzene	$350,000 per plant	approx. $0 per plant	-
CFCs	1988 estimate to reduce emissions by 50% within 10 years: $2.7 billion	1992 estimate to phase out CFCs within 8 years: $3.8 billion	41%
CFCs-Auto Air Conditioners	$650 - $1,200 per new car	$40-$400 per new car	63% - 2,900%
Coke Oven Emissions OSHA 1970s	$200 million - $1 billion	$160 million	29% - 525%
Coke Oven Emissions EPA 1980s	$4 billion	$250 - 400 million	900% - 1,500%
Cotton Dust	$700 million per year	$205 million per year	241%
Halons	1989: phase out not considered possible	1993: phase out considered technologically and economically feasible	-
Landfill Leachate	Mid-1980s: $14.8 billion	1990: $5.7 billion	159%
Sulfur Dioxide	$4 billion - $5 billion	-	100% - 300%
Surface Mining	$6 - $12 per ton of coal	$0.50 - $1 per ton	500% - 2,300%
Vinyl Chloride	$109 million per year	$20 million per year	445%

SOURCE: Hodges (1997)

Fig 18.2

18.2 Mastering the new art – the next 'Lean'

The Forum of the Future, WWF UK and the Climate Group, with the support of British Telecom, launched a Net-Positive Initiative in 2010 in order to guide companies towards net-positive business management. The group has identified twelve principles companies have to embrace in order to become net positive. We have been working with clients of different size, in different industries and across all continents for the last eight years, helping them in their journey towards better environmental and social outcomes. We found that there is a set of functional skills companies need to learn. Once they have embraced them, they are a source of true competitiveness. An analogy that we often use when discussing this change with corporate leaders is 'LEAN' operations. This is the operations philosophy that Toyota pioneered from the 1960s onwards, and that has been on every global executive's mind since the 1980s. In brief, it consists of going after waste along a company's whole value chain, and teaching employees at all levels to identify and address different types of waste. This has become so hugely popular because it allows companies to identify and address improvement opportunities they never 'saw' before. Says 'LEAN' veteran Shigeo Shingo: 'The most dangerous kind of waste is the waste we do not recognize.'[7] And importantly, this global movement was created out of nothing but a powerful new idea and a new way of looking at supply chains and operations. Notably, there have been no regulation or subsidies that have achieved results as good as LEAN's. The innovation will go far beyond what we or anyone else can foresee today.

So think of the ReSOLVE examples we described earlier in Chapter 8 as the first wave of innovation and growth if the world turns on this opportunity – hugely important in themselves, but still only a first step. There is so much system waste in our economy, and it has been so neglected compared to the size of the opportunity, that ReSOLVE strategies will be fertile ground for value creation for decades to come. Look at what happened in clean energy: when the 'market' understood how hugely important it was and there were consistent policy signals that society wanted this development, an amazing technology revolution was set loose. So we expect that once the world acknowledges for real that these opportunities exist, and starts pursuing them, we will see a second and third wave of opportunities that no one can foresee today.

18.3 Internalizing complexity – managing system-level change

By definition, an accretive economy takes entrepreneurs outside chartered territory. Consumers are unaware and cautious, capital markets are poorly organized and policed, industry standards are absent, value chains are optimized for the less negative products, regulation is unhelpful or adverse and employees are sceptical and ill-trained. Any product or service needs to match the industrial system around it, but this time pioneer offerings are built for a new system which is only slowly coming into place. Judging from experience, what can entrepreneurs do to prevail and shape the new system as, say, mobility, energy or net-positive agriculture pioneers?

Many pioneers took on the complexity of systemic change by internalizing it: the support functions, the supply chain, the R&D, the development of skills and the funding. Tesla decided to build up its own network of superchargers rather than wait for public infrastructure to evolve. Nespresso concluded that the best way to close the loop on its highly sought after coffee capsules was to develop a proprietary takeback system. The Port of Rotterdam, together with Rabobank, Bikker and Van Gansewinkel, decided in the absence of national legislation to establish its own Circularity Center and launched a set of concrete projects such as plastic, phosphorus and CO_2 recovery. Some companies internalized the R&D that is within more mature systems provided by the suppliers. Recognizing that the market did not deliver the positive materials that Lego required, the company started a Sustainable Materials Centre in order to develop the next generation of bio-based and non-toxic plastics. Development of net-positive skills is another demand not freely available on the market. While the Net-Positive Initiative is providing helpful guidance, NGOs such as the Ellen MacArthur Foundation offer training and awareness building to their constituents (such as the CE 100 Group) or the open public (such as the Disruptive Innovation Festival), and institutes like the Cradle-to-Cradle Products Innovation Institute offer so-called catalyst programmes. Companies struggled to get the right skills through public education so started offering in-house vocational programmes and sustainability academies. Daimler launched a green demonstration and learning centre in which it trains aspects of energy-efficient manufacturing.

A major barrier for system-level pioneers is funding. Conventional capital markets are unable to assess the opportunities and risks that come with radically new designs, system architectures or business models. One way to deal with the slow speed of capital is royalty financing. Instead of raising debt or equity and planning for liquidity events later on, pioneer innovators are licensing investor capital.

Companies are paying their investors a royalty of typically 2–6 per cent of revenues, until a defined multiple of the initial principal is reached. Royalty financing is a $100 billion market today; it is much easier to process and comes at a lower risk.[8]

Most importantly, system innovators learn to break out of silos. Internally they regularly convene the different experts that, in more mature companies, rarely need each other: product developers, marketeers, supply chain managers, procurement officers, scrap handlers. It is these different disciplines that jointly own the new system. Similarly across companies planet-positive innovations are team sports. They form and join consortia, often with government or NGO participation, which have the reach and muscle to define the future system: the New Plastic Economy, the blueprint for a Trash-free Sea, hydrogen-based mobility, an accelerated energy transition or the compliance of business with SDG principles. The ability to work with third parties on questions of system design is an increasingly critical competitive skill.

18.4 Think long term – taking back the company

More and more research is indicating that short-term orientation is a response to short-term incentives which have crept in. In this way we are not only inflicting costs on society, we are also losing economic value. It is time for owners to take back their companies and for managers to act like owners. So the heart of this agenda is that companies need to adjust their governance to focus on long-term health and act more like family-owned businesses. In his *Harvard Business Review* article, McKinsey managing director Dominic Barton hints at a couple of possible levers:[9] more focused board members with more time available, a more strategic dialogue between the board and the management team, executive compensation linked to long-term performance, longer evaluation cycles for executives, executives with (at least) a year's salary invested, contracts that ensure a bigger say for long-term investors. But it also requires a cultural shift: CEOs who can play within their industries but also in the social and private sectors. The new reality is this: companies are served better by shielding themselves against shocks that come with product liabilities, feedstock markets, consumer activism, than by optimizing short-term returns. Many examples, from British Petroleum and Exxon to Foxfire and Mattel, have proven this case. In that environment, CEOs need to act as long-term custodians and leaders, not as short-term managers.

Also with regard to the net-positive economy, there is movement and a change of perspective. On 24 November 2015, German insurance giant Allianz announced plans to divest from the coal industry almost entirely. It is a sizeable and private sector-led move in a much broader investor stampede away from fossil fuels. A coalition of 2,000 individuals and 400 institutions with assets under management worth $2.6 trillion have now divested from the coal, oil and gas industry. Among them are the world's largest sovereign wealth fund, from Norway, and two of the world's largest pension funds, from California.[10] This already adds up to the largest act of shareholder activism ever. Partly, this is good citizenship and a response to consumer and government expectations. Partly, it is an attempt to reduce the mounting portfolio risk associated with the fossil fuel industry. And partly, it is an expression of a convergent view on the future of our energy sector shared by many CEOs as they grow more confident and vocal. Apple's CEO Tim Cook told environment-sceptic investors to exit from their stock if they disagree with the company's green, more longer-term initiatives. He, like others, refuses to be a 'slave to ROI'.[11]

Chapter 19

The great reconciliation – entering the upward spiral

An object either remains at rest or continues to move at a constant velocity, unless acted upon by a net force.

Isaac Newton

The starting point and the trigger for this book has been a very fundamental question, one you could feel in the air on that June day in 2015 when the European Commission started its consultation for the Circular Economy package. Can we afford such an experiment?

Our work with corporate and government leaders, the many discussions and interviews and the analyses we undertook confirmed to us that we can. More than that: we can't afford not to shift from a net to an accretive system of wealth creation. We are more convinced than ever that capital accretion rapidly needs to take the place of income optimization. In the short term they might look like antagonisms, but in the long term they are not. All the data presented so far is showing how exhausted ecosystems, rising cost of extraction, uncontrollable resource markets, global dependencies, consumer fatigue and mounting externalities are starting to affect GDP growth, even today. A planet-positive strategy could reconcile economic growth with the build-up of manufactured, human and social capital in the long term. It is the stock of that capital that determines whether we thrive as individuals and societies. To allow for that great reconciliation to happen, we need to turn our eyes from protecting the old to creating the new. And we need to embrace the benefits that such a new system design could yield.

19.1 First order benefits – affordable, productive, clean

There is a massive shift in thinking underway. In the past it was almost inevitably correct to suspect higher costs through recycling, renewable energy or stricter material standards. And if costs were not higher, convenience was lower. These truisms are proving wrong in today's world of cheap renewable energy, sharing, component harvesting, condition-based maintenance, nutrient recovery, industrial collocation and large-scale soil rehabilitation. All of these are manifestations of a more circular, regenerative and ultimately accretive economy. The immediate benefits are at hand.

Affordability. Shared, electrified, autonomous mobility will make families more mobile than today's system of car ownership. Pay-per-use power tools, refurbished printers, compostable cutlery, shared office space are all significantly more affordable and come, if well organized, at higher convenience and performance. In Germany and many other European countries, the discount revolution had similar effects. There are estimates that the proliferation of this radical retail model brought end-user prices significantly down and kept inflation at bay.[1] However this came at a price for inner cities, for suppliers all the way up to the milk farmers, and often for quality. The systems outlined in Part II of this book could deliver affordability with fewer downsides.

Productivity. High-volume production and automation continue to drive productivity up and costs down. However, since labour productivity has been pursued for so long, and since resource markets are getting increasingly volatile, boosting resource productivity might be the better option. Desso is translating returned carpets into new ones at a better cost, Renault is successfully remanufacturing passenger cars, Girsberger is giving its office furniture a second use cycle, thereby saving inputs and fighting grey markets,[2] and JustPark is managing parking space in cities, thereby massively boosting the productivity of the urban mobility system. All of these solutions are positive and boost the productivity of the provider and the customer at the same time.

Sustainability. The third immediate benefit accrues to society at large and partially to producers through the reduction of external costs which are hitting our books today. Time lost in congestion, start-ups unable to contract affordable office space, treatment plants cleaning effluents replete with mineral fertilizer run-off or waste-to-energy plants managing chlorides represent real cost to the economy. They were all triggered by products or industrial processes that were either bad or less bad, but clearly not good.

Our numbers indicate that the immediate benefits are real today even as the regulatory environment, our supply chains and our consumer mindsets continue to be deeply entrenched in the linear model. So why don't companies flock to capture the opportunity? It is fair to say that many of these opportunities come with additional complexity, new skill requirements, additional risks and higher transaction costs. So for the average company it continues to be the more costly option. For pioneers, foresighted and agile players, however, they are the real opportunity today.

19.2 Second-order benefits – resilient growth and employment

More importantly, the new competitive dynamic of a planet-positive economy will change the pattern of how we generate and share wealth. It would be unduly optimistic to state that fixing the resource economy will eradicate the major shortcomings of secular stagnation, jobless growth and impending risk of market shocks. And yet if seconded by the right macro policies, the second-order effects can make it an important pillar as we seek to derisk our economies.

Growth. We have seen that GDP growth and other measures of wealth such as the Genuine Progress Indicator or the Inclusive Wealth Index have started to take different paths from the mid-1980s onwards.[3] GDP growth seemed increasingly unrelated to the development of our capital stock. In many countries growth became uneconomic. Thirty years into this process, growth itself seems to stutter, and some of the reasons are linked to the way we are exhausting our planetary resources. It seems clear that recapitalizing our planet and our social systems will ultimately lead to higher GDP growth. It must, because there are more productive assets to work with. What is new is this: the analysis shows that even during the transition towards an accretive, net-positive capital stock, the GDP growth will benefit. The reason is straightforward: eliminating structural waste from the economy frees up productive resources. For example, people will spend less time in congestion, less valuable land will be devoted to parking space, and fewer buildings will be unnecessarily torn down.[4] As discussed in chapter 9, the positive impact on Europe's GDP could be up to 7 percentage points until 2030, or almost half a percentage point additional growth per year. We believe this makes this one of the most attractive reform opportunities available to European (and other) policy makers, perhaps as attractive as the creation of the internal European market was when it was initiated in the 1990s, until now.

Employment. Sharing, reuse, higher asset utilization or reducing agricultural inputs will decrease primary industrial output and the associated employment. Ironically, less pollution clean-up, less frequent product controls and fewer accidents will also negatively affect the job market. There is reason to be concerned about employment in a circular, regenerated economy. The meta-study conducted by the Institute for the Future of Labour, however, implies the opposite.[5] It points out the significant infrastructure programmes needed to build the circular economy. It shows how circular economy principles are formalizing work in domains formerly dominated by informal labour. It also shows that recovery, remanufacturing, refurbishment and reuse are essentially service-driven sectors which require labour, often more than highly automated industrial environments. We need to recognize that during the transition jobs would be lost. They are less specific to a certain sector, although primary sectors such as mining, oil and gas production clearly will have to reinvent themselves. It will be more a race between the fast and slow, the adaptive and the laggard. There is a neutral role to play for government during the transition – not to fight the new trend but to quickly transition people into the new economy and to help them acquire the necessary skills. Governments have to make the shift faster, not slower, to serve people best.

Resilience. Much of our post-war economic ups and downs can be described as a story of the oil price. It is the most visible dependency on resource markets that we have. High resource prices such as those experienced in the early 1970s caused crisis in resource-dependent economies. But low energy or resource prices, too, come with their downsides. They have destabilized commodity exporting countries like Russia, Nigeria and South Africa, deferred efficiency investments among heavy user nations and deflated currencies. Commodities have been used in trade wars, winning access to critical resources such as oil, phosphorus or rare earth metals, and any costs often came at a high political price. A net-positive economy is massively levelling the playing field (with a slight benefit for countries with a high solar income) and reducing the exposure to risks and increasingly volatile markets.

19.3 Third-order benefits – generous, equal and replete with possibility

We believe that the benefits of an accretive economy go further. Moving from a paradigm of scarcity to one of abundance might be one of the most pervasive changes society can undergo. It might change our dialogue and mitigate some of the most concerning trends that dominate the recent debate: polarizing societies that are increasingly afraid of sharing their wealth with others.

Generosity. The notion of scarce resources might not be the only reason for greed – but it is a very significant one. Admittedly, our discussion has moved on from scarce resources in general to a more modern notion that some resources are scarce while others are not, but that the conversion of any of them is linked to high environmental costs. The view that the earth, its resources and the wealth we can extract from it is limited and hard, if not impossible, to expand is shaping our view on two towering themes: population and migration. A population of 7.5, then 9, 10 and 11 billion is a truly unsettling perspective at a moment when Earth Overshoot Day has already moved to 13 August. The outlook has sparked global family planning programmes, agitated debates and more deeply a sense of overwhelm, which starts to translate into an inability to embrace and welcome a new life. It brought us to the brink of moral surrender. Declaring a newborn child a *persona non grata* on the planet is a new low point. It is particularly dramatic if it translates into active rejection and erodes our compassion. That is a tonality that increasingly governs our reflex to the incipient mass migration that we see in Europe, in Australia, along the Mexican border, in Chinese cities and within Africa. In a paradigm of scarce resources, exhausted biosystems, wars for water and CO_2 budgets, the influx of more human beings has to be a threat. Let's turn it around now.

How would our perception change if we believed that abundant energy derived from the sun is the ultimate source of wealth and that there is a 5x, 10x, or 50x resource productivity lever available to any country that is able to organize high-performance systems to tap this wealth? It would be naive to believe that adversity, greed and angst are entirely resolved in an age of abundant energy and high-performance mobility, housing or industrial systems. At the same time, if we developed the capability to massively restore ecosystems, particularly in geographies with high population growth and migrant source regions; if we could massively slow down the pace of global warming and if we were able to fulfil more needs with fewer manufactured assets, some of the explosiveness of today's trend could be dampened. A culture of generosity essentially needs to ride on the back of an economic paradigm of generosity.

Equality. Inequality has grown dramatically within most societies. Even some of the more egalitarian ones such as Germany or the Nordics have taken a turn for the worse. Inequality remains high in the US and increasingly appears as an unavoidable side effect of economic growth in aspiring BRICS countries. There are many reasons for this: it is linked to globalizing labour markets, technology substitution or merely to the dynamics of capital markets. Sometimes it is amplified by labour legislation in poorly regulated capital markets. How would that change in the accretive economy? A number of aspects would come into play: prosumption where consumers produce content (as on Facebook), products (as in 3D printing) or energy (as in rooftop PV) clearly come with a migration of value from producers to consumers. Prosumption underlies many of the net-positive business models outlined before. Also, the rent-taking of resource owners – oil, rare earth metals, phosphorus, land, water – could be reduced. In recent years much of the market power has moved upwards towards the resource owners and in a circular economy that would of course be systematically reversed.

Additionally, the circular, regenerative economy denotes an accelerated shift into the knowledge economy. It will come with less conventional industrial work and more modern occupations, as all the new job examples listed in Part II illustrated. Jobs would be harder to replace, less mechanical, more customer-centric and, hopefully, better paid. And by eradicating harmful substances and waste more broadly, a lot of the ecological poverty could be addressed. It is known that much of the environmental burden is carried by the economically weak across communities, countries or the globe.

Possibility. What we most like about the accretive economy is what it does to our imagination, our sense of opportunity and our ability to dream. We have had the opportunity to share our experiences with hundreds of young people, the so-called millennial generation. Each time we are astonished and pleased to see what accretive thinking and secular principles do to the mind. It releases people out of the inherited hard trade-offs between prosperity and good stewardship and is perceived as truly liberating. In a net-positive world the sky is the limit. Courses for cradle-to-cradle are oversubscribed, consulting associates are queueing up to be considered for circular economy projects and any related job opening is quickly filled. Producing nutrients rather than waste, improving earth systems with every economic activity and building capital on the way are too attractive concepts to put the pencil down. We observed it with our colleagues, students, and out children. We had to tell them 'lights out' because they were dreaming on and on. This is Alice's wonderland – powered by new technology and principles delivered by nature.

A decoupled, largely dematerialised and circular economy may or may not deliver all these much-desired benefits. But clearly and differently from the scale-governed industrial economy of the last century it is able to deliver a much broader set of societal goods – if only we shape it accordingly.

Chapter 20

The good singularity – not wasting our best chance

In all of your deliberations in the Confederate Council, in your efforts at law making, in all your official acts, self-interest shall be cast into oblivion. Cast not over your shoulder behind you the warnings of the nephews and nieces should they chide you for any error or wrong you may do, but return to the way of the Great Law which is just and right. Look and listen for the welfare of the whole people and have always in view not only the present but also the coming generations, even those whose faces are yet beneath the surface of the ground – the unborn of the future Nation.

Constitution of the Iroquois Nation

We have reached a singular moment where the case for change is imminent, the new forces available to us are infinite and the outcomes are undefined. Tangibly so. The conversations we have with business executives, public sector leaders, scientists, friends or our children are replete with a sense of new opportunity mixed with massive anxiety over how we consume, travel and live. In the course of this book we have tried to assemble factual evidence that helps to comprehend the historic point at which we have arrived and to characterize it as a unique departure point – if only we take the opportunity. Where are we? Over the course of the twentieth century we have generated unprecedented wealth, raised billions out of poverty, defeated illnesses, connected with each other and developed the modern, secure and comfortable lifestyle shared by billions. However, in the late twentieth century, a number of developments started to take a different turn. The period between 1985, when the great divergence started, and 2015, when the new technology and business platform started being robust enough, might go down in history as an era 'off-track' or, more optimistically, of inflexion. It was within the mid-1980s as elaborated in Chapter 3 when GDP, employment, real income and income distribution started to diverge. And it was in that same period when we had to wake up to the reality that we are overusing our planetary resources in sometimes irreversible ways. And we were exposing ourselves to ever bigger system shocks – erratic commodity markets (see steel in 2008, or oil in 2014), weather events (see Sandy), supply chain failure (see the Thailand shut-down), geopolitical disruptions (see the European refugee crisis) or big infrastructure failure (see Fukushima). What looked like side effects that could be managed along the way by better legislation, incremental improvements and sustainability self-commitments have now turned out to be something entirely different. This is a flaw deeply embedded into our economic model which continues for all practical purposes to be built on extraction, exploitation, exhaustion. The costs of that model are starting to outpace the benefits. In many sectors and geographies we have entered into a spiral of uneconomic growth.

We have shown that during that period our resource-intense model of growth turned essentially into one of massively diminishing returns. Luckily – and this is the core message of the book – now in 2016 and beyond, there is a new vector for growth available that is consistent with the new realities of a denser planet: the technology and business model disruption that started happening in front of our eyes, in the media, financial services, telecom industry, and now in energy and mobility, and soon across all industrial sectors right into agriculture and ecosystem management. The power of those new systems to generate wealth out of our given stock of resources is staggering. There is no system where we couldn't find – with conservative assumptions – a factor 3 to 5 improvement in resource productivity. Moving the productive use of vehicles for example from 2 per cent to 20–40 per cent demonstrates that there is an upside to those numbers. By doubling the annual improvement of our resource productivity from 1.5 to 3 per cent we would tap into our single biggest source of growth and redefine the competitive game between companies, sectors and economies. The end point is not only a more resource-productive economy; it is a planet-positive system with a completely different dynamic and based on a new set of accepted norms.

This book has tried to move beyond the case for action and cost of inaction. We have to describe the transition that is ahead of us. It will be an era of creative destruction, fundamental redesign, testing of orthodoxies, experimentation, shift of economic value between actors and overall high penalties for laggards. To get there we need a set of new design principles replacing the old ones, a plan for how to manage the tipping points ahead of us, and we need real leadership instead of management. We have made proposals for each of those points. It is particularly important to build the three building blocks of the new accretive system: abundant sources of renewable energy, a cradle-to-cradle material bank and a high-productivity positive industrial system built on circular and regenerative principles – in summary, delivering our human needs. These building blocks will be picked up like Lego bricks by the next generation, to build the future they desire.

Throughout our history, phases of scepticism, disorder and anxiety have been alternating with episodes of momentum and collective confidence. They have proven to be turning points – sometimes for bad and sometimes for good. The key reason why we have written this book is to point to the massive opportunity ahead of us. It's ours to lose. We, the authors of this book, could not think of a more exciting, more rewarding and more deserving time in which to live.

PART V: Appendices

Five perspectives on the necessary transition

The transition we describe in this book is incremental but systemic. It involves new technology, behaviours, industrial practices, governance systems and – eventually – societal norms. To reach a holistic understanding of it, we chose to interview five leading minds from different disciplines. We selected them with purpose. They have – in very different ways – influenced our work and thinking. And each of them is a disruptive thinker and has been – again in their very own way – part of a transformation in their field. It is striking how they all advocate deep and disruptive changes to our current industrial model. Their perspectives have influenced many parts of the book, but we also want to provide the original interviews, as we feel many good points were made that would otherwise be lost. The conversations have been shortened, but we have kept as much as possible of the original language. As you'll notice, each interview emphasizes different aspects of the transition, and together they make a strong case for a good disruption.

- *Jean-Marc Duvoisin* is the CEO of Nespresso, which has fundamentally disrupted the coffee value chain, and established a new business model which decommoditizes coffee with benefits along the entire value chain. Duvoisin describes how 'net positive' is a realistic vision for Nespresso, and how crucial it is for companies to develop new, environmentally-positive, and often disruptive, business models rather than tinkering at the edges of old business models with a built-in conflict between profitability and environment.
- *Bishop Heinrich Bedford-Strohm* is the leader of the Protestant church in Germany, and as such the informal leader of the Protestant church worldwide. He discusses how the necessary 'reformation' towards a planet-compatible economy needs to become an issue of hearts and souls, as well as wallets, and how social norms and financial incentives need to come together to ensure the transition succeeds.

- *Professor Lord Nicholas Stern* is the author of *The Stern Review of the Economics of Climate Change,* and one of the world's most respected climate-change economists. He underscores how system productivity and circular material flows need to complement low-carbon energy to keep climate change under control. He also elaborates on how a clean and healthy environment will be a key competitive advantage for cities and countries in the future.
- *Professor Dr. Michael Braungart* is a leading environmental thinker and the father of the cradle-to-cradle concept used extensively in this book. He sees the transition ahead as an enormous industrial innovation opportunity, and argues that it is just the sort of renewal and revitalization that the economy needs, even disregarding the enormous huge environmental benefits.
- *Muhammad Yunus* is a social entrepreneur and a Nobel laureate, recognized for establishing micro-finance as a pillar of economic and social development. He explains that our economic model must reflect both the selflessness and the selfishness of humans, not just the latter. He describes the immense power of innovation and new technology as building blocks of that new model, how misdirected he feels that innovation is today, and how much good 'social technology' could do if it was directed at the real issues facing our society.

Interview with Jean-Marc Duvoisin, CEO of Nespresso

Q: Knowing that the environment is a high priority for you, what strategies does Nespresso pursue?

A: Sustainability is built into our business model and embedded within our brand. We do this through creating shared value to ensure that not only our customers, and of course the business, benefit, but that the farmers do, as well.

We work with more than 70,000 farmers around the world through our AAA Sustainable Quality programme. We have more than 300 agronomists in the coffee-growing countries who help those farmers one-on-one to achieve the highest quality, environmental and social standards. Because the coffee these farmers grow is such high quality, we pay them 30 to 40 per cent more than they would get paid in the commodity coffee market.

With this focus on quality, we are able to 'decommoditize' coffee for the benefit of consumers and farmers. This allows consumers to know exactly where the coffee comes from, and by making a direct link from the coffee to the farmer that grew it, customers better understand our approach to creating shared value and they start to care more about the coffee-growing communities and their conditions. We believe this makes a difference to the choices consumers will make.

We are also reducing the carbon footprint of our supply chain, and are working on developing more circular solutions for the aluminium capsules. The question of 'why aluminium' comes up often, and the fact is that it is the best material we have found to preserve the freshness and aromas of our coffee and it is infinitely recyclable. We encourage and enable recycling around the world, and are working on some new approaches to the capsules' lifecycle that we will scale up in the coming years.

When you look at the entire lifecycle of portioned coffee, it is about resource efficiency: when you brew a cup of Nespresso coffee, you use exactly the right amount of coffee and water, and our machines are energy-efficient: they are not wasting energy by heating too much water and remaining on longer than they need to be. So with portion coffee, there is less waste than with, for instance, drip coffee.

Q: What are your views about the much-discussed contradiction between competitiveness on one hand, and environment on the other? Can companies afford to proactively 'go green' or will they just lose market share to others that don't?

A: There is certainly tension between the two that can be difficult to manage when companies have a short-term vision, looking for quicker gains. But this tension disappears when you have a long-term approach. Then sustainability and competitiveness become complementary and reinforce each other. Sustainable corporate behaviour is now a must for companies that want to be competitive and consumers, regulators and financial markets will ask more from us in the future.

Another important aspect of the competitiveness discussion that I often feel is neglected is talent. Before becoming the CEO of Nespresso, I was Head of HR for the Nestlé Group, and I spent a lot of time making sure Nestlé was attractive to young talent. If you want to recruit the best talent and engage and inspire your employees, you must be a responsible company with values that employees share. Sound values are a major competitive advantage in the talent market.

Q: Nespresso is a clear 'disruptor' of the coffee value chain. How do you think about industry disruption in relation to creating a planet-compatible economy?

A: I don't think it is a coincidence that so many of the disrupting companies we see today are also leaders in sustainability. They've often found a way to improve efficiency dramatically and reinvent their value chains, and at the same time, they are creating environmental benefits.

I will stress again that for Nespresso, having a business model that inherently supports sustainability is non-negotiable. The more we grow and consolidate our business, the more we will differentiate ourselves from the commodity coffee market, and the more sustainable we will get. So it is a positive reinforcement cycle.

Disruption, however, is not a quick and easy thing to do. If you have to discuss trade-offs, and if sustainability is an extra burden, you won't get too far. Disruption forces companies to reassess their strategies and business models but, as I said, reinventing yourself comes with benefits for the society, environment and the company itself.

Q: How far can a company such as Nespresso go towards becoming 'net-positive' in its environmental footprint? Is the vision we are painting in the book realistic for a company such as yours, which after all deals with physical products, and relies on complex global supply chains?

A: Yes, I would say it is a realistic aspiration over the next years. Today, Nespresso is at a stage where we know our footprint very well, and we have improved considerably in many of our largest opportunity areas. We have investigated whether to set a 'net-positive' target for ourselves, and we concluded that it is not at all out of reach. We have the dedication and the strategy to achieve it.

Interview with Bishop Heinrich Bedford-Strohm

Q: What are the deeper tectonic shifts that you feel are happening beneath society's feet that will be relevant to how these changes are playing out?

A: Well, I think one factor is a growing feeling of uncertainty, of complexity. The world is no longer as simple as it seemed to be in the past. For example, in the East-West conflict there

used to be two sides; now we have many sides. Look at the situation in Syria: there are so many players that almost nobody finds a way through. That is just one example. Current issues are so complex that people are no longer able to understand them. At the same time, however, growing numbers of people in Germany understand that certain changes must happen, especially in terms of our lifestyles and our way of doing business. But I think beyond Germany, if you look at Paris and the Climate Summit for example, it is becoming apparent that with our current way of doing business we will not be able to lift poorer countries out of poverty. With an ever higher need for resources, there is no way that our present economy will continue to work. By calculating all of the resource needs in the different countries of the world, the World Wildlife Fund has come to the conclusion that we need a second Earth in the year 2030 if we continue on our path of economic and business growth. In climate studies, we have seen that it can take a long time for the results of academic research to feature in political debates or even reach the hearts of the people. However, in the end it comes down to political decisions. Church figures have spoken about climate issues for decades and the numbers that are the goals for CO_2 emissions have been part of church documents since at least the 1990s. Now we find them appearing again in political documents.

Q: Is there reason for optimism or pessimism?

A: For me, it is a story of hope. Some people say it has taken too long, but it is a story of hope in terms of the effectiveness of civil society. Many people, who not that many years ago were marginalized for their political ideas, have now moved to the centre ground. In my experience as a religious leader, church leaders are in demand among economic leaders. They want to talk to us and we want to talk to them, precisely because these issues have now become so important. So for me, that is a message of hope. There is a tectonic shift happening. We are going to experience a deep transformation of society and lifestyles which will be inseparably linked to our way of doing business. The task at hand is how to manage this tectonic shift.

Q: Many people tell us that if we cannot make the economic case for this transformation, then don't make the case at all because no one will do it, no one will follow you – either we're doing it for economic reasons or we won't do it. What you're saying is different: you're saying that there can be moral, political, judicial, and spiritual cases for this transition. Are we wrong to overemphasize the economic case that we have to deliver?

A: Yes, I think there is a danger of overemphasizing that. I do understand the importance of economic factors – prices, for example. I know there is research into environmental issues in Germany that shows very high results in terms of public awareness. But when it comes to spending money on it, then the follow-up activity is quite limited. So I am very aware that among people with lower incomes economic factors are very important. But I disagree with the Marxist view that only economic factors move history. I think that ideas and moral conviction have a strong meaning for people, although to different degrees. The power of moral ideas *has* moved history. I also think religion plays a huge role in moving the hearts of people. This is because religion is a factor that not only reaches your head, but also your soul, as we would say. Whatever reaches your soul will move you. I think we as churches have a great responsibility to promote good theology. And by good theology I mean that a spiritual search can never be separated from political change, from public engagement, nor from caring for other human beings and for the Earth. Because if we pray to God as the creator of heaven and Earth, it is very clear that our view of non-human nature must change. If we confess, it is very clear that we do not consider nature as a thing. If we see ourselves as creatures of God and we see non-humans as creations of God, that must change our relationship to non-human nature. If we see nature as our co-creation, then there is an intricate value to it. When we look at biblical texts it is very clear that the Earth is entrusted to human beings. There is a famous passage about the dominion of the Earth by humans, which is often quoted to justify the exploitation of nature. If you look more carefully at the words, however, you will see that this is a misuse of that quote. The king of the Old Testament was someone who had to care for the poor – that was his mandate given from God. A king in the Old Testament never had a licence to exploit his people; rather he was expected to care for the people and particularly for the vulnerable. If you transfer this analogy to being king of the Earth, it must mean caring for all of the Earth.

Q: Is it helpful to use an economic argument for this cause? Or do we risk achieving the opposite of what we want – we devalue the planet and commoditize nature?

A: I would say that we should look for the convergence of both motives, especially knowing that human beings don't always do what they know in their hearts is right, which is what the Bible means by the word 'sin'. You need to implement an incentives-based ethic as a complementary element to a moral-based ethic in order for people to identify the right goals. I think it is a mistake if we as churches only sketch out an ideal way of living with each other and alongside non-human nature. An invaluable best-case scenario would be if the moral ideal and the spiritual power in our hearts were so strong that we consciously act in that way.

But if, and this is perhaps more realistic, we take into account that most people are more short-sighted then we also need to make use of incentives. We need to think about ways to make it easier for people who are less driven by moral ideas. Ecological taxes would be such an instrument, for example. We should set prices that tell the ecological truth and tax them accordingly. People can then choose to buy less of a certain product. Such taxes will help them to buy those goods that are ecologically more valuable because they're cheaper. This is just one example of how you can support moral ideas by using appropriate structural measures.

Q: What is the historical precedent, or analogy from which we can learn? When were we actually able to make such a transition?

A: I am, of course, tempted to go back to the history with which I am most familiar: the Reformation, which happened nearly 500 years ago. It changed history to a degree that no one could have imagined. The role of the church as the agent of deciding on good and evil, or heaven and hell, to put it that bluntly, was absolutely unquestioned at that time. The church administered the system very well and nobody would have thought about experiencing salvation without the church.

And then Martin Luther said 'Solus Christus': only Christ is the decisive centre of my life. He argued that the church is important, but it is not decisive in terms of your salvation; the relationship with Christ decides that. Luther had this wonderful image of the 'happy exchange' – you live with a feeling of inner freedom because you're freed of all your sins and burdens, the fears of hell and eternal darkness. This was an essential revolution the extent of which cannot be overestimated. It was something that no one could have imagined, but it changed history and moved many people. This is one example within the church where there has been a change – a global and historic one – that nobody could have foreseen.

Q: What lessons can we take from this in terms of dealing with our ecological crisis? Do you think we should focus on defining an attractive target state? Or should we cherish the fact that things will be different, and look at building more effective stepping stones?

A: Perhaps the first thing is that we should never underestimate the possibilities of concrete human action. Nobody would have thought that a monk from Wittenberg could change history. This should be an encouragement for all those who are trying to change the world. Many of these people are being told: you're naive, you're an idealist, you can never change the world. It's not true. You can change the world through human action.

The second thing we learn is that if you want to change history, you need to move souls. It's not enough to move money; it's not even enough to move intellectual ideas. You need to reach the souls of the people. In terms of ecological change there may even be a third factor: a pressure for change. In Luther's time that pressure came from the fears of the people. They were afraid of pestilence and disease. It was an apocalyptic mindset and people were tormented by the fear of hell. Luther's new doctrine liberated their souls.

To move souls, however, first, you need a vision. The church has a role in that. We need a vision that touches people's souls in a way that makes people say that this is the way they want to live. I do believe, and maybe it's a naive view, that people are happier when they know that they are not living in conflict with other human beings or non-human nature. Religion can offer many fruitful grounds for this vision. My hope is that we as a church can reach the people more than we have in recent decades and that young people understand that there is more to life than money. Material possessions may be attractive in the short term, but only a spiritual basis in life can be a source of deep happiness. The results of 'happiness' research' show very clearly that factors for happiness are linked to biblical content. The research says: 'Try to live thankfully' which is a core theme in the Bible. Gratitude is an indispensable dimension of prayer. It makes a difference if you celebrate life, rather than taking it for granted.

Second, you need to learn to forgive. 'Our father, forgive us our trespasses, as we forgive those who trespass against us' is a core teaching. Third, live in the present rather than worrying about the future. Again, you can quote the Bible: Look at the birds of the air; they neither sow nor reap nor gather into barns, and yet your heavenly Father feeds them. So do not worry; it's the same thing. I think religion is a decisive force in modern times just as much as it has been in the past. And this force could help to strengthen the vision of a new life in the future where everyone can live in dignity and without destroying nature in the process. That would be wonderful. This is my big hope.

Q: One final question: what is your most concrete vision of how that future would look? How will we live? In the most positive of visions, what would that look like?

A: I think we will have fewer material goods, as we start to consume less. Relationships will play a bigger role in our lives, because it is very clear that a lack of relationships will lead to higher levels of consumption. You do not need to compensate for empty relationships by consuming. We will be more in touch with nature. People will realize that mobility can mean using a bike, enjoying your ride without adding to CO_2 emissions, and they will be happier than they were when they used to drive a car.

It will seem natural to people that how we use material goods is part of a circular economy. Such things will be absolutely normal – by then it will have been normal for fifty years. You need a generation inbetween, because young people will have forgotten why older people threw things away. Like throwing away good wine – that's how they will feel about what we are doing today. When we look back, the striking feature of a circular economy will be the naturalness: it will work to everyone's advantage as it will be cheaper; you won't have a garbage problem. The only thing you will have to deal with will be the sins of the past. The nuclear waste that people created 100 years ago... why did they do that? They created and left behind dangerous materials that will remain hazardous for millions of years. This will be the stuff that people in the future will need to understand, in the same way as historians today try to understand why people for example voted for what turned out to be dictators.

Interview with Professor Lord Nicholas Stern

Q: Given the massive changes that have happened in recent decades, we should be taking comfort from the fact that deeply-embedded issues – like our carbon-intensive and material-intensive economies – can be transformed into something that is different in terms of both systems and in principle. Is there a single analogy that you are using here?

A: I look at analogies here in two different ways. One is disruption that I have experienced myself, and the other is from the point of economic history.

The one I experienced myself was the Green Revolution in northern India: after major investment in irrigation, which arose as a possibility because of land reform, the cultivator had much greater rights to the land. These people were then willing to invest, particularly in terms of irrigation. From an institutional change – legal reform – other benefits were made possible.

And once that happened, other developments took place: essentially people started getting involved in the maintenance of pumping equipment and so became personally invested in the mechanization. As a result, incomes went up and people started to build houses. And those people who started by becoming involved in agriculture learned new skills – nothing high-tech, but enough to be involved in building houses.

So here you have a development triggered by two things: institutional change and the technological change associated with the water pumps. And this led to something transformational. It started in the 1950s and extended into sectors outside agriculture through the 1980s and 1990s. And it was these that I was able to observe closely as a researcher.

Q: And the second analogy?

The second analogy comes from economic history – although I am more an economist than an economic historian. We have to learn from economic history, and in particular the work of Chris Freeman (who died in September 2010), who wrote extensively on the history of technology, often influenced by Josef Schumpeter.

He puts the first wave of technology in the industrial revolution in the second half of the eighteenth century, when mechanization was starting to take off. He then puts two in the twentieth century: the mass production of automobiles early on and then the great wave at the end in terms of digital technology.

Who knows where we are headed – we are probably near the beginning of a new wave, but we don't yet know. Whilst I am not a historian, I think there have been at least five waves. But we are now in a sixth, where you have digital material, biotech, the circular economy, climate change and energy revolutions. I think that it will be bigger than all the rest of the things going on at the same time. And that's why I feel we are probably in the most exciting period in economic history the world has ever known – particularly since there is an urgency in terms of climate change at a time when we need to be investing in our cities and energy systems. Building energy systems needs to happen just when we are running out of climate space.

Q: It sounds as if you put a lot of trust in technology, but reading your books I know that you do not believe that technology alone will 'fix' things. What are the real mechanisms where technology and the way we embed it into society and economies come together?

A: It's technology, it's socialization and it's sound economic policy. Land and social reform in India was a critical social change that grew around independence, and around politics. And then other technology developed and we witnessed better economic policies in India – it all happened a bit slowly, but these things are interdependent.

I don't think a 'technological fix' is a helpful form of language. But I do think that technology lies at the heart of so many of the issues we currently face – such as efficiency, sustainability, recycling, renewal and so on. Technology allows all kinds of social change. And the rise of sharing is very much a social phenomenon enabled by technology. So although I think 'technological fix' itself is a difficult term, it's the combination that's a fascinating and critical success. All social organizations will put policy into economic incentives. And we are becoming better at doing that.

Q: Where are the places that will get that mix right – where there is the right access to technology, or where societies are adapting to their political economies? Is it the Silicon Valley-side of the spectrum or is it the Nordic model?

A: There is nowhere that is perfect. There are places like Singapore or the Scandinavian countries, where you have a lot of things coming together. But then places where you might be a bit pessimistic are starting to move as well.

I think the combination of tax reform in Mexico and better energy policies is an example where things can change. Or cities like Bogotà, which are innovating with rapid bus transit systems, which in turn depend on the management of the public transport and information.

We are at the early stage at the country level and it seems to me that's why this ground is so fertile. But we are not so early that we are without good examples. And such examples are contagious.

Q: The point we are trying to make in the book is that the entire industrial engine continues to operate in an astoundingly resource-intensive way, and we are depicting it as a second pillar next to decarbonisation: a dematerialization pillar. No one has observed the climate change debate like you. Is there an opportunity to learn how we can accelerate that agenda?

A: The time pressure for acting on climate change is intense. Whether we have any chance of holding to two degrees, depends on our actions over the next twenty years, particularly in cities. We know that between now and mid-century our cities will grow from roughly three and a half billion people to roughly six and a half billion. After that, population growth slows. So the shape of these cities is absolutely fundamental. We have to do things differently, much more efficiently, and much less carbon-intensively.

Doing things differently earns a much more – or should I say a much less – heavy economy in the material sense. We can do that in many ways: efficiency, sharing, services, etc. And we have to place that in the context of systems where the different pieces fit together effectively. An obvious example is electricity. Where the different sources of electricity supply have to fit together in a system – electrical grid systems are normally the ways of doing it as well – and these need to be matched with demand, a process which we can influence in much more subtle ways than we could before.

Or take transport, as another example. Public transport, private transport and now driverless cars are morphing into a new platform through better management. For centuries, we have managed public and private transport systems largely in separation. With digital technology and much better management of information than ever before, we can do it in different ways. So you have both information and control, and thus better access to city centres.

Material systems provide another good example. The use of construction steel in buildings is a major opportunity. To date, most of our buildings have encased steel in concrete. To dismantle the building, it is incredibly difficult to get the steel out. Either we need to use alternatives to steel or we find different systems for separating the materials.

Q: What's your most positive scenario – even if that involves some wishful thinking – of how this could actually create a race to the top, a positive competition between regions? How would you depict that?

A: I see competition between countries and cities, particularly cities, as being enormously important. We are now in a world where capital is mobile, labour is mobile, ideas are mobile, and information is mobile. So where do you go? You go where it is most creative and productive and nicest to work. You go to cities where you can breathe. You go to cities where you can move around and which have good transport systems. You go to cities where your children are safe and they can be educated and they can be exposed to all kinds of exciting cultural experiences.

So the design of cities as places to live, work, breathe and enjoy yourself is going to be enormously important. And the places which design themselves in the best ways are the ones that are going to prosper. So I see the competition between cities as, in many ways, the most important way to amplify success. The cities that don't do well in terms of those factors will lose the future.

Interview with Professor Michael Braungart

Q: What is the analogy that you would use to show that this deep systemic change is actually do-able. What is the historical analogy that resonates?

A: Basically, central Europe missed out on key future technology – genetic engineering for good and bad reasons; nano-technology for good and bad reasons; electronics from the beginning – because we thought it was not relevant for Europe, as it was all done by Chinese and Japanese companies. We missed out on digital thinking and digital work.

In infrastructure we are fifteen to twenty years behind, compared to other countries. But what we can do is make things good instead of less bad. We can organize products out of forty years of blame and shame. We can test out innovation with digital thinking. And cradle-to-cradle thinking makes sense. It means we can make materials that are designed for both the technosphere and biosphere.

To do this, it needs defined new spirits; it needs material management upon management, which means that these two opponents can be used again and again. We can now use any negative thinking about the environment as a great innovation entry. This makes the notion of a circular economy useful and will generate competitive advantage for European countries.

Q: You have been part of this discussion for thirty years. Apart from digitalization, what has changed in politics, in the way we are running our companies, and in society at large? What's different nowadays?

A: We need to see that all great ideas require a lot of time. The mobile phone took about 50 years and the Internet took about 40 years till they were actually accessible. So we need to learn to be patient.

This is not about ethics, it's about quality. It's not about feeling responsible, it's about innovation. We can demonstrate how innovation can happen differently – for example, through the circular economy, or cradle-to-cradle thinking. And the really interesting thing is that in a world of social networks the young people, this new selfie generation, want to be proud of what they are doing. For them recognition via social networks is at least as important as money. Anyone who is creating waste is just an idiot, and nobody today wants to be seen as stupid on social media. This is a massive change.

Q: What do you think our lifestyles will look like in twenty years' time. What will make us shake our heads at how we did it twenty years ago? Can you explain what a positive life will look like, from a future perspective?

A: Whenever students analyzed a TV set in 1986, I asked them: 'Do you want to own 4,360 different chemicals or do you want to watch TV?' At that time I was playing at being a Communist, because I was questioning ownership. In the Cold War we believed in ownership; it was a religion. But the generation which was basically organized and influenced by the Cold War is fast disappearing. Young people today understand that service is far more comfortable. Service allows you to have far more choices than just owning things. So now we will see a lot of new products coming through. And this is changing more swiftly than I expected, because it's amazing how young kids want to *use* things instead of *own* things. Of course, companies like Uber or Airbnb are just services. They have done all these things before, but now this context of true innovation is exploding.

Q: But does that also imply that we have to run through a post-materialistic fatigue in order to get to that new service and consumption model? And if that is true, will we ever get the Chinese and the Indians on board?

A: First of all: it's not about dematerialization, it's about rematerialization. It's not about zero-materials, it's about materials and services: 3-D materials are amazingly dangerous for health and environment. And the material base of the digital age is amazingly poor.

So it's less about minimizing the damage, and more about celebrating abundance. It's building on generosity. It's celebrating human footprints on this planet, not telling people to be 10 per cent less bad. Because when you question human existence on this planet, when you say it's better that you are not here, people become greedy and angry. When they feel safe, when they are accepted, people are always friendly and then even the poorest people feel comfortable sharing. So it's important to understand that, as we celebrate 10 billion people on this planet, we should not see humans as a burden. Because when you treat people as a burden, they will behave like a burden and when you treat them as an opportunity, they behave like that as well.

You can see this in schools that have embraced cradle-to-cradle thinking. There are schools in Sweden and Netherlands where there is no longer any vandalism, because these children are respected. They like to be a part of a positive story.

Q: So there is something in it for everyone. I clearly get that point. And yet, who are the most likely winners in this race – which companies and which countries?

A: First of all, we have been investing a lot in Europe, specifically in Germany, to encourage 'less bad' behaviour. For example, we have spent enormous amounts of money to reduce the number of toxic chemicals in printing products from ninety to fifty. But there is no benefit. What's the difference whether you get shot fifty or ninety times? We really need to learn to think from the goal, from the effect, instead of optimizing the wrong things and making them 'perfectly' wrong.

We have to look at how we can actually make healthy stuff from the beginning. So we have to define goals. It's no longer about efficiency, it's about effectiveness. That means that, in a traditional sense, East Germany has, in practice, been protecting the environment much better than West Germany. This has been through inefficiency – the system was so inefficient that they couldn't destroy all the weapons.

I was just in northern Germany and I was there twenty-five years ago after the unification and you just have tears in your eyes. It's an agricultural desert because, despite all of our environmental legislation, we cannot protect the environment from efficient destruction. We need to come up with completely new ideas on how to organize human activity on this planet.

We also need a completely different form of agriculture, so the winner will be a garden-based agriculture. We need learn to enter the food chain on a basic diet at a much lower level, using algae and bacteria, along with mushrooms, so that beef will be a celebration food on Sundays and not a day-to-day hamburger any more.

And we need to learn how to support society far more effectively. People suffering from chronic diseases such as Alzheimer's need far more attention; right now they are losing their dignity in retirement homes and hospitals. If we do that the whole of society will be the winner.

We need to learn that we should not optimize the wrong things. That tyres, for example, will last much longer than they did 30 years ago or twice as long is great but tyre dust is extremely dangerous, and very unhealthy. Previously, rubber hit the road and it stayed there; now we are inhaling the rubber dust and this should not be the case. We have to reinvent all the stuff that we consume so easily – like shoe soles, brake pads, tyres, etc – all of which have to be designed to go into biological systems.

Q: So in a society that is getting ever younger, what is your best prediction? What was the year of the tipping point for that whole agenda?

A: Right now we are losing vitality every year because we are trying to do the same things that India and China can do much more cheaply. And at a certain point we cannot change the system any more because we no longer have the right skills to do it.

Let me give you an example: it took us twenty-four years to develop a leather that is perfectly compostable. Traditionally, people used 20 per cent of the world's chromium for leather tanning. And the last school teaching tanning closed in Reutlingen in 2009. There is no big tanning company left any more. The new BMW comes with a leather that every i3 electric BMW has, but at a certain point in time we will not have the strength, the skills or the vitality any more. So we need to act now.

The tipping point can apply to both sides. We can either use the forty years of blame and shame as a real engine for innovation or we learn how to become a museum for tourists from India and China, which might be a nice thing as well. Munich is a great museum for visitors. But on the other hand, if we don't make a blueprint that can be used by India and China, the whole system will destroy itself. We need to be able to generate blueprints because we cannot have another forty-year cycle of blame and shame that plays out in India and China.

This is why things are so urgent. The vitality of our own system is depleting every day. If we continue to compete with the same stupid products that can be made somewhere else much cheaper, we will only lose our strengths and advantages.

So, for the best of all worlds, I hope that we are beyond the tipping point.

Interview with Mohamed Yunus

Q: Where have you seen a revolution work? Where have you seen a big shift in thinking and acting? Where has a new social standard been established in a very effective way? What are the examples we should turn to?

A: I use the example of sustainable development goals, seventeen goals and 169 targets. They are excellent goals and ambitious goals to achieve. We should read these seventeen goals as our report card. In school you get a report card on how you've done; this is our report card for the whole universe, the whole world. Because these are the things we have produced, the wrong things that we created ourselves.

So I look at the wrong things we have done, how we have done them, how we created these problems. Then I pose the question: suppose by some kind of miracle we have achieved all these goals by 2030 – fully accomplished them. There would be celebrations globally that we have achieved everything we said we would. Now I ask the question: how can we guarantee that they will not come back? The machines are the same, still produce the same problems. The moment you shift your eyes those problems will be back – and many more besides. So I think goals are important, but you have to tackle the root issues that created those problems so that they can no longer create more.

As long as the economy is a greed-based economy the basic tenacity of the machine will remain the same. It will still be making the old stuff – i.e. more money. You may tweak it a little bit, you could camouflage it a little, but the whole purpose of the machine is to make money.

So I suggest you have to deviate from that. This is why we have to understand basic human qualities. We can look at humans as being basically greedy, trying to get as much as they can, rather like a child in a toy shop grabbing things. And that grabbing comes because of the way we have designed our businesses – to maximize profit. In order to make businesses more human, we can look at human nature as one of both selfishness and selflessness, and build businesses on both: selfish business and selfless business. Selfless business will become more and more important.

Q: Which is what we seem to have today, right?

A: This is what we have today. And tomorrow it could be worse. Today, sixty-two people own more wealth than the bottom half of the world's population. Can reusing of assets save us from that? No – because we have not redesigned the machine itself. The machine is something that is sucking up all the steam from the bottom. That machine is not going to stop. So you have to redefine 'business'. Then possibly all of these things will make sense.

Q: So you are saying that what we need is not just a redesign of the political economy, but also a redesign of society, of our culture?

A: It can include everything. At the moment you have wealth concentration, but at the same time you also have power concentration. They go hand in hand, and they dominate our society.

Q: If you think through the solutions for all of this, the one big consolation comes from technology; why is that?

A: I have said that technology is the greatest force that's coming and it has the potential to change the world, and to change it very quickly. But technology must be designed for a purpose. Today, all technologies are designed by profit-makers, who want to build systems so that they can make more money. Technology is driven by profit; they will create fifteen versions of something, launch a new technology for this feature or that feature and so on, so that they can make more money.

Q: So there is pressure to throw one product away and buy a new one?

A: Yes! Because that is how the technology has been designed. The same people who are designing these things could design beautiful new technology to solve the education of the imperilled. But they won't do so because that doesn't make the levels of money that they need. As long as profit-makers are in control, this is what they design.

Technology is being used to design fancy furniture, fancy cars and fancy gadgets. But that is not solving the problems. I could take the same group of people and say: design a costless healthcare system. They may be able to design it, but this is not their focus. As long as profit is the driver of technology, there is no chance of using it in another way.

Q: Can you give me a good example of where technology is playing the role it should?

A: We have not done it. Look at the Internet – we didn't develop the Internet for a good use.

Q: For money?

A: No, it's not for money. Today, technology is driven by money-makers and war-makers. Don't forget that: the Internet was designed by the war-makers. It was not the money-makers who designed it: it was *released* to the money-makers.

Q: Could we follow up on that example where the sense of crisis will be so strong that we almost have to wage war against these collective challenges? Will there be a moment when we have to reconvene and pit technology and our collective solutions against those new crises?

A: That's where social technology comes in. I've said that the social technology guys who sit at the design pulpit are problem-solvers; they should solve problems. For most current technologies, the origins go back to secondary technology. As I said, the Internet was developed for safe communication in times of war; it is now the foundation stone of every business around the world. But look at the costs of development – you could remove poverty in the whole world. It is a trillion-dollar business they run – every year! If you put a trillion dollars behind something, you get a lot of things done.

Q: In a way what you did was a considerable revolution – a more formalized financial sector around the poor was unthinkable before you did it. What can we learn from this point?

A: It happened because it didn't need investment, from the government or from anybody. If it needed a trillion-dollar investment, it wouldn't have happened. So we created something that was generated from just our money. We didn't go to any donor, we didn't go to any bank. We had a licence to become a bank, so we just used the deposit as money to expand, just as a new banker would do, to take deposits and lend money. Why not? I could do it. At the time, nobody knew it could be done, simply because it hadn't been done before. That it hadn't been done before, didn't mean it couldn't be done; that was the lesson.

Q: Let's have one last question. What's your best and most optimistic view of how we might be living in thirty years if we embraced some of these principles? How will it look if technology, government, the social sector and the markets and business sector are doing the right things? What's your most positive picture of that?

A: I am a compulsive optimist. And the reason that I am a compulsive optimist is blind faith in human destiny. Human beings ultimately will always win. So no matter what mistakes they make along the way and so on, their creative power will lead them to find the right path.

Furthermore I have faith in the young people today. The younger generation is different from the young generation of my age. In our youth, we were desperately trying to find a way to make it: to get a job, to get a house, to get a first car, an education. That's our generation, the post-war generation, all over the world. Because they lost everything, they needed everything, so they had to build up something. They had to have the first home – very proud – the first car – very proud – sending a child to college for the first time – very proud.

But young people now have already done everything. Their parents have done it for them. They have a house, they have cars – not one car but probably multiple cars – they have education. They didn't ask, they didn't struggle for it like their parents who struggled for every penny, working hard in a restaurant washing dishes and so on to pay for college. This generation don't have to go through that. They've made it.

And they have an enormous power in their hands – technology. So they have enormous capacity to be connected with each other, and enormous capacity to access knowledge. Without an effort you just push a button and knowledge is right in front of you, in exactly the shape and size you wanted it. Their parents had to go to the library, waiting early in the morning before it opened to be the first one to get a book.

The younger generation is more likely to respond to social issues than the older generation. But we have to reach them before others lure them into more fascinating things. Our education system is a kind of factory that produces job-seekers. At the end, they receive a piece of paper saying he is a good worker. We have made him job-ready for you. That's a fantastic achievement for all colleges and universities. Nobody says: 'I make these young people critical, and capable of being in business'.

We have to tell them: a job is too humiliating for you. As a human being you should not be dreaming about serving in somebody else's business. You are a free person and should do your own thing. By nature, human beings are entrepreneurs. So we need to create that environment – not a world of job-seekers, but one of job-makers and entrepreneurs.

That will be a welcome sensation: everybody is an entrepreneur. So you can be an entrepreneur, and I can be an entrepreneur.

Q: Educate them into independence?

A: Truly! Educate them into independence. Never let them feel that they can't do anything on their own. I am a creative human being. I am a problem-solver. As a human being I was born onto this planet as a problem-solver. That's why I survive.

Seeds of a better economy – visiting the frontline

In this appendix, we will show that a new and better economy is already in the making. We have compiled six interesting case examples from all over the world of companies that are innovating in a way that creates real growth and at the same time resolves many of the issues we have described. We hope they will inspire you, and make you start dreaming of a better economy. One thing you should note is that all of them imply disruptive change for markets and for resource productivity: the improvements are often a *factor* 5–10, not 5–10 *per cent* improvement. However, we must also warn that inspiring as these cases are, they don't even add up to 1 per cent of our current economy.

1. Beyond Meat – eating meat, not animals[1,2,3]

'I couldn't tell the difference,' wrote Bill Gates on his blog in 2013.[4] He had just tried a sample of Chicken-Free Strips, the first commercial product of start-up Beyond Meat, which produces meat substitutes from soybeans and peas. Mark Bittman, a food journalist with the *New York Times*, agreed: 'You won't know the difference between that [Beyond Meat] and real chicken. I didn't, at least, and this is the kind of thing I do for a living.'[5] Since then, Beyond Meat has added a product line for beef, including Beefy Crumbles for tacos and ground beef dishes, and the Beast Burger, to the same raving reviews. Beyond Meat is expanding quickly, and at the end of 2014 their products were available at 6,000 stores across the US – not only at Whole Foods but also at mainstream stores such as Safeways, Targets and Publix. Between 2013 and 2014, sales were up 250 per cent, compared to the 0.5 per cent growth for the rest of the meat substitute segment. Beyond

Meat's products are still more expensive than traditional meat but less expensive than premium meats.

Having grown up on a dairy farm in Maryland, with a philosopher father who was teaching environmental ethics, it was perhaps no surprise that Ethan Brown, the founder and CEO of Beyond Meat, should start to ask himself if there wasn't a better way to provide meat than the traditional one. Originally it came from concern about the welfare of the animals. 'It wasn't emotional,' he says. 'It was a question of fairness. Why should we treat our dog so well, but not the pig?' Later on, while working at a fuel cell company during his early career, he also got to understand the massive impact meat production has on climate change, deforestation, soil erosion and water pollution. 'I started thinking,' says Brown, 'why can't you just create animal protein with plants? What are the biological reasons you can't do that? And I started looking around at people who were answering that question.'

Eventually he found Fu-hung Hsieh and Harold Huff, two professors at the University of Missouri, who had already been working for almost a decade to get their vegetarian chicken substitute 'as close to the look and feel of real chicken as possible'. They had been experimenting with different inputs and combinations of heat and pressure to replicate the 'meatiness' of the chicken, and had found that a mix of soy and pea proteins gave a texture very close to that of real chicken. The texture has always been the issue with meat substitutes. Getting to something that tastes and smells like meat has been possible for decades, but, so far, the chewy, fibrous texture of meat has eluded researchers. Many consumers consider tofu and other substitutes mushy, and perhaps that is why they have remained niche products. The three decided it was time to take the research to market, and Hsieh and Huff started to license their technology to Beyond Meat in 2010.

Now, Beyond Meat has set a vision of a 25 per cent reduced global meat consumption by 2020.[6] This is of course wildly ambitious, but if they succeed with even a fraction of that, it is a massive deal. Global meat demand has increased by a factor of three over the last forty years, and with current trends, it could double again by 2050. At present, the global cattle headcount stands at about 1.5 billion, and as much as 33 per cent of scarce arable land is used for grazing globally.[7] What's more, meat production is directly responsible for about 18 per cent of global greenhouse gas emissions, and even more if one includes the indirect effects of ranchers clearing forests to expand grazing land.

The resources required to produce substitutes are a small fraction of ordinary meat: it takes only 400 grams of soy and pea protein to produce a kilogram of Beyond Meat's chicken (a chicken is about 60 per cent water). An ordinary chicken, by comparison, requires more than 3 kilograms of feed to produce 1 kilogram of chicken. In caloric terms, the differences become even clearer. For chicken, the ratio between feed and meat calories is 9:1, for pork it is 11:1 and for beef it is a full 36:1.

Substitutes could also be healthier than ordinary meat. The Beast Burger has more protein than ordinary ground beef, more calcium than milk, more omega-3 than salmon and more antioxidants than blueberries.[8] And it is guaranteed to be free of the antibiotics-resistant bacteria that is a major problem for ordinary ground beef.[9] So a long list of benefits. 'But isn't it unnatural, processed Frankenfood?' some consumers have asked. It is of course processed food, but, says Brown, 'if you are willing to eat bread, you should be willing to eat our products. It goes through heating, cooling, and pressure and that's it'.

'We think it can be as big as the meat industry is today,' says Amol Deshpande from venture capitalist Kleiner Perkins, who is one of the big owners (Bill Gates is another). 'If you can remove the main bottleneck to meat production, which is the livestock, and get the price down, it could happen.' Says Brown: 'There aren't any obstacles to us underpricing beef as we scale up. The industry is large and established, yet it's facing huge cost challenges. The price slope for beef since 2010 has been pretty steep; we're already competitive with certain grades.'

Our feeling is that the global meat industry – a $740.5 billion industry[10] – could face a classic case of technology disruption over the next ten years. Beyond Meat, or some of its competitors, will develop a meat substitute that consumers broadly feel is good enough to replace the real thing, and it will be cheaper, healthier and better for the environment. 'If our product is higher quality than meat at a much lower cost, imagine how much we can disrupt the market', as Brown says.

2. Not missing the biogas bus – from waste to wheels

Biogas-fuelled buses have started to appear in some of the world's cities. To us, they are a beautiful example of capturing multiple benefits at once. The city of Stockholm, as an example, started producing biogas from its wastewater in 2010. Before this, the wastewaster sludge was dried and burned in a combined heat and power plant, the heat from which was used to feed the district heating system in Stockholm.

The way it works is that the largest sewage treatment plant was equipped with anaerobic digestion chambers, where the sludge digests in the right temperature and chemical environment for 2–3 weeks, releasing gas in the process. Approximately 70 per cent of the energy content of wastewater can be captured this way. The 'raw gas' that is produced consists of approximately 55 per cent methane, 40 per cent carbon dioxide, and 5 per cent sulphuric gases. This raw gas is then upgraded in a scrubber, producing a transport gas that consists of 98 per cent methane, which can be used in the same way as any natural gas. Since 2010, an increasing share of Stockholm households also separate out solid food waste, and this waste is now also digested in the same system. In total, the biogas production in Stockholm reached 108 gigawatt hours (GWh) per year in 2013[11], enough to fuel more than 259 local biogas buses,[12] and replacing the same amount of diesel buses. The lowered heat production for the district heating network has partly been met with energy efficiency measures, and partly with importing municipal waste from warmer countries with less demand for heating. Importing municipal waste may seem like a strange procedure, but actually makes sense when you consider that heat is not worth much in many parts of the world, but it is in Scandinavia with its long and cold winters, and its well-built-out district heating systems.

The project comes with a long list of benefits, environmental as well as economic: first, replacing diesel buses with biogas in inner-city traffic reduces CO_2 emissions by 70–80 per cent. But it also reduces particle emissions (responsible for many respiratory problems) to near zero, and it reduces traffic noise. So for the local environment in Stockholm it is a great improvement. But the waste remaining after the biogas extraction process is also brought back to the fields as bio-fertilizer. So a closed-loop system for phosphorus as well as nitrogen has been created. This is an equally important environmental advantage, since the global biophysical flows of both nitrogen and phosphorus are deeply disturbed. Economically, the project has been a gain for Stockholm, since the production cost for biogas is lower than the cost of purchasing diesel, on an energy content basis. Gas buses do not cost substantially more than diesel buses, and the biogas distribution costs are very low, as the biogas is piped the short distance between the sewage plant and the bus depot.

Based on the successes to date, further biogas production facilities are now being constructed around Stockholm. We find this an elegant way of solving a waste management problem at the same time as making the bus fleet cleaner, solving a nitrogen and phosphorus problem, and reducing the burden on Stockholm tax payers.

There is no reason why this solution could not be used in many other parts of the world. Most large cities are struggling with the same waste and local transport issues. If a large share of the world's inner-city buses were shifted from diesel to biogas, this would be a big step forward from many perspectives.

3. AutoLib – the French commute[13,14]

AutoLib is a successful car-sharing scheme in Paris, and illustrates many of the benefits of shared mobility. As a customer, you register once, and pay an annual fee of €120. Then when you need a car, you reserve one through your smartphone, specifying when and where you would like to pick up and return the car. AutoLib has more than 900 reserved parking locations in Paris, so there are good chances there is one close by. You unlock the car with a code delivered to your smartphone, and there is no direct interaction with any AutoLib personnel. All cars are electric, so you just unplug and drive off. For a standard car, the fee is €5.50 per half-hour of use.

This scheme has proven highly attractive to customers. Operations started as recently as 2011, but AutoLib already had 155,000 registered customers and 3,000 cars in 2014, and almost triples in size every year. There are several important customer benefits: you avoid the hassle of owning a car, you don't have to search for a parking space and the car is always fully charged. And the price point is in between that of taking a taxi and taking the metro. If you are not a major car user, even a generous usage of AutoLib will cost you much less than owning a car.

But also from a societal point of view, there are many benefits: much less parking space is needed (as the cars spend much less time parked), and the higher utilization pattern tilts the drivetrain economics towards electricity with its associated benefits for reducing pollution, greenhouse gas emissions and noise. There are further environmental benefits from upstream material savings: AutoLib claims each of their cars replaces seven privately owned cars.[15] This would mean that seven times less steel, copper and other metals is tied up in cars. Finally, the cost efficiency of the sharing scheme releases household spending for other areas, acting as an economic stimulus.

4. Joule – sun fuel

Massachusetts-based Joule Unlimited is pioneering a very interesting approach to produce liquid hydrocarbon fuels out of essentially CO_2, sunlight and water, through cleverly designed enzymes. If Joule succeeds in bringing down costs for this 'sun fuel', it will be disruptive for global fuel markets. The way Joule's process works is that large amounts of waste CO_2 (for instance from a chemical plant – there are many industrial processes that produce large amounts of CO_2 as a by-product) is injected into a mix of water, catalysts and micro-nutrients, and exposed to strong sunlight. This stimulates a sort of photo-synthesis, but instead of producing oxygen as ordinary photo-synthesis does, tailor-made catalysts convert the solar energy into liquid fuels, either ethanol or diesel. These fuels can then be separated and purified. In a way Joule's process mimics how fossil hydrocarbons were produced in the first place, only hundreds of thousands times faster.

Joule believe they will be able to produce these fuels at approximately $50 per barrel of oil equivalent. If they succeed, this fuel has enormous advantages: it is CO_2 neutral, the key inputs are readily available in most countries across the world, which will create local jobs and reduce geopolitical tension, and the production process poses few health and safety risks. Joule are now building their first commercial-scale production facilities. Joule estimates that commercial-scale plants will cover an area of 6–7 square kilometres, and be located in sunny facilities.

Carbon Recycling International ('CRI') in Iceland has a similar ambition. CRI produces renewable methanol, a fuel that can replace fossil fuels in many types of vehicles, from CO_2 and hydrogen. The hydrogen, in turn, is produced from water and renewable energy). On a lifecycle basis, this reduces greenhouse gas emissions by more than 90 per cent, according to the CRI. Again, this is not a story of incremental improvements of an existing system, but of a groundbreaking new technology that could fundamentally change fuel markets.

5. The Amazon forest – saving the jungle[16]

Home to approximately 30 per cent of the world's remaining forests, large-scale deforestation in Brazil has long been a major environmental issue. Illegal logging has been a big part of the problem, but also slash-and-burn agriculture has contributed: cattle farmers have cut down rainforest to create grazing land for their cattle, and grain farmers have cleared new land instead of using fertilizers and crop rotation to maintain their existing land. The result: an average of 19,559 square kilometres of rainforest (or half the size of Denmark) were cleared every year between 1996 and 2005. This implied huge carbon emissions: almost 1 billion tons of CO_2 were released into the atmosphere every year from Brazilian forests alone – approximately four times Germany's emissions. Deforestation also led to other severe environmental issues such as soil degradation and loss of habitat for many animal species. And there were social issues; it is hard to create good housing, health care and schooling when families keep moving around.

Several factors contributed to this situation: many of the farmers are acutely poor and are not able to pay for fertilizers or modern agricultural equipment, and monitoring has been a real issue – there has simply not been a good way of detecting land clearing before it is too late. Issues of weak governance and corruption have not helped either. For all these complicated reasons, deforestation was long seen as near impossible to stop, in spite of its very harmful effects.

Until now. During the last years deforestation in Brazil has decreased dramatically: in 2014 deforestation was 5, 012 square kilometres, down 75 per cent from the 1996–2005 baseline, and the trend suggests it could soon stop altogether. Already, the CO_2 emission reductions are down by more than 700 million tons CO_2 per year, more than the combined UNFCCC climate pledges of the US and the EU until 2020. What's more, several promising land rehabilitation approaches have now emerged, and there is a very real chance that Brazil will go into reforestation during the next ten years. Beyond solving many local issues, this would also mean Brazil would act as a large-scale carbon sink.

What has led to this great turn of events? Several factors: first, Brazil has pioneered a satellite-based monitoring system (DETER) which provides a deforestation update every second week, and it has established a rapid-response team that quickly takes action. Second, the large slaughterhouses and soybean producers adopted new codes of conduct, which made it hard for suppliers to get away with slash-and-burn agricultural practices. International food producers and restaurant chains also used their purchasing power to create more sustainable farming practices. Third, Brazil adopted a new forest code in 2010, establishing a stronger legal framework around deforestation and land use. Importantly, it contained innovative financing mechanisms to help boost farm productivity, reducing the need for farmers to slash and burn. The Amazon Fund was established in 2008 to help finance many of these changes. It is open to contributions from governments and philanthropy. The Norwegian government was the first contributor to the fund, and remains the largest. This example nicely illustrates the good disruption concept and its drivers: new technology is coming together with a new powerful meso-economy (this time in the form of an industrial cooperation and an international fund) and improved governance to solve a massive issue that was broadly believed to be unsolvable only a decade ago.

Turning to land rehabilitation, the Clean Air Action Corporation (CAAC) is an interesting example. The CAAC works with subsistence farmers in Africa and India, supporting them to reforest their land. The CAAC provides a very modest upfront capital infusion for the tree plants, basic training, and it monitors the results. Farmers benefit primarily through a stable supply of fodder and firewood, but there are many other 'co-benefits' in the form of improved agricultural productivity, less soil degradation, and a more enjoyable landscape. The results of this simple approach are impressive: CAAC now works with 75,000 farmers, more than 90 per cent of whom stick with the programme. Carbon uptake is on average 22 tons per hectare per year in Kenya, and 31 tons in Uganda, according to the external verifications made – far beyond the 1–3 tons per hectare per year that the literature suggests is possible.

There are other approaches as well, for instance the Holistic Planned Grazing approach championed by the Savory Institute.[17] As a thought experiment, if these and similar results could be scaled to only 10–15 per cent of the 2 billion hectares of degraded land globally, it would offset all of the US's greenhouse gas emissions for decades. Again, these are not incremental changes but order-of-magnitude improvements.

6. Balbo Sugar – from agriculture to ecosystem[18,19]

São Paolo state in southern Brazil is perhaps not where you would expect to look for inspiration as to what the future of agriculture could look like. But Leontino Balbo Junior, the CEO of Balbo Sugar, is on a thirty-year quest to revolutionize conventional sugar production, and is achieving impressive results. It started in the mid-1980s, when the young Leontino had just graduated from his agronomy studies and returned to the family sugar business, Balbo Sugar, one of the largest in Brazil. Back then, Balbo Sugar's production approach was very much in line with the standard principles of modern agriculture:

large monoculture areas, where productivity is increased through intensive use of fossil fertilizers, pesticides, modified seeds and ever more mechanization.

Leontino Balbo Junior was having none of it. His aim was to 'achieve agricultural self-sufficiency, a way to preserve the natural resources we need now – water, soil fertility, biodiversity and the atmosphere'. A strong believer in nature's ability to self-regulate, he developed an approach he called 'ecosystem revitalizing agriculture' (ERA), with the core idea that if he was able to restore the soil to the quality and structure it had before intensive agriculture, this would simultaneously increase productivity, reduce resource inputs and revitalize the surrounding ecosystem.

Balbo set aside 16,000 hectares of sugarcane plantations for his large-scale experiment. The first change was to stop crop burning. Many sugarcane farmers start fires before harvesting to burn off leaves, insects and snakes. But this forces harvesters not only to collect the cane but also the melted sugar that has dripped into the soil. So the sugar needs cleaning, in Balbo's case by 3 million litres of water per hour, and burning also removes valuable nutrients from the soil. Instead, he spent five years in developing a mechanical harvester that avoids the need for crop burning, meaning 20 tons of leaves could instead be returned to each hectare of soil, returning nitrogen and helping to keep weeds down.

Second, he changed all the tyres on the farm's machinery to ultrasoft tyres that Balbo partially deflates to reduce the impact on the soil. 'Farm equipment is heavy, and wherever you drive you compress the soil, changing its geometric structure and reducing its ability to hold water.' Next in line were the by-products: the farm started to sprinkle back the liquid sugar residue onto the fields, and the dry matter is burned for steam and electricity. Finally, Balbo stopped using fossil fertilizers and pesticides altogether. They were simply not needed, as more nutrients were returned to the soil, and as earthworms, termites and fungi started to keep pests under control. Per hectare, 1,200 wasps were released, eating the moths that would otherwise have harmed the sugarcanes.

At the start, results were disappointing. Between 1992 and 2000, production figures were bad, and the environmental results also did not readily materialize. But over time, when several years of mulch had revitalized the soil, the results came in, and beyond expectations. 'A fourfold increase in the soil's ability to retain water, a fivefold increase in erosion resistance and a threefold increase in organic content.' The sugarcane plants can now muster six or seven cuts, compared to the five of conventional farms, and Balbo is hoping they might soon not have to remove the canes at all. But the new farming practices have also translated to commercial success: Productivity is 23 per cent above that of the average conventional producer, and with its 75,000 tons of organic sugar, Balbo now has 34 per cent of the world market for organic sugar, under the Native brand. As many high-profile food companies are willing to pay a premium for organic sugar, revenues per ton are higher than for conventional sugar and less volatile. Again, an inspiring case of improving revenue, productivity, and environment all at once, in a classical commodity industry.

Notes

Introduction

1 Stiftungsfond für Umweltökonomie und Nachhaltigkeit (Foundation for Environmental Economics and Sustainability).

A new narrative emerging

1 Fink (2015).
2 The World Bank (2016a).
3 The World Bank (2015b).
4 United Nations (2015).
5 Dobbs et al. (2015b).
6 McKinsey Center for Business and Environment, Ellen MacArthur Foundation and SUN (2015).
7 The 2030 Water Resources Group (2009).
8 McKinsey Center for Business and Environment, Ellen MacArthur Foundation and SUN (2015).
9 Global Ocean Commission (2014).
10 Ellen MacArthur Foundation (2016).
11 Ceballos et al. (2015).
12 Ripple et al. (2014).
13 Steffen et al. (2015).
14 Earth Overshoot Day (2015a).
15 Trucost (2013).
16 European Commission (2014).
17 The UN's Human Development Index ('HDI') is often discussed, and has improved significantly over the last two decades. Crucially, this index focuses on annual income, education and health, and does not include any measure of natural capital development.
18 UNEP (2014a).
19 Trucost (2013).
20 Eurostat (2015a).
21 McKinsey Center for Business and Environment, Ellen MacArthur Foundation and SUN (2015).
22 An average of 1.2 tons of car is used to transport 100 kilograms of human
23 Wikipedia (2016) Eco-efficiency.
24 Jolly (2015).

25   IEA (2015a).
26   McDonough and Braungart (2002).
27   IEA (2015c).
28   McKinsey Center for Business and Environment, Ellen MacArthur Foundation and SUN (2015).
29   Just-in-time, system takt, visual performance indicators, variability as waste, continuous improvement, to name just a few.
30   Haub (2011).
31   Frey and Osborne (2013).
32   Dobbs et al. (2011).
33   Steffen et al. (2015).
34   IEA (2015a).
35   The New Climate Economy (2014).
36   Gapminder (2011).
37   Kuhn (1962).
38   Painter (2014).
39   Tomnod (2014).
40   Stine (2011).
41   EITI (2016).
42   Shirky (2009).
43   Pfeil (2013).
44   Bailey et al. (2015).
45   GSIR (2014).
46   Sustainable Brands (2015).

Chapter 1: Desired – celebrating growth

1   FAOSTAT (2015a).
2   Dargay/Gately/Sommer (2007).
3   Brandmeir et al. (2015).
4   Dobbs et al. (2011).
5   *The Economist* (2013).
6   Phelps and Crabtree (2013).
7   Own calculations.
8   The World Bank (2016b).
9   Deaton (2013).
10   King (2013).
11   Dobbs et al. (2015b).
12   United Nations (2015).
13   Afdb 2016 http://www.afdb.org/en/knowledge/publications/african-economic-outlook/
14   http://www.economist.com/news/

briefing/21679781-fertility-rates-falling-more-slowly-anywhere-else-
africa-faces-population

15 Dobbs et al. (2015b).
16 Barton (2011).
17 Roesti (2015).
18 Bartels (2013).
19 Krugman (2013).
20 See, for example, Germany's Stability Bill of 1967.

Chapter 2: Fuelled – resource-based growth

1 Johnston and Williams (2014).
2 Solow (1956).
3 Solow (1957).
4 OECD (2015a).
5 Ayres and Warr (2005).
6 Ayres and Voudouris (2014).
7 The exception is the recession in 1960–1. See Hamilton (2013).
8 In fact, Hamilton performs another set of tests to create further
   conviction that hypothesis II is not correct. He observes that if there is
   some third underlying factor causing both oil price increases and recessions, then some macroeconomic time series should show an unusual
   behaviour *prior* to the oil price increases. He statically tests relevant
   candidates and shows that there is no significant statistical pattern.

Chapter 3: Borrowed – a growth of liabilities

1 Mongabay (2011).
2 Miettinen et al. (2012).
3 National Geographic Society (2008).
4 Thompson (2013).
5 Global Footprint Network (2015). The methodology is very visual, and
   thought-provoking, but has the methodological challenges of any highly
   aggregating index number. The Global Footprint Network is very transparent about the approach and its limitations.
6 Earth Overshoot Day (2015b).
7 Pope Francis (2015).
8 Steffen et al. (2015).
9 Gleick (1993).
10 The 2030 Water Resources Group (2009).
11 UNEP (2004).
12 Wang (2014).
13 Josephs (2013).

14 Elhadj (2008).
15 Mauser (2009).
16 Dwyer (2015).
17 Ellen MacArthur Foundation (2016).
18 Laist (1997).
19 McKinsey Center for Business and Environment and Ocean Conservancy (2015).
20 UNEP (2014c).
21 European Commission, Directorate General for Environment (2015).
22 McKinsey & Company (2015b).
23 Dobbs et al. (2011).
24 McKinsey Center for Business and Environment, Ellen MacArthur Foundation and SUN (2015).
25 McKinsey & Company (2015b).
26 FAO (2011b).
27 Roser (2015).
28 EIA (2016).
29 Stuchtey (2015).
30 Ceballos et al. (2015).
31 Ripple et al. (2014).
32 Watson et al. (2012).
33 Global Ocean Commission (2014).
34 Stern (2006).
35 UNEP (2014b).
36 McKinsey & Company (2009).
37 Trucost (2013)
38 United Nations (2016).
39 The World Bank (2015d).
40 Eurostat (2015a).
41 Eurostat (2015b).
42 Earth Overshoot Day (2015a).
43 Mauser (2009).
44 The term was first used in the 1980s by an ecologist, Eugene F. Stoermer. It has been brought to broader attention by atmospheric chemist, Paul Crutzen.
45 Schwägerl (2016).
46 Dobbs et al. (2015a).
47 Barton (2011).
48 Confino (2015).
49 Gordon (2014).
50 McKinsey & Company (2014).

51 Dobbs et al. (2015a).
52 *The Economist* (2015a).
53 Stallknecht (2012).
54 Putnam (1995).
55 Steingart (2013).
56 Edelman (2015).
57 The trust index is an average of a country's trust in the institutions of government, business, media and NGOs.
58 Stürmer (2012).
59 Sander and Putnam (2010).
60 Putnam et al. (1993).
61 Piketty (2014).
62 Slater (2015).
63 Kaufman (2014).
64 Charities Aid Foundation (2014).
65 Lecoutere et al. (2015).
66 WLOG – without loss of generality is used by mathematicians before any assumption in a proof which narrows the premise to some special case.

Chapter 4: Lost – the great divergence

1 Gordon (2012a).
2 Kaiser (2016).
3 The New Climate Economy (2014).
4 Stiglitz et al. (2010).
5 UNEP (2014a).
6 A joint initiative of the United Nations University International Human Dimensions Programme (UNU-IHDP) and the United Nations Environment Programme (UNEP) in collaboration with the United Nations Educational, Scientific and Cultural Organization (UNESCO).
7 Inclusive Wealth Project (2014).
8 Sagar and Najam (1998).
9 Kubiszewski et al. (2013.)
10 Neumayer (2010).
11 A note of caution: satisfaction indices have a roof, given the 1–5 scale, and so have to stagnate at some stage.
12 Herman Daly (2005).
13 Inclusive Wealth Project (2012).
14 Kuznets (1962).
15 Trucost (2013).
16 Investopedia (2016).
17 Bradford DeLong (1998).

18 Some externalities have already been addressed through environmental regulation, for instance wastewater treatment standards, and vehicle standards.
19 Trucost (2013).
20 Ayres (2014).
21 Carbon Tracker Initiative (2013).
22 Carbon Tracker Initiative (2014)
23 Welzer (2013).
24 Daly (1973).
25 La Décroissance (2002).
26 Miegel (2010).
27 Mill (1848).
28 Daly (2005).
29 The University of California Museum of Paleontology (2016).
30 Jackson (2009).
31 Ekins and Max-Neef (1992).
32 Smith (2015).
33 Mathiesen (2014).
34 INSM (2012).
35 Plastindia Foundation (2014).
36 UN and DOE EIA (2007).
37 Jackson (2009).
38 UK Department of Energy and Climate Change (2009).
39 Mearns (2013).
40 Goldenberg (2014).
41 FAO (2015).
42 McKinsey Center for Business and Environment and Ocean Conservancy (2015).
43 Lomborg (2015).
44 Atsmon et al. (2011).
45 United States Department of Agriculture (2016).
46 OECD (2016b).

Chapter 5: Wasted – system waste as a new resource

1 McKinsey Center for Business and Environment, Ellen MacArthur Foundation and SUN (2015).
2 European Commission – Press release (2015).
3 Domestic material consumption equals direct material input minus exports.
4 Eurostat (2015a).
5 This material value retention ratio is defined as the sales of secondary

(i.e. recycled) materials plus the sales of waste-generated energy in Europe, divided by the sales of raw materials (adjusted for net imports).

6   OEA (2016).
7   Geyer and Blass (2009).
8   PlasticsEurope (2013).
9   McKinsey Center for Business and Environment and Ocean Conservancy (2015).
10 Ellen MacArthur Foundation (2016).
11 Umweltbundesamt (2015).
12 McKinsey Center for Business and Environment, Ellen MacArthur Foundation and SUN (2015).
13 FAO (2011a).
14 WRAP (2013).
15 Hirshon (2008).
16 European Environment Agency (2015).
17 Dobbs et al. (2011).
18 Holly Gibbs and Meghan Salmon, *Mapping the World's Degraded Lands*, 2015; estimates by Campbell et al. (2008) (60 million hectares), GLADA (65 million hectares), Dregne and Chou (1992) (94 million hectares), Cai et al. (2011) (104 million hectares) and GLASOD (158 million hectares).
19 Direct user cash-out cost includes annualized rent or purchase price, maintenance, utility costs (energy and water), insurance, appliances and accommodation services (e.g. hotels). Societal cash-out costs include office space and government expenses for social housing, community development, street lighting and waste management. Opportunity costs include CO_2 emissions, health effects due to indoor air quality, and transport time to and from work as this is strongly related to urban design and virtual offices.
20 In EU27 countries according to Eurostat (2013).
21 European Commission – Mobility and Transport (2011).
22 Arsova (2010).
23 The World Bank (2014).
24 IEA (2014).
25 For instance just-in-time supply chains, takt-based manufacturing, variability as a source of waste, visual performance indicators.
26 TNS Political and Social (2014).

Chapter 6: Broken – the unfulfilled sustainability dream

1   Grober (1999).
2   Wikipedia (2016) Environmentalism history.
3   McKie (2012).

4 McDiarmid (2011).
5 Kelly (2015).
6 Wikipedia (2016) Brundtland Commission.
7 The formal name was the World Commission on Environment and Development. It was led by the former Norwegian prime minister, Gro Harlem Brundtland, and delivered its final report, *Our Common Future*, in 1987.
8 Wikipedia (2016) Eco-efficiency.
9 European Commission (2016).
10 Kimura (2010).
11 WEO (2014).
12 WEO (2015).
13 Dobbs et al. (2011).
14 CDIAC (2011).
15 FAO (2008).
16 Dobbs et al (2011).
17 Hebebrand (2013).
18 Jolly (2015).

Chapter 7: Three pillars of a better growth model

1 Tsanova (2015).
2 Liebreich (2015a).
3 Parkinson (2015a).
4 IEA (2015b).
5 IEA (2015c).
6 *The Economist* (2015c).
7 The World Bank (2014a).
8 *The Economist* (2015d).
9 Potočnik (2015).
10 McDonough and Braungart (2002).
11 McKinsey Center for Business and Environment, Ellen MacArthur Foundation and SUN (2015).
12 Jambeck et al. (2015).
13 Ellen MacArthur Foundation (2013).
14 World Urbanization Prospects (2014).
15 Hirsch (2015).
16 McKinsey Center for Business and Environment, Ellen MacArthur Foundation and SUN (2015).

Chapter 8: The 'net-positive' norm – accretive, productive, healthy

1 McKinsey Center for Business and Environment, Ellen MacArthur Foundation and SUN (2015).

Chapter 9: A European case example – positive for economy and environment

1 McKinsey Center for Business and Environment, Ellen MacArthur Foundation and SUN (2015).
2 Mezue et al. (2015).
3 Rogelj et al. (2015).
4 Stuchtey (2015).
5 European Commission (2015).
6 Clark et al. (2014).
7 Fallows (2015).
8 Such as CAPM Alpha, Fama-French Alpha, Sharpe Ratio, Information Ratio and Total Return.
9 Balkissoon and Heaps (2014).
10 Satariano (2015).

Chapter 10: Disruptive trends – the world at a turning point

1 The World Bank (2010).
2 The New Climate Economy (2014).
3 World Urbanization Prospects (2014).
4 Dobbs et al. (2015b).
5 The New Climate Economy (2014).
6 The World Bank (2013a).
7 Wikipedia (2016) Khan Academy.
8 Noer (2012).
9 Khan Academy (2016).
10 Brynjolfsson and McAfee (2014).
11 Naugthon (2012).
12 Rao and Primack (2015).
13 Goulart (2015).
14 Wan (2015).
15 edX (2016).
16 Rifkin (2014).
17 GSV EDU (2012).
18 Rifkin (2014).
19 Gabbatt (2011).
20 IFR Statistical Department (2015).
21 Rus (2015).

22 United Nations (2000).
23 Keller (2014).
24 UN Department of Economic and Social Affairs (2015).
25 UN Department of Economic and Social Affairs (2004).
26 *The Economist* (2015b).
27 UN Department of Economic and Social Affairs (2015).
28 Ip (2015).

Chapter 11: Digitizing the physical world – the next revolution

1   The New Climate Economy (2014).
2   The figure includes all investment in energy, land use and urban infrastructure.
3   McKinsey Center for Business and Environment, Ellen MacArthur Foundation and SUN (2015).
4   Shaheen and Cohen (2013).
5   McKinsey Center for Business and Environment, Ellen MacArthur Foundation and SUN (2015).
6   Clearpath Foundation (2015).
7   Google (2016).
8   Company website, December 2014. A fully autonomous vehicle involves additional costs. For example, LiDAR for the Google car costs €64,000. Companies like Quanergy are promising flash LiDARs (lower resolution) for €90–230 by 2016.
9   McKinsey Center for Business and Environment, Ellen MacArthur Foundation and SUN (2015).
10 Ziegler (2015).
11 World Economic Forum (2012).
12 CEMA (2015).
13 Stuchtey (2015).
14 Global TraPs Project (2013).
15 Anaerobic Digestion (2016).
16 Weber and Herrlein (2011).
17 Parry et al. (2015).
18 Plant Chicago (2016).
19 The World Bank (2007).
20 McKinsey Center for Business and Environment, Ellen MacArthur Foundation and SUN (2015).
21 Baker (2015)
22 GSA Office of Government wide Policy (2011).
23 Woetzel et al. (2014).
24 *Smart home* refers to a residence equipped with computing and

information technology devices that anticipate and respond to the needs of the residents – enhancing comfort, convenience, security and entertainment.

25 Calthorpe (2013).
26 The New Climate Economy (2014).
27 Jetpissova (2013).

Chapter 12: Disrupted – for better or for worse?

1 Wolf (2015).
2 The term economists use to describe the difference between how a consumer truly values a product or service and what they actually pay for it.
3 Wolf (2015).
4 Gordon (2012b).
5 SBDCNet (2012).
6 Frey (2013).
7 Boerse.de (2016).
8 YCharts (2016).
9 Oxfam (2016).
10 Autor and Dorn (2013).

Chapter 13: Turning innovation into a force of good

1 Arthur (2009).
2 Webopedia.
3 Mazzucato (2011).
4 Wolf (2013).
5 The formal name is Advanced Research Projects Agency (ARPA), but the organization is most often referred to as DARPA.
6 DARPA (2016).
7 Mazzucato (2011).
8 Ellen MacArthur Foundation (2015).

Part IV: THE GREAT RECONCILIATION – HOW TO CROSS THE CHASM

1 Potočnik (2015).

Chapter 14: Ten years that matter – the case for change

1 Steffen et al. (2015).
2 IEA (2015a).
3 Dobbs et al. (2011).
4 FAO (2003).

5   Lloyd and Wire Reports (2015).
6   Reuters (2015).
7   Burgis and Blas (2009)
8   Hecking (2015).
9   *The Economist* (2015e).
10 Grantham Research Institute (2014).
11 The New Climate Economy (2014).
12 Umweltbundesamt (2015).
13 McKibben (2012).
14 Parkinson (2015b)
15 Harvey (2014).
16 Zumbrun and Cui (2015).
17 Bailey et al. (2015).
18 Mooney (2016).
19 Gapminder (2011).
20 Plant For The Planet (2016).
21 Manrodt (2014).
22 Schott (2014).
23 FAZ (2014).
24 Doyle (2015).
25 These so-called INDCs (Intended Nationally Determined Contributions)
    are the voluntary plans submitted by each participating country to the
    annual UN-hosted climate negotiations.
26 Jeffery et al. (2015).
27 Rogelj et al. (2015).
28 IPCC (2015).
29 UBS (2015).
30 The New Climate Economy (2014).

Chapter 15: An intuition reset – structure of a good revolution

1   Eisenhammer (2015).
2   Aphra Behn, based on Aesop's *Fables*; Wikipedia (2016) Aphra Behn.
3   Wikipedia (2016) The fox and the grapes.
4   Festinger (1957).
5   In experiments, an educational video that ended with refutational
    statements emphatically denying content of the video information
    was remembered and comprehended by most students after five
    months.
6   Guzzetti et al. (1993).
7   McKie (2012).
8   RoSPA (2016).

9   Lacey (1995).
10 Simon (2015).
11 Naughton (2012b).
12 Kuhn (1962).
13 USMA (2012).
14 Xie et al. (2011).
15 Groth (2011).
16 Gladwell (2002).
17 Wikipedia (2016) The Tipping Point.

Chapter 16: Shaping, not gaping – government's new role

1   The World Bank (2016b).
2   McKinsey Center for Business and Environment and Ocean Conservancy (2015).
3   Shaw (2015).
4   Shackleton (2013).
5   McKinsey Global Institute (2011).
6   Ex'Tax (2015).
7   McDonough and Braungart (2002).
8   Kelly (2016).
9   Wertstoffgesetz-Fakten (2015).
10 Greenpeace (2016).
11 The World Bank (2012).
12 European Environment Agency (2013).
13 McKinsey Center for Business and Environment and Ocean Conservancy (2015).
14 TEEB (2010).
15 The Nature Conservancy (2014).
16 IUCN (2013).
17 Ecosystem marketplace (2008).
18 McKinsey Center for Business and Environment, Ellen MacArthur Foundation and SUN (2015)
19 Roepke (1952).
20 OECD (2007).
21 Mezue et al. (2015).
22 Engel et al. (2016).
23 Dopfer et al. (2004).

Chapter 17: More is different – the unstoppable crowd

1   Walker and Mathiesen (2013).
2   Watts (2008).

3 Shirky (2009).
4 Gertz (2015).
5 Weaver and Gajanan (2015).
6 eMarketer (2014).
7 Crowdsourcing LLC (2016).
8 *The Economist* (2015f).
9 *The Economist* (2015g).

Chapter 18: The new capitalist – the rise of long-term entrepreneurism

1 McKinsey Global Institute (2015).
2 Sebastian (2015).
3 McDonough and Braungart (2002).
4 Heck and Rogers (2014).
5 Hodges (1997).
6 Mendeloff (1979).
7 Leading Edge Group (2015).
8 Entrepreneur Media (2016).
9 Barton (2011).
10 Carrington and Howard (2015).
11 Winston (2014).

Chapter 19: The great reconciliation – entering the upward spiral

1 Thomasson and Davey (2014).
2 Girsberger Holding AG (2014).
3 Kubiszewski et al. (2013).
4 McKinsey Center for Business and Environment, Ellen MacArthur Foundation and SUN (2015).
5 Horbach et al. (2015).

Appendix 2: Seeds of a better economy – visiting the frontline

1 Gunther (2013)
2 Jacobsen (2014)
3 Ringen (2014)
4 Gates (2013)
5 Bittman (2012)
6 Sparkes (2014)
7 FAO (2006)
8 Nassauer (2014)
9 Food and Beverage Close-Up (2013)
10 MarketLine (2014)
11 Lönnqvist et al. (2015)

12 The Baltic Biogas Bus Project (2012)
13 Bolloré (2014)
14 Henley (2014)
15 Sevcenko (2011)
16 Ministry of Climate and Environment (2016)
17 The Savory Institute (2016)
18 Baker (2013)
19 World Forum for a Responsible Economy (2011)

Bibliography

ACTeon. (2012). *Gap Analysis of the Water Scarcity and Droughts Policy in the EU.* Retrieved from European Commission: http://ec.europa.eu/environment/water/quantity/pdf/WSDGapAnalysis.pdf (accessed 1 August 2016).

Alesina, A., Glaeser, E. and Sacerdote, B. (2001). 'Why Doesn't the United States Have a European-Style Welfare State?' *Brookings Papers on Economic Activity*, 1–69.

Allsopp, M., Walters, A., Santillo, D. and Johnston, P. (2006). *Plastic Debris in the World's Oceans.* Retrieved from UNEP: http://www.unep.org/regionalseas/marinelitter/publications/docs/plastic_ocean_report.pdf (accessed 6 April 2016).

Anaerobic Digestion (2016). Website. Retrieved from BiogasInfo: http://www.biogas-info.co.uk/ (accessed 11 April 2016).

Armstrong, T. (2012). *The Cement Industry in Figures.* International Cement Review.

Arsova, L. (2010). *Anaerobic digestion of food waste: Current status, problems and an alternative product.* Retrieved from Columbia University: http://www.seas.columbia.edu/earth/wtert/sofos/arsova_thesis.pdf (accessed 18 March 2016).

Arthur, W. B. (2009). *The Technologature: What It Is and How It Evolves.* New York: Free Press.

Askerov, E. (2012). *Global economic outlook and steel demand trends.* Retrieved from Worldsteel Association: http://www.worldsteel.org/dms/internetDocumentList/downloads/media-centre/2012-04-23_Ukraine/document/Global%20economic%20outlook%20and%20steel%20demand%20trends.pdf (accessed 8 April 2016).

Atsmon, Y., Kertesz, A and Vittal, I. (2011). *Is your emerging-market strategy local enough?* Retrieved from McKinsey Quarterly April 2011: http://www.mckinsey.com/global-themes/employment-and-growth/is-your-emerging-market-strategy-local-enough (accessed 18 April 2016).

Australian Government – Productivity Commission. (2005). *Trends in Australian Agriculture.* Retrieved from: http://www.pc.gov.au/research/supporting/agriculture/agriculture.pdf (accessed 20 April 2016).

Autor, D. H. and Dorn, D. (2013). 'The Growth of Low-Skill Service Jobs and the Polarization of the US Labor Market'. *American Economic Review* 103 (5); 1553–97. http://dx.doi.org/10.1257/aer.103.5.1553

Ayres, R. (2014). *The Bubble Economy: Is Sustainable Growth Possible?* Cambridge, MA: MIT Press.

Ayres, R., and Voudouris, V. (2014). 'The economic growth enigma: Capital, labour and useful energy?' *Energy Policy,* 64: 16–28. doi:10.1016/j. enpol.2013.06.001

Ayres, R., and Warr, B. (2005). Accounting for growth: the role of physical work. *Structural Change and Economic Dynamics* 16 (2): 181–209. doi:10.1016/j.strueco.2003.10.003

Ayres, R. and Warr, B. (2009). *The Economic Growth Engine: How Energy and Work Drive Material Prosperity.* Cheltenham: Edward Elgar Publishing Limited.

Bailey, J., Godsall, J., Oppenheim, J. and Titel, E. (2015). *Global impact investing market in 2015.* McKinsey & Company, Internal document.

Baker, D. (2013). *Post-organic: Leontino Balbo Junior's green farming future.* Retrieved from Wired.co.uk: http://www.wired.co.uk/magazine/ archive/2013/08/features/post-organic (accessed 17 March 2016).

Baker, M. B. (2015). *Barclays: Airbnb Usage To Surpass Hotel Cos., But Not For Business Travel.* Retrieved from Business Travel News: http://www. businesstravelnews.com/Hotel-News/Barclays-Airbnb-Usage-To-Surpass-Hotel-Cos-But-Not-For-Business-Travel?ida=Hotel%20Chains (accessed 11 April 2016).

Balkissoon, K. and Heaps, T. (2014). *Performance and Impact: Can Low Carbon Equity Portfolios Generate Healthier Financial Returns?* Retrieved from SSRN: http://dx.doi.org/10.2139/ssrn.2519803 (accessed 22 March 2016).

Bartels, L. (2013). *Obama Toes the Line.* Retrieved from The Monkey Cage: http://themonkeycage.org/2013/01/obama-toes-the-line/ (accessed 4 April 2016).

Barton, D. (2011). 'Capitalism for the long term'. *Harvard Business Review* 89 (3): 84–91.

Bennett, J. (2012). *Nylon-12 Haunts Car Makers.* Retrieved from *The Wall Street Journal:* http://www.wsj.com/articles/SB100014240527023044327045773 49883297625686 (accessed 14 April 2016).

Bhattacharyya, S. (2013). *What is the impact of natural resource booms on income inequality? Some lessons from Australia.* Retrieved from CSAE – Centre for the Study of African Economies: http://blogs.csae.ox.ac.uk/2013/08/ what-is-the-impact-of-natural-resource-booms-on-income-inequality-some-lessons-from-australia/ (accessed 6 April 2016).

Bittman, M. (2012). *A Chicken Without Guilt.* Retrieved from *The New York Times:* http://www.nytimes.com/2012/03/11/opinion/sunday/finally-fake-chicken-worth-eating.html?pagewanted=all&_r=0 (accessed 16 March 2016).

Boerse.de (2016) (German). *Energie und Rohstoffe – Versorger-Aktien*. Retrieved from Boerse.de: http://www.boerse.de/aktien/Versorger/kursliste (accessed 19 April 2016).

Bolloré (2014). *Blue Solutions for optimization of urban transport – Company presentation*. Retrieved from: http://www.fondationecologiedavenir.org/Colloque_Stockage_Energie/Jacques_Mercier.pdf (accessed 21 March 2016).

Bradford DeLong, J. (1998). *Estimating World GDP, One Million B.C. – Present*. Retrieved from Holtz: http://holtz.org/Library/Social%20Science/Economics/Estimating%20World%20GDP%20by%20DeLong/Estimating%20World%20GDP.htm (accessed 23 March 2016).

Brandmeir, K., Grimm, M., Heise, M. and Holzhausen, A. (2015). *Global Wealth Report 2015*. Retrieved from Allianz.com: https://www.allianz.com/v_1444215837000/media/economic_research/publications/specials/en/AGWR2015_ENG.pdf (accessed 4 April 2016).

Brynjolfsson, E. and McAfee, A. (2014). *The Second Machine Age: Work, Progress, and Prosperity in a Time of Brilliant Technologies*. New York: W. W. Norton & Co., Inc.

Burgis, T., and Blas, J. (2009). *Madagascar scraps Daewoo farm deal*. Retrieved from *Financial Times*: http://www.ft.com/cms/s/0/7e133310-13ba-11de-9e32-0000779fd2ac.html#axzz44Hwhvo00 (accessed 29 March 2016).

Calthorpe, P. (2013). *Urbanism in the Age of Climate Change*. Washington, DC: Island Press.

Cambridge Econometrics and Bio Intelligence Service (2014). *Study on modelling of the economic and environmental impacts of raw material consumption*. Retrieved from European Commission: http://ec.europa.eu/environment/enveco/resource_efficiency/pdf/RMC.pdf (accessed 22 March 2016).

Carbon Tracker Initiative (2013). *Unburnable Carbon – Are the world's financial markets carrying a carbon bubble?* Retrieved from Carbon Tracker: http://www.carbontracker.org/wp-content/uploads/2014/09/Unburnable-Carbon-Full-rev2-1.pdf (accessed 23 March 2016).

Carbon Tracker Initiative (2014). *Investors challenge fossil fuel companies*. Retrieved from Carbon Tracker: http://www.carbontracker.org/news/investors-challenge-fossil-fuel-companies/ (accessed 23 March 2016).

Carrington, D. and Howard, M. (2015). *Institutions worth $2.6 trillion have now pulled investments out of fossil fuels*. Retrieved from *The Guardian*: http://www.theguardian.com/environment/2015/sep/22/leonardo-dicaprio-joins-26tn-fossil-fuel-divestment-movement (accessed 18 April 2016).

CDIAC (2011). *Annual Global Fossil-Fuel Carbon Emissions*. Retrieved from CDIAC: http://cdiac.ornl.gov/trends/emis/glo_2011.html (accessed 15 March 2016).

Ceballos, G., Ehrlich, P. R., Barnosky, A. D., Gracía, A., Pringle, R. M. and Palmer, T. M. (2015). 'Accelerated modern human-induced species losses: Entering the sixth mass extinction'. *Science Advances* 1 (5, e1400253): 1–5. doi:10.1126/sciadv.1400253

CEMA (2015). *Precision Farming – producing more with less*. Retrieved from CEMA: http://www.cema-agri.org/page/precision-farming-0 (accessed 20 April 2016).

Charities Aid Foundation (2014). *World Giving Index 2014 – A global view of giving trends*. Retrieved from CAF Online: https://www.cafonline.org/docs/default-source/about-us-publications/caf_wgi2014_report_1555awebfinal.pdf (accessed 6 April 2016).

Clark, G. L., Feiner, A. and Viehs, M. (2015). *From the stockholder to the stakeholder*. Retrieved from Arabesque: http://www.arabesque.com/index.php?tt_down=51e2de00a30f88872897824d3e211b11 (accessed 22 March 2016).

Clark, T. (2015). *Between Debt and the Devil by Adair Turner review – should the government start printing money?* Retrieved from *The Guardian*: http://www.theguardian.com/books/2015/nov/25/between-debt-and-devil-adair-turner-review (accessed 6 April 2016).

Clearpath Foundation (2015). *Tesla Electrifies the Auto Industry*. Retrieved from Clearpath Foundation: http://www.clearpath.org/en/why-clean-energy/promise-of-clean-energy/tesla-nearly-twice-valuable-as-chrysler.html (accessed 7 April 2016).

Coady, D., Parry, I. W., Sears, L. and Shang, B. (2015). *How Large Are Global Energy Subsidies?* Retrieved from IMF: https://www.imf.org/external/pubs/ft/wp/2015/wp15105.pdf (accessed 1 August 2016).

Collier, P. (2011). *The Plundered Planet: Why We Must – and How We Can – Manage Nature for Global Prosperity*. Oxford: Oxford University Press.

Confino, J. (2011). *Paul Polman: 'The power is in the hands of the consumers'*. Retrieved from *The Guardian*: http://www.theguardian.com/sustainable-business/unilever-ceo-paul-polman-interview

Confino, J. (2015). *Public trust in business hits five-year low*. Retrieved from *The Guardian*: http://www.theguardian.com/sustainable-business/2015/jan/21/public-trust-global-business-government-low-decline (accessed 18 April 2016).

Coyle, D. (2012). *The Economics of Enough: How to Run the Economy as If the Future Matters*. Princeton, NJ: Princeton University Press.

Coyle, D. (2014). *GDP – A brief but affectionate history*. Princeton, NJ: Princeton University Press.

Crowdsourcing LLC (2016). *Global Crowdfunding Market To Reach $34.4B in 2015, Predicts Massolution's 2015CF Industry Report*. Retrieved from Crowdsourcing LLC: http://www.crowdsourcing.org/editorial/

global-crowdfunding-market-to-reach-344b-in-2015-predicts-massolutions-2015cf-industry-report/45376 (accessed 15 April 2016).

Daly, H. E. (1973). *Towards a Steady-State Economy*. San Francisco: W. H. Freeman.

Daly, H. E. (2005). 'Economics In A Full World'. *Scientific American* 293 (3): 100–7.

Damodaran, A. (2016). *Return on Equity by Sector (US)*. Retrieved from New York University: http://pages.stern.nyu.edu/~adamodar/New_Home_Page/datafile/roe.html (accessed 30 March 2016).

Dargay, J., Gately, D. and Sommer, M. (2007). *Vehicle Ownership and Income Growth, Worldwide: 1960–2030*. Retrieved from ECON NYU: http://www.econ.nyu.edu/dept/courses/gately/DGS_Vehicle%20Ownership_2007.pdf (accessed 4 April 2016).

DARPA (2016). *Budget*. Retrieved from DARPA: http://www.darpa.mil/about-us/budget (accessed 8 April 2016).

Deaton, A. (2013). *The Great Escape: Health, Wealth, and the Origins of Inequality*. Princeton, NJ: Princeton University Press.

Destatis (2016). *Volkswirtschaftliche Gesamtrechnungen – Private Konsumausgaben und Verfügbares Einkommen*. Retrieved from Destatis: https://www.destatis.de/DE/Publikationen/Thematisch/VolkswirtschaftlicheGesamtrechnungen/Inlandsprodukt/KonsumausgabenPDF_5811109.pdf?__blob=publicationFile (accessed 18 April 2016).

Dobbs, R., Oppenheim, J., Thompson, F., Brinkman, M. and Zornes, M. (2011). *Resource revolution: Meeting the world's energy, materials, food, and water needs*. Retrieved from McKinsey Global Institute: http://www.mckinsey.com/insights/energy_resources_materials/resource_revolution (accessed 16 March 2016).

Dobbs, R., Madgavkar, A., Barton, D., Labaye, E., Manyika, J., Roxburgh, C., Lund, S. and Madhav, S. (2012). *The world at work: Jobs, pay, and skills for 3.5 billion people*. Retrieved from McKinsey Global Institute: http://www.mckinsey.com/global-themes/employment-and-growth/the-world-at-work (accessed 8 April 2016).

Dobbs, R., Oppenheim, J., Thompson, F., Thompson, F., Mareels, S., Nyquist, S. and Sanghvi, S. (2013). *Resource Revolution: Tracking Global Commodity Markets*. Retrieved from McKinsey Global Institute: http://www.mckinsey.com/~/media/McKinsey/Not%20Mapped/TEST%20Copy%20of%20Resource%20revolution%20Tracking%20global%20commodity%20markets/MGI_Resources_survey_Full_report_Sep2013.ashx (accessed 19 April 2016).

Dobbs, R., Lund, S., Woetzel, J. and Mutafchieva, M. (2015a). *Debt and (not much) deleveraging*. Retrieved from McKinsey Global Institute: http://www.

mckinsey.com/insights/economic_studies/debt_and_not_much_delever-aging (accessed 6 April 2016).

Dobbs, R., Manyika, J. and Woetzel, J. (2015b). *No Ordinary Disruption*. McKinsey and Company. New York: Public Affairs.

Doom, J. (2012). *Battery Prices for Electric Vehicles Fall 14%, BNEF says*. Retrieved from Bloomberg: http://www.bloomberg.com/news/articles/2012-04-16/battery-prices-for-electric-vehicles-fall-14-bnef-says (accessed 7 April 2016).

Dopfer, K., Foster, J. and Potts, J. (2004). 'Micro-meso-macro'. *Journal of Evolutionary Economics* 14 (3): 263–79.

Doyle, A. (2015). *16 quotes from world leaders on the Paris climate agreement*. Retrieved from World Economic Forum: https://www.weforum.org/agenda/2015/12/16-quotes-from-world-leaders-on-the-paris-climate-agreement/ (accessed 20 April 2016).

Dwyer, M. (2015). *Breastfeeding may expose infants to toxic chemicals*. Retrieved from Harvard T.H. Chan School of Public Health: http://www.hsph.harvard.edu/news/press-releases/breastfeeding-may-expose-infants-to-toxic-chemicals/ (accessed 6 April 2016).

Eadicicco, L. (2015). *Google May Be Making a Big Move to Take on Uber*. Retrieved from *TIME*: http://time.com/4151289/google-uber-self-driving-cars/ (accessed 12 April 2016).

Earth Overshoot Day (2015a). *August 13th is Earth Overshoot Day this year*. Retrieved from Earth Overshoot Day: http://www.overshootday.org/newsroom/press-release-english/ (accessed 5 April 2016).

Earth Overshoot Day (2015b). *Past Earth Overshoot Days*. Retrieved from Earth Overshoot Day 2015: http://www.overshootday.org/newsroom/past-earth-overshoot-days/ (accessed 20 April 2016).

Edelman (2015). *2015 Edelman Trust Barometer: Executive Summary*. Retrieved from Edelman: http://www.edelman.com/insights/intellectual-property/2015-edelman-trust-barometer/trust-and-innovation-edelman-trust-barometer/executive-summary/ (accessed 6 April 2016).

edX (2016). *The Leading Open Source, Nonprofit Online Learning Destination*. Retrieved from edX: https://www.edx.org/sites/default/files/mediakit/file/edx_mediakit_final_feb_2016v2.pdf (accessed 15 March 2016).

eMarketer (2014). *Smartphone Users Worldwide Will Total 1.75 Billion in 2014*. Retrieved from Emarketer: http://www.emarketer.com/Article/Smartphone-Users-Worldwide-Will-Total-175-Billion-2014/1010536 (accessed 14 April 2016).

Entrepreneur Media (2016). *An Introduction to Royalty Financing*. Retrieved from Entrepreneur Media: https://www.entrepreneur.com/article/52738 (accessed 18 April 2016).

EIA (2016). *Short-Term Energy And Summer Fuels Outlook.* Retrieved from EIA: https://www.eia.gov/forecasts/steo/report/global_oil.cfm (accessed 18 April 2016).

Eisenhammer, S. (2015). *Brazil mining flood could devastate environment for years.* Retrieved from Reuters: http://www.reuters.com/article/us-brazil-damburst-environment-idUSKCN0T40PY20151115 (accessed 14 April 2016).

EITI (2016). *EITI Countries – Facts & Figures.* Retrieved from EITI: https://eiti.org/countries (accesed 31 March 2016).

Ekins, P. and Max-Neef, M. (1992). *Real-Life Economics: Understanding Wealth Creation.* London: Routledge.

Elhadj, E. (2008). *SAUDI ARABIA'S AGRICULTURAL PROJECT: FROM DUST TO DUST.* Retrieved from Middle East Review of International Affairs: http://www.rubincenter.org/meria/2008/06/elhadj.pdf (accessed 14 April 2016).

Ellen MacArthur Foundation (2013). *Towards The Circular Economy Vol. 1 – Economic and business rationale for an accelerated transition.* Retrieved from Ellen MacArthur Foundation: http://www.ellenmacarthurfoundation.org/assets/downloads/publications/Ellen-MacArthur-Foundation-Towards-the-Circular-Economy-vol.1.pdf (accessed 22 March 2016).

Ellen MacArthur Foundation (2015). *Project Mainstream Launches Three New Programmes.* Retrieved from Ellen MacArthur Foundation: http://www.ellenmacarthurfoundation.org/news/project-mainstream-launches-three-new-programmes (accessed 14 April 2016).

Ellen MacArthur Foundation (2016). *The New Plastics Economy.* Retrieved from Ellen MacArthur Foundation: http://www.ellenmacarthurfoundation.org/assets/downloads/EllenMacArthurFoundation_TheNewPlasticsEconomy_15-3-16.pdf (accessed 23 March 2016).

Emmott, S. (2013). *Ten Billion.* New York: Vintage Books.

Engel, H., Stuchtey, M., and Vanthournout, H. (2016). *Managing waste in emerging markets.* Retrieved from McKinsey & Company: http://www.mckinsey.com/business-functions/sustainability-and-resource-productivity/our-insights/managing-waste-in-emerging-markets (accessed 30 March 2016).

EU Parliament Directorate-General for Internal Policies (2014). *Precision agriculture: an opportunity for EU farmers – potential support with the CAP 2014-2020.* Retrieved from EU Parliament Directorate-General for internal policies: http://www.europarl.europa.eu/RegData/etudes/note/join/2014/529049/IPOL-AGRI_NT(2014)529049_EN.pdf (accessed 8 April 2016).

European Commission (2014). *On the review of the list of critical raw materials for the EU and the implementation of the Raw Materials Initiative.* Retrieved from European Commission: http://eur-lex.europa.eu/legal-content/EN/TXT/PDF/?uri=CELEX:52014DC0297&from=EN (accessed 12 April 2016).

European Commission (2015). *Sewage Sludge.* Retrieved from European Commission: http://ec.europa.eu/environment/waste/sludge/ (accessed 22 March 2016).

European Commission (2016). *Reducing CO_2 emissions from passenger cars.* Retrieved from European Commission: http://ec.europa.eu/clima/policies/transport/vehicles/cars/index_en.htm (accessed 15 March 2016).

European Commission – Agriculture and Rural Development (2013). *Facts and figures on organic agriculture in the European Union.* Retrieved from European Commission – Agriculture and Rural Development: http://ec.europa.eu/agriculture/markets-and-prices/more-reports/pdf/organic-2013_en.pdf (accessed 11 April 2016).

European Commission, Directorate General for Environment (2015). *Our Oceans, Seas and Coasts – Marine Litter.* Retrieved from European Commission Environment: http://ec.europa.eu/environment/marine/good-environmental-status/descriptor-10/index_en.htm (accessed 6 April 2016).

European Commission, Directorate General for Regional and Urban Policy (2013). *Urban Development in the EU: 50 Projects supported by the European Regional Development Fund during the 2007-2013 period.* Retrieved from: http://ec.europa.eu/regional_policy/sources/docgener/studies/pdf/50_projects/urban_dev_erdf50.pdf (accessed 11 April 2016).

European Commission – Mobility & Transport (2011). *Roadmap to a Single European Transport Area.* Retrieved from European Commission Mobility & Transport: http://ec.europa.eu/transport/strategies/facts-and-figures/all-themes/index_en.htm (accessed 18 March 2016).

European Commission – Press release (2015). *Closing the loop: Commission adopts ambitious new Circular Economy Package to boost competitiveness, create jobs and generate sustainable growth.* Retrieved from European Commission: http://europa.eu/rapid/press-release_IP-15-6203_en.htm (accessed 21 March 2016).

European Environment Agency (2013). *Managing municipal solid waste – a review of achievements in 32 European countries.* Retrieved from European Environment Agency: http://www.eea.europa.eu/publications/managing-municipal-solid-waste (accessed 19 April 2016).

European Environment Agency (2015). *Agriculture.* Retrieved from European Environment Agency: http://www.eea.europa.eu/soer-2015/europe/agriculture (accessed 17 March 2016).

Eurostat (2012). *Final consumption expenditure of households by consumption purpose.* Retrieved from Eurostat: http://www.eea.europa.eu/data-and-maps/data/external/household-consumption-coicop-eurostat (accessed 17 March 2016).

Eurostat (2013). *Overview of the composition of EU27 expenditure in 2011.* Retrieved from Eurostat: http://ec.europa.eu/eurostat/statistics-explained/index.php/File:Overview_of_the_composition_of_EU27_expenditure_in_2011.png (accessed 18 March 2016).

Eurostat (2015a). *Domestic material consumption – tons per capita.* Retrieved from Eurostat: http://ec.europa.eu/eurostat/tgm/table.do?tab=table&init=1&language=en&pcode=t2020_rl110&plugin=1 (accessed 16 March 2016).

Eurostat (2015b). *Municipal waste generation and treatment, by type of treatment method.* Retrieved from Eurostat: http://ec.europa.eu/eurostat/tgm/refreshTableAction.do?tab=table&plugin=1&pcode=tsdpc240&language=en (accessed 6 April 2016).

Eurostat (2015c). *Expenditure on pensions, 2012 (% of GDP).* Retrieved from Eurostat: http://ec.europa.eu/eurostat/statistics-explained/index.php/File:Expenditure_on_pensions,_2012_(%25_of_GDP)_YB15-de.png (accessed 18 April 2016).

Ex'Tax (2015). *IMF Recommends Tax Shift.* Retrieved from Ex'Tax: http://www.ex-tax.com/news/extax/imf-recommends-tax-shift/ (accessed 20 April 2016).

Fallows, J. (2015). *The Planet-Saving, Capitalism-Subverting, Surprisingly Lucrative Investment Secrets of Al Gore.* Retrieved from *The Atlantic*: http://www.theatlantic.com/magazine/archive/2015/11/the-planet-saving-capitalism-subverting-surprisingly-lucrative-investment-secrets-of-al-gore/407857/ (accessed 22 March 2016).

FAO (2003). *World Agriculture: Towards 2015/2030. An FAO perspective.* Retrieved from FAO: http://www.fao.org/docrep/005/y4252e/y4252e05b.htm (accessed 19 April 2016).

FAO (2006). *Livestock's long shadow: environmental issues and options.* Retrieved from FAO: ftp://ftp.fao.org/docrep/fao/010/a0701e/a0701e.pdf (accessed 16 March 2016).

FAO (2008). *Forecasting Long-term Global Fertilizer Demand.* Retrieved from FAO: ftp://ftp.fao.org/agl/agll/docs/globalfertdemand.pdf (accessed 19 April 2016).

FAO (2011a). *Global food losses and food waste – Extent, causes and prevention.* Retrieved from FAO: http://www.fao.org/docrep/014/mb060e/mb060e.pdf (accessed 17 March 2016).

FAO (2011b). *Current world fertilizer trends and outlook to 2015.* Retrieved from FAO: http://www.fao.org/3/a-av252e.pdf (accessed 6 April 2016).

FAO (2011c). *Germany: Per capita food supply.* Retrieved from FAO: http://faostat.fao.org/site/368/default.aspx#ancor (accessed 18 April 2016).

FAO (2013). *FAO Statistical Yearbook 2013 – Feeding the world.* Retrieved from FAO: http://www.fao.org/docrep/018/i3107e/i3107e03.pdf (accessed 19 April 2016).

FAO (2015). *World Fertilizer Trend and Outlook to 2018.* Retrieved from FAO: http://www.fao.org/publications/card/en/c/db95327a-5936-4d01-b67d-7e55e532e8f5/ (accessed 20 April 2016).

FAOSTAT (2015a). *Food Security – Suite of Food Security Indicators.* Retrieved from FAOSTAT: http://faostat3.fao.org/browse/D/*/E (accessed 4 April 2016).

FAOSTAT (2015b). *Production Indices.* Retrieved from FAOSTAT: http://faostat3.fao.org/browse/Q/QI/E (accessed 17 March 2015).

Faßbender, H., and Kluge, J. (2006) (German). *Perspektive Deutschland: Was die Deutschen Wirklich wollen.* Berlin: Econ.

FAZ (2014) (German). *Autofahren ist out, Smartphones werden wichtiger.* Retrieved from Frankfurter Allgemeine: http://www.faz.net/aktuell/technik-motor/auto-verkehr/fuehrerschein-kein-statussymbol-autofahren-ist-out-smart-phones-werden-wichtiger-13346242.html (accessed 21 April 2016).

Fehrenbacher, K. (2015). *Goldman Sachs to invest $150 billion in clean energy.* Retrieved from *Fortune*: http://fortune.com/2015/11/02/goldman-sachs-clean-energy/

Festinger, L. (1957). *A Theory of Cognitive Dissonance.* Stanford, CA: Stanford University Press.

Festinger, L., Riecken, H. W. and Schachter, S. (1956). *When Prophecy Fails.* Minneapolis, MN: University of Minnesota Press.

Fink, L. (2015). *Our Gambling Culture – The craving for immediate gratification has spread well beyond Wall Street.* Retrieved from McKinsey&Company: http://www.mckinsey.com/insights/strategy/our_gambling_culture (accessed 8 April 2016).

Fondation de France (2015). *An overview of philanthropy in Europe.* Retrieved from Fondation de France: https://www.fondationdefrance.org/sites/default/files/atoms/files/philanthropy_in_europe_2015_0.pdf (accessed 18 April 2016).

Food & Beverage Close-Up (2013). *Beyond Meat Launches Transparency Challenge to Poultry Producers.* Retrieved from HighBeam Research: https://www.highbeam.com/doc/1G1-345793400.html (accessed 20 April 2016).

FoodDrink Europe (2015). *Promoting an EU Industrial Policy for Food and Drink – Competitiveness Report 2013-2014.* Retrieved from FoodDrink Europe: http://www.fooddrinkeurope.eu/uploads/publications_documents/Promoting_an_EU_industrial_policy_for_food_and_drink.pdf

Francis (2013). *Evangelii Gaudium : Apostolic Exhortation on the Proclamation of the Gospel in Today's World*. Vatican: Vatican Press.

Frey, C. B. and Osborne, M. A. (2013). *The Future of Employment: How Susceptible Are Jobs to Computerisation?* Retrieved from Oxford Martin School – University of Oxford: http://www.oxfordmartin.ox.ac.uk/downloads/academic/The_Future_of_Employment.pdf (accessed 11 April 2016).

Fukuyama, F. (1989). 'The End of History?' *The National Interest* (Summer).

Gabbatt, A. (2011). *IBM computer Watson wins Jeopardy clash*. Retrieved from *The Guardian*: http://www.theguardian.com/technology/2011/feb/17/ibm-computer-watson-wins-jeopardy (accessed 11 March 2016).

Gapminder (2011). *The World has reached Peak Number of Children!* Retrieved from Gapminder: http://www.gapminder.org/news/world-peak-number-of-children-is-now/ (accessed 29 March 2016).

Gates, B. (2013). *The Future of Food*. Retrieved from http://www.gatesnotes.com/About-Bill-Gates/Future-of-Food (accessed 16 March 2016)

Gertz, E. (2015). *Watch How a Gadget in Your Pocket Is Helping Save Endangered Orangutans*. Retrieved from: http://www.takepart.com/article/2015/03/11/sumatra-aceh-smartphones-forest-orangutans-tigers (accessed 14 April 2016).

Gesis (2009). *Wohnen in Deutschland: Teuer, komfortabel und meist zur Miete*. Retrieved from Gesis : http://www.gesis.org/fileadmin/upload/forschung/publikationen/zeitschriften/isi/isi-41.pdf (accessed 18 April 2016).

Geyer, R. and Blass, V. D. (2009). 'The economics of cell phone reuse and recycling'. *The International Journal of Advanced Manufacturing Technology* Retrieved from: https://link.springer.com/content/pdf/10.1007%2Fs00170-009-2228-z.pdf (accessed 16 March 2016).

Girsberger Holding AG (2014). Website. Retrieved from Girsberger Holding AG: https://www.girsberger.com/de/ (accessed 31 March 2016).

Gladwell, M. (2002). *The tipping point*. London: Abacus.

Gleick, P. H. (1993). *Water in Crisis: A Guide to the World's Freshwater Resources*. Oxford: Oxford University Press.

Global Carbon Project (2016). *Global Carbon Budget*. Retrieved from Global Carbon Project: http://www.globalcarbonproject.org/carbonbudget/15/presentation.htm (accessed 15 April 2016).

Global Footprint Network (2015). *Glossary*. Retrieved from Global Footprint Network: http://www.footprintnetwork.org/en/index.php/GFN/page/glossary/#Ecologicalfootprint (accessed 5 April 2016).

Global Ocean Commission (2014). *A Living Ocean – Managing our ocean to its full economic potential*. Discussion document.

Global TraPs Project (2013). *Response of the Global TraPs Project to the EC Consultative Communication on the Sustainable Use of Phosphorus*. Retrieved from Global&TraPs Project: http://www.globaltraps.ch/tl_files/bilder/start/12-01-13_Respose_to_EUSUP.pdf (accessed 11 April 2016).

Goldenberg, S. (2014). *CO₂ emissions are being 'outsourced' by rich countries to rising economies.* Retrieved from *The Guardian*: http://www.theguardian.com/environment/2014/jan/19/co2-emissions-outsourced-rich-nations-rising-economies (accessed 31 March 2016).

Google (2016). *Google Self-Driving Car Project.* Retrieved from: https://www.google.com/selfdrivingcar/ (accessed 12 April 2016).

Gordon, R. J. (2012a). *Discussion of Fixler and Johnson.* Retrieved from the U.S. Bureau of Economic Analysis: www.bea.gov/about/ppt/DCA_BEA_Fixler%26Johnson_121116.pptx (accessed 11 April 2016).

Gordon, R. J. (2012b). *Is U.S. Economic Growth Over? Faltering Innovation Confronts The Six Headwinds.* Retrieved from The National Bureau of Economic Research: http://www.nber.org/papers/w18315 (accessed 7 April 2016).

Gordon, R. J. (2014). 'The Demise of U.S. Economic Growth: Restatement, Rebuttal, and Reflections'. *NBER Working Paper No. 19895.* doi:10.3386/w19895

Goulart, J. (2015). *What an amazing year 2015 has been for edX and for our learners!* Retrieved from edX: http://blog.edx.org/edx-year-in-review?track=blog&utm_source=twitter&utm_medium=social-post&utm_content=blog-promotion-year-in-review&utm_campaign=year-in-review (accessed 11 March 2016).

Grafton, R. Q. and Horne, J. (2014). *Water markets in the Murray-Darling Basin.* Retrieved from ResearchGate: https://www.researchgate.net/publication/259994068_Water_markets_in_the_Murray-Darling_Basin (accessed 30 March 2016).

Grantham Research Institute (2014). *The impacts of environmental regulations on competitiveness.* Retrieved from The London School of Economics and Political Science: http://personal.lse.ac.uk/dechezle/Impacts_of_Environmental_Regulations.pdf (accessed 29 March 2016).

Greenpeace (2016). *Italy's largest fashion supply chain pledges to Detox hazardous chemicals.* Retrieved from Greenpeace: http://www.greenpeace.org/international/en/press/releases/2016/Italys-fashion-supply-chain-Detox-hazardous-chemicals/ (accessed 20 April 2016).

Grober, U. (1999) (German). Der Erfinder der Nachhaltigkeit. *Die Zeit, 48,* 98.

Groth, A. (2011). *Scientists Reveal The 'Tipping Point' For Ideas Is When There's A 10% Consensus.* Retrieved from Business Insider: http://www.businessinsider.com/scientists-reveal-the-tipping-point-for-ideas-is-when-theres-a-10-consensus-2011-7?IR=T (accessed 14 April 2016).

GSA Office of Governmentwide Policy (2011). *Workspace Utilization and*

Allocation Benchmark. Retrieved from GSA: http://www.gsa.gov/graphics/ogp/Workspace_Utilization_Banchmark_July_2012.pdf (accessed 18 March 2016).

GSIA (2014). *Global Sustainable Investment Review 2014*. Retrieved from GSI-Alliance: http://www.gsi-alliance.org/wp-content/uploads/2015/02/GSIA_Review_download.pdf (accessed 18 April 2016).

GSV EDU (2012). *Education Sector Factbook 2012*. Retrieved from GSV EDU: http://gsvadvisors.com/wordpress/wp-content/uploads/2012/04/GSV-EDU-Factbook-Apr-13-2012.pdf (accessed 11 March 2016).

Gunther, M. (2013). *The Bill Gates-backed company that's reinventing meat*. Retrieved from *Fortune*: http://fortune.com/2013/10/03/the-bill-gates-backed-company-thats-reinventing-meat/ (accessed 16 March 2016).

Guzzetti, B., Snyder, T., Glass, G. and Gamas, W. (1993). 'Promoting conceptual change in science: A comparative meta-analysis of instructional interventions from reading education and science education'. *Reading Research Quarterly* 28 (2): 116–59. http://www.jstor.org/stable/747886

Hajer, M. (2014). *Europe needs 'smart urbanism' not 'smart cities'*. Retrieved from *The Parliament Magazine*: https://www.theparliamentmagazine.eu/articles/feature/europe-needs-smart-urbanism-not-smart-cities (accessed 11 April 2016).

Hamburgh, R. (2015). *The common good: the rise and rise of the UK cooperative movement*. Retrieved from *Positive News*: http://positivenews.org.uk/2015/economics_innovation/17836/common-good-rise-and-rise-uk-cooperative-movement/ (accessed 6 April 2016).

Hamilton, J. D. (1983). 'Oil and the Macroeconomy since World War II'. *The Journal of Political Economy* 91 (2): 228–48.

Hamilton, J. D. (1996). 'This is what happened to the oil price-macro-economy relationship'. *Journal of Monetary Economics* 38 (2): 215–20. doi:10.1016/S0304-3932(96)01282-2

Hamilton, J. D. (2009). 'Causes and Consequences of the Oil Shock of 2007-08'. *Brookings Papers on Economic Activity, Economic Studies Program, The Brookings Institution,* 40 (1): 215–83. doi:10.3386/w15002

Hamilton, J. D. (2013). Historical Oil Shocks. In R. E. Parker and R. Whaples (ed.), *Routledge Handbook of Major Events in Economic History,* 239–65. New York: Routledge.

Harvey, F. (2014). *'Carbon bubble' poses serious threat to UK economy, MPs warn*. Retrieved from *The Guardian*: http://www.theguardian.com/environment/2014/mar/06/carbon-bubble-threat-uk-economy-fossil-fuels-mps (accessed 29 March 2016).

Hastings-Simon, S., Pinner, D. and Stuchtey, M. (2014). *Myths and realities of clean technologies*. Retrieved from McKinsey & Company – Insights &

Publications: http://www.mckinsey.com/insights/energy_resources_materials/myths_and_realities_of_clean_technologies (accessed 20 April 2016).

Haub, C. (2011). *How Many People Have Ever Lived on Earth?* Retrieved from Population Reference Bureau: http://www.prb.org/Publications/Articles/2002/HowManyPeopleHaveEverLivedonEarth.aspx (accessed 18 April 2016).

Hebebrand, C. (2013). *Global Fertilizer Production and Use: Issues and Challenges.* Retrieved from IFA: http://www.fertilizer.org/imis20/images/Library_Downloads/2013_AG_Beijing_Hebebrand_slides.pdf?WebsiteKey=411e9724-4bda-422f-abfc-8152ed74f306&=404%3bhttp%3a%2f%2fwww.fertilizer.org%3a80%2fen%2fimages%2fLibrary_Downloads%2f2013_AG_Beijing_Hebebrand_slides.pdf (accessed 19 April 2016).

Heck, S., Kaza, S. and Pinner, D. (2011). *Creating Value In The Semiconductor Industry.* Retrieved from McKinsey & Company: www.mckinsey.com/~/media/McKinsey/dotcom/client_service/Semiconductors/PDFs/MOSC_1_Value_creation.ashx (accessed 8 April 2016).

Heck, S. and Rogers, M. (2014). *Resource Revolution: How to Capture the Biggest Business Opportunity in a Century.* Boston and New York: Houghton Mifflin Harcourt Melcher Media.

Hecking, C. (2015) (German). *Umweltschutz: Was wurde eigentlich aus dem Waldsterben?* Retrieved from *Der Spiegel*: http://www.spiegel.de/wissenschaft/natur/umweltschutz-was-wurde-aus-dem-waldsterben-a-1009580.html (accessed 29 March 2016).

Helbing, D. (2010). 'Systemic Risks in Society and Economics'. *Social Self-Organization*, 261–84. http://link.springer.com/chapter/10.1007/978-3-642-24004-1_14#page-1

Helbing, D. (2013). 'Globally networked risks and to respond'. *Nature* 497: 51–9. doi:10.1038/nature12047

Henley, J. (2014). *Electric 'Boris cars' are coming to London – how do they work in Paris?* Retrieved from *The Guardian*: http://www.theguardian.com/cities/2014/jul/09/electric-boris-car-source-london-how-work-paris-autolib (accessed 17 March 2016)

Hensley, R., Newman, J. and Rogers, M. (2012). *Battery technology charges ahead.* Retrieved from McKinsey & Company – Insights & Publications: http://www.mckinsey.com/insights/energy_resources_materials/battery_technology_charges_ahead

Hirsch, J. (2015). *Major auto industry disruption will lead to robotic taxis, Morgan Stanley says.* Retrieved from *LA Times*: http://www.latimes.com/business/autos/la-fi-hy-end-of-human-driving-20150407-story.html (accessed 23 March 2016).

Hirshon, B. (2008). *Nitrogen Pollution.* Retrieved from Science NetLinks: http://sciencenetlinks.com/science-news/science-updates/nitrogen-pollution/ (accessed 17 March 2016).

Hodges, H. (1997). *Falling Prices : Cost of Complying With Environmental Regulations Almost Always Less Than Advertised.* Retrieved from Economic Policy Institute Briefing Paper: http://www.epi.org/files/page/-/old/brief-ingpapers/bp69.pdf (accessed 06 April 2016).

Horbach, J., Rennings, K. and Sommerfeld, K. (2015). *Circular Economy and Employment.* Retrieved from IZA: http://www.iza.org/conference_files/environ_2015/horbach_j11332.pdf (accessed 31 March 2016).

IEA (2014). *Energy Efficiency Market Report 2014.* Retrieved from IEA: https://www.iea.org/Textbase/npsum/EEMR2014SUM.pdf (accessed 18 March 2016).

IEA (2015a). *Energy Climate and Change – World Energy Outlook Special Report.* Retrieved from IEA: https://www.iea.org/publications/freepublications/publication/WEO2015SpecialReportonEnergyandClimateChange.pdf (accessed 15 March 2016).

IEA. (2015b). *Key Coal Trends – Excerpt from the publication Coal Information (2015 edition).* Retrieved from IEA: http://www.iea.org/publications/freepublications/publication/KeyCoalTrends.pdf (accessed 22 March 2016)

IEA (2015c). *Global coal demand stalls after more than a decade of relentless growth.* Retrieved from IEA: https://www.iea.org/newsroomandevents/pressreleases/2015/december/global-coal-demand-stalls-after-more-than-a-decade-of-relentless-growth.html (accessed 22 March 2016).

IFR Statistical Department (2015) (German). *World-Robotics-Studie: Industrie-Roboter erobern die Welt.* Retrieved from World Robotics: http://www.worldrobotics.org/uploads/tx_zeifr/09_30_2015_Press_Release_IFR_Industrieroboter_deutsch.pdf (accessed 11 March 2016).

Inclusive Wealth Project (2012). *2012 Findings.* Retrieved from Inclusive Wealth Project: http://inclusivewealthindex.org/numbers-/#2012-findings-numbers (accessed 12 April 2016).

Inclusive Wealth Project (2014). *The Inclusive Wealth Approach.* Retrieved from Inclusive Wealth Project: http://inclusivewealthindex.org/inclusive-wealth/#our-approach (accessed 12 April 2016).

INSM (2012) (German) *Kampagne 'Wachstum'.* Retrieved from INSM: *http://www.insm.de/insm/ueber-die-insm/INSM-Anzeigen/Anzeigen-Wachstum-2012.html (accessed 18 April 2016).*

International Labour Organization Online (2009). *Coops and the global financial crisis.* Retrieved from ILO Newsroom: http://www.ilo.org/global/about-the-ilo/newsroom/features/WCMS_105073/lang--en/index.htm

Investopedia (2016). *Externality*. Retrieved from Investopedia: http://www. investopedia.com/terms/e/externality.asp (accessed 23 March 2016).

Ip, G. (2015). *The World's New Population Time Bomb: Too Few People*. Retrieved from *The Wall Street Journal*: http://www.wsj.com/articles/ how-demographics-rule-the-global-economy-1448284890 (accessed 11 March 2016).

IPCC (2008). *Climate Change 2007: Synthesis Report*. Retrieved from IPCC: https://www.ipcc.ch/publications_and_data/ar4/syr/en/mains5-4.html (accessed 14 April 2016).

IRI (2015). *Indonesia on track to have the worst fire season since 1997*. Retrieved from Medium.com: https://medium.com/@climatesociety/indonesia-on-track-to-have-the-worst-fire-season-since-1997-49b55e19be5f#.sh98h9bgn (accessed 13 April 2016).

IUCN (2013). *Why we need biodiversity*. Retrieved from IUCN: https://www. iucn.org/what/biodiversity/about/biodiversity/ (accessed 30 March 2016).

Jackson, T. (2009). *Prosperity Without Growth: Economics for a Finite Planet*. Abingdon: Earthscan.

Jacobsen, R. (2014). *This Top-Secret Food Will Change the Way You Eat*. Retrieved from Outside: http://www.outsideonline.com/1928211/top-secret-food-will-change-way-you-eat (accessed 16 March 2016).

Jambeck, J., Geyer, R., Wilcox, R., Siegler, T. R., Perryman, M., Andrady, A., Narayan, R. and Law, K. (2015). *Plastic waste inputs from land into the ocean*. Retrieved from : http://www.iswa.org/fileadmin/user_upload/ Calendar_2011_03_AMERICANA/Science-2015-Jambeck-768-71__2_.pdf (accessed 19 April 2016)

Jeffery, L., Alexander, R., Hare, B., Rocha, M., Schaeffer, M., Hohne, N., Fekete, H., Breevoort, P. van and Blok, K. (2015). *How close are INDCs to 2 and 1.5 °C pathways?* Retrieved from Climate Action Tracker: http:// climateactiontracker.org/assets/publications/briefing_papers/CAT_ EmissionsGap_Briefing_Sep2015.pdf (accessed 14 April 2016).

Jetpissova, S. (2013). *Planning and Financing Low-Carbon, Livable Cities*. Retrieved from The World Bank: http://www.worldbank.org/en/news/ feature/2013/09/25/planning-financing-low-carbon-cities (accessed 19 April 2016).

Johnston, L., and Williamson, S. H. (2016). *What Was the U.S. GDP Then?* Retrieved from MeasuringWorth: http://www.measuringworth.com/ usgdp/ (accessed 5 April 2016).

Josephs, J. (2013). *Green Light For Red-Dead Sea Pipeline Project*. Retrieved from Water & Wastewater International: http://www.waterworld.com/articles/ wwi/print/volume-28/issue-6/technology-case-studies/water-provision/ green-light-for-red-dead-sea-pipeline-project.html (accessed 14 April 2016).

Jolly, D. (2015). *Despite Push for Cleaner Cars, Sheer Numbers Could Work Against Climate Benefits*. Retrieved from *The New York Times*: http://www.nytimes.com/2015/12/08/business/energy-environment/despite-push-for-cleaner-cars-sheer-numbers-could-work-against-climate-benefits.html?_r=0 (accessed 15 March 2016).

Kaiser, T. (2016) (German). 'Das Ende des Traums vom ewig wachsenden Wohlstand'. Retrieved from Die Welt: http://www.welt.de/wirtschaft/article153795855/Das-Ende-des-Traums-vom-ewig-wachsenden-Wohlstand.html (accessed 11 April 2016).

Kaufman, A. (2014). *Getting Walmart Workers Off Food Stamps Would Cost Customers Barely Anything*. Retrieved from *Huffington Post*: http://www.huffingtonpost.com/2014/04/09/walmart-workers-food-stamps_n_5092262.html (accessed 12 April 2016).

Keller, J. (2014). *App Store has 1.2 million apps, 75 billion apps downloaded to date*. Retrieved from iMore: http://www.imore.com/app-store-has-12-million-apps-75-billion-apps-downloaded-date (accessed 11 March 2016).

Kelly, S. (2015). *A New Blue Marble*. Retrieved from The White House: https://www.whitehouse.gov/blog/2015/07/20/new-blue-marble (accessed 14 March 2015).

Kelly, S. M. (2016). *Inside Liam, Apple's super-secret, 29-armed robot that tears down your iPhone*. Retrieved from Mashable: http://mashable.com/2016/03/21/apple-liam-recycling-robot/#MLVfoQH8tqq3 (accessed 29 March 2016).

Khan Academy (2016). Website. Retrieved from Khan Academy: https://www.khanacademy.org/ (accessed 15 March 2016).

Kimmel, L. (2016). *What Business Leaders Can Learn From the Trudeau Effect*. Retrieved from Edelman: http://www.edelman.com/post/what-business-leaders-can-learn-from-the-trudeau-effect/ (accessed 14 April 2016).

Kimura, O. (2010). *Japanese Top Runner Approach for energy efficiency standards*. Retrieved from CRIEPI: http://criepi.denken.or.jp/en/serc/research_re/download/09035dp.pdf (accessed 15 March 2016).

King, N. (2013). *Why do we need GDP to grow anyway?* Retrieved from Marketplace: http://www.marketplace.org/2013/04/26/economy/why-do-we-need-gdp-grow-anyway (accessed 4 April 2016).

Krautkraemer, J. (1998). 'Nonrenewable Resource Scarcity'. *Journal of Economic Literature* 36 (4): 2065–107. Retrieved from http://www.jstor.org/stable/2565047 (accessed 1 August 2016).

Kroll, C. (2015). *Sustainable Development Goals: Are the rich countries ready?* Retrieved from Bertelsmann Stiftung: https://www.bertelsmann-stiftung.de/fileadmin/files/BSt/Publikationen/GrauePublikationen/Studie_NW_Sustainable-Development-Goals_Are-the-rich-countries-ready_2015.pdf

Krugman, P. (2013). *Oh Yes They Can*. Retrieved from *The New York Times*: http://krugman.blogs.nytimes.com/2013/09/10/oh-yes-they-can/ (accessed 13 April 2016).

Kubiszewski, I., Costanza, R., Franco, C., Lawn, P., Talberth, J., Jackson, T. and Aylmer, C. (2013). 'Beyond GDP: Measuring and achieving global genuine progress'. *Ecological Economics* 93: 57–68. doi:10.1016/j.ecolecon.2013.04.019

Kuhn, T. (1962). *The Structure of Scientific Revolutions*. Chicago: University of Chicago Press.

Kümmel, R. (2011). *The Second Law of Economics – Energy, Entropy, and the Origins of Wealth*. New York: Springer Science+Business Media.

Kümmel, R., and Lindenberger, D. (2013). 'The Sledge on the Slope or: Energy in the Economy, and the Paradox of Theory and Policy'. *EWI Working Paper, No. 13/03*. http://www.econstor.eu/bitstream/10419/74377/1/746671865.pdf

Kuznets, S. (1962). How to judge quality. *The New Republic*, 20: 29-32.

La Décroissance. (2002). Website. Retrieved from *La Décroissance*: http://www.ladecroissance.net/ (accessed 15 April 2016).

Lacey, H. (1995). *The smokers' last gasp*. Retrieved from *The Independent*: http://www.independent.co.uk/life-style/the-smokers-last-gasp-1538510.html (accessed 14 April 2016).

Laist, D. W. (1997). *Impacts of Marine Debris: Entanglement of Marine Life in Marine Debris Including a Comprehensive List of Species with Entanglement and Ingestion Records*. Retrieved from Researchgate: https://www.researchgate.net/profile/David_Laist/publication/235768493_Impacts_of_Marine_Debris_Entanglement_of_Marine_Life_in_Marine_Debris_Including_a_Comprehensive_List_of_Species_with_Entanglement_and_IngestiOn_Records/links/02bfe5136037d75c73000000.pdf (6 April 2016).

Lamb, K. (2015). *Indonesia's fires labelled a 'crime against humanity' as 500,000 suffer*. Retrieved from *The Guardian*: http://www.theguardian.com/world/2015/oct/26/indonesias-fires-crime-against-humanity-hundreds-of-thousands-suffer (accessed 1 August 2016).

Leading Edge Group. (2015). *Top 20 Quotes for Lean Business Inspiration*. Retrieved from Leading Edge Group: http://www.leadingedgegroup.com/top-20-quotes-lean-business-inspiration/ (accessed 18 April 2016).

Leamer, E. E., Maul, H., Rodriguez, S. and Schott, P. K. (1999). 'Does natural resource abundance increase Latin American income inequality?' *Journal of Development Economics* 59: 3–42.

Lecoutere, E., D'Exelle, B., Campenhout, B. van (2015). 'Sharing Common Resources in Patriarchal and Status-Based Societies: Evidence from Tanzania'. *Feminist Economics*, 21 (3): 142–67. doi:10.1080/13545701.2015.1024274

Liebreich, M. (2015a). *Future of Energy Summit Shanghai.* Bloomberg New Energy Finance.

Liebreich, M. (2015b). *GLOBAL TRENDS IN CLEAN.* Retrieved from Bloomberg New Energy Finance: http://about.bnef.com/content/uploads/sites/4/2015/10/Liebreich_BNEF-Summit-London.pdf (accessed 20 April 2016).

Lloyd, J. and Wire Reports. (2015). *Governor, California Lawmakers Unveil $1B Emergency Drought-Relief-Plan.* Retrieved from NBC Southern California: http://www.nbclosangeles.com/news/local/Governor-Jerry-Brown-California-Drought-Relief-296861521.html (accessed 20 April 2016).

Lönnqvist, T., Sanchez-Pereira, A. and Sandberg, T. (2015). 'Biogas potential for sustainable transport – a Swedish regional case'. *Journal of Cleaner Production* 108 (A), 1105–14.

Lomborg, B. (2015) (German). *Deutschlands gescheiterte Klimapolitik.* Retrieved from Frankfurter Allgemeine Zeitung: http://www.faz.net/aktuell/wirtschaft/energiepolitik/bjoern-lomborg-ueber-klimawandel-und-gescheiterte-klimapolitik-13580487.html (accessed 31 March 2016).

Lovins, A. L. (2013). *Re-Inventing the Fire: Bold business solutions for the new energy era.* White River Junction, VT: Chelsea Green Publishing.

Manrodt, A. (2014). *The New Face of Teen Activism.* Retrieved from TeenVogue: http://www.teenvogue.com/story/teen-online-activism (accessed 21 April 2016).

Manyika, J., Lund, S., Auguste, B., Mendonca, L., Welsh, T. and Ramaswamy, S. (2011). *An economy that works: Job creation and America's future.* Retrieved from McKinsey Global Institute: http://www.mckinsey.com/global-themes/employment-and-growth/an-economy-that-works-for-us-job-creation (accessed 8 April 2016).

Manyika, J., Sinclair, J., Dobbs, R., Strube, G., Rassey, L., Mischke, J., Remes, J., Roxburgh, C., George, K., O'Halloran, D. and Ramaswamy, S. (2012). *Manufacturing the future: The next era of global growth and innovation.* Retrieved from McKinsey Global Institute: http://www.mckinsey.com/business-functions/operations/our-insights/the-future-of-manufacturing (accessed 8 April 2016).

MarketLine (2014). *Meat, Fish, and Poultry: Global Industry Guide.* Retrieved from MarketLine: http://store.marketline.com/Product/meat_fish_poultry_global_industry_guide?productid=ML00016-329 (accessed 16 March 2016).

Materialflows (2015). *Material consumption per capita and day in 2007.* Retrieved from Materialflows: http://www.materialflows.net/trends/analyses-1980-2011/material-consumption-per-capita-and-day-in-2007/

Mathiesen, K. (2014). *Climate change and poverty: why Indira Gandhi's speech matters*. Retrieved from *The Guardian*: http://www.theguardian.com/global-development-professionals-network/2014/may/06/indira-gandhi-india-climate-change (accessed 15 April 2016).

Mauser, W. (2009) (German). *Wie lange reicht die Ressource Wasser?* Retrieved from Boku Wien: https://multimedia.boku.ac.at/MutzurNachhaltigkeit/Einheit05_Mauser/Resource %20Wasser%20Mauser%20Wien.pdf (accessed 13 April 2016).

Mazzucato, M. (2011). *The Entrepreneurial State*. London: Demos.

McDiarmid, H. Jr. (2011). *When our rivers caught fire*. Retrieved from Michigan Environmental Council: http://www.environmentalcouncil.org/priorities/article.php?x=264 (accessed 14 March 2016).

McDonough, W. and Braungart, M. (2002). *Cradle to Cradle: Remaking the Way We Make Things*. New York: North Point Press.

McDonough, W. and Braungart, M. (2013). *The Upcycle: beyond sustainability – designing for abundance*. New York: North Point Press.

McKibben, B. (2012). *Global Warming's Terrifying New Math*. Retrieved from *Rolling Stone*: http://www.rollingstone.com/politics/news/global-warmings-terrifying-new-math-20120719?page=3 (accessed 29 March 2016).

McKie, R. (2012). *Rachel Carson and the legacy of Silent Spring*. Retrieved from *The Guardian*: https://www.theguardian.com/science/2012/may/27/rachel-carson-silent-spring-anniversary (accessed 29 March 2016).

McKinsey Center for Business and Environment & Ocean Conservancy (2015). *Stemming the Tide: Land-based strategies for a plastic-free ocean*. Retrieved from Ocean Conservancy: http://www.oceanconservancy.org/our-work/marine-debris/mckinsey-report-files/full-report-stemming-the.pdf (accessed 31 March 2016).

McKinsey Center for Business and Environment, Ellen MacArthur Foundation & SUN (2015). *Growth Within: A Circular Economy Vision for a Competitive Europe*. Retrieved from Ellen MacArthur Foundation: http://www.ellenmacarthurfoundation.org/publications/growth-within-a-circular-economy-vision-for-a-competitive-europe (accessed 17 March 2016).

McKinsey & Company (2009). *Explosive increase in water demand for generating energy at the end of the oil era*. Internal document.

McKinsey & Company (2014). *The bias for now – example US government*. Internal document.

McKinsey & Company (2015a). *Effective Peatland Management –a preliminary fact base*. Internal document.

McKinsey & Company (2015b) (German). *Der Schutz des Bodens – Eckpunkte einer handlungsorientierten Agenda*. Internal document.

McKinsey Global Institute (2015). *Playing to win: The new global competition for corporate profits*. Retrieved from: http://www.mckinsey.com/business-functions/strategy-and-corporate-finance/our-insights/the-new-global-competition-for-corporate-profits (accessed 18 April 2016).

Mearns, E. (2013). *Energiewende: Germany, UK, France and Spain*. Retrieved from: http://euanmearns.com/energiewende-germany-uk-france-and-spain/ (accessed 18 April 2016).

Mendeloff, J. (1979). *Regulating Safety: An Economic and Political Analysis of Occupational Safety and Health Policy*. Cambridge, MA: MIT Press.

Merkel, A. (2012). *Speech by Federal Chancellor Angela Merkel given at the international symposium – 'Towards Low-Carbon Prosperity: National Strategies and International Partnerships'*. Retrieved from Die Bundeskanzlerin: http://www.bundeskanzlerin.de/ContentArchiv/EN/Archiv17/Reden/2012/2012-05-09-rede-wbgu-symposium_en.html

Mezue, B. C., Christensen C. M. and Bever, D. van (2015). *The Power of Market Creation – How Innovation Can Spur Development*. Retrieved from Foreign Affairs: https://www.foreignaffairs.com/articles/africa/2014-12-15/power-market-creation (accessed 30 March 2016).

Miegel, M. (2010) (German). *Trends der wirtschaftlichen und gesellschaftlichen Entwicklung im 21. Jahrhundert*. Retrieved from Markenverband: http://www.markenverband.de/veranstaltungen/jahrestagungen-mv/copy_of_Jahrestagung-2010/redeMiegel (accessed 20 April 2016).

Miettinen, J., Hooijer, A., Shi, C., Tollenaar, D., Vernummen, R., Liew, S. C., Malins, C. and Page, S. (2012). *Extent of industrial plantations on Southeast Asian peatlands in 2010 with analysis of historical expansion and future projections*. Retrieved from Wiley Online Library: http://onlinelibrary.wiley.com/doi/10.1111/j.1757-1707.2012.01172.x/full (accessed 13 April 2016).

Mill, J. S. (1848). *Principles of Political Economy*. New York: The Colonial Press.

Mills, L. (2015). *Global Trends in Clean Energy Investment*. Retrieved from Bloomberg New Energy Finance: http://about.bnef.com/presentations/clean-energy-investment-q4-2014-fact-pack/content/uploads/sites/4/2015/01/Q4-investment-fact-pack.pdf

Ministry of Climate and Environment (2016). *Brazil*. Retrieved from Regjeringen: https://www.regjeringen.no/en/topics/climate-and-environment/climate/climate-and-forest-initiative/kos-innsikt/brazil-and-the-amazon-fund/id734166/ (accessed 23 March 2016).

Mobbs, P. (2014). *What MH370 told us – the oceans are awash with trash*. Retrieved from *The Ecologist*: http://www.theecologist.org/blogs_and_comments/commentators/2345236/what_mh370_told_us_the_oceans_are_awash_with_trash.html (accessed 14 April 2016).

Mongabay (2011). *Indonesia Forest Information and Data*. Retrieved from Mongabay.com: http://rainforests.mongabay.com/deforestation/2000/Indonesia.htm (accessed 13 April 2016).

Mooney, A. (2016). *Pension funds looking for infrastructure investments*. Retrieved from *Financial Times*: http://www.ft.com/intl/cms/s/2/fb18e676-475b-11e5-af2f-4d6e0e5eda22.html#axzz46NkY9CUw (accessed 20 April 2016).

Murray, J. (2014). *Clean-tech venture investment is on the rise, report says*. Retrieved from GreenBiz: https://www.greenbiz.com/blog/2014/01/13/clean-tech-venture-investment-rise (accessed 8 April 2016).

Narayan, S. (2016). *Trojans*. Retrieved from TinyCent: https://www.tinycent.com/trojans (accessed 14 April 2016).

Nassauer, S. (2014). 'Meatless Burgers Meet the Mets', *The Wall Street Journal*, 26 June.

National Geographic Society. (2008). *Human Footprint*. Retrieved from *National Geographic*: http://www.nationalgeographic.com/xpeditions/lessons/14/g68/HumanFootprint.pdf (accessed 5 April 2016).

Naughton, J. (2012a). *Welcome to the desktop degree ...* Retrieved from *The Guardian*: http://www.theguardian.com/technology/2012/feb/05/desktop-degree-stanford-university-naughton (accessed 11 March 2016).

Naugthon, J. (2012b). *Thomas Kuhn: the man who changed they way the world looked at science*. Retrieved from *The Guardian*: https://www.theguardian.com/science/2012/aug/19/thomas-kuhn-structure-scientific-revolutions (accessed 14 April 2016).

Neumayer, E. (2010). *Human Development and Sustainability*. Retrieved from United Nations Development Programme: http://hdr.undp.org/sites/default/files/hdrp_2010_05.pdf (accessed 15 April 2016).

NOAA (2014). *Climate model shows Australia's rainfall decline due to human-caused climate change*. Retrieved from NOAA: http://research.noaa.gov/News/NewsArchive/LatestNews/TabId/684/ArtMID/1768/ArticleID/10658/Climate-model-shows-Australia's-rainfall-decline-due-to-human-caused-climate-change.aspx (accessed 20 April 2016).

Noer, M. (2012). *One Man, One Computer, 10 Million Students: How Khan Academy Is Reinventing Education*. Retrieved from *Forbes*: http://www.forbes.com/sites/michaelnoer/2012/11/02/one-man-one-computer-10-million-students-how-khan-academy-is-reinventing-education/ (accessed 11 March 2016).

Nyquist, S. (2015). *Lower oil prices but more renewables: What's going on?* Retrieved from McKinsey & Company – Insights & Publication: http://www.mckinsey.com/insights/energy_resources_materials/lower_oil_prices_but_more_renewables_whats_going_on

OEA (2016). *Aluminium Recycling in Europe – The Road to High Quality Products*.

Retrieved from Recycling World Aluminium: http://recycling.world-aluminium.org/uploads/media/fl0000217.pdf (accessed 16 March 2016).

OECD (2007). *Innovation and Growth: Rationale for an Innovation Strategy.* Retrieved from: http://www.oecd.org/science/inno/39374789.pdf (accessed 30 March 2016).

OECD (2015a). *Health Status.* Retrieved from OECD Data: https://data.oecd.org/healthstat/life-expectancy-at-birth.htm

OECD (2015b). *OECD Employment Outlook 2015.* doi:10.1787/empl_outlook-2015-en

OECD (2015c). *Trade in Value Added (TiVA): Origin of Value Added in Gross Exports.* Retrieved from OECD.Stat: http://stats.oecd.org/Index.aspx?DataSetCode=TIVA2015_C2 (accessed 5 April 2016).

OECD (2015d). *Towards sustainable public finances.* Retrieved from OECD: http://www.oecd.org/statistics/towards-sustainable-public-finances.htm (accessed 18 April 2016).

OECD (2016a). *Gross domestic product (GDP).* Retrieved from OECD Data: https://data.oecd.org/gdp/gross-domestic-product-gdp.htm (accessed 14 April 2016).

OECD (2016b). *Level of GDP per Capita and Productivity.* Retrieved from OECD Data: https://stats.oecd.org/Index.aspx?DataSetCode=PDB_LV# (accessed 18 April 2016).

Oxfam (2016). *An Economy For the %: How privilege and power in the economy drive extreme inequality and how this can be stopped.* Retrieved from Oxfam: https://www.oxfam.org/sites/www.oxfam.org/files/file_attachments/bp210-economy-one-percent-tax-havens-180116-en_0.pdf (accessed 20 April 2016).

Painter, K. L. (2014). *DigitalGlobe crowdsource search reboots with new Malaysia plane images.* Retrieved from *The Denver Post:* http://www.denverpost.com/business/ci_25322840/digitalglobe-crowdsource-search-reboots-new-malaysia-plane-images (accessed 31 March 2016).

Parkinson, G. (2015a). *German grid operator sees 70% wind + solar before storage needed.* Retrieved from RenewEconomy: http://reneweconomy.com.au/2015/german-grid-operator-sees-70-wind-solar-storage-needed-35731 (accessed 22 March 2016).

Parkinson, G. (2015b). *Citigroup sees $100 trillion of stranded assets if Paris succeeds.* Retrieved from RenewEconomy: http://reneweconomy.com.au/2015/citigroup-sees-100-trillion-of-stranded-assets-if-paris-succeeds-13431 (accessed 29 March 2016).

Parry, A., James, K. and LeRoux, S. (2015). *Strategies to achieve economic and environmental gains by reducing food waste.* Retrieved from The New Climate Economy: http://2014.newclimateeconomy.report/wp-content/

uploads/2015/02/WRAP-NCE_Economic-environmental-gains-food-waste.pdf (accessed 11 April 2016).

Pfeil, M. (2013) (German). *Raiffeisen-Wunder*. Retrieved from Zeit Online: http://www.zeit.de/2013/05/Genossenschaftsbanken (accessed 1 April 2016).

Phelps, G. and Crabtree, S. (2013). *Worldwide, Median Household Income About $10,000*. Retrieved from Gallup: http://www.gallup.com/poll/166211/worldwide-median-household-income-000.aspx (accessed 4 April 2016).

Piketty, T. (2014). *Capital in the Twenty-First Century*. Cambridge, MA: Harvard University Press.

Pison, G. (2005). 'France 2004: Life expectancy tops 80 years'. *Population & Societies*, 410: 1–4.

Plant Chicago (2016). Website. Retrieved from Plant Chicago: http://plantchicago.org/ (accessed 11 April 2016).

Plant For The Planet (2016) (German). *Idee und Ziel*. Retrieved from Plant For The Planet: http://www.plant-for-the-planet.org/de/informieren/idee-ziel (accessed 29 March 2016).

Plas, A. van der (2015). *Five invaluable lessons kids taught me about the circular economy*. Retrieved from 2degrees: https://www.2degreesnetwork.com/groups/2degrees-community/resources/five-invaluable-lessons-kids-taught-me-about-circular-economy/ (accessed 1 August 2016).

PlasticsEurope (2013). *Plastics – the Facts 2013*. Retrieved from PlasticsEurope: http://www.plasticseurope.org/documents/document/20131014095824-final_plastics_the_facts_2013_published_october2013.pdf (accessed 17 March 2016).

Plastindia Foundation (2014). *Report on Indian Plastics Industry 2013–2017 – Edition 2*. Retrieved from PlastIndia: http://www.plastindia.org/Upload/CkEditor/Indian%20Plastics%20Industry%20Report%202014.pdf (accessed 31 March 2016).

Pope Francis (2015). *Encyclical Letter Laudato Si' Of The Holy Father Francis On Care For Our Common Home*. Retrieved from the Vatican: http://w2.vatican.va/content/dam/francesco/pdf/encyclicals/documents/papa-francesco_20150524_enciclica-laudato-si_en.pdf (accessed 5 April 2016).

Potočnik, J. (2015). *Natural Resource Management Solutions For Climate Change Problems*. Paris: International Resource Panel.

Putnam, R. D. (1995). Bowling Alone: America's Declining Social Capital. *Journal of Democracy* 6 (1): 65–78. Retrieved from American Studies at the University of Virginia: http://xroads.virginia.edu/~HYPER/DETOC/assoc/bowling.html (accessed 6 April 2016).

Putnam, R. D. (2007). E Pluribus Unum: Diversity and Community in the Twenty-first Century. *Scandinavian Political Studies* 137 (174): 137–74.

Putnam, R. D., Leonardi, R. and Nanetti, R. Y. (1993). *Making Democracy Work: Civic Traditions in Modern Italy*. Princeton, NJ: Princeton University Press.

Rao, L. and Primack, D. (2015). *Online Education Company Udacity is Tech's Latest Unicorn*. Retrieved from *Fortune*: http://fortune.com/2015/11/11/udacity-funding/ (accessed 11 March 2016).

Raskin, P. (2014). *A Great Transition? Where We Stand*. Retrieved from Great Transition Initiative: http://www.greattransition.org/images/GTI_publications/Raskin_A_Great_Transition_Where_We_Stand.pdf

Reuters, T. (2015). *Lake Poopo, Bolivia's 2nd-largest lake, dries up*. Retrieved from CBCNews: http://www.cbc.ca/news/technology/lake-poopo-bolivia-dries-up-1.3371359 (accessed 29 March 2016).

Rifkin, J. (2011). *The Third Industrial Revolution: How lateral power is transforming energy, the economy, and the world*. New York: St. Martin's Press.

Rifkin, J. (2014). *The Zero Marginal Cost Society*. New York: Palgrave Macmillan.

Ringen, J. (2014). *Tastier, Healthier, And Animal-Free: Can Ethan Brown Reinvent Meat?* Retrieved from FASTCODESIGN: http://www.fastcodesign.com/3035034/innovation-by-design/ethan-browns-quest-to-make-meat-tastier-healthier-and-animal-free (accessed 16 March 2016).

Ripple, W. J., Estes, J. A., Beschta, R. L. and Wilmers, C. C. (2014). 'Status and Ecological Effects of the World's Largest Carnivores'. *Science* 343 (6167). doi:10.1126/science.1241484

Roepke, W. (1952). *The Social Crisis of Our Time*. New Brunswick and London: Transaction Publishers.

Roesti, M. (2015): *Degrowth – Leidet auch der Wohlfahrtsstaat?* Retrieved from: http://www.postwachstumskritik.de/koennen/wohlfahrtsstaat (accessed 1 August 2016).

Rogelj, J., Hare, B. and Schaeffer, M. (2015). *Timetables for Zero Emissions and 2050 Emissions Reductions: State of the Science for the ADP Agreement*. Retrieved from Climate Analytics: http://climateanalytics.org/files/ca_briefing_timetables_for_zero_emissions_and_2050_emissions_reductions.pdf (accessed 14 April 2016).

Roser, M. (2015). *Fertilizer and Pesticides*. Retrieved from Our World In Data: http://ourworldindata.org/data/food-agriculture/fertilizer-and-pesticides/ (accessed 14 April 2016).

Roser, M. (2016). *GDP Growth Over the Last Centuries*. Retrieved from Our World In Data: http://ourworldindata.org/data/growth-and-distribution-of-prosperity/gdp-growth-over-the-last-centuries/ (accessed 4 April 2016).

RoSPA (2016). *Seat Belts: History*. Retrieved from RoSPA: http://www.rospa.com/road-safety/advice/vehicles/in-car-safety-and-crashworthiness/seat-belts-history/ (accessed 14 April 2016).

Rus, D. (2015). *The Robots Are Coming: How Technological Breakthroughs Will Transform Everyday Life*. Retrieved from *Foreign Affairs*: https://www.foreignaffairs.com/articles/2015-06-16/robots-are-coming (accessed 11 March 2016).

Safaei, H. and Keith, D. (2015). 'How much bulk energy storage is needed to decarbonize electricity?' *Energy Environ. Sci.*: 3409–17. doi:10.1039/C5EE01452B

Sagar, A. D. and Najam, A. (1998). 'The Human Development Index: A Critical Review'. *Ecological Economics* 25 (3): 249–64. doi:10.1016/S0921-8009(97)00168-7

Salmon, F. and Stokes, J. (2010). *Algorithms Take Control of Wall Street*. Retrieved from Wired: http://www.wired.com/2010/12/ff_ai_flashtrading/ (accessed 11 March 2016).

Sander, T. H. and Putnam, R. D. (2010). 'Still Bowling Alone? The Post-9/11 Split'. *Journal of Democracy*, 21 (1): 9–16. doi:10.1353/jod.0.0153

Satariano, A. (2015). *Putting the Good in Greed*. Retrieved from Bloomberg Business: http://www.bloomberg.com/news/articles/2015-12-01/putting-the-good-in-greed (accessed 22 March 2016).

SBDCNet (2012). *Convenience Store 2012*. Retrieved from SBDCNet: http://www.sbdcnet.org/small-business-research-reports/convenience-store-2012 (accessed 7 April 2016).

Schirrmacher, F. (2013) (German). *Ego: Das Spiel des Lebens*. Guetersloh, Germany: Karl Blessing Verlag.

Schott, V. (2014). *Junge Leute – Abwendung vom Auto?* Retrieved from VDA: https://www.vda.de/dam/vda/publications/2014/junge-leute-abwendung-vom-auto.pdf (accessed 21 April 2016).

Schwägerl, C. (2016) (German). *Erdepoche „Anthropozän" – Die Narben der Zivilisation*. Retrieved from Frankfurter Allgemeine: http://www.faz.net/aktuell/wissen/erde-klima/erdepoche-anthropozaen-die-narben-der-zivilisation-14009147.html (accessed 6 April 2016).

Sebastian, M. (2015). *Marketers to Boost Global Ad Spending This Year to $540 Billion*. Retrieved from Advertising Age: http://adage.com/article/media/marketers-boost-global-ad-spending-540-billion/297737/ (accessed 18 April 2016).

Sevcenko, M. (2011). *Paris tests Autolib' electric car-sharing program*. Retrieved from Deutsche Welle: http://www.dw.com/en/paris-tests-autolib-electric-car-sharing-program/a-15469794 (accessed 22 March 2016).

Shackleton, R. (2013). *Total Factor Productivity Growth in Historical Perspective*. Retrieved from Working Paper Series Congressional Budget Office: http://www.cbo.gov/sites/default/files/cbofiles/attachments/44002_TFP_Growth_03-18-2013.pdf (accessed 29 March 2016).

Shaheen, S. and Cohen, H. (2013). *Innovative Mobility Carsharing Outlook: Carsharing Market Overview, Analysis, and Trends*. Retrieved from Transportation Sustainability Research Center: http://tsrc.berkeley.edu/node/629 (accessed 7 April 2016).

Shallenberger, K. (2015). *Updated: Tesla Gigafactory will cut battery costs 50%, analyst says*. Retrieved from UtilityDive: http://www.utilitydive.com/news/updated-tesla-gigafactory-will-cut-battery-costs-50-analyst-says/405970/ (accessed 8 April 2016).

Shaw, V. (2015). *China: PV installed capacity grows to almost 30 GW in 2014*. Retrieved from *PV Magazine*: http://www.pv-magazine.com/news/details/beitrag/china--pv-installed-capacity-grows-to-almost-30-gw-in-2014_100018231/#axzz45nbjzNsp (accessed 14 April 2016).

Shirky, C. (2009). *How social media can make history*. Retrieved from TED: https://www.ted.com/talks/clay_shirky_how_cellphones_twitter_facebook_can_make_history/transcript (accessed 31 March 2016).

Simon, S. (2015). *Celebrating 25 Years of No Smoking in Airplanes*. Retrieved from Cancer.org: http://www.cancer.org/cancer/news/features/celebrating-25-years-of-no-smoking-in-airplanes (accessed 14 April 2016).

Slater, J. (2015). *Richest 1% will own more than all the rest by 2016 – Oxfam*. Retrieved from Oxfam: http://www.oxfam.org.uk/blogs/2015/01/richest-1-per-cent-will-own-more-than-all-the-rest-by-2016 (accessed 6 April 2016).

Slezak, M. (2016). *Coal plants use as much water as 1 billion people and consumption set to double: report*. Retrieved from *The Guardian*: http://www.theguardian.com/environment/2016/mar/22/world-water-day-coal-plants-use-as-much-water-as-1-billion-people-and-its-set-to-double (accessed 11 April 2016).

Smith, J. A. and Paxton, P. (2008). *America's Trust Fall*. Retrieved from Greater Good Berkeley: http://greatergood.berkeley.edu/article/item/americas_trust_fall/ (accessed 6 April 2016).

Smith, R. (2015). *Green Capitalism: The God that Failed*. Bristol: WEA Books.

Solow, R. (1987). 'We'd better watch out'. *New York Times Book Review*, 36. Retrieved from: http://www.standupeconomist.com/pdf/misc/solow-computer-productivity.pdf (accessed 1 August 2016).

Solow, R. M. (1956). 'A Contribution to the Theory of Economic Growth'. *The Quarterly Journal of Economics*, 70 (1): 65–94. http://www.jstor.org/stable/1884513 (accessed 1 August 2016).

Solow, R. M. (1957). 'Technical Change and the Aggregate Production Function'. *The Review of Economics and Statistics* 39 (3): 312–20. http://www.jstor.org/stable/1926047 (accessed 1 August 2016).

Sparkes, M. (2014). *Bill Gates turns attention to latest project: fake chicken*. Retrieved from *The Telegraph*: http://www.telegraph.co.uk/technology/bill-gates/10792629/Bill-Gates-turns-attention-to-latest-project-fake-chicken. html (accessed 22 March 2016).

Stallknecht, M. (2012) (German). *Da gräbt einer nach der knappen Ressource Solidarität*. Sueddeutsche Zeitung 21/22 July, 13.

Steffen, W., Richardson, K., Rockström, J., Cornell, S., Fetzer, I., Bennett, E. M., Biggs, R., Carpenter, S. R., Vries, W. de, Wit, C. A. dem Folke, C., Gerten, D., Heinke, J., Mace, G. M., Persson, L. M., Ramanthan, V., Reyers, B. and Sorlin, S. (2015). 'Planetary Boundaries: Guiding human development on a changing planet'. *Science* 347 (6223). doi:10.1126/science.1259855

Steingart, G. (2013) (German). *Unser Wohlstand und seine Feinde*. Munich, Germany: Albrecht Knaus Verlag.

Stern, N. (2006). *STERN REVIEW: The Economics of Climate Change – executive Summary*. Retrieved from The World Bank: http://siteresources.worldbank. org/INTINDONESIA/Resources/226271-1170911056314/3428109-1174614780539/SternReviewEng.pdf (accessed 14 April 2016).

Stiglitz, J. E., Sen, A. and Fitoussi, J.-P. (2008). *Report by the Commission on the Measurement of Economic Performance and Social Progress*. Retrieved from Insee: http://www.insee.fr/fr/publications-et-services/dossiers_web/stiglitz/doc-commission/RAPPORT_anglais.pdf

Stiglitz, J. E., Sen, A. and Fitoussi, J.-P. (2010). *Mis-Measuring Our Lives – Why GDP Doesn't Add Up*. New York: The New Press.

Stine, R. (2011). *Social media and environmental campaigning: Brand lessons from Barbie*. Retrieved from Ethical Corporation: http://www.ethicalcorp. com/supply-chains/social-media-and-environmental-campaigning-brand-lessons-barbie (accessed 31 March 2016).

Stock, J. H. and Watson, M. W. (2003). 'Has the Business Cycle Changed and Why?' *NBER Marcoeconomics Annual*, 159–230. Retrieved from National Bureau of Economic Research: http://www.nber.org/chapters/c11075.pdf (accessed 1 August 2016).

Stockholm Resilience Center (2015). *Figures and data for the updated Planetary Boundaries*. Retrieved from Stockholm Resilience Center: http://www. stockholmresilience.org/research/planetary-boundaries/planetary-bound aries-data.html (accessed 1 August 2016).

Stuchtey, M. (2015). *Rethinking the water cycle*. Retrieved from McKinsey & Company – Insights & Publications: http://www.mckinsey.com/insights/sustainability/rethinking_the_water_cycle (accessed 22 March 2016).

Stürmer, M. (2012) (German). *Als Schröder Stoiber im Hochwasser versenkte*. Retrieved from *Die Welt*: http://www.welt.de/politik/deutschland/

article108607179/Als-Schroeder-Stoiber-im-Hochwasser-versenkte.html
(accessed 18 April 2016).

Sustainable Brands. (2015). *European Commission Offering €24B to 'Help Risk-Takers Make The Leap' to a Circular Economy*. Retrieved from Sustainable Brands: http://www.sustainablebrands.com/ news_and_views/next_economy/sustainable_brands/european_ commission_offering_%E2%82%AC24b_help_risk-takers_ma (accessed 12 April 2016).

Talberth, J., Cocc, C., and Slatery, N. (2007). *The Genuine Progress Indicator 2006: A Tool for Sustainable Development*. Retrieved from Redefining Progress: http://rprogress.org/publications/2007/GPI%202006.pdf (accessed 16 April 2016).

TEEB (2010). *The Economics of Ecosystems and Biodiversity – Mainstreaming the Economics of Nature: A synthesis of the approach, conclusions and recommendations of TEEB*. Retrieved from TEEB: http://doc.teebweb.org/wp-content/ uploads/Study%20and%20Reports/Reports/Synthesis%20report/TEEB%20 Synthesis%20Report%202010.pdf (accessed 30 March 2016).

The 2030 Water Resources Group (2009). *Charting Our Water Future*. Retrieved from McKinsey&Company: http://www.mckinsey.com/ business-functions/sustainability-and-resource-productivity/our-insights/ charting-our-water-future (accessed 6 April 2016).

The Baltic Biogas Bus Project (2012). *Biogas – the natural choice for city buses*. Retrieved from Tartu: http://www.tartu.ee/data/BBBAugust2012Low.pdf (accessed 17 March 2016).

The Economist (2013). *Poverty – Not always with us*. Retrieved from *The Economist*: http://www.economist.com/news/briefing/21578643-world- has-astonishing-chance-take-billion-people-out-extreme-poverty-2030-not (accessed 8 April 2016).

The Economist (2015a). *Pulled back in – the world is entering a third stage of a rolling debt crisis, this time centred on emerging markets*. Retrieved from *The Economist*: http://www.economist.com/news/briefing/21678215-world- entering-third-stage-rolling-debt-crisis-time-centred-emerging (accessed 11 March 2016).

The Economist (2015b). *The young continent*. Retrieved from *The Economist*: http://www.economist.com/news/briefing/21679781-fertility-rates-falling- more-slowly-anywhere-else-africa-faces-population (accessed 11 March 2016).

The Economist (2015c). *King Coal's misrule*. Retrieved from *The Economist*: http://www.economist.com/news/china/21679263-rise-and-fall-corrupt- coal-fuelled-economy-king-coals-misrule (accessed 23 March 2016).

The Economist (2015d). *Second-best solutions*. Retrieved from *The Economist*:

http://www.economist.com/news/special-report/21678959-if-best-method-tackling-climate-change-not-offer-try-something (accessed 23 March 2016).

The Economist (2015e). *Green tape – Environmental regulations may not cost as much as governments and businesses fear.* Retrieved from *The Economist*: http://www.economist.com/news/finance-and-economics/21637411-environmental-regulations-may-not-cost-much-governments-and-businesses (accessed 29 March 2016).

The Economist (2015f). *The promise of the block chain : the trust machine.* Retrieved from *The Economist*: http://www.economist.com/news/leaders/21677198-technology-behind-bitcoin-could-transform-how-economy-works-trust-machine (accessed 5 April 2016).

The Economist (2015g). *The great chain of being sure about things.* Retrieved from *The Economist*: http://www.economist.com/news/briefing/21677228-technology-behind-bitcoin-lets-people-who-do-not-know-or-trust-each-other-build-dependable (accessed 15 April 2016).

The Nature Conservancy (2013). *Green Infrastructure Case Studies.* Retrieved from The Nature Conservancy: http://www.nature.org/about-us/working-with-companies/case-studies-for-green-infrastructure.pdf (accessed 22 March 2016).

The Nature Conservancy (2014). *Urban Water Blueprint: Mapping conservation solutions to the global water challenge.* Retrieved from The Nature Conservancy: http://water.nature.org/waterblueprint/#/section=overview (accessed 30 March 2016).

The Nature Conservancy (2016). *Rivers and Lakes – Water Funds: Investing in Nature and Clean Water.* Retrieved from The Nature Conservancy: http://www.nature.org/ourinitiatives/habitats/riverslakes/water-funds-investing-in-nature-and-clean-water-1.xml (accessed 30 March 2016).

The New Climate Economy (2014). *Better Growth, Better Climate – The New Climate Economy Report.* Retrieved from New Climate Economy: http://newclimateeconomy.report/TheNewClimateEconomyReport.pdf (accessed 11 March 2016).

The Savory Institute (2016). Website. Retrieved from The Savory Institute: http://www.savoryinstitute.net/ (accessed 17 March 2016).

The University of California Museum of Paleontology (2016). *The Ecology of Human Populations: Thomas Malthus.* Retrieved from The University of California Museum of Paleontology: http://evolution.berkeley.edu/evolibrary/article/history_07 (accessed 15 April 2016).

The World Bank (2007). *Restoring China's Loess Plateau.* Retrieved from The World Bank: http://www.worldbank.org/en/news/feature/2007/03/15/restoring-chinas-loess-plateau (accessed 11 April 2016).

The World Bank (2010). *Cities and Climate Change: An urgent agenda*. Retrieved from The World Bank: http://siteresources.worldbank.org/INTUWM/Resources/340232-1205330656272/CitiesandClimateChange.pdf (accessed 11 March 2016).

The World Bank (2012). *What A Waste – A Global Review of Solid Waste Management*. Retrieved from The World Bank: http://siteresources.worldbank.org/INTURBANDEVELOPMENT/Resources/336387-1334852610766/What_a_Waste2012_Final.pdf (accessed 19 April 2016).

The World Bank (2013a). *Planning and Financing Low-Carbon, Livable Cities*. Retrieved from The World Bank: http://www.worldbank.org/en/news/feature/2013/09/25/planning-financing-low-carbon-cities (accessed 15 March 2016).

The World Bank (2013b). *Prosperity for all – ending extreme poverty*. Retrieved from The World Bank: http://econ.worldbank.org/WBSITE/EXTERNAL/EXTDEC/EXTDECPROSPECTS/0,,contentMDK:23553788~pagePK:64165401~piPK:64165026~theSitePK:476883,00.html (accessed 1 August 2016).

The World Bank (2014a). *Fossil fuel energy consumption*. Retrieved from The World Bank: http://data.worldbank.org/indicator/EG.USE.COMM.FO.ZS/countries?display=graph (accessed 23 March 2016).

The World Bank (2014b). *Energy use (kg of oil equivalent per capita)*. Retrieved from The World Bank: http://data.worldbank.org/indicator/EG.USE.PCAP.KG.OE/countries/DE?display=graph (accessed 18 April 2016).

The World Bank (2015a). *Agriculture, value added (%of GDP)*. Retrieved from The World Bank: http://data.worldbank.org/indicator/NV.AGR.TOTL.ZS/countries/1W?display=graph (accessed 1 August 2016).

The World Bank (2015b). *World Bank Open Data*. Retrieved from The World Bank: http://data.worldbank.org/ (accessed 1 August 2016).

The World Bank (2015c). *Poverty – Overview*. Retrieved from The World Bank: http://www.worldbank.org/en/topic/poverty/overview#1 (accessed 8 April 2016).

The World Bank (2015d). *CO_2 emissions (metric tons per capita)*. Retrieved from The World Bank: http://data.worldbank.org/indicator/EN.ATM.CO2E.PC/ (accessed 1 August 2016).

The World Bank (2016a). *GDP at market prices (current US$)*. Retrieved from The World Bank: http://data.worldbank.org/indicator/NY.GDP.MKTP.CD/countries?display=graph (accessed 8 April 2016).

The World Bank (2016b). *World Development Indicators*. Retrieved from The World Bank: http://data.worldbank.org/data-catalog/world-development-indicators (accessed 13 April 2016).

Thomasson, E. and Davey, J. (2014). *Analysis – Low food inflation tightens squeeze on Europe's grocers*. Retrieved from Reuters: http://uk.reuters.com/article/uk-retail-europe-analysis-idUKKCN0JB1M220141127 (accessed 18 April 2016).

Thompson, C. (2013). *This is the man Bill Gates thinks you absolutely should be reading*. Retrieved from *Wired*: http://www.wired.com/2013/11/vaclav-smil-wired/ (accessed 5 April 2016).

Thompson, D. (2012). *A Giant Statistical Round-Up of the Income Inequality Crisis in 16 Charts*. Retrieved from *The Atlantic*: http://www.theatlantic.com/business/archive/2012/12/a-giant-statistical-round-up-of-the-income-inequality-crisis-in-16-charts/266074/ (accessed 1 August 2016).

TNS Political & Social (2014). *Attitudes of Europeans towards Waste Management and Resource Efficiency* . Retrieved from European Commission: http://ec.europa.eu/public_opinion/flash/fl_388_en.pdf (accessed 18 March 2016).

Tomnod (2014). *Global Forest Watch: Sumatra*. Retrieved from Tomnod: http://www.tomnod.com/campaign/indonesiafires012014/map/1uux9y9b (accessed 31 March 2016).

Topper, J. (2012). *Future Coal Demand: Roadmap For Coal-Fired Power Plant Efficiency And Interaction With CCS*. Retrieved from IEA Clean Coal Centre: https://usea.org/sites/default/files/event-file/512/IEA-CCCPresentation.pdf (accessed 8 April 2016).

Trucost (2013). *Natural Capital at Risk: The Top 100 Externalities of Business*. Retrieved from Trucost: http://www.trucost.com/published-research/99/natural-capital-at-risk-the-top-100-externalities-of-business (accessed 23 March 2016).

Tsanova, T. (2015). *Overview – How low will solar prices go in 2015?* Retrieved from Seenews Renewables: http://renewables.seenews.com/news/overview-how-low-will-solar-prices-go-in-2015-500228 (accessed 21 March 2016).

Turner, A. (2015). *Between Debt and the Devil: Money, Credit, and Fixing Global Finance*. Princeton, NJ: Princeton University Press.

Turner, G. M. (2008). 'A comparison of The Limits to Growth with 30 years of reality'. *Global Environmental Change* 18 (3): 397–411. doi:10.1016/j.gloenvcha.2008.05.001

UBS (2015) Global Research Paper '*Global Utilities*'

U.S. Department of Health, Education, and Welfare (1968). *Lifetime Allocation of Work and Leisure*. Washington: United States Government Printing Office.

U.S. Energy Information Administration (2014). *U.S. Energy-Related Carbon Dioxide Emissions*. Retrieved from EIA.gov: http://www.eia.gov/environment/emissions/carbon/pdf/2014_CO$_2$analysis.pdf (accessed 1 August 2016).

U.S. Energy Information Administration (2015). *International Energy Statistics*. Retrieved from EIA: http://www.eia.gov/cfapps/ipdbproject/iedindex3. cfm?tid=5&pid=5&aid=2&cid=regions&syid=1999&eyid=2014&unit =TBPD (accessed 1 August 2016).

UK Department of Energy and Climate Change (2009). *60th Anniversary Digest of United Kingdom Energy Statistics*. Retrieved from: https://www.gov. uk/government/uploads/system/uploads/attachment_data/file/65896/1_ 20090729135638_e____dukes60.pdf (accessed 18 April 2016).

Umweltbundesamt (2011). *Emissionsentwicklung 1990 – 2009 für klassische Luftschadstoffe*. Retrieved from Umweltbundesamt: https://www. umweltbundesamt.de/sites/default/files/medien/419/dokumente/em_ entwicklung_in_d_trendtabelle_luft_v1.3.0_out.xls (accessed 25 April 2016).

Umweltbundesamt (2015). *Einfluss der Nutzungsdauer von Produkten auf ihre Umweltwirkung: Schaffung einer Informationsgrundlage und Entwicklung von Strategien gegen „Obsoleszenz'* . Retrieved from Umweltbundesamt: http://www.umweltbundesamt.de/sites/default/files/medien/378/ publikationen/texte_10_2015_einfluss_der_nutzungsdauer_von_ produkten_auf_ihre_umwelt_obsoleszenz_17.3.2015.pdf (accessed 17 March 2016)

UN (2000). *We the People*. Retrieved from United Nations: http://www.un.org/ en/events/pastevents/pdfs/We_The_Peoples.pdf (accessed 11 March 2016).

UN (2015). *The Millennium Development Goals Report 2015*. Retrieved from United Nations: http://www.un.org/millenniumgoals/2015_MDG_ Report/pdf/MDG%202015%20rev%20(July%201).pdf (accessed 11 March 2016).

UN (2016). *Sustainable Development Goals*. Retrieved from United Nations: http://www.un.org/sustainabledevelopment/sustainable-development-goals/ (accessed 14 April 2016).

UN & DOE EIA (2007). *Energy demand and GDP per capita (1980 – 2002)*. Retrieved from Wordpress: https://notable.wordpress.com/2007/04/07/ us-energy-usage-trends/ (accessed 18 April 2016).

UN Department of Economic and Social Affairs (2004). *World Population To 2300*. Retrieved from UN Department of Economic and Social Affairs: http://www.un.org/en/development/desa/population/publications/pdf/ trends/WorldPop2300final.pdf (accessed 24 March 2016).

UN Department of Economic and Social Affairs (2014). *World Urbanization Prospects, 2014 Revision*. Retrieved from UN Department of Economic and Social Affairs: http://esa.un.org/unpd/wup/highlights/wup2014-highlights.pdf (accessed 23 March 2016).

UN Department of Economic and Social Affairs (2015). *World Population Prospects, the 2015 Revision*. Retrieved from UN Department of Economic

and Social Affairs: http://esa.un.org/unpd/wpp/Download/Standard/
Population/ (accessed 11 March 2016).

UNEP (2004). *The Great Man-Made River of Libya*. Retrieved from UNEP: www.
unep.org/GC/GCSS-VIII/Libya_IWRM.doc (accessed 14 April 2016).

UNEP (2011a). *Ban Calls For A Green Economy As Crucial For a Sustainable
Future*. Retrieved from UNEP Press Releases: http://www.unep.org/
Documents.Multilingual/Default.asp?DocumentID=655&ArticleID=6888
&l=en&t=long (accessed 1 August 2016).

UNEP (2011b). *Waste – Investing in energy and resource efficiency*. Retrieved from
UNEP: http://www.unep.org/greeneconomy/Portals/88/documents/ger/
GER_8_Waste.pdf (accessed 11 March 2016).

UNEP (2014a). *Inclusive Wealth Report 2014 – Measuring progress toward sustainability*. Retrieved from MGIEP – UNESCO: http://mgiep.unesco.org/
wp-content/uploads/2014/12/IWR2014-WEB.pdf (accessed 18 April 2016).

UNEP (2014b). *United Nations Environment Programme Annual Report 2014*.
Retrieved from UNEP: http://www.unep.org/annualreport/2014/en/
message_BKM.html (accessed 6 April 2016).

UNEP (2014c). *Valuing Plastic – The Business Case for Measuring, Managing and
Disclosing Plastic Use in the Consumer Goods Industry*. Retrieved from UNEP:
http://www.unep.org/pdf/ValuingPlastic/ (accessed 6 April 2016).

US Department of Agriculture (2016). *Real GDP (2010 dollars) Projections*.
Retrieved from United States Department of Agriculture Economic
Research Service: http://www.ers.usda.gov/data-products/international-
macroeconomic-data-set.aspx#26198 (accessed 18 April 2016).

US Department of Transportation (2016). *Table 1-40: U.S. Passenger-Miles
(Millions)*. Retrieved from United States Department of Transportation:
http://www.rita.dot.gov/bts/sites/rita.dot.gov.bts/files/publications/national_
transportation_statistics/html/table_01_40.html (accessed 20 April 2016).

USGS (2016). *Copper – Statistics and Information*. Retrieved from USGS: http://
minerals.usgs.gov/minerals/pubs/commodity/copper/ (accessed 19 April
2016).

USMA (2012). *Social Cognitive Network Academic Research Center*. Retrieved
from USMA: http://www.usma.edu/nsc/siteassets/sitepages/workshops/
wallace%20center_scnarcwestpoint2012.pdf (accessed 29 March 2016).

Voudouris, V. (2015). Introduction to: The enigmo of economic growth:
Beyond Solow-type macroeconomic perspectives. *Energy Policy* 86: 1–2.

Voudouris, V., Ayres, R., Serrenho, A. C. and Kiose, D. (2015). 'The economic
growth enigma revisited: The EU-15 since the 1970s'. *Energy Policy* 86:
812–32. doi:10.1016/j.enpol.2015.04.027

Wagner, W. and Weitzman, M. L. (2015). *Climate Shock: The Economic
Consequences of a Hotter Planet*. Princeton, NJ: Princeton University Press.

Wald, M. L. (2012). *Toward a Greener Soday Can*. Retrieved from *The New York Times*: http://green.blogs.nytimes.com/2012/06/12/toward-a-greener-soda-can/?smid=pl-share&_r=1

Walker, P. and Mathiesen, K. (2013). *Greenpeace activists climb London's Shard*. Retrieved from *The Guardian*: http://www.theguardian.com/environment/2013/jul/11/greenpeace-activists-climb-london-shard (accessed 14 April 2016).

Wan, T. (2015). *Coursera Charts Course for International Expansion With $49.5M in Series C Funding*. Retrieved from edSurge: https://www.edsurge.com/news/2015-08-25-coursera-charts-course-for-international-expansion-with-49-5m-in-series-c-funding (accessed 11 March 2016).

Wang, Y. (2014). *Chinese Minister Speaks Out Against South-North Water Diversion Project*. Retrieved from *Forbes*: http://www.forbes.com/sites/ywang/2014/02/20/chinese-minister-speaks-out-against-south-north-water-diversion-project/#4a893abf6b44 (accessed 14 April 2016).

Waste Land (2010). [Film] Dir. Lucy Walker. USA/Brazil: Midas Filmes.

Watson, R. A., Cheung, W. W. L., Anticamara, J. A., Sumaila, R. U., Zeller, D. and Pauly, D. (2012). 'Global marine yield halved as fishing intensity redoubles'. *Fish and Fisheries* 14 (40): 493–503, December 2013. doi:10.1111/j.1467-2979.2012.00483.x

Watts, J. (2008). *Sichuan quake: China's earthquake reconstruction to cost $150 bn*. Retrieved from *The Guardian*: http://www.theguardian.com/world/2008/aug/15/chinaearthquake.china (accessed 14 April 2016).

Weaver, M. and Gajanan, M. (2015). *Cecil the lion hunter Walter Palmer faces calls for prosecution*. Retrieved from *The Guardian*: http://www.theguardian.com/world/2015/jul/29/cecil-the-lion-calls-for-prosecution-us-dentist-walter-palmer (accessed 14 April 2016).

Weber, B. and Herrlein, S. (2011). *The Challenge of Food Waste – Retailers step up to the next level of inventory management*. Retrieved from Planet Retail: http://www.gs1.org/docs/casestudies/foodwaste_planetretail.pdf (accessed 21 April 2016).

Webodpedia (2016). *What is Moore's Law?* Retrieved from Webopedia: http://www.webopedia.com/TERM/M/Moores_Law.html (accessed 08 April 2016).

Weizsäcker, E. von, Lovins, A. B. and Lovins, L. H. (1998). *Factor Four: Doubling Wealth, Halving Resource Use*. Abingdon: Earthscan.

Welzer, H. (2013) (German). *Selbst Denken: Eine Anleitung zum Widerstand*. Frankfurt am Main: S. Fischer Verlag.

WEO (2010). *WORLD ENERGY OUTLOOK 2010*. Retrieved from WEO: http://www.worldenergyoutlook.org/media/weo2010.pdf (accessed 8 April 2016).

WEO (2014). *WORLD ENERGY OUTLOOK 2014 FACTSHEET*. Retrieved from WEO: http://www.worldenergyoutlook.org/media/weowebsite/2014/WEO2014FactSheets.pdf (accessed 15 March 2016).

WEO (2015). *WEO 2015 Fossil Fuel Subsidies Database.* Retrieved from
WEO: http://www.worldenergyoutlook.org/media/weowebsite/2015/
Subsidies20122014.xlsx (accessed 15 March 2016).

Wertstoffgesetz-Fakten (2015) (German). *Interview Professor Dr. Michael
Braungart.* Retrieved from Wertstoffgesetz-Fakten.de: http://wertstoff-
gesetz-fakten.de/statement-professor-dr-michael-braungart/ (accessed 19
April 2016).

Wijkman, A. and Rockström, J. (2013). *Bankrupting Nature. Denying Our Planetary
Boundaries. A Report to the Club of Rome.* New York: Earthscan/Routledge.

Wikipedia (2016). *Aphra Behn.* Retrieved from Wikipedia: https://
en.wikipedia.org/wiki/Aphra_Behn (accessed 29 March 2016).

Wikipedia (2016). *Brundtland Commission.* Retrieved from Wikipedia: https://
en.wikipedia.org/wiki/Brundtland_Commission (accessed 21 March 2016).

Wikipedia (2016). *Eco-efficiency.* Retrieved from Wikipedia: https://
en.wikipedia.org/wiki/Eco-efficiency (accessed 21 March 2016).

Wikipedia (2016). *Environmentalism History.* Retrieved from Wikipedia:
https://en.wikipedia.org/wiki/Environmentalism#History (accessed 14
March 2016).

Wikipedia (2016). *Genuine progress indicator.* Retrieved from Wikipedia:
https://en.wikipedia.org/wiki/Genuine_progress_indicator (accessed 21
April 2016).

Wikipedia (2016). *Khan Academy.* Retrieved from Wikipedia: https://
en.wikipedia.org/wiki/Khan_Academy (accessed 13 April 2016).

Wikipedia (2016). *The fox and the grapes.* Retrieved from Wikipedia: https://
en.wikipedia.org/wiki/The_Fox_and_the_Grapes (accessed 14 April 2016).

Wikipedia (2016). *The Tipping Point.* Retrieved from Wikipedia: https://
en.wikipedia.org/wiki/The_Tipping_Point (accessed 06 April 2016).

Williamson, S. H. (2015). *What Was the U.K. GDP Then?* Retrieved from
MeasuringWorth: http://www.measuringworth.com/ukgdp/

Winston, A. (2014). *The 10 Most Important Sustainable Business Stories from 2014.*
Retrieved from *Harvard Business Review*: https://hbr.org/2014/12/the-10-
most-important-sustainable-business-stories-from-2014 (accessed 31
March 2016).

Woetzel, J., Ram, S., Mitschke, J., Garemo, N. and Sankhe, S. (2014). *Tackling
the world's affordable housing challenge.* Retrieved from McKinsey & Company
– Insights & Publications: http://www.mckinsey.com/insights/urbani-
zation/tackling_the_worlds_affordable_housing_challenge (accessed 11
April 2016).

Wolf, M. (2013). *A much-maligned engine of innovation.* Retrieved from *Financial
Times*: http://www.ft.com/cms/s/2/32ba9b92-efd4-11e2-a237-00144feabdc0.
html#axzz45FGFSBh3 (accessed 8 April 2016).

Wolf, M. (2015). 'Same as It Ever Was'. *Foreign Affairs* (July/August): 15–22.

World Bank Group (2012). *Toward a Green, Clean, and Resilient World for All: A World Bank Group Environment Stratefy 2012-2022.* Retrieved from WDS Worldbank: http://www-wds.worldbank.org/external/default/ WDSContentServer/WDSP/IB/2013/08/19/000333037_2013081911 5200/Rendered/PDF/804820WP0ENV0E0Box0379805B00PUBLIC0.pdf (accessed 6 April 2016).

World Bank Group (2014). *Doubling the Rate of Improvement of Energy Efficiency.* Retrieved from WDS Worldbank: http://www-wds.worldbank.org/ external/default/WDSContentServer/WDSP/IB/2015/02/27/090224b0 82b6d434/2_0/Rendered/PDF/Doubling0the0r0of0energy0efficiency.pdf (accessed 18 March 2016).

World Co-Operative Monitor (2015). *Exploring the Co-Operative Economy – Report 2015.* Retrieved from World Co-Operative Monitor: http:// monitor.coop/sites/default/files/WCM_2015%20WEB.pdf (accessed 6 April 2016).

World Economic Forum (2012). *What If the World's Soil Run Out?* Retrieved from: http://world.time.com/2012/12/14/what-if-the-worlds-soil-runs-out/ (accessed 12 April 2016).

World Forum for a Responsible Economy (2011). *Native's Success Story: 15000 ha of sugar cane 30% more profitable thanks to organic culture.* Retrieved from Bipiz: http://www.bipiz.org/en/advanced-search/natives-success-story-15-000-ha-of-sugar-cane-30-more-profitable-thanks-to-organic-culture.html (accessed 17 March 2016).

Worldwatch Institute (2012). *Cooperative Membership Hits 1 Billion Worldwide.* Retrieved from Worldwatch Institute: http://www.worldwatch.org/system/ files/Cooperative %20News.pdf (accessed 14 April 2016).

WRAP (2013). *Household Food and Drink Waste in the United Kingdom 2012.* Retrieved from WRAP: http://www.wrap.org.uk/sites/files/wrap/hhfdw-2012-summary.pdf (accessed 17 March 2016).

Wright, M. (2014). *LEDs will slash energy use for lighting by 95%.* Retrieved from RenewEconomy: http://reneweconomy.com.au/2014/leds-will-slash-energy-use-for-lighting-by-95-12875 (accessed 22 March 2016).

YCharts (2016). *Stocks.* Retrieved from YCharts, Inc.: https://ycharts.com/ stocks (accessed 19 April 2016).

Xie, J., Sreenivasan, S., Korniss, G., Zhang, W., Lim, C. and Szymanski, K. (2011). 'Social consensus through the influence of committed minorities'. *Physical Review* E 84 (1). Retrieved from: https://pdfs.semanticscholar. org/21ce/52e518edef55a4eb05edb19286132c5eb1a6.pdf (accessed 29 March 2016).

Ziegler, C. (2015). *Google's self-driving cars have been in 11 accidents, but none were the car's fault*. Retrieved from The Verge: http://www.theverge.com/2015/5/11/8586661/google-self-driving-car-11-accidents-not-at-fault (accessed 12 April 2016).

Zumbrun, J. and Cui, C. (2015). *Glut of Capital and Labor Challenge Policy Makers*. Retrieved from *The Wall Street Journal*: http://www.wsj.com/articles/global-glut-challenges-policy-makers-1429867807?mod=e2tw&utm_content=buffer32cbd&utm_medium=social&utm_source=facebook.com&utm_campaign=buffer (accessed 29 March 2016).

Index

The letter *f* after an entry indicates a page that includes a figure.